RASPUTIN
THE HOLY DEVIL

Rasputin was the most mysterious figure of old Russia who swayed men and nations by the power of his eyes. Contents: Rasputin; The Cellar Preacher; Before the High Priests; The Fateful Idyll of Tsarskoe Selo; The Friend; The Penitential Journey of the Great Sinner; In the Holy of Holies; The Revolt Against the Holy Devil; The Murderer with the Guitar; The Death Ship; Bibliography; Index.

Renee Fulop-Miller

ISBN 1-56459-599-4

Kessinger Publishing's Rare Mystical Reprints

THOUSANDS OF SCARCE BOOKS ON THESE AND OTHER SUBJECTS:

Freemasonry * Akashic * Alchemy * Alternative Health * Ancient Civilizations * Anthroposophy * Astrology * Astronomy * Aura * Bible Study * Cabalah * Cartomancy * Chakras * Clairvoyance * Comparative Religions * Divination * Druids * Eastern Thought * Egyptology * Esoterism * Essenes * Etheric * ESP * Gnosticism * Great White Brotherhood * Hermetics * Kabalah * Karma * Knights Templar * Kundalini * Magic * Meditation * Mediumship * Mesmerism * Metaphysics * Mithraism * Mystery Schools * Mysticism * Mythology * Numerology * Occultism * Palmistry * Pantheism * Parapsychology * Philosophy * Prosperity * Psychokinesis * Psychology * Pyramids * Qabalah * Reincarnation * Rosicrucian * Sacred Geometry * Secret Rituals * Secret Societies * Spiritism * Symbolism * Tarot * Telepathy * Theosophy * Transcendentalism * Upanishads * Vedanta * Wisdom * Yoga * *Plus Much More!*

DOWNLOAD A FREE CATALOG AT:
www.kessinger.net

OR EMAIL US AT:
books@kessinger.net

INTRODUCTION

"THE HOLY DEVIL" is the title of a scurrilous pamphlet against Rasputin, from the pen of his opponent, the dreaded monk-priest Iliodor; the statements and accusations contained in it have contributed not a little to create the false picture in which Rasputin appears as a cunning charlatan, and even as the man mainly responsible for the ruin of the old Russia.

This picture, distorted with the hatred of an unsuccessful enemy, has hitherto served as a model for all portraits of Rasputin, and as such has been offered to the public. The confusion of the Revolution long rendered an impartial correction of it impossible, for, in the making of revolutionary catchwords, destined for the use of the day, veracity was of no account whatever; efficacy in political warfare was all that mattered. From this point of view, it would scarcely have been possible to have found a more suitable historical portrait than this, or one more eminently fitted to reveal the utter abomination of the old regime and its representatives.

For revolutionary Russia in its attack on a system such as tsarism, that undoubtedly had had its day, and that was, therefore, corrupt in many respects, the distortion of persons and situations may appear, if not justifiable, at least excusable. But even without that motive lurking in the background, the bourgeois love of scandal and sensation seized on the figure of Rasputin, and did its part in drawing the untrue picture, which is also flat and uninteresting because it is in simple black and white, of a commonplace "devil in human shape."

Immediately after the collapse, it became necessary to supply the masses as quickly as possible with blood-curdling stories about the Imperial Court, in order to rouse and maintain in them the spirit of rebellion, and, for that reason, this figure of Rasputin was offered to the public as the one authentic portrait. No critical investigation was made; and the utter unimaginativeness of sensation-mongers, and the incapacity of the mob for critical thought, have brought it about that this convenient picture, so easy to grasp in its commonplace simplicity, has remained almost unchallenged.

Indeed, in order to give a semblance of historical truth to this false picture, an equally ill-founded life of Rasputin was concocted. With wonderful academic pedantry, a collection of false facts and dates, wrong names of persons and places, was put together with an air of exactness that is hardly ever to be met with in biographies founded on fact. Anyone who studies the literature on Rasputin comes up continually against a mass of seemingly precise information, which, by its apparent precision, blinds the reader to the fact that it is without any foundation whatever. Freiherr von Taube alone, in his excellent book, refused to accept unquestioningly the reports about Rasputin; he subjected them to critical examination, with the result that his is the only work of any value on the subject.

One shy, quiet voice passed almost unheard in the chorus of lies about Rasputin: his daughter Matriona essayed in a short pamphlet the almost hopeless task of defending her father's memory. Doubtless what the daughter called "The Truth about Rasputin" is only half the truth; her love and reverence caused her to leave out all the dark shadows and to depict only the kind and dearly loved being whom Matriona knew as her father. But how much nearer the truth is this picture, one-sided though it be! Of course, Rasputin was not merely a simple and lovable man; but he was that too; and this side of him not only outweighs many of his defects and weaknesses, but enriches and completes his personality, and makes him appear as a truly fascinating character, supremely interesting from the human, historical, and psychological standpoint.

It was the recognition, after an unprejudiced investigation of all the available material, that it was no longer possible to assign Rasputin with justice to either of those two commonplace categories, charlatan or holy starets, that led the author to write this book. Rasputin was neither entirely bad nor entirely good, he was neither altogether a libertine nor a saint.

INTRODUCTION

He was a man of rich nature and exuberant vitality, endowed with many good qualities and cursed with many weaknesses, a man so many-sided, complex, and contradictory that an adequate delineation of his character calls for a far more exact and careful examination of all the pros and cons than anyone has yet attempted.

Believing that the contradictory and opposing elements in a human life are the one and only reality, the author has wrested his weapons from Rasputin's enemy in order to use them in defence of this reality, and has chosen "The Holy Devil," the title invented by Iliodor, as the title of his own book.

The representation of Rasputin and his environment is based entirely on official documents, police records, diaries, letters, depositions of witnesses, and other adequately documented and authentic sources. The picture of Rasputin, in its seeming incredibility, stands out from these documents with a vividness that nothing else could give to it; for they belong to an epoch which, for uneasy agitation, has scarcely a parallel in history. The men and women, too, whom we meet derive from a strange and a most peculiar state of society: for we are here dealing with Russian society immediately before the earthquake of the Bolshevik Revolution.

The author expresses his thanks to all those of the old and the new regime, to the Russian Government Departments, and to the curators of museums and of collections of manuscripts and pictures, who so kindly placed their records at his disposal. A special debt of gratitude is due to Percy Eckstein, the friend of the author, who gave him valuable help in completing the book.

RENÉ FÜLÖP-MILLER

VIENNA — HINTERBRÜHL, *Autumn, 1927.*

CONTENTS

		PAGE
INTRODUCTION		v

CHAP.		
I.	RASPUTIN	3
II.	LEHR- AND WANDERJAHRE	11
III.	THE CELLAR PREACHER	33
IV.	BEFORE THE HIGH PRIESTS	52
V.	THE FATEFUL IDYLL OF TSARSKOE SELO	70
VI.	THE FRIEND	130
VII.	THE PENITENTIAL JOURNEY OF THE GREAT SINNER	172
VIII.	STAIRCASE NOTES	181
IX.	FATHER GRIGORI RECEIVES	201
X.	IN THE HOLY OF HOLIES	241
XI.	THE DANCING STARETS	267
XII.	THE REVOLT AGAINST THE HOLY DEVIL	289
XIII.	THE GREAT FISH SUPPERS	305
XIV.	THE MURDERER WITH THE GUITAR	321
XV.	THE DEATH SHIP	369
SOURCES AND BIBLIOGRAPHY		375
INDEX		381

RASPUTIN
THE HOLY DEVIL

CHAPTER I

RASPUTIN

A TALL peasant of about forty, broad-shouldered, of robust but lean frame, clad in a peasant's shirt of coarse linen bound with a simple leather girdle, and in wide trousers and heavy top-boots: such was Grigori Efimovich Rasputin when he appeared for the first time in the salon of the Countess Ignatiev, amid that circle of Petersburg society ladies, clerical dignitaries, monks, politicians, schemers, adventurers, charlatans, and Court toadies who met three times a week in the house of the aged Countess.

They had been awaiting, with lively curiosity, the arrival of the "new saint," the "miracle-worker" from Pokrovskoe. And when he entered, peasant-like, with great noisy strides and ungainly movements, and bowed his greetings, his coarse, even ugly face seemed at first to disappoint their anxious expectations. His big head was covered with unkempt brown hair, carelessly parted in the middle and flowing in long strands over his neck. On his high forehead a dark patch was visible, the scar of a wound. His broad, pock-marked nose stood out from his face, and his thin pale lips were hidden by a limp, untidy moustache. His weather-beaten, sunburned skin was wrinkled and seamed in deep folds, his eyes were hidden under his projecting eyebrows, the right eye disfigured by a yellow blotch. The whole face was overgrown by a dishevelled light brown beard. But the assembled company were accustomed to such apparitions and, at first, he made no unusual impression on them.

When, however, he went up to the guests one by one, seized their hands between his own broad, horny palms, and looked searchingly into their eyes, they all felt somehow disturbed. For those eyes had a peculiar urgency. Small, bright, and waterblue, they gazed from under the meeting, bushy brows; restlessly, as if all the while seeking something, they probed, tried, and penetrated everything within their range. If they rested for a moment on anyone they immediately became keen and piercing, as if they could see right to the bottom of the soul; the next instant they would suddenly assume an indescribable expression of understanding, kindness, and wise toleration.

His harsh peasant's voice, too, could take on a beautiful, deep, and charmingly animated tone. When he spoke he put his head a little on one side, as priests are wont to do when they take confessions, and his speech, then, like his glance, was filled with a thoughtful, monastic benevolence. At such moments the Countess's guests felt him as a good and holy Father in whom they could trust implicitly.

But his glance and speech would change: it was as if an all-devouring sensual desire flamed up in this strange man, his eyes began to blaze, his voice became excited, violent and passionate, confidential and insinuating. His glances and words became lewd, cynical, and full of scarcely concealed suggestiveness, until, unexpectedly, his attitude again changed entirely, and he spoke of mystical and religious things with poetic ardour and genuine flaming enthusiasm.

As he spoke his unbeautiful face acquired an extraordinary animation. Sometimes the quick play of his features and gestures was almost theatrical. In these movements his horny peasant's hands became visible: they were coarse but well formed with long, bony fingers.

Soon a wide circle of women from all classes of society, ranging from ladies of the highest rank down to servant maids, peasant women, and sempstresses, looked on Rasputin as a higher, divine being. Men, too, of all ranks and callings thronged round the miracle-worker—ministers and officials, brokers and spies. Grigori Efimovich was immoderately pampered, admired, and worshipped by them all.

Rasputin's external appearance changed in accordance with the improvement in his social position. He wore costly blouses of pale blue, brilliant red, mauve, or light yellow silk, made specially for him by the most distinguished ladies of the Court and Society, and embroidered with flowers. The plain leather girdle of the peasant gave place to a silk cord, raspberry-coloured or sky-blue, with big tassels; he wore trousers made of striped English cloth or of black velvet, and boots of the softest leather. In winter, he was wrapped in an expensive fur coat, with a beaver cap on his head and English snow-boots on his feet.

But even in these fine clothes, to which admiring women had accustomed him, he in no way changed his careless, forthright, peasant nature. In spite of everything, he continued to be the *muzhik* with the unkempt hair and beard, dirty hands, and the native, even unseemly, speech of the peasant.

All the characteristics which had made him seem coarse and common on his first entry into the drawing-rooms of St. Petersburg underwent a peculiar transfiguration in the eyes of his credulously enthusiastic women worshippers. While they nervously awaited his coming a stifling atmosphere of overwrought excitement hung over the expectant company. When at last the door opened and revealed Rasputin on the threshold, a tremor passed through all present, as at the announcement of a miraculous event. If he stopped before the women to kiss them three times with bowed head after the manner of the wandering monks, they thrilled with the ecstasy of a religious experience, and called him by names proper only to a saint. They were convinced that God revealed Himself in his words, that the Holy Ghost met them in the glance of his little, water-blue eyes, that his touch transmitted even to their sinful bodies the grace dwelling in him, and that his kisses and embraces sanctified each one of his faithful disciples.

Sometimes he would rise in the midst of the conversation and, à propos of nothing, call on the women to sing him those melancholy folk songs that recall Church music, and of which he was particularly fond. Then he took a few paces forward, remained standing in the midst of the assembly, stuck his hands in his silk girdle, and began to rock himself slowly in time to the singing. Next, he stamped noisily on the parquet floor with his peasant's boots, and began to dance. With circling motions he seductively drew nearer to the women and invited them to dance with him; his beard waved, his boots set the time, and his keen eyes took stock of his partner, who followed his glance confusedly and ecstatically, as if spellbound. The rest of the men and women sat attentive and absorbed in a circle about them, and looked upon the dancing peasant as if they were taking part in a religious service.

Many people, of course, attempted to withstand Rasputin's magic. They tried to keep their heads, and fought with all their might against his compelling influence. But even the few who succeeded, and continued to see the human being with his common features, small, cunning eyes, and unkempt beard, could not quite escape his mysterious power.

Some spoke of hypnotism, and tried to break the strange spell of the miracle-worker with a dry, scientific word; but this was of little avail against the living impression of Rasputin's personality.

"How peculiar his eyes are," confesses a woman who had made efforts to resist his influence. She goes on to say that every time she met him she was always amazed afresh at the power of his glance, which it was impossible to withstand for any considerable time. There was something oppressive in this kind and gentle, but at the same time sly and cunning, glance; people were helpless under the spell of the powerful will which could be felt in his whole being. However tired you might be of this charm, and however much you wanted to escape it, somehow or other you always found yourself attracted back and held.

A young girl who had heard of the strange new saint came from her province to the capital, and visited him in search of edification and spiritual instruction. She had never seen either him or a portrait of him before, and met him for the first time in his house. When he came up to her and spoke to her, she thought him like one of the peasant preachers she had often seen in her own country home. His gentle, monastic gaze and the plainly parted light brown hair around the worthy simple face, all at first inspired her with confidence. But when he came nearer to her, she felt immediately that another quite different man, mysterious, crafty, and corrupting, looked out from behind the eyes that radiated goodness and gentleness.

He sat down opposite her, edged quite close up to her, and

his light blue eyes changed colour, and became deep and dark. A keen glance reached her from the corner of his eyes, bored into her, and held her fascinated. A leaden heaviness overpowered her limbs as his great wrinkled face, distorted with desire, came closer to hers. She felt his hot breath on her cheeks, and saw how his eyes, burning from the depths of their sockets, furtively roved over her helpless body, until he dropped his lids with a sensuous expression. His voice had fallen to a passionate whisper, and he murmured strange, voluptuous words in her ear.

Just as she was on the point of abandoning herself to her seducer, a memory stirred in her dimly and as if from some far distance; she recalled that she had come to ask him about God. As she gradually awoke more clearly to the original purpose of her visit, the heaviness disappeared from her limbs, and she began to struggle in his toils.

He was at once aware of the increasing inner resistance, his half-shut eyes opened again, he stood up, bent over her, lightly stroked her girlishly parted hair, and pressed a passionless, gentle, fatherly kiss on her forehead. His face distorted with desire became smooth again, and was once more the kindly face of the wandering preacher. He spoke to his visitor in a benevolent, patronizing tone, his right hand raised to his forehead in blessing. He stood before her in the attitude in which Christ is depicted on old Russian ikons; his glance was again gentle and friendly, almost humble, and only in the depth of those little eyes still lurked, almost invisible, the other man, the sensual beast.

Painfully disappointed and confused, the girl rose, stammered a few words of farewell, and left Rasputin's house. In her heart she carried with her the terrifying question, Was this man a saint or a libertine?

Another woman, a St. Petersburg society lady, declared with scorn to the French Ambassador that Rasputin had filthy hands, black nails, and a dirty beard. "Faugh," she cried when she spoke of him. But she had to confess that, after a few words, it was impossible for anyone to be indifferent to the glimmering, inscrutable change in Rasputin's glance, bearing, and words, the cleverness, mystery, goodness, violence, familiarity, ardour, poetry, and attraction of his nature.

* * * * *

Rasputin's influence was not, however, confined to women. The French Ambassador himself was impressed the first time he met him. M. Paléologue had received unfavourable reports of Rasputin from his agents; he regarded him as a corrupt charlatan, and hated him particularly for urging Russia to make peace.

Once, while the Ambassador was visiting a lady of his acquaintance, the door of the reception room suddenly opened with a great uproar. Rasputin came in, boisterously embraced the lady of the house, and talked with her for some time. Paléologue meanwhile watched him with the mixture of strained attention and distrust that a diplomat usually accords to a suspicious political character. He recorded that the miraculous monk had an "ordinary face," but that its whole expression was concentrated in his eyes, which were as blue as flax. The Ambassador was fascinated for the moment, and had to admit that Rasputin's eyes were at once penetrating and caressing, childlike and cunning, direct and yet remote, and that when his talk became more animated, it seemed that his pupils "became magnetic."

M. Gilliard, the French tutor of the Crown Prince, met the despicable charlatan and hated opponent of war only once, in the antechamber of the imperial apartments, as Rasputin was leaving the Palace. A strange, unpleasant sensation took possession of the tutor. As his glance crossed that of Rasputin he formed the firm conviction that he was in the presence of a powerful and dangerous man. Profoundly disturbed, he made haste to escape from Rasputin's eyes, and at once left the room.

But even the man who had hated Rasputin from the beginning, who set out with the preconceived opinion that the existence of this miracle-worker was a disaster for Russia, that Prince Yusupov who coolly and deliberately wormed his way into Rasputin's favour in order to prepare a murderous attack upon him—even he had difficulty in escaping the charm that Grigori Efimovich exercised.

When he saw him for the first time, heard his voice for the first time, all the horrible and repulsive things he had previously been told about this man seemed to be confirmed by the sight of him. This peasant, so coddled by women, inspired him with profound disgust: his features were coarse and lacked all trace of refinement; the laugh with which he turned to his audience seemed unwholesome, sensual, and cruel. His face recalled a sly, rank satyr; everything about him aroused suspicion and mistrust.

Prince Yusupov had hardly ever beheld anything more repellent than those little, almost colourless, eyes, set too close together in their unusually deep sockets. They often seemed to be lost in their hollows, and then it was not easy to decide whether they were open or shut. Only an uncanny, uneasy feeling told the Prince that Rasputin was watching him.

But, at the same time, the proud young aristocrat was forced to recognize clearly that there was something unusual in this hated peasant face, and that a strong, mysterious, almost supernatural power lurked in the glance of those unpleasant eyes.

Yusupov was later to learn the full power of Rasputin's gaze. With the object of insinuating himself into his enemy's confidence, he visited him in his own house on the pretext of asking him for medical advice. The young Prince, on an impulse of curiosity, obeyed all Rasputin's instructions, followed him into his bedroom, and lay down on the sofa. At first, when Rasputin was trying to put him to sleep by gazing at him and making stroking movements, Yusupov still retained the power of cool observation, and concluded that the whole healing process of the miracle-worker was nothing but "hypnotism of the worst kind."

Rasputin gazed fixedly into his eyes, slowly stroked his breast, neck, and head, and then knelt down and began to pray, laying his hands lightly on Yusupov's head. He remained in this attitude for a while, then rose and continued the hypnotic stroking. Yusupov set his will against this treatment, but had soon to recognize that a strange warmth was spreading over his whole body, and complete paralysis taking possession of it.

His tongue no longer obeyed him, and he tried in vain to utter a sound or to rise. His limbs lay there lifeless, as if made of lead. Close in front of him he saw Rasputin's eyes, big and powerful. They shone with a kind of phosphorescent glimmer; two tapering rays radiated from them, fused and became a circle of fire, which now approached, now receded. Yusupov's eyelids became heavier and heavier, and slowly dropped; he was on the point of falling asleep and yielding to the will of the nauseous charlatan; but summoning the last remnant of his energy to resist, and struggling despairingly, he finally succeeded in breaking the spell. He left Rasputin's house with the firm determination to destroy this man as soon as possible.

CHAPTER II

LEHR- AND WANDERJAHRE

GRISHA, the little son of the carter, Efim Andreevich Rasputin, of Pokrovskoe, loved being in the stable. There he could squat for hours on the low balk under the lantern, and gaze with bright, wide-open eyes at the great beasts, and listen with indrawn breath to the scraping of their hoofs and the snorting of their nostrils. Out on the village street Grisha was a wild and unruly, even alarming, youngster, a ringleader in all the pranks of the peasant children. But as soon as he entered the stable behind his father or one of the men, in his long, wide trousers of white canvas, he became transformed. His childish face took on a peculiar seriousness; his eyes were all eager attention, and his whole countenance had an intense look, as if he must display especial dignity and manliness. With firm, measured steps he marched in behind the grown-ups, feeling that he was entering a holy place where you had to be quiet and serious, as in church.

Best of all were the times when he was allowed to remain alone with the horses. Then he crept up softly and cautiously, and raised his little body on tiptoe, until he was able to stroke and caress the warm bodies of the beasts with his outstretched hand. At such times he showed a tenderness which he never displayed either to his parents, his brothers and sisters, or anybody else in the world. Often he would run cautiously to the door and peer out into the yard to see if anyone were coming. Then with the agility of a monkey he climbed up onto the wooden manger, seized the iron bars of the hay rack, and boldly swung himself onto the back of one of the horses. He pressed his hot cheeks to the animal's neck, and carried on long, wonderful, and tender conversations in a language which his child's heart had invented, and which no one understood but himself and the horses.

To be with the horses was the boy's greatest happiness. He loved the dim light from the stable lantern hanging slantwise from the wall, that strange half-darkness, in which could be distinguished here and there only the shining of a horse's coat or a heap of straw. He breathed in the smell of the stable, and he was never tired of touching the steaming bodies of the animals with hand or cheek. However much he enjoyed running about the meadows with the peasant lads or watching his father sitting angling with the other fishermen on the bank of the Tura, he would have given up all these pleasures for his horses, whom he looked upon as his dumb comrades and secret allies. And it soon came about that Grisha learned to give better advice in any difficulty about horses than the most experienced old carters of Pokrovskoe, so that when anything out of the ordinary happened to their beasts, they more than once sent for Grisha Efimovich.

But what a wonderful place the stable became for him after that evening on which his father first read aloud to him, from the big book with its beautiful pictures, the story of the birth of the Christ-child! Grisha listened to every word of the tale of Saint Joseph, Mary, and the new-born infant, who lay in the crib when the three Kings of the East came to worship him. Henceforward, everything in his father's stable, the great wooden manger and the dimly glimmering lantern, was full of a mysterious meaning which only he knew and of which he spoke to no one.

Once, when old Efim was not at home, Grisha stole into the big room, climbed on a chair, and reached down from the chimney-piece the big book with its wealth of pictures from which his father had read to him. He turned over the heavy folio in its thick covers until he found the picture which showed the stable with the crib and the Christ-child in colours of blue, red, and gold. He waited impatiently for the evening, when he could beg his father after supper to read aloud to him again, and, sitting on old Efim's knee, he looked eagerly at the pictures, while his father read to him the rest of the life of the Christ-child, how he grew up and became the Saviour of the world.

Evening after evening Efim Andreevich, in response to the

boy's entreaties, had to reach down the big book. Soon Grisha knew all the pictures; and as he listened to his father reading aloud, painfully tracing with his finger word by word and line by line, he himself learned the letters and the art of combining them to form words. So Grisha grew up between two equally mysterious worlds: on the one side the stable with its marvels, and on the other the big book with the beautiful pictures and the black signs.

When Grisha was twelve a catastrophe occurred in his life, the effects of which were long felt. He was playing with his elder brother Misha on the bank of the Tura, when Misha suddenly fell backwards into the stream. Without reflection Grisha sprang in after him, and both boys would have been drowned if a passing peasant had not rescued them. Misha fell ill the same day of a serious inflammation of the lungs, and died almost immediately. Grisha's life was saved; but he was so shaken by this accident that he fell into a heavy fever. He recovered rapidly, and was soon playing again and busy with his beloved horses, but there was a change in him. His face, once so plump and rosy, was now hollow-cheeked and pale; and although in the evenings it was covered with a reddish flush, this was not the fresh ruddiness of health, but the hectic stain of fever. His nature also underwent a peculiar change, which caused his parents no little anxiety. No one could say exactly what was really wrong, and even the village herbalist could give no advice; and the lad again fell into violent fever and semiconsciousness, a condition that lasted several days and even weeks.

There was nothing to be done but to make up a bed for the invalid in the "black half," the dark part of the big kitchen. In winter as it now was, while outside the Siberian storms blew from the fields through the village street, this was the warmest and most comfortable place in the house. Besides, the kitchen was everybody's favourite spot, so that someone was always there to keep an eye on the sick child.

At twilight the peasants from the neighbourhood used to assemble and seat themselves on the broad benches round the big stove. The hosts handed round schnapps and Siberian sweetmeats, and the talk went on until late into the evening, about everything that had happened in the village itself and the news that penetrated to Pokrovskoe from the neighbouring market towns.

On one of these evenings they were all talking in whispers, because Grisha was very ill again. To the anxiety of the household, he had lain for hours completely apathetic, with his pale face turned to the wall and his eyes closed. So his parents and their guests lowered their voices, though they had a particularly important affair to discuss that evening. The night before, a crime had been committed of a kind calculated to excite the minds of all the peasants of Pokrovskoe in the highest degree. One of the poorest carters of the village had had his one horse stolen from the stable, and the poor man was in misery and despair. The kindly peasants of Pokrovskoe, old and young, had searched from early morning for the thief and his booty, but all their efforts had been fruitless.

The peasants were all in a state of furious resentment over the occurrence, for in the eyes of these Siberian carters horse-stealing is the meanest crime, worse and more loathsome even than murder. These men, whose villages not infrequently had originally been settlements of exiled criminals, for the most part regarded even the greatest sinners as "poor weak brothers"; but for horse thieves they had neither understanding nor pity. Anna Egorovna, Efim's wife, had had more than once to point to the sick child, and beg for greater quietness, when the excitement of her guests took a noisy form. Outside it was quite dark, and only a single lamp in the middle of the table threw a dim light on the peasants crouching round the stove.

Suddenly the sick child rose from his bed and walked up to the peasants in his trailing white night-shirt, with cheeks pale as death and an almost awesome glitter in his eyes. Before they had recovered from their amazement the child was already in their midst; he stared fixedly in front of him for a second or two, sprang with a leap onto a giant of a fellow, threw his arms round his legs, climbed up to his shoulders, and sat astride on his back. Then he shrieked out: "Ha! ha! Petr Alexandrovich! You stole the horse! You are the thief!" He burst into unrestrained, childish laughter and, trembling with delight, beat the peasant on the chest with his feet, as if trying to spur him on, and went on shouting that Petr Alexandrovich was the thief. His voice rang so shrill, and his eyes shone with such a strange light, that all present felt eerie. They had no idea what to make of the boy's accusation, for Petr Alexandrovich was a most respectable and well-to-do man, who had been particularly indignant over the theft, and from the start had demanded a ruthless prosecution of the criminal.

Old Efim and his wife were most disturbed by the incident. If Grisha had not already lain so long sick with a high fever his father would have given him a sound thrashing on the spot, for he was a man who knew how to keep discipline in his own house. Anna Egorovna exerted herself to dispel all memory of the painful incident, and apologized many times to worthy Petr Alexandrovich. The other visitors also tried to restore peace, and even the grossly insulted Petr Alexandrovich finally looked friendly, and expressed his concern for Grisha's serious illness. By the time the peasants departed the same peaceful atmosphere prevailed as before the distressing incident. Nevertheless, some of Efim's guests could not forget the words of the sick boy; they went on ruminating, as peasants do, and at last, here and there, in this cabin and that, several got up and stealthily stole to Petr Alexandrovich's farm. There, in the darkness, one met the others who, uneasy like him, had risen to find out the true state of affairs. Soon quite a number had collected. As they crawled noiselessly on their bellies up to the fence of Petr Alexandrovich's homestead, they suddenly saw him, also observing the greatest secrecy, come out of his house, look round for a few seconds to see if anyone were watching, and then, thinking himself alone, go to a dark hole situated in the furthest recesses of the yard. Immediately afterwards the peasants, to their amazement, saw Petr Alexandrovich lead out the stolen horse and disappear with it into the darkness.

Early next morning the peasants one by one knocked at the door of Efim's house and, making the sign of the Cross, with many invocations of the holy Mother of God and Saint George, related how Grisha had in his fever discovered the truth, and that it was really Petr Alexandrovich who had stolen the horse.

They told how they had crept up behind the criminal, had finally captured him and beaten him senseless. They were all convinced that God himself had spoken through the sick child.

Whatever may be the explanation of this "miracle," whether the boy, his sensitiveness further heightened by fever, had noticed something doubtful in the attitude and words of Petr Alexandrovich or whether in his wanderings through the Pokrovskoe stables he had on previous occasions seen something suspicious, which led to his accusation, in any case the incident caused the peasants of the district, even later, when Grisha was completely cured, to eye him with strange glances, and ask themselves what they were really to think of this queer rascal.

Grigori Efimovich Rasputin gradually developed into a peasant lad like all the rest, frequented public-houses, ran after the girls, and fell into a disorderly and dissipated life. Although he diligently did his share when there was any farm work to be done, he would get dead drunk every night afterwards.

He made very little change in this way of life when later, at one of those Siberian "sessions" at which all the young people of the village assemble to gamble, sing, and dance, he met the beautiful fair-haired Praskovia Fedorovna Dubrovina and fell in love with her. Even when the dark-eyed, slim girl became his wife Grisha could not abandon his dissipated life, and relapsed from time to time into unsavoury intercourse with boon companions and village girls.

Then he underwent his second great experience, which made a profound impression on him, and of which he spoke only to his trusted friend, the peasant lad Mikhail Pecherkin, once when the two were strolling along the bank of the Tura, and, after desultory talk of the harvest, cattle, horses, and girls, came to speak about God. According to his story Rasputin had been striding along the field after the plough, had reached the end of a furrow, and was about to turn the horse when suddenly, behind him, he heard a wonderful anthem like those the village girls sang in chorus. As he turned round he dropped the plough in amazement, for right in front of him he saw a marvellous image, the holy Mother of God swinging on the golden rays of the noonday sun. In the air echoed solemn music from a thousand angels' throats, in which the Virgin Mary joined.

The vision lasted only a few minutes, he told his friend, and immediately disappeared again. Grigori Efimovich, shaken and stirred to the depths, stood in the middle of the empty field with trembling hands, and was unable to go on with his work. When he went into the stable in the evening to attend to the horses he felt an inexplicable melancholy. Something in him seemed to tell him that God had some special design on him, and at the same time he knew that, for the sake of this special and higher thing, he would have to leave the horses, the public-house, home, father, wife, and the village girls. So he deemed it better not to think any more about this miraculous vision, and to say nothing about it except to his friend Pecherkin.

* * * * *

When he reached the proper age Rasputin at first went on with his father's trade, and conveyed passengers and goods over the long straight roads to the neighbouring villages, sometimes as far as Tobolsk and Tiumen, or, in the other direction, to Verkhoture, at the foot of the Urals. For it was only in summer that boats plied up to Pokrovskoe on the Tura, and conveyed traffic downstream to Tiumen, or down the Tobol to Tobolsk. Travellers in these districts in winter were dependent on carriages or sledges, and so the young carrier Grigori more than once drove people into remote localities in the Governments of Tobolsk and Perm.

It was when he was thirty-three that one of his passengers was destined to make a fundamental change in his life, and to inspire him with a completely new spirit. One day he had to drive the novice Mileti Zaborovski, a student of the college of divinity, to the monastery of Verkhoture. During the journey a conversation started between the driver and his clerical fare on faith and the Church, in which the seminarist, to his amazement, was forced to recognize how extraordinarily conversant this simple peasant was with religious matters. The youthful theologian tried to convince his driver how sinful it was to waste all these capacities, and his words made a great impression on Rasputin; for Grigori, even as a boy, had been passionately addicted to meditation on God and the things of faith.

But it was a new doctrine that he heard from his passenger—not the strict Orthodox faith that held out no hope of salvation for a poor and weak sinner like himself, but the joyful gospel that even a sinful man could participate here on earth in heavenly bliss, if only he followed certain biddings of a mysterious "true" faith in God. The seminarist finally succeeded in persuading Rasputin to remain in the monastery instead of turning back and going home.

Verkhoture was one of those peculiar Siberian monastic communities which, in their aspect and the conduct of their inhabitants, resemble big farms rather than places for the practise of the contemplative life of faith. While the monks of Verkhoture strictly fulfilled all the monastic rules, and were diligent in the prescribed spiritual exercises, they also cultivated their lands and pursued occupations of a worldly nature. It was not, therefore, too difficult for the peasant Grigori to take his place in this half-monastic, half-agricultural community.

Soon he discovered, to his astonishment, that the brotherhood of the monastery was divided into two groups, one of whom played the part of prisoners and the other that of jailers, although this relation was as far as possible veiled and concealed. Rasputin learned that the brothers who were thus carefully supervised and watched were open or secret adherents of heretical creeds, "Khlysty" and other sectarians, who had been sent to Verkhoture to be reformed and brought back into the bosom of the Orthodox Church.

And Rasputin recalled the strange talk of the young seminarist he had driven to the monastery. He remembered how greatly the doctrines of his passenger differed from the ordinary faith of the Church, and it dawned on him that the young man had tried to convert him to sectarianism. He also perceived that the apostate monks who had been banished to Verkhoture, and who were distinguished by strict observance of the rules of the Church, had only pretended to abjure their orthodoxy, and that many of the "prison warders" had already been captured by the beliefs of the sectarians. In fact, the whole monastery of Verkhoture followed the rules of the Church purely in externals, and was in reality a hotbed of sectarianism.

To almost all these monks the strict rites of the Church seemed a mere useless formality, which they were obliged to observe in order to avoid coming into conflict with the authorities, while each one bore hidden in his soul the true faith, of which he would speak only in secret to those holding the same conviction, true to the precept of that Danila Filipich who had founded the brotherhood of the "Men of God," the "Khlysty," more than two hundred years before, and had enjoined upon his followers: "Keep my laws secret, entrust them neither to your father nor to your mother, be steadfast and silent even under the lash or the flames; thus you will enter into the Kingdom of Heaven, and even here on earth receive the bliss of the spirit."

The Khlysty sect drew their greatest strength from mystery, and in order to preserve this mystery, to protect the truth from any profanation, the founders of the new doctrine prescribed that their adherents should strictly observe in externals the forms of the "false faith," Orthodoxy, and even distinguish themselves by special zeal in observance.

Little by little Rasputin learned from his brethren how the customs, prayers, and practices of the Church were necessary only for men who were still unawakened, who still remained in the darkness of common existence, how the Church and the priesthood had missed the right road to God, and how only the prophet of the secret brotherhood could set his disciples on the true way. For the doctrines of the Church clung to the letter, were earthly and lacked inspiration, while the word of the prophet revered by the Khlysty was given him direct from God. The man who, through grace, was in direct communion with the Holy Ghost and with God no longer had need of the laws and forms of the Church devised by human reason. It was only at the beginning, before his enlightenment, that Danila Filipich had been a zealous student of the Gospels and the other religious writings; later, after grace had been vouchsafed to him, he threw all his books into the Volga, in order thenceforward to seek the meaning of truth in the "golden book of life" alone.

Thus Rasputin, the novice in the Khlysty faith, became gradually estranged from the "letter doctrines" of the Church, and drew nearer to the mystical, direct "experience of God." He entrusted himself to the guidance of the Holy Spirit, and had become a true "Son of God," an "imitator of Christ," a convinced adherent of the Khlysty sect. Now if he took the communion, went to confession, and bowed countless times to the ground before the ikons of the monastery chapel, he felt that it was meaningless to seek in external ceremonies the divinity that could be found only in the living prophet. To Rasputin, as to all Khlysty, this pretence of Orthodoxy was no sin and no conflict with true piety. By this means they preserved in their hearts the pure true faith, the "istinnaia vera."

This true faith of the "people of God" opened up to Rasputin a world of unique promises, hopes, and possibilities; for according to this doctrine, man here on earth, at any time and in any place, can be united with God, the Lord is ever anew reincarnated among men, and the marvellous birth of Nazareth, when the Son of God became man, was not an event happening once, but is ever repeated afresh.

But to commune with God and participate in all the glories of Heaven the sinful man must first die the "mysterious death of Christ," death in the living body, which is followed by the mystical resurrection. The man who is born only once in the flesh bears in him the doom of Adam, persists in sin, and thereby incurs death. Only the man born a second time in the spirit escapes the laws of mortality and is able to grow towards a higher life. The Khlysty teach that the "mysterious death" can be attained only through complete self-denial and absolute submission to the will of the Holy Spirit, by the subduing of every passion, for rebirth is possible only if the sinful man is completely overcome. But he who has once undergone the mystical resurrection can perform miracles, heal the sick, and foresee the future, by the might of the divine spirit dwelling in him; he can raise the dead from the grave, he has the power to bind and to loose, to rescue sinful souls from Hell and lead them to Heaven, and on the day of the Last Judgment he will apportion rewards and punishments. He rises to a new nature filled with the Holy Spirit, which is at once God and man, a new Christ.

Rasputin learned how God had become reincarnate countless times since the days of Jesus of Nazareth, and had walked among the people in the form of simple Russian peasants. It even appeared as if the Lord loved to linger in holy Russia and to reveal Himself in lowly Russian men.

God the Father Himself had descended to Russian soil in a fiery chariot surrounded by angels on a mountain in the government of Vladimir in the district of Starodub, in the county of Murov, and had there become incarnate in the body of the peasant Danila Filipich, a one-time deserter. From then onwards the God of Sabaoth had lived in the fleshly envelope of Danila Filipich, wandered through the villages of the Kostroma government, spoken the language of simple people, and shown the peasants the true way to salvation.

Christ, the Son of God, also appeared again on earth at that time, and like the Lord Himself, chose as his abode the body of a sinful muzhik. A peasant woman a hundred years old belonging to the village of Maksakov, also in the Vladimir government, to the mockery of the inhabitants of the village, became pregnant by an old man of a hundred. Ivan Timofeevich Suslov, the child of this strange pair, grew up in the house of his parents, a simple peasant's son like the rest, drank with the village lads and led a careless life, until Danila Filipich, the incarnate God of Sabaoth, encountered him, recognized him as his Son, Christ, and summoned him to his house in the Vladimir government.

Rasputin heard how from this simple peasant house, where Danila Filipich and Ivan Suslov, God the Father and Christ, lived together, a straight road led to Heaven, and how pious and enlightened peasants had often seen the two wonderful men journeying on high. Ivan Suslov had chosen twelve peasants to be his apostles, and with them had wandered along the banks of the Volga, until the Tsar Alexander Mikhailovich arrested them, brought them to Moscow, and there by the Saviour's Gate crucified Ivan Suslov on the wall of the Kremlin. On Saturday, however, the third day after his death, Suslov rose from his grave and appeared to his apostles. He was captured a second time by police spies, flayed and nailed to the cross, but once again the dead rose. He was again caught and, on the day on which he was to be executed for the third time, the Tsaritsa gave birth to a son, Petr Alexeevich, who later bore the name of Peter the Great. In celebration of this happy event the Tsar released Ivan Suslov from prison, and he lived for thirty years in Moscow, and finally, at the age of a hundred, was raised to Heaven in glory to be reunited to Danila Filipich, his Father.

After the new Ascension of Christ the Saviour again became incarnate on Russian earth and wandered once more among his beloved Russian peasants: this time he chose the body of a "strelets," a humble archer, Prokopi Lupkin, in the Baturin regiment, which had mutinied against Peter the Great and had been exiled to Novgorod.

When the earthly body of Prokopi Lupkin departed this life, the Redeemer descended into the body of Andrei Petrov, a dumb peasant looked upon as mad, who stammered and made meaningless gestures and, summer and winter, clad only in a shirt, roamed through the villages. But the peasants, who know, immediately recognized the Saviour in the fool, fell on their knees before him, and cried: "Christus Andriushka, bless us and save our souls." For the peasants knew that in those who had "died mysteriously and risen again" it is not the man who is revealed, but the Spirit of God; but the revelations of the Holy Spirit are too high for the ordinary human reason to grasp at all times, and so it happens that much in the words and actions of the resurrected may appear like foolishness or madness, for the wisdom of God hides behind the mask of witlessness.

But the story of God's advent in the form of the prophet Radaev came to Rasputin as an illumination. For Radaev, who had wandered among men but a few decades past, was, according to the standards of earthly reason, a depraved and wicked sinner, whose licentiousness was far greater and more serious than anything of which Rasputin himself had ever been guilty. Radaev had practised every kind of carnal sin, and had lived with thirteen women at once in open intercourse. Nevertheless, he had been a great prophet, and, in spite of all his sinful deeds, the Holy Spirit had spoken from his mouth.

Radaev's sins were no sins, for they were inspired by the Spirit of God: even the ugliest deeds of which he, the mysteriously resurrected, might be guilty were, in the eyes of the Lord, more precious and pleasing than the best and purest acts of ordinary men. In him sin had lost all its power, and thus nothing that he did was to be condemned or rejected. When the self-righteous informers of the Tsar reproached him with his vicious life, and demanded that he do penance, Radaev answered, proudly conscious that God Himself spoke from his mouth: "I know no reason why I should do penance. You know my sins, but the grace of God in me you do not know."

When the divine prophet was arraigned before a worldly court for his depravity and debauchery, he declared that the power of the Holy Spirit had worked in him and compelled him to do every one of his actions. "I was well aware that I was transgressing the law, but I was also aware that my acts proceeded from the will of the Lord. Therefore, all these women who have sinned with me are better and more pleasing in the sight of God than those who resisted me and remained virtuous. For the Lord has appeared in me, put on flesh and sinned in the flesh, that sin might thereby be destroyed. It is only the man who debases himself through sin whose penitence is truly acceptable to God. I have debased the women who sacrificed their chastity to me that they might not be proud and vain of their virtue. What can bring pride lower than abasement through sin?"

And Grigori Rasputin heard that, since the death of Radaev, the Redeemer had appeared again in the form of Russian peasants, and even yet, often in different places at the same time, tarried awhile among the faithful. Wherever the adherents of the secret brotherhood, the "people of God," assemble for solemn ceremonies, the Holy Ghost descends upon the community and chooses the earthly envelope of the worthiest among them, so that Christ may become flesh anew. Close to the Russian earth, too, lies the heavenly paradise of God; the way thither may often be near at hand, somewhere in the village, in one of those houses where the community of the faithful assembles, in order to ascend to Heaven in the "ship," the "ark of the righteous," in the living body.

In this faith Rasputin found the promise of all that he had most deeply yearned for since his earliest childhood. If he could only succeed in opening his heart completely to the Holy Ghost and die the mysterious death, then no sin could tempt him thereafter or seduce him from the path, for whatever he did would be sanctified by the blessing of the Spirit. Henceforth, Grigori Efimovich was swayed by only one longing, only one zealous struggle to tread towards perfection on the way opened up by the doctrines of the Khlysty.

Before Rasputin left the monastery of Verkhoture he decided to visit the holy starets Makari. The hut of this anchorite was at no great distance from the monastery, and no one liked to leave it without having asked for the blessing of this holy man. Not only the monks of Verkhoture, but also men and women of various social classes from far and near came to Father Makari, when they had any heavy burden to bear, any injustice to suffer, or any evil deed to repent. Among the pilgrims who often for days traversed the endless woods and huts of Siberia, barefooted and bareheaded, with a bread bag on their backs and a staff in their hands, to visit the wise Elder, were to be seen beggars and rich peasants, men of the middle classes and aristocrats, common soldiers and officers. No one had ever left the anchorite's hut without a word of consolation, advice, and edification; and, with the homecoming pilgrims, the fame of Makari spread all over Russia.

Rasputin had learned from his secret brothers in the faith that the pious starets had in former times been a great sinner, to whom no passion and no sensual intoxication was unknown. He had experienced all the allurements of the world, tasted to the full all the joys of life, and abandoned himself to all temptations as long as a drop of sin remained in his blood. But when he had purified himself by this sin, when not the slightest evil remained either in his feeling or his thoughts, he had humbly offered to God his purified heart, flesh, and senses.

At first, the story ran, he entered a monastery, and there for many years had subjected himself to the severest mortifications, in order to test his flesh once more, and discover whether he were truly ready to serve the Almighty alone. Then, when at last he was sure that the old man in him had really died the mysterious death, he went into the forest and settled in his hut. There he dwelt, in the "pure joy of the Lord," free from all worldly desire and earthly weakness, and even the iron chains he had fastened round his emaciated limbs were not burdensome. All earthly limitations had fallen from him; he lived beyond space and time, and could see into the fate of men.

Rasputin's visit to the anchorite was to decide whether he should return home to his wife and children and his jolly boon companions, to his horses and his stable, or whether he should devote his life to a higher task, to which a divine power had summoned him while he was yet a boy.

As a preparation for his visit Grigori went to the reliquary in which the bones of Saint Simeon of Verkhoture were preserved. There, in long and fervent prayer, he found the strength and purity of soul he needed for his meeting with the Starets.

Makari's dwelling lay deep in the forest, and it was a long journey to reach it. It was a poor, desolate hut, in which there was scarcely room for one man. There the old Elder lived in utter poverty and deprivation. But his glance spoke of joy, and a perpetual sunny smile played round his colourless lips. His voice was so weak and low as to be scarcely more than a breath. But it held a note of warmth and vitality.

On arriving at the Elder's cell Grigori threw himself on the ground and covered with kisses the bony hands of the old man in their iron fetters. Then, with the greatest simplicity, he told him of the reasons that had brought him thither, without trying to extenuate or conceal anything. He confessed his sinful life, his evil thoughts, the lust of the flesh that had continued to trouble him in the monastery, and also the strange visions that had been vouchsafed to him. He spoke of his weakness and doubts, how sometimes an inner voice whispered to him that he must dedicate himself to the service of God, but how at the same time there often came over him a longing for his wife and children, earthly possessions, and the tavern.

Rasputin made this confession with head humbly bowed; then he looked up and saw that Makari was smiling at him with kindness and understanding. He felt the skeleton right hand of the saint on his head, its chains rattling slightly: "Rejoice, my son," said the voice of Father Makari, "for among many thousands the Lord hath chosen you. Great things lie before you. Leave your wife and children, leave your horses, hide yourself, go forth and wander! You will hear the earth speak and learn to understand its words. Then and not till then return to the world again, and proclaim to men what the voice of our holy Russian earth says to them!"

* * * * *

Rasputin returned to Pokrovskoe only to take farewell of his family. Father Makari had sent him wandering, and he himself recognized that all external exercises, penitence, and mortification could only mean a first stage, a preparation for the real "way." In order to be able to tread this "inner way" he must needs take the "outer way" also, the "wandering" or "pilgrimage." Wandering—*uīti v stranstvo*—is one of the chief acts in Russian mysticism: men of all ages suddenly break off work in the fields or the farm, abandon their former names, throw away their clothes, burn their papers, forget father and mother, wife and children, and plunge into the unknown. They never write or give any sign of life; for years their family and friends do not hear a word of them; they have become "wanderers," "stranniki."

To all sectarians marriage is an intolerable, even accursed, bond, for it is the closest tie that binds a man to possessions and home. According to the Khlysty, among whom this belief is strongest, marriage is a sin against the Holy Ghost, and every "man of God" is bound to separate from his wedded wife, or at least to refrain from marital intercourse with her. But although they condemn legal marriage, blessed by the priest, and therefore in their eyes sealed with the seal of Antichrist, they permit all other forms of love, because these do not bind men for ever to earth and home. Every adherent of the Khlysty sect is thus justified in substituting for the priest-consecrated tie one or several "marriages in the spirit," blessed by God Himself.

Thousands of these wandering sectarians continually roam all over Russia, either without any definite aim, in obedience to the dictates of their feelings, or on pilgrimages to the holy places of the Christian faith, to Athos, Jerusalem, or even Mount Sinai.

In nearly every Russian village there are simple peasants who also belong in secret to the brotherhood of the Wanderers, and whose duty it is to give shelter to the Stranniki. Their steadings contain a special room, a hay-loft, a closet without windows in the courtyard, or cellar under the "izba" itself, where wanderers in need of protection and rest are lodged. Sometimes whole villages are in sympathy with the Stranniki, and then practically every izba has an underground lodging in readiness for them.

As the strannik goes from one dark hole to another and becomes a "podpol'nik" or "underground man," he gradually strips himself of everything belonging to his former existence that may still encumber him. No one knows his real name or anything of his past, and no one asks whence he comes or whither he intends to go. Free from all earthly restraints, he lives henceforth for his soul alone, and abandons himself to spiritual exercises pleasing to God. Little by little he attains prestige as a being apart, and the peasants are happy when he visits them. The esteem for these "podpol'niki" is extraordinarily great, and far exceeds that given to the priests of the Church. When the wanderer feels that the time of his roaming is at an end, he sometimes gains a reputation for special sanctity: he becomes a "wise man," a "starets," and from all over the country the faithful make pilgrimages to beg for his counsel and blessing. He has completely freed himself from all external things, has banished even from his heart everything binding him to the false world of appearance. His sinful feelings and thoughts are gradually obliterated, and there begins in him the wonderful process of the mysterious death.

Rasputin lived a life of vagabondage for many years, and this period was of the greatest importance for his whole development. In the underground rooms of the peasant houses he continually encountered all sorts of men who, like him, for their souls' sake, had exchanged their ordinary life for the unsettled existence of the "podpol'nik." In intercourse with adherents of the most varied sects, champions of the most fantastic ideas, and in intimate contact with enthusiasts and religious fanatics of all kinds, he penetrated the deepest secrets of the soul of the Russian people, and absorbed the real feelings, thoughts, and wishes of the peasantry. During this eternal vagabondage, and subject to the perpetual persecution of the police and the priests, he became expert in watching men unobtrusively, discovering their most secret designs, and noting their weaknesses and peculiarities, and he extended his knowledge of humanity to an extraordinary degree.

He came in contact with "Old Believers," those fanatics of the letter who rebelled against the reform of the Church books by the Patriarch Nikon, and who believed that by this sacrilegious change in the method of writing, the word of God became the tool of Antichrist and the Orthodox Church the Whore of Babylon. Other sectarians, again, were ruthlessly persecuted by the authorities because they refused to perform military service; firmly believing in the word of God that he who takes the sword must perish by the sword, they rejected all war. Other fanatical peasants refused to pay taxes because they did not wish to hand over their property to the agents of Satan. They fled from the Government and dreamed of the coming of a new kingdom, the fourth great age, in which the Holy Ghost would assume sovereignty over the earth, punish the servants of Antichrist, and exalt the righteous.

But however different might be the ideas of all these sectarians about the coming redemption, whether they preached the renewal of man through repentance, or tried to participate in the divine grace by rebellion against the world of sin, they were all united by the common desire to overcome the sinful world here on earth, and to enter the Kingdom of Heaven in the living body. None of them was content with the consolations of the Orthodox Church, or prepared to wait patiently for salvation in a life beyond the grave. The firm bond that united all these "underground men" in an inner brotherhood was their concealment in face of the world, their secrecy about their hopes, their faith, and their cult.

In his intercourse with these innumerable pilgrims and wandering monks Rasputin gradually deepened his theological knowledge, and acquired that skill in the use of biblical texts which was later to excite amazement even among the highest dignitaries of the Church. Thus in every respect these years of vagabondage were a most important period of apprenticeship for him, and there is hardly a feature in his later life which cannot be traced back to this time of pilgrimage and "underground" life.

* * * * *

But Rasputin's greatest and most decisive experience during his wanderings was his real initiation into the mysteries of the Khlysty. What had deeply interested and fascinated him when he vaguely learned of it at Verkhoture, he now encountered in person during his roamings through the countless villages of the vast Russian Empire. For the first time he saw with his own eyes the concealed peasant rooms, monastery cells, or barns in which the great mystery of the "wonderful transfiguration" was enacted. In these "ships" of the People of God Rasputin first truly experienced the miracle of the mysterious death, and found in all this the fulfilment and completion for which he had long been preparing himself by mortification and wandering and the renunciation of a settled life and earthly possessions.

These mystical rites of the Khlysty are strange enough. The insignificant peasant house in which the miracle is to take place looks just the same as all the other huts of the village. On crossing the threshold you pass into a simple, everyday peasant room with rough benches along the walls and a plain table and two chairs in the middle. On Saturday evening one peasant, then another, and many a peasant woman, steal into this house. When "the red sun has set" the window is covered with thick curtains; and the members of the community silently seat themselves on the benches, the men on the right and the women on the left. They sit in the same attitudes as when they crouch round the samovar in their own huts after their work in the fields is done. Even the two peasants, a man and a woman, who take their places in the seats of honour at the table, are no different from the other members of the community: they wear coarse clothes and the dust of the village street still clings to their clumsy boots. But the "people of God," whose hearts know, tremble as soon as their gaze lights on the two figures at the table, for there, in the persons of two simple peasants, are beings endowed with the grace of God.

Now begins the singing of the long-drawn-out hymns resembling litanies, psalms, and folk songs, in which is expressed the longing of the Khlysty for the advent of the Kingdom of Heaven, for God's becoming man, and for the outpouring of the Holy Spirit. Gradually the singing becomes more jubilant, rapturous, and ecstatic, for the hymns proclaim the appearance of the Saviour in the midst of his shining host of angels. Then the peasants strip off their clothes and shoes, and each puts on a white shirt made of muslin, in memory of the marvellous resurrection of the Christ, Ivan Suslov, on whose body, when flayed by the police informers, the white linen became a new skin. But, at the same time, the donning of the white shirt, the "garment of the departed spirits and angels," signifies to the people of God that they themselves have exchanged their earthly covering for a spiritual one, and have been transformed into beings endowed with special powers.

Clad in their white shirts, by the light of twelve wax candles, they continue the singing, which swells to ever greater heights of rapture and passion, until at last one rises and begins to turn round in a circle. Then others step out of the ranks, men and women, form pairs, and begin a sort of peasant round dance, keeping time to the singing, now following each other round in a circle and now slowly turning round alone.

And soon the simple dance, by a mystical transformation, becomes the dance of the disciples round Jesus Christ as told in the secret writings of the hidden true faith; and just as, in accordance with these secret writings, in the dance of the disciples round the Lord, all the powers of Heaven, sun, moon, and stars, turn in joyful measures around Jesus, the Son of God become man, so the same cosmic event repeats itself at the feast of the dancing people of God. The whole universe dances with the exultant sectarians until "the Lord shows himself in the circle, sounds a blast on the golden trumpet, and gives the world to know that all sinners are pardoned."

Now come different forms of the dance: the faithful, one after the other, traverse the room with skipping steps; then they run crosswise up and down raising their arms aloft and fervently calling on the Holy Ghost. When the ecstasy reaches a certain height, the people of God feel above their heads the beat of the wings of the Holy Ghost, and the great transfiguration is fulfilled in which everything earthly becomes heavenly. The benches, the table, the chairs, the whole stuffy peasant's room becomes the unearthly "ark of the righteous," the vessel that bears the company through the stormy, swelling sea of the profane external world into the kingdom of bliss. The peasant man and woman in the places of honour at the table become Jesus Christ and the Mother of God, and both steer the ship of the brotherhood of the faithful towards the Heavenly Kingdom.

Now the word is fulfilled, the miracle has happened anew: the Almighty Spirit of God has once again taken on flesh. In frenzied rapture breaks from the people of God the cry: "The Holy Ghost is among us," and they repeat this cry until their tongues are paralysed and a blissful numbness gradually overpowers their movements. The dance ends, the song is silent, and the divine helmsman rises in his seat. He begins to speak, but his voice has changed and sounds now deep and sinister like the cry of an animal, now stammers like a child, and again is jubilant with joyful excitement.

Only those who have been initiated into the mysteries of the Khlysty understand that he who speaks, stammers, and cries, who now breaks into childish laughter and now distorts his face in grimaces, is moved by the Holy Spirit; only they know that it is man newly risen, innocent, and once again as a child, who stammers with his voice. Filled with happy reverence, the sectarians huddle on the ground round the divine helmsman, weep and tremble with rapture, cross themselves, and listen to the blessed words uttered by the prophet.

Then the dancing starts again, even wilder and more unrestrained than before, and lasts till dawn. The voices, the stamping of the dancing feet, and the rustling of the garments mingle in a single confused noise; faces and voices are blurred, shirts billowed out by the whirling are like rotating pillars, and the floor is wet with the sweat of the dancers. Suddenly, amid the mad, ever faster gyrations, the sectarians bare their bodies to the waist and, one by one, half-naked, step up to the prophet, who flagellates them with a staff made of twisted osier switches to signify the fecundation and generation of the new man in Adam's body.

Then, just as Christ cast off the husk of mortality to rise again in the spirit, the Khlysty, both men and women, cast all their garments from them during their wild dance. Here and there, one of them is seized with convulsions and sinks to the ground senseless; the lights are extinguished, the women with unbound hair fall on the men and embrace and kiss them passionately. In "sinful encounter" the people of God roll on the ground and copulate, regardless of age and relationship.

Only in this mad intoxication of the senses are earthly consciousness and self-will completely extinguished, for in the "sinful encounter" the earthly ego has no more influence, but only the will of the invisible spirit.

Grigori Efimovich Rasputin, the sensual but believing peasant of Pokrovskoe, learned in these Khlysty orgies to understand the real meaning of the peculiar mysteries of rebirth through sin. He perceived that the true inner life was granted only to him who could arouse the old man in himself through the "sinful encounter" and struggle with him, in order to slay him in the mysterious way of sin and attain to "holy passionlessness." Man could never completely overcome all the ties binding him to earth until he had annihilated the last remnants of arrogance and pride in his soul, the arrogance of the ascetic, and the pride of the virtuous. The way to true submission and humility henceforth for Rasputin must be followed through the "sinful encounter," through the casting away of the final barriers, through the deepest self-abasement in carnal sin.

CHAPTER III

THE CELLAR PREACHER

MANY years had passed since Grigori Efimovich had slung on his bread sack, taken his alms bowl and staff in his hand, and set out on his wanderings. For long his family in Pokrovskoe had had no news of him, and his father, old Efim, was heavy-hearted over his son's absence. Efim Andreevich Rasputin had by his industry in the course of the years enlarged considerably the steading he had inherited. He had erected a fairsized, two-story house in place of the old family cabin, extended the stables, and increased the stock of horses to several dozen. His property had thus become a neat, prosperous-looking farm such as is seldom to be met with in Siberia.

But on him, as on Job, one blow of fate after another had fallen. First, God had within a brief period robbed him of two sons and then of his faithful, industrious wife, Anna Egorovna, who, up to the end, tall, slim, and fair, with her silver-grey hair and smiling eyes, had directed the household and sat at the spinning-wheel. She had caught a chill when journeying from Tiumen to Pokrovskoe in the damp autumn weather, and a few days after was carried off. Grigori only had been left to him, a great support to his old father in spite of his drinking habits.

But however keenly the old man might feel about the separation from his son, he never complained, for he was a pious and God-fearing peasant. Had not the wise and reverend Father Makari of Verkhoture decided his Grisha to leave hearth and home, father, wife, and children? Efim Andreevich had given his son a father's blessing and let him go in the pious conviction that work in the service of the Lord was of more account than the work of the world.

And even now, some years after Grigori's departure, the old man still tried to comfort his grief with the thought that God

Himself had need of his Grigori. This conviction gave him a feeling of proud superiority, such as is not infrequently felt by those who are convinced that God has called them to a great task, to make a heavy sacrifice, or to endure an overwhelming sorrow. As this idea took hold of him old Efim spent more and more of his time in church or in the large, ground-floor room, where hung the miracle-working picture of the Holy Virgin of Kazan. There he would pray for hours on end, and gradually he came to neglect his worldly occupations.

He avoided the neighbours and other chance visitors and, even when sitting with Praskovia Fedorovna, the wife of his absent son, and her growing children, he no longer told them wonderful stories of the old times as he used to do, but remained for the most part sunk in a deep, meditative silence. When asked for his orders about the farm work, it was not uncommon for him to look at the questioner in amazement and with a glance that seemed to say: "We, my son and I, now live only for the service of God."

The long absence of her husband also weighed heavily on the spirits of Grisha's young wife. She, too, was religious, and sought refuge from her grief in the wonder-working picture of the Mother of God; but she lacked the firm, proud faith which could comfort old Efim to some extent for the loss of his son. The earthly longing of a young and lonely woman was stronger in her than meek submission to the divine decree. So Praskovia Fedorovna spent far less time in contemplating the holy ikons than in looking at the well-worn picture of her husband, taken by a travelling photographer from Tobolsk. It showed Grigori with a contented, merry face, the straightly-parted hair smoothed down with grease, the face, with its slight light-brown moustache, fresh, rosy, and sunburned. His features and his whole figure breathed strength and gay vitality; but the look in his eyes was both far-away and yet piercing.

Fortunately, the young wife was too much occupied by the work of the household to have much time to devote to her gloomy thoughts. But her heart could not be glad and, as the years passed, she too became silent, quiet, and reserved; she aged quickly and her pretty features assumed a careworn, melancholy expression.

It not infrequently happened that strange pilgrims, wanderers, or tramps, came to the village and, in accordance with ancient custom, begged for a night's shelter in Efim's house. On these occasions Praskovia Fedorovna immediately became talkative again, and put a thousand questions to the strangers, for she kept on hoping that each new arrival would be able to give her news of Grigori.

In the time immediately following Grigori's departure it really had happened sometimes that one or another of the wanderers declared that he had met a man answering to Praskovia's description. Many pilgrims even thought that they had spoken with Grigori Efimovich and accompanied him for a time on his way. One man reported having met him in a monastery hostel in the Urals; according to another story he had been seen on the high road travelling in the direction of the town of Kazan; other pilgrims believed that they had encountered him in the woods quite close to Pokrovskoe, on the opposite bank of the Tura. But there was never any certainty that they were really talking of Praskovia's husband, for none of them ever called him by name.

But, in the course of time, such news became rarer and more doubtful and, finally, even these few untrustworthy reports ceased entirely. On the other hand, in the third year after Rasputin's disappearance, strange rumours began to circulate among the peasants about a strannik who was causing much talk on account of the numerous miracles he had performed.

More and more frequently travellers came to Pokrovskoe telling of these amazing deeds and also of the curious and novel teaching of this mysterious man. According to these accounts he had appeared first among the fishermen on the upper Tura, had spent many days among them, helped them to bring in the nets, and taught them to sing psalms and other sacred songs. He had also revealed to the fishermen that he was sent by God, and that in him the Holy Ghost had descended among men. According to other stories he had appeared among a group of farm men and women in a field, helped them in the harvesting and, in the evenings, told them that the priests of the Church had forgotten the true meaning of the Gospel and the real words of the Saviour; that they no longer knew anything of the joyful message that all sin could be wiped out by repentance, and that God valued the lost sheep more than all the rest of the flock.

Another story had it that this peculiar wanderer held strange services in the depths of the forests with pretty young girls and women. He first made crosses from boughs, and prayed before them with his disciples. When his devotions were over he threw his arms about the women, fondled and kissed them, and then all sang and danced. In explanation he declared that these kisses, caresses, songs, and dances, formed part of the divine service and rejoiced and cheered the Lord.

Soon more serious rumours began to be current among the peasants. It was said that, at these forest services, the stranger did not restrict himself to caressing his "sisters," as he called his women disciples. There were whispers of festivals at which the unknown and his train of women kindled huge fires of leaves and branches, sent up fervent prayers, and sang hymns. Then they all danced round the flames, until the women were seized by a mad delirium, and the prophet cried in a strange voice, "Abase yourselves through sin! Try your flesh!" Of what happened afterwards the horrified peasants dared speak only in whispers, for in the darkness of the forest, lit only by the stars of heaven, the pilgrim committed the most horrible sins with the women.

Soon a report was abroad that this sinister starets was accompanied on his wanderings through the forests and over the steppes by a band of women and girls, who had all left husbands and parents to follow the preacher, in the faith that he alone could save their souls. It was said that, in some more distant villages, the stranger had been seen in the public baths displaying himself to the women completely naked, and making them undress also. The "sisters" had then to wash his dusty feet. He declared that this extreme humiliation of his pupils served to kill the last remnants of their pride and self-righteousness.

At the outset most of the peasants of Pokrovskoe were of the opinion that this wanderer was a false prophet and an emissary of Satan, especially after the local priest, Father Petr, had given forcible expression to this view. But news came of fresh signs, great miracles, such as can be worked only by saints: that he had driven the devil out of a nun, and that elsewhere he had prophesied events that actually came to pass soon after.

But that which had the most convincing effect on the peasants, and which did more than anything else to establish the fame of the wanderer among them, was the story of how he, on one occasion when the outraged fathers and husbands of his disciples went to attack him personally, raised his arm threateningly, and cried in a terrible voice: "Let there be no rain for three months." And this curse was fulfilled! For twelve weeks the sun blazed in a cloudless sky and burned up the fields, and not until the period had expired did the rain come again. Who but a messenger from God could have the power to stop the rain? Whatever Father Petr might say, the stranger was a holy man, perhaps holier than the priest himself, who was not yet able to command the weather!

There were also people in Pokrovskoe who, on the first news of the appearance of the new starets, had exchanged understanding glances. These were the peasants, men and women, of whom rumour had long had it that they were only in outward appearance pious Christians, and that, in fact, they adhered to the heretical doctrines of the "people of God." No one, it is true, could bring any definite charge against them; but, every now and again, little signs were noticed which indicated that these peasants belonged to the secret brotherhood.

When these heretics assembled on Saturday evenings in their clandestine meetings they, too, discussed the reports about the miracle-worker. But while the other peasants, steeped in the Orthodox faith, were doubtful and argued among themselves whether the strange wanderer was a saint or a devil, the sectarians knew beyond all doubt that this wanderer preaching the doctrine of the meaning of sin was one of themselves. They talked exultantly of the advent of the newly risen Saviour, in whom once again, as so often before, God had become incarnate on earth, in accordance with the eternal rules. All the actions of the stranger that seemed odd and repulsive to the orthodox peasants presented themselves in a different light to the sectarians. Did not the great Radaev act in this way too? Had not that divine master also proclaimed the truth that man can by carnal vice master his sin, and thus free his soul from all evil? Now another had arisen to preach this doctrine, and the divine spirit was again incarnate on earth, as once before in Radaev and before him in Ivan Suslov and Danila Filipich.

It was not only the sectarians who were exercised by the unknown starets. There was also much talk of him in the house of old Efim Andreevich, when in the evenings the farmer, his daughter-in-law, the servants and neighbours were assembled round the table and on the great bench by the stove. None of the villagers and none of the wanderers who lodged at Efim Andreevich's had ever yet seen the starets personally. But a Pokrovskoe peasant had once met a feeble old man from another village at the market at Tiumen, who reported that he had seen the saint and a crowd of young girls break from the woods and proceed through his village. The old man described the miracle-worker as a lean man of middle size, with a great flowing beard and hair parted on his forehead, and falling over his shoulders like the hair of Christ on the ikons. His eyes had a piercing glance, his face was pale from mortifications and privations, and furrowed like that of an old man; but his voice was gentle and melodious. Although his whole appearance gave the impression of a good and holy man, the old peasant had had a feeling of inexplicable horror at the sight of him.

* * * * *

Many a long evening passed in such talks and discussions, until one night the great event happened, and Grigori Efimovich came home. Whenever Praskovia Fedorovna looked back on this first meeting with Grisha on his return from years of wandering, it always seemed one of the turning-points of her life. She had had household work to do that evening that had kept her longer than usual from her bed. Suddenly there was a knock at the gate and, looking out, she saw an old, bearded man standing before the door. She took him at first for one of the wandering folk who came to Efim Andreevich's to beg a night's shelter, and she hastened to open the door. Then she knew him; it was his small, light blue eyes that betrayed him. Although they peered forth from a wrinkled face covered with an unkempt beard, Praskovia immediately recognized the look of cheerfulness and cunning in them.

What followed was as surprising as this first encounter. While they all ran joyfully to greet the returned pilgrim, they could not help noticing the change that had taken place in him. He was glad to see his family again after so long an absence; but his gladness was quite different from theirs, and had nothing of worldly happiness in it. His first words of greeting were uttered in a strangely solemn tone and, as his family clung round his neck, he seemed to ward off their caresses with a gesture that, though tender and kind, was grave and firm. He raised his right hand above their heads in blessing, and made the sign of the cross with priestly dignity; there was a strange expression on his lips, and his eyes seemed to look through them into the far distance. There was something so solemn about his thin figure that father, wife, and children were embarrassed, and shrank back from him.

Before her husband Praskovia had a feeling of reverence, as before a person of high birth or great saintliness. As she set about preparing his bed in the usual place her glance fell upon his thin figure, with its stern and solemn attitude, and, seized with awe and embarrassment, she immediately desisted, and hung her head humbly like a frightened maidservant.

But Grigori asked that the door of the secret cellar should be opened for him. Usually it was only wandering pilgrims in flight from the authorities who found refuge there, or those who, from some inner need, wished to withdraw from men. Whenever Praskovia had descended the dark, narrow steps into the comfortless and windowless room, it had been to conduct some such wanderer to his quarters for the night, and now it was her own husband she was leading down! As the door with its iron fastenings opened, she felt on her face the musty air that comes from damp masonry. The bare room with its low, vaulted roof was lit by oil lamps, in the flickering light of which the beribboned pictures of the saints in the ikon-niche seemed to live a ghostly life.

Grigori Rasputin stayed in this tiny, remote chamber of the

prosperous farmhouse and, day and night, stretched in abasement on the bare floor, he mortified his sinful body and did penance. As Praskovia lay at night on her bed waiting for sleep the despairing prayers and lamentations of the penitent reached her from the depths of the cellar. The anguish of his voice cut sharply through the silence of the night, followed by groaning and wailing. Then the lamentation changed to the jubilant singing of psalms and sacred songs, after which the groaning and wailing began again.

The morning after the first night Praskovia and old Efim went down the dark stairs to the penitent. They remained standing on the threshold shattered by the sight before their eyes. They found Grisha on his knees, his thin body painfully bent in convulsive tremors, and his face almost touching the ground. His sing-song lamentation sounded like a weird monotonous groaning, that began with the repetition a hundred times over of the words: "Lord have mercy upon us." Then the words dissolved into despairing cries that burst, one by one, from the cramped body until they merged again into a single, long-drawn-out, and horrifying shriek, when the penitent suddenly became quiet, as if God had had mercy on his woes. His cramped body began gradually to relax, and his head, with its long hair falling backwards, rose from the ground. Grigori's face, turned towards the ikons, seemed, in the glimmer of the oil lamps, blissfully transfigured, as though bathed in golden light.

As he began to sing psalms with trembling lips there came over Praskovia and old Efim a wonderful feeling such as they had never had before. An irresistible force constrained them, too, to kneel down and join in Grigori's chanting. But this happy change again gave place to despairing outbursts of abasement and remorse, and Praskovia and Efim also bowed their heads, and prayed God for grace and forgiveness for their sins.

More and more frequently Efim and Praskovia, in obedience to the voice from the cellar, with its alternations of lamentation and jubilation, descended to the penitent's dark retreat and took part in his prayers. They began to neglect their worldly occupations, and often spent whole days and nights sharing Grigori's penitential exercises. How it had happened they themselves could hardly explain; but from the moment when his terrible lamentations and the joyful song that immediately followed them had first forced them to their knees, a curious change took place in them also, and the ecstasy of the penitent raised them to unknown heights of religious enthusiasm.

As soon as this great conversion in themselves had taken place they became certain that Grisha had been sent on his wanderings by God Himself, in order that he might become a saint; nor did it surprise them that this rare and divine grace should have been vouchsafed to their Grigori. In their pure and simple faith they had no thought of trying to search out the ways and decrees of God.

* * * * *

When, in the course of a day or two, the news of Rasputin's return and of the wonderful change in him became known among the peasants of Pokrovskoe, there were many who felt very doubtful about his conversion into a saint; they remembered too well the careless peasant lad he had been, always loafing in public-houses, picking quarrels, and running after women.

An old peasant who, as a member of the local church council, had frequent occasion to call on Efim Andreevich, made up his mind to be the first to go to his house and convince himself personally of the truth of all these curious rumours. Accompanied by his man, he proceeded to the farm and explained that he had heard of the wonderful conversion that God had wrought in Grisha, and earnestly desired to visit the penitent in his cellar. Old Efim immediately showed him the way through the courtyard, and begged him to go down the steps to Grisha's underground room.

While he was crossing the yard the visitor heard the wailing voice coming up from under the ground, and the nearer he approached the steps the more uneasy he felt. The farm servant accompanying him would have preferred to turn and flee, and he was heartily thankful when his master told him to remain in the yard while he himself prepared to descend the stairs.

Even the old peasant hesitated for an instant, but his curiosity, behind which was the curiosity of the whole village, won the day; he stuck the point of his stick firmly into the ground once or twice in peasant fashion, and disappeared into the opening of the cellar.

With craning neck and eyes half out of his head with excitement, the servant stared after the old man until he disappeared into the darkness. Then he remained motionless by the opening, his heart beating in agitated expectation, for the uncanny and terrifying voice of the penitent continued to rise from the hole. But when the voice suddenly stopped he became really anxious.

A considerable time passed before the heavy steps of the peasant again sounded from the darkness of the cellar stair, and the anxious servant heard his master's stick tapping on the steps. At last the old man himself emerged from the narrow opening and stepped into the yard. The curious servant threw an inquisitive glance at his master; but, when he saw his face, he was so terrified that, in spite of his curiosity, he could not put a single question to him, and he turned and followed his master at some distance as he, with heavy step and thoughtfully bowed head, slowly returned to the village.

Soon the whole of Pokrovskoe was in a ferment of excitement over the old peasant's report of his visit to Grisha, his tales of his lamentations and songs of jubilation, and the strange words he had spoken. The servant's reports about the queer change in his master when he came up from the cellar added not a little to the excitement.

Many of the peasants, after these accounts, were ready without further ado to believe that Grigori Rasputin had been transformed into a saint, especially as they were struck by the resemblance between the descriptions of the old peasant and his servant, and the rumours about the legendary stranger. The conviction gained ground that Grisha was none else than that mysterious pilgrim about whom so many wonderful tales were current. The thought that, of all the villages in the government, it was Pokrovskoe that had been singled out to be the birthplace of a saint was thrilling enough to keep all the inhabitants agog with excitement.

Next day many peasants with their heavy boots and staffs, and many peasant women in wide skirts with gaily coloured kerchiefs on their heads, proceeded to old Efim's farm. Among them were believers, but also not a few doubters; they were all moved by the same curiosity, to see and hear Grisha. And every one of them had the same experience as the old member of the church council. As they crossed the yard and heard the uncanny wailing voice of the saint coming up from the cellar, they hesitated a while before they made up their minds to descend the steep steps. And when one after the other crawled out of the dark opening again, those who had remained above noticed how strangely their faces had changed and, in awed embarrassment, they refrained, in spite of their excitement, from immediately questioning the others about their experiences.

The same thing befell every one of these men and women: they went down to the cellar full of earthly and profane curiosity and they came out transformed. Among those who visited him were men of his own age, who had spent many a night drinking with him and had played many a stupid prank in his company. It was these peasants who had put least faith in the tale of his saintliness, and they had gone down the stairs firm in their unbelief in their old boon companion. But in Rasputin's presence they fared no better than all the rest.

The new saint made a particularly deep impression on the young women and girls of the village. When they returned to the light of day their relations or friends who had remained outside noticed a delicate flush on their faces, such as love alone is wont to paint on the cheeks of young women. A radiant light shone in their eyes, and a slight smile played about their lips, as if those eyes and lips were aware of a happy secret.

Very soon hardly a single inhabitant of Pokrovskoe doubted that something extraordinary had happened to Grigori Efimovich Rasputin. It is true that much of what the penitent told his visitors of redemption through sin was in flat contradiction of all the traditions of the Orthodox faith and, therefore, it was difficult for many of the peasants to acclaim Grisha as the new Saviour, for as such he was already revered by a large part of the village. This worship of Rasputin originated chiefly with the women and girls, and it seems that it was they who from the start really grasped the meaning of his new doctrines. While the old peasants still stood before their doors in the evenings, leaning on their heavy staffs, and tried laboriously to bring the preaching of the cellar into harmony with the doctrines of the Orthodox Church, the women, untroubled by any scruples, were asserting Grigori's saintliness in rapturous and enthusiastic words. Every day saw an increase in the number of Grisha's followers of both sexes, and very soon every cabin contained a peasant, old man or young, a girl or an old woman, who was unreservedly devoted to the preacher in the cellar.

One man held out, the venerable Father Petr, the village priest. Both at first, when only vague rumours about the "new saint" reached his ears, and also later, when the sermons from the cellar were known all over Pokrovskoe, Father Petr attacked this impious and villainous false doctrine with the fighting spirit of a truly orthodox servant of the Church. He unflinchingly proclaimed at every opportunity that Grisha was a messenger of Hell, and his preaching of redemption through sin the satanic lie itself, which alone would dare to blaspheme the true word of God. The apostate Grisha was accursed, as also was everyone who fell a victim to his false teachings.

In such or similar ways Father Petr thundered day in and day out; his dumpy little figure stiffened whenever the conversation turned on Grisha, and his eyes blazed furiously. His disproportionately large head, round which the red hair stood up like a halo, his face covered with a curly red beard, and his flashing eyes all gave the impression that the angry little priest might burst into flames at any moment. But in spite of all his anathemas Father Petr had to admit that the number of those who went down to the cellar kept on increasing, and that even the most faithful of his parishioners found pleasure in the shameless doctrines of the false preacher. He remained for whole days in his little house on the hill in the middle of Pokrovskoe, or sat sulking at his window. He no longer went into the village itself, among the peasants who had fallen into the snares of Satan, for his pure faith forbade him to seek any contact with evildoers. So he lay in wait for passers-by in his parsonage, in order to learn what new and terrible blasphemies the devil in the cellar had been uttering.

On the next great Church festival Father Petr prayed long in his chamber before the ikons in the corner, and fervently implored God to give him strength for his sermon; for that day, after the prescribed prayers and ceremonies were ended, he must take up the fight against Satan, and lead his flock back to the true path. When the hour of divine service arrived, he had the bells tolled especially loud and long, so that their pure metallic clangour might penetrate into the remotest cabins and there proclaim the one true faith of the Church.

But it was as if a frightful curse lay over Pokrovskoe. However clear and invitingly the bells might peal from the church tower, it seemed that they were drowned by the wailing voice of the penitent in his underground vault. The peasants listened only to this devilish voice, and instead of gathering in the church, one by one they descended the dark stairs in Efim Andreevich's yard.

The venerable Father Petr who, for so many years, had been a real pastor in his village, a true father and adviser to his congregation, stood before the ikonostas sad at heart on that festival for which he had made such earnest preparations. Only a few old women and a handful of particularly loyal peasants came to partake of mass; for the rest there were the beggars, the halt, and the blind who regularly appear at every church service. The respected members of the church council, the rich peasants and their wives, the well-dressed girls and lads did not appear, for they were all standing in Efim's courtyard waiting to be admitted to the presence of the diabolical Grisha. Sadly Father Petr celebrated the divine rites; then, waiting until the few faithful sons and daughters of the Church had departed, he knelt in prayer before the ikonostas and implored God to give him light and show him the way whereby he might be enabled to fight Antichrist.

Next day he wakened with a new and unshakable resolution. He would no longer look on in silence and inactivity while the devil took possession of his flock; rather, like a brave soldier of the heavenly kingdom, he would go down into Satan's burrow and conquer him with the weapon of the true word of the Gospel. With flaming eyes he hastened down to the village from his church on the hill and on to old Efim's house. The peasants, when they saw him coming, thought that they were looking on Saint George himself issuing with fiery courage to do battle with the dragon. A shudder ran over them, for they believed that the decisive hour of the battle between the priest and the prophet of the new faith was at hand.

As Father Petr passed through Efim's yard the peasants who were standing about quickly moved aside to make way for the priest. Though it was long since they had been to church, yet now, when they saw their pastor approaching with firm steps, they felt once more their old reverence for the man of God, and bowed before him in deep humility. But he scarcely heeded these faithless, who had fallen away from the truth to follow a false prophet.

With chest well forward, his little figure erect, head thrown back, and his chin with its reddish beard thrust forward at an acute angle, he stepped boldly up to the cellar stairs. At that moment there was undoubtedly something proud and brave about him, and all his movements betrayed a desire for battle as he disappeared into the deep, dark hole. After he had descended the peasants crowded round and, craning their necks, stared down full of fearful expectation of what was going to happen. An excited whisper passed from lip to lip as the wailing voice from the underground dungeon was suddenly stilled, as if snapped off. The peasants held their breath.

All at once the voice of the penitent cut sharply through the stillness, like the whipping out of a peasant knife. One cry followed another, like knife-thrust on knife-thrust; never had the voice of the holy Grigori seemed so terrifying to the peasants. While they were still listening shudderingly to these sinister sounds, the figure of Father Petr crawled out of the dark cave again. But what a pitiable look the combative priest had now! Broken, shaken, and with a furtive glance, like a poor, beaten cur he slunk as fast as his legs would carry him through the rows of peasants, and hurried over the yard to the road. The voice from below continued to curse in a mighty succession of cries, as if it wished still to pursue the fleeing village priest. Like one bereft of his senses, the little cleric ran through the lanes to the church on the hill, and did not recover until he was close to the tower, and the devilish voice from the cellar no longer echoed in his ears. Then he stood still, drew a deep breath, and gradually won back his dignity and self-control. What had befallen him? He knew now that in the cellar, as the hideous voice of the penitent ruthlessly bore down on him, Antichrist had gained power over his soul too. He had had to take to flight, to the derision of all the peasants, men and women, who had been witnesses of his humiliation. But he knew that if he had remained a moment longer he, too, would have fallen a victim to the might of the false prophet.

Now, when he thought of his rebellious congregation, Father Petr was considerably more lenient towards their sinful weakness. Nevertheless, he knew that he must not abandon the fight against the devil. As soon as the enchantment of the satanic voice of the penitent had fallen from him he felt that enlightenment had been granted to him, showing him the right way. He hurried into the house, first said a prayer, and then took a quill pen from a drawer and wrote down on a large sheet of paper everything bad he knew about the former life, the actions, and the preaching of the devil-possessed Grigori Efimovich. He also added much he really did not know but which, nevertheless, it seemed to him imperative to say in the interest of the holy cause. Finally, at the end of his report, he declared that beyond doubt the doctrine preached by Grisha was the accursed heresy of the Khlysty, and that Grisha himself was an emissary of that sinful brotherhood. It therefore seemed necessary to him, for the honour of the true faith and for the salvation of the parish of Pokrovskoe, that the authorities should without delay intervene in the most drastic fashion against the propagator of this dangerous doctrine, that is, take legal proceedings against the former carrier, Grigori Efimovich Rasputin. This letter he signed, placed in a large envelope, and sent to the Bishop of Tiumen. Then, with the peaceful feeling of having done the right thing, he awaited the outcome.

It was not long before a commission appeared in Pokrovskoe, with the Very Reverend Lord Bishop at its head. They made the parsonage their headquarters, and one by one all the adherents to the false doctrine were summoned for examination by the local police. Every single person who was known to Father Petr as having been in the cellar had to appear before the commission, young men and girls, old peasants and white-haired old women.

The young women were examined first, and for this purpose the Lord Bishop sent all the other members of the commission and even the clerk from the room, and questioned the women in a fatherly tone as if he were their confessor. But to his consternation he had to listen to words of the highest praise of the saintly Grisha from every one of them; with glowing cheeks they declared, one after the other, that Grigori Efimovich was a holy and truly God-fearing man and that his words had inspired them with the deepest piety. Even the old peasants and their wives, usually so garrulous, refused to admit that they had heard anything in the cellar which could possibly be construed in an evil sense. In fact, it seemed that the whole village was in a conspiracy to protect the false prophet from the authorities. They all asserted that Grisha spoke divine words, prayed, fasted, mortified his flesh, and served God in the deepest contrition and submission.

The Bishop became impatient, the clerk played nervously with his quill pen, and the other gentlemen of the commission were thinking of rising and declaring the official proceedings at an end. Then Father Petr jumped up from his seat, his whole body shaking with rage, crossed himself hurriedly three times, and cried out in an agitated voice: "The peasants are all under the spell of Antichrist! The spirit of lying speaks from them! Let the high commission convince itself of the blasphemous conduct of this accursed preacher!"

The commission thereupon resolved to send Father Petr to Efim's house accompanied by a policeman. The two men set off and the cleric conducted the official to the entrance of the cellar, and waited while the policeman descended in a dignified, official manner. When he entered the cellar Grisha was again lying on the ground and praying fervently. His devotions were so profound and produced such an effect that the policeman, also a simple, God-fearing peasant, was overcome, fell on his knees on the threshold of the vault, and joined in the prayers of the peni-

THE CELLAR PREACHER

tent. Grisha noticed the man who had come "to take proceedings" against him, and who was now devoutly kneeling, went up to him, made the sign of the cross over him, and spoke words more wonderful than the policeman had ever heard. Deeply moved, he seized and kissed the hand of the penitent, which was raised in blessing over him. From his coarse peasant lips burst the words: "Father Grigori, forgive me my sins." On the return journey to the church the policeman spoke only in monosyllables, although the priest walking by his side kept pressing him to say whether he was not convinced of the blasphemous words of Antichrist. He briefly reported to the commission that he had observed nothing suspicious, which statement was duly entered in the minutes. Under the circumstances the Bishop saw no possibility of taking any steps against Grigori Efimovich Rasputin, and confined himself to the resolve that the preacher in the cellar should in future be under official supervision. Thereupon the commission left Pokrovskoe, and Father Petr, to his infinite disappointment, had to acknowledge that practically nothing had happened. The miraculous conversion of the policeman very quickly spread among the peasantry, and served as a further proof of the saintliness of "Father Grigori"—the name which the policeman was the first to apply to the penitent. This designation flew from mouth to mouth. From a peasant lad Grisha had become a "Father," a "starets," and thus the last stage in the canonization of this Russian muzhik was complete.

The fame of the new starets spread far beyond Pokrovskoe and penetrated into the neighbouring governments. Old Efim's house became a place of pilgrimage, and swarms of peasants crowded round the cellar into which Grigori, one of the long line of pious stranniki, had crept, so that from the womb of Mother Earth he might proclaim anew to the world the unadulterated word of the Russian earth, the gospel of the pilgrims, the truth of the "underground men."

Nothing contributed more to Rasputin's prestige than the fact that the authorities were trying to persecute him: had not the spies of the temporal powers from earliest times tried to put God's emissaries in chains, imprison them, and nail them to the cross? In the same way Grisha, now persecuted for his saintly teaching, became a martyr and a witness to the true word of God.

In the fields and the spinning-rooms, on the benches in front of the house doors, among the fishermen, and in the concealed underground holes of the sectarians, everywhere there was talk of the miracles of the new saint. It was recalled how he had commanded the rain to cease, and how he had saved a nun from the devil's clutches; for none now doubted that the mysterious stranger was Father Grigori.

Three weeks had passed since Grisha had entered on his penance in the cellar; on the twenty-first day he was to appear again among men. Early in the morning of this important day a crowd assembled in Efim's courtyard and in the road before his house, in order to be present at the solemn first appearance of the holy man. They once again heard the wailing cries followed by a joyful psalm; then the voice of the wonderful man ceased, and the crowd stood waiting in a silence charged with emotion; silent and still, they stood expectantly, as in the framework of the door that led to the underground dungeon, appeared in the semi-darkness the stern, lean figure of the penitent. His face was pale and yellowish, as if made of wax, and his nose stood out sharp and prominent from cheeks worn and hollow with prolonged mortifications.

With slow, dignified steps he left the doorway and passed through the waiting crowd to the street. His form spoke of a high seriousness, but the bright glance of his pale blue eyes shone with kindliness, gaiety, and joy. The peasants threw themselves at his feet, kissed his hands and the hem of his kaftan, crying "Father Grigori! Our Saviour!"

He stopped, bent over the devout crowd, blessed them, and said: "I am come to preach to you the joyous message which our Mother Earth taught me down there, the message of salvation through sin."

He slowly proceeded down the long road to the bank of the Tura and, wherever he appeared, men kneeled before him and paid homage to him. And gradually a circle of young girls and women formed about him, surrounding him like a wreath. Again and again he turned to them with a radiant, joyful glance, and blessed them. Then a peasant or two began also to kiss the garments of the women whom the saint had chosen as his disciples.

On the bank of the river he stopped, turned to the crowd, uttered a solemn prayer, blessed the many who had followed him, and dismissed them; only his women disciples remained.

The peasants, deeply moved, turned to go; and looking back on their homeward way, they saw how the saint, encircled by the host of his disciples, took the road to the forest rising behind the steppe and disappeared into its depths.

CHAPTER IV

BEFORE THE HIGH PRIESTS

IN the long corridor leading to the hostel of the monastery the students and professors of the Academy of Theology had for several hours surrounded the Siberian muzhik who, already honoured as a holy man in his own country, had appeared as a simple pilgrim in the capital. They were accustomed even in their leisure hours to dispute ceaselessly about the correct interpretation of a word or a letter in the Holy Scriptures, and they listened with intense interest to the strange peasant's unusual talk.

They had at first regarded him, when he had appeared that morning at early prayers, merely with the passing interest due a wanderer from some far Siberian province. It was no uncommon thing for simple muzhiks to stop at the Petersburg seminary, and make use of its hostel; and the young seminarists put a question or two in passing to this queer-looking codger, with the condescension with which learned students in the higher branches of theology always treat simple people of the lower classes. They did this less for the purpose of learning anything worth knowing than of deriving entertainment from the simplicity of the stranger.

But his answers soon made the seminarists prick up their ears, for they were marked by a clear-cut assurance that could not fail to make an impression. The students put more and more questions; others came along, and soon a growing group was formed; it was joined by teachers as they passed and, in a little while, the peasant was surrounded by a circle of questioners, who showed an ever keener interest in his pertinent answers.

Some of the seminarists were famous for their skill in confusing opponents in theological discussions, and in involving them in contradictions by the subtlety of their argument. One of these was inspired to show off his art on this simple muzhik, and put to him some very complex questions on the trinity and similar thorny subjects. The audience looked excitedly at the peasant to see how he, who could not possibly be accustomed to the difficult processes of theological speculation, would answer.

Grigori Efimovich Rasputin, the Siberian muzhik, followed the complicated argument with the quiet attentiveness native to the peasant. His bright little eyes regarded the young theologian without the least embarrassment, and he waited until he had finished what he had to say. He was silent for a few seconds, as if turning over in his mind the words he had just heard, and then came his answer. It was quite short, and consisted only of a few clear words; and yet what he said seemed amazing and convincingly right. One by one, other redoubtable disputants tried their luck, and the same fate befell each of them: after they had posed their difficult problems they received from Rasputin a brief but pertinent answer, and the audience had to confess that none of them could have answered the questions so quickly and with such unfailing correctness.

After this interrogation had lasted for a while its character underwent a considerable change. The conceited young seminarists, who had at first merely wished to make fun of the simple peasant, now felt a kind of respectful admiration for the man whom nothing could confuse, and who had a plain, serious, and correct rejoinder to everything. Their questions were no longer put in order to embarrass Rasputin, but because they were really anxious to hear his answer, and receive enlightenment on many problems they themselves did not understand. They became more and more ashamed of their arrogance and conceit and, for the first time, they had a glimmering of the idea that book-learning is not the only path to wisdom. Many of them thought of the Gospels, and remembered that the words of the Holy Scriptures are also simple and plain, exactly like the talk of this peasant. He seemed to know by intuition what they had in vain tried to understand as, night after night, they pored over their books. How was it that he did not, like themselves and even their teachers, get lost in tedious arguments, discussions, and speculations, but was able in a few words to express clearly and unerringly what was important?

So deeply absorbed were the students in their discussion with Grigori Efimovich that they did not notice that their revered teacher, Father Feofan, the rector of the Academy, had quietly joined their group. The frail old man had been observing the pilgrim with his dreamy blue eyes for some time before his well-known voice made itself heard. There was a sudden silence, and the students awaited with excitement the conversation between their rector and the wonderful peasant. Father Feofan addressed the starets with the modesty so characteristic of him: "Just one question if *you* * will allow me, little father." He said this in a voice so weak that his words were hardly audible. Rasputin looked up and glanced straightforwardly and good-naturedly at the grey-haired archimandrite. The latter asked for his opinion on a passage in the Scriptures; he was silent for a moment, and then answered without embarrassment, not in the least overawed by the high dignity of the priest. His reply was again brief, clear, and pertinent. The pupils observed with surprise that the answer of the pilgrim had clearly made a strong impression on Father Feofan. He nodded his fine grey head slightly and said: "Yes, little father, that is correct, *you* speak the truth." Then he put further questions, which were always answered in the same way, until at last he came to the difficult problem of sin, and inquired of the starets what he thought about that. "*You* have said, little father," he began in an even shyer tone than before, "that sin is indispensable before God. But how can that be possible when our Saviour and all the great saints of the Orthodox Church have denounced sin as the work of Satan?" This time Grigori answered without a moment's reflection: in his pale eyes had appeared a peculiar expression, a blend of humility, gentleness, slyness, and craft. "Certainly, little father," he said, "our Saviour and the holy fathers have denounced sin, since it is a work of the Evil One. But how can *you* drive out evil, little father,

---

* Owing to the importance of its use in certain passages, the second person singular has been rendered by the second person plural in italics throughout this translation. (*Translators' note.*)

except by sincere repentance? And how can *you* sincerely repent, if *you* have not sinned?"

He paused a second, and his eyes seemed to have lost all humility; then he continued his speech, but it was no longer quiet and friendly, but noisy, vehement, even reproachful. His words became more and more violent, and finally sounded like the uncontrolled abuse of an angry peasant. "Away with your Scriptures!" he thundered. "Scriptures! Truly, I warn *you*, little father, cease this vain and useless labour so that you may stand before the Lord. Take life as it is, for it alone is given you by God. And let me say this to you. Be not for ever brooding on whence comes sin, on how many prayers a man must say a day, and how long he must fast to escape from sin! Sin, if sin still lurks in you; only in this way can you overcome it! Sin, then you will repent and drive evil from you. So long as you bear sin secretly within you, and fearfully cover it up with fasting, prayer, and eternal discussion of the Scriptures, so long will you remain hypocrites and good-for-nothings, and such are hateful to the Lord. The filth must be expelled, do *you* hear, little father? Only then will your savour be well pleasing to the Lord!"

The students looked anxiously at their teacher; the craziness of these words and the unseemly, disrespectful tone in which they were uttered amazed and troubled them. Some of them became indignant, and would have sharply corrected the muzhik, in spite of his reputation as a saint. But gentle, dreamy Father Feofan remained still, gazing in front of him, as if he were collecting his forces for a reply. So the seminarists, too, kept silent and waited expectantly for what was to happen.

It did not happen. The rector began to speak slowly, started to raise objections to what Rasputin had said; but when he looked at the peasant he stumbled, repeated himself, became confused, and could only stammer out one or two disconnected sentences. His eyelids drooped, he reeled; everything was swimming, and only Rasputin's two bright, glittering eyes seemed to be fixed points. Meanwhile Grigori Efimovich went on talking, and his words beat down on the archimandrite like a shower of stones, so that his whole body began to tremble.

Father Feofan rapidly recovered from his strange attack of

weakness. By the time he had come to himself again, all trace of anything sinister had vanished from Rasputin's aspect. His eyes were clear and friendly, his voice was calm, and his words simple and shrewd, so shrewd that the rector was again reduced to a state of respectful admiration, and fell once more completely under his spell. He resumed his questioning, and the students observed that, after each answer, almost even after each word, he bowed his little grey, bird-like head in approval, saying assentingly: "Yes, little father, that is correct, *you* speak the truth."

Meanwhile, it had become very late, and the archimandrite at last prepared to go to bed. According to his custom he blessed each of his scholars, and then approached the pilgrim and raised his hand. But it seemed as if a stronger power made his hand fall back, and from his lips burst the words: "*You* bless me, little father." Somewhat confused, he hurried off to his room with his quick little steps but, turning round on the stairs, he called to the peasant: "Come to my room early to-morrow, little father. The Venerable Lord Bishop Hermogen will be there, and I should like him to hear *you*."

The students were long in going to bed that night; they discussed the queer incident, and could not still their uneasiness. Many of them were attacked by fearful doubts: what was really the use of all this study and striving, if a simple peasant could come nearer to the truth than they? They felt that the living word had been heard to-day for the first time in this abode of book-learning, and that they must, with shame, confess their powerlessness in face of this living word.

Father Feofan, too, was long troubled by similar thoughts. He could not deny that Grigori Efimovich could explain the meaning of the Gospel words better and more clearly than himself. Was it really true, then, that all acquaintance with commentaries and the most exact theological knowledge was as nothing compared with the direct, God-given intuition of a simple peasant? The old priest struggled in vain to find a way out of his doubts. If Grigori Efimovich was really a saint, what of his blasphemous words about sin? Were these, too, part of divine truth? Or was Rasputin no saint, but an emissary of Satan, sent to confuse the minds of the pious? The only comfort Father Feofan could find was in his hopes of the coming meeting between Rasputin and Bishop Hermogen: this truly God-fearing and learned man, with his deep knowledge of human nature, would tell him what to think of Grigori Efimovich and his doctrine of sin.

* * * * *

It was still very early when, next morning, Hermogen, Bishop of Saratov, knocked at the door of his friend Feofan. The rector, who was still agitated over the events of yesterday, began immediately in words tumbling over each other with excitement to tell his visitor about the extraordinary peasant from Tobolsk, who had made such a strangely powerful impression on him. He spoke with such haste that the words in his toothless mouth finally became an incomprehensible mumbling. The Bishop had again and again to interrupt him with: "What was that, little father? Please say it again."

Father Feofan had not told the half of his tale when the door burst open violently and the peasant from Tobolsk broke noisily into the room. Stopping himself with difficulty, he paused a moment on the threshold, looked fixedly round the room, inspected the two men in front of him, sniffed, and went close up to them as if he wished to smell them. He then turned to the ikon-corner, bowed once and a second and third time, making the sign of the cross; afterwards he sprang to the table, stroked the moustache that covered his broadly smirking lips, and cried out heartily: "Here I am, little father."

He next looked at Bishop Hermogen, over whose delicate features played the kindly, comfortable smile so characteristic of him. The gigantic Bishop sat broadly ensconced on the old leather sofa by the window, and observed with amusement the strange peasant, who had fixed his cunning eyes on him.

"Is that *your* bishop *you* spoke of yesterday?" inquired Rasputin.

Somewhat taken aback by this disrespectful form of question, Feofan nodded assent; Grigori Efimovich first rushed up to the frail little rector and next to the good-natured Bishop of Saratov, threw arms round them, and, peasant-fashion, kissed them three times, first from right to left and then from left to right, so boisterously that both were alarmed.

"Little father, little father," cried the Bishop, laughing good-humouredly, *"you'll* crush me."

From the first Hermogen liked Rasputin: he was delighted with his jolly, animated little eyes, with the genuine sincerity and simplicity that breathed from his whole being, but especially with the piquant and sometimes even slightly coarse flavour of Rasputin's language, which abounded in mother-wit and peasant slyness, and which, with its beautiful, deep tones, and its distinctive Siberian dialect, seemed particularly charming to the Bishop. Grigori, too, from the start felt sympathetic to this comfortably smiling man. The two found the right tone immediately, and a few minutes later they were talking away as unconstrainedly as if they had been old friends. Grigori suddenly seized the Bishop's hand, pressed it affectionately, and cried "I like *you.*" Hermogen burst out laughing, much cheered by this spontaneous proof of friendship, while gentle little Father Feofan again made vain attempts to bring the conversation round to sacred subjects. For the rector earnestly desired to introduce his episcopal friend to the pilgrim's singular capacity for expounding the Gospels, and to hear his verdict on it.

The Bishop was not so sensitive to direct impressions, and not so easily carried away by enthusiasm as the rector; but his benevolent mind and serenity of spirit brought him all the more quickly into touch with the Siberian peasant. He did not immediately succumb to admiration for the "new saint," but none the less, his liking for this vital peasant was at least as great as the rapture of gentle Father Feofan. During his talk with Grisha he was more and more captivated by his clarity and sagacity; but what really attracted him to Grigori was not so much his theological skill as the direct sensuous effect of his words.

Hermogen was a militant servant of the Church and a great preacher; he at once saw how great an influence Rasputin might exercise, and how valuable his co-operation might be in the service of the Orthodox cause. It seemed to the Bishop that the clergy, in their fight against the tendency towards complete Westernization then prevailing in Russian politics, needed just such a man as this Grigori Efimovich who, with his native and original speech, so exactly embodied the best type of muzhik. As Hermogen listened to the pilgrim he was hard at work thinking how he could best arrange to secure this impressive, fundamentally Russian personality for his political purposes. When Grigori Efimovich had finished his discourse Hermogen, his mind full of such schemes, turned to Father Feofan with the remark that they must at once take the starets to the famous monk-priest Iliodor. Father Feofan had not yet grasped the Bishop's far-reaching projects, and had merely noticed what extraordinary pleasure he found in this peculiar Siberian peasant. At the same time, he felt somewhat disappointed, for he could not help thinking that Grigori was to-day making a less favourable impression than he had made yesterday; in particular, the rough manner in which he talked to Hermogen offended the rector. But when Hermogen invited him and Grigori Rasputin to go with him to Iliodor, he suppressed his disappointment, and followed the other two with little steps, quiet and gentle as was his wont, to visit the monk-priest.

* * * * *

Iliodor, the monk-priest of Tsarytsin, or, to give him his real name, Sergei Trufanov, had the reputation of being the greatest church orator in Russia, and his sermons were beginning to surpass in fame even those of John of Kronstadt. He was a tall, thin monk with wild, burning eyes, whose voice, though sharp and unpleasant, had a compelling power. On account of his austere life and his fanatical zeal in the faith, he had been nicknamed "the Knight of the Heavenly Kingdom." As a personality he was powerful, feared, and at the same time idolized; thousands of muzhiks flocked to him, and even the Tsar was accustomed to listen reverently to his words. When, at Epiphany, he descended from his monastery to the banks of the Volga to conduct the time-honoured festival of the Church, under a white baldaquin adorned with flowers and surrounded by glittering ikons, the crowds fell on their knees and, as with one voice, broke into sacred songs. Behind Iliodor came the monks of his monastery, like Greek charioteers standing in chariots to which girls and old women had harnessed themselves. As this triumphal procession approached, the enraptured crowd ecstatically acclaimed the "Knight of the Heavenly Kingdom."

Iliodor had wished to build a great monastery, but the funds of his parish were inadequate. He ascended a hill in the town and addressed the people: "Whoever has a plank he does not need," ran his appeal, "let him bring me that plank; whoever has a rusty nail, let him give that nail; and let him who possesses nothing, sacrifice himself and help to delve earth!" As a result of this sermon the whole population contributed tiles, timber, and other building materials, and hundreds of volunteer workers offered their services; and very soon there rose from the soil, in a formerly disreputable part of the town, a great monastery with a large hall, which put many another Russian monastery in the shade.

This successful effort added appreciably to the fame and power of Iliodor. Soon the new church would not hold the crowds that flocked from near and far to hear sermons of the monk-priest. Iliodor then hit upon a curious plan. He appealed to his disciples to dig cellars under the monastery, and to shovel together the earth thus removed, so as to form an artificial hill, a "Mount Tabor." His intention was to build on this hill a "transparent tower" overgrown with flowers and, from this height, to address his "sermons on the Mount" to the assembled multitude. This curious plan was immediately put into effect, and Iliodor's adherents, especially the famous boxer and heavyweight champion, Saikin, began to delve and collect the earth. "Mount Tabor," however, was never completed.

As a strict and zealous adherent of the Orthodox faith, Iliodor became first a supporter and then a champion of extreme nationalistic pan-slavism and monarchism. In innumerable sermons he supported the absolute autocracy of the Tsar. He joined the "Union of the True Russian People," that powerful and dangerous association of political reactionaries. His monarchism was, however, shot with popular ideas of a peasant communism, in which the Tsar alone should be master, and the whole people, without distinction of rank or class, should be brothers with equal rights. Although he championed that absolute power of the Tsar, at the same time he fought against all other class privileges, and this brought him great popularity.

His patriotism did not prevent him from inveighing against bad government officials, governors, and administrators; indeed, he particularly enjoyed doing so, in order to show that not the Tsar but his servants were to blame, if everything were not for the best in the Empire. Often he preferred violent charges against the authorities; but his great reputation as a "true champion of the monarchist idea" protected him from prosecution. His speeches were of an unrestrained, filthy, almost heretical coarseness, and this earned him the nickname of the "curser." He was particularly violent in his denunciation of the "diabolical corruption of morals," that pestilence with which, according to him, the intelligentsia, officials, and Jews, in their coquetting with the West, were infecting the uncorrupted Russian people.

The sermons of this "Russian Savonarola" became every day more gross and outrageous: first he would attack the governor, and shout that it would have been better for him to have stayed on his estates and milked the cows; then he would thunder against the chief of police, and he was never tired of declaring that the administration of the Tsarytsin district was in Satan's clutches. When his attacks became intolerable, Kurlov, one of the chief police officials, tried to call him to order as considerately and circumspectly as possible. He sent for Iliodor, and submitted to him the report of one of his speeches, in which he had openly incited to resistance against the commands of the authorities. He asked him whether the text had not been somewhat distorted. Iliodor, however, replied proudly and defiantly that the document corresponded, word for word, with his sermon, and that he saw no necessity for withdrawing a single one of his utterances. Kurlov timidly tried to point out that such incitements to violence could not be suffered; whereupon the monk-priest turned to him with a voice of thunder, abused him, and declared that his one aim was to protect the people and the Tsar from incapable and treacherous administrators.

The authorities tried to take steps against Iliodor through the agency of the Holy Synod; but the monk refused to appear and justify himself before his spiritual superiors. He barricaded himself in the church of his monastery, from there sent out letters of invective against the Synod, and called upon his followers to defend him. So violent a popular movement began in his favour that no one dared to proceed against him.

After that Iliodor carried on a veritable reign of terror in Tsarytsin. During Lent he went about the town at night in his black cowl, appeared at masked balls and drove away the guests, forced his way into gambling rooms, and visited brothels. There he stared at the women in silence, but so threateningly that they fled into the street with hysterical cries of fear, and for a long time did not dare to return to the house. Next day articles appeared in the newspapers in which Iliodor described his "impressions" during his nocturnal expeditions, and gave the names of all the "honourable citizens" he had met in disreputable places.

He nourished a particular hatred for the intellectuals, whom he always called "Jews," without any inquiry about their faith. On one occasion he had a big doll in a Jewish caftan carried in a procession, and it was afterwards burned with great solemnity. Close to the entrance of the monastery church he had built, was a large picture of the Last Judgment, in which Jewish lawyers and journalists were depicted in the forefront of the sinners condemned to everlasting punishment in Hell.

From time to time, voices were heard declaring that Iliodor was nothing but a "pusher," who would do anything to make himself popular; but the masses revered him unreservedly and exalted him as a "Knight of the Heavenly Kingdom." His huge following was devoted to him; it consisted of resolute, brave men and fanatical women who were ready to do anything at the command of their leader.

When the fame of Iliodor spread from Tsarytsin to St. Petersburg, the Imperial couple summoned him to Tsarskoe Selo. During his stay there he formed a friendship with Bishop Hermogen and with the Archimandrite Feofan, the confessor of the Empress. After his visit he returned, loaded with honours, to his home, where he was now able to play the part of a despotic ruler.

* * * * *

When Bishop Hermogen, accompanied by Father Feofan and Grigori Efimovich, knocked at the monk-priest's cell, he received no answer. He opened the door carefully and quietly, and the three men peered into the half-darkened room. The monk lay in one corner of it, where innumerable ikons hung, with little oil lamps burning before them. He was absorbed in profound prayer, and had bowed his head until it was touching the ground, so that his visitors could see only his hindquarters sticking up in the air, with the stiff monastic robe standing out like a board; below, appeared the broad soles of his gigantic boots. The unusual picture made by the praying monk strongly impressed the three visitors, and although they really had urgent business to discuss with Iliodor, they simultaneously fell on their knees and joined in his prayers.

Gentle Father Feofan had had such years of practice that he could at once automatically become absorbed in deep devotion as soon as the golden light of an oil lamp fell on his eyes; so now he let his eyelids drop and was immediately in a state of devotional ecstasy. But good Bishop Hermogen could not on the moment attain to the proper importance of his mission, and was impatient for Iliodor to finish his prayers, so that he could discuss with him the newly discovered champion of the faith.

But Iliodor did nothing of the kind. Although he must have observed the arrival of his visitors, he behaved as though he thought himself quite alone, and continued to pray unmoved. Under other circumstances Bishop Hermogen would have been the first to admire this strict, even fanatical, zeal in prayer; but this time he felt in his heart that there had been enough of piety. The obstinate devotion of the monk gradually approached maliciousness; and the great Iliodor was malicious, as Hermogen had had frequent occasion to convince himself. But however that might be, there could be no thought of disturbing the monk's devotional exercises, and the Bishop had no resource but to go on kneeling, raging in his heart.

Rasputin was neither restless nor impatient; in his soul he had brought with him to St. Petersburg the peace of the infinite steppes of Siberia; he knew how to wait. Nothing disturbed his equanimity, in which respect he really had something of a "holy temper." The whole position even gave him a sincere pleasure. He could examine the monk closely, with the serenity native to the peasant, and estimate his importance and value. The fact that he had seen the redoubted Iliodor for the first time in an unusual situation and attitude was, as Rasputin at once felt instinctively, an important advantage, for he would never lose the grotesque picture of the suppliant with his cassock standing stiffly out and his enormous soles exposed, whatever awe-inspiring and superior attitudes he might afterwards assume.

Grisha the peasant was, in any case, accustomed to encounter the most important personages with natural unconcern; this time he had been particularly confident from the start. But at a moment when Iliodor finished a prayer, he felt that the monk's praying had lasted long enough and, to the infinite dismay of the gentle Archimandrite and Bishop Hermogen, he rose, crossed himself, and stepped up to him, saying: "Brother . . . brother." The "curser," furious at anyone's having the audacity to interrupt his devotions, leapt up precipitately and glared at Rasputin with angry, blazing eyes. Father Feofan and the Bishop, terrified to death, waited for the awful outburst to come. Iliodor raised his arm and drew a breath before loosing a flood of terrible invective on the foolhardy intruder, when he felt the unknown peasant lay his right hand on his shoulder and saw the pale little eyes, smiling good-humouredly, turn on him and take his own glance captive. And a voice sounded very melodious, but at the same time strong as steel, saying: "*You* pray well, brother."

Iliodor stared at his visitor in amazement, and this amazement was further increased when the peasant went on in all innocence: "Now cease persecuting God with *your* prayers; even He wants a rest sometimes. Come, those two there," pointing to Feofan and Hermogen, "have something to discuss with *you*."

* * * * *

Later, whenever Iliodor recalled this first meeting with Rasputin, there stirred in his heart the same confused feeling he had felt then, the same wrath, which had made him start up like a wounded animal, that anyone should dare to disturb him at his devotions, the same agitation under the glance of this man who displayed so little respect for him, this dirty peasant with his imperturbable assurance and friendly smile. When he remembered that Grisha had from the beginning addressed him with the familiar *you* and called him "brother," a wave of anger always broke over him afresh; but at the same time he experienced the same queer state of impotence that had then overpowered him like a paralysing spell. Something terrible happened to the monk-priest in Rasputin's presence. The invective, the divine power such as none but the great prophets of old had possessed before him, seemed to vanish whenever he felt the diabolical pale eyes of this peasant resting on him. He had struggled in vain to find words, and had exerted all his strength to produce at least one of his favourite formulas of execration; but, instead of this, he had been silent, and had even in the end clasped in friendly fashion the rough hand which this disrespectful peasant had offered him with a peaceful smile.

This divided state of mind, a blend of anger, disgust, impotence, fear, and admiration, Iliodor never lost. On that first day, when he sat with Feofan and Hermogen and discussed Grisha, a force he could not explain impelled him not only openly to share their enthusiasm, but even to fan the flame of Feofan's childish faith in the saintliness of Rasputin, and of the worthy Hermogen's optimistic conviction of the political importance of the peasant. Although, at this meeting, Iliodor could not for an instant overcome his repulsion and distrust, he yet approved the plan of introducing Grisha to the committee of the "true Russian people," and was even a passionate advocate of the idea. He felt quite clearly that this ugly lout of a peasant was utterly distasteful to him, and his instinct warned him of danger threatening; but whenever he began to talk about Grigori Efimovich it was as if his tongue were governed by an alien power, and he always declared that he was a real saint, a God-sent champion of the true faith.

So it happened that, although it was the venerable Father Feofan and the highly respected Bishop Hermogen who introduced Rasputin to the Central Committee of the "true Russian people," as an important fellow-combatant, the decision to accept him was brought about solely by the enthusiastic speeches of Iliodor. There was more than one incredulous person, more than one cynical sceptic, among the members of the Central Committee, and these would never have been convinced of the saintliness of Rasputin by Feofan and Hermogen alone. They had listened to their explanations in silence, shaking their heads, and Hermogen, to his dismay, had to note that the case of the Tobolsk peasant was not particularly favourable.

But then the "great curser" rose and, under the influence of his persuasive eloquence, the atmosphere immediately underwent a complete change. In all that followed, Iliodor had to confess that during this session he was, in his inmost heart, of the opinion of the head-shaking sceptics; nevertheless, he jumped up furiously, thundered at the doubters, and declared that even the "true Russian people" were plainly corrupted by the devilish spirit of the West, by that disintegrating search for enlightenment which was trying to destroy true faith in God and in the holiness of the Russian nation. With flaming eyes he told Rasputin's opponents that their patriotism was no better than that of the impious Jews, lawyers, and journalists who believed in nothing, and wanted to drag everything through the mire. With uplifted hands the great preacher bewailed the fact that the reign of Antichrist was at hand, since even the Union of the True Russian People had succumbed to the influence of scepticism. "Woe, woe, for poor holy Russia!"

After a brief pause Iliodor proceeded to the practical side of his proposals, appealed to the "clear political reason" of his audience, and tried to convince them how important it was for the aims and objects of the Union to enlist Grigori Rasputin as a working tool. He argued that the Union must have the support of the people in its political efforts, for that was the best means of successfully stemming the advance of the ideas of freedom and scepticism from the West. In his opinion they must show that the Russian muzhik, as representative of the "God-fearing people," was the embodiment of the highest form of humanity; and Grisha, the Siberian peasant, was the very man to convince everyone, by his simple but profound words, of the muzhik's wisdom and heaven-inspired clear-sightedness.

Iliodor explained to his political friends how the greatest national thinkers, a Dostoevski, even a Tolstoi (otherwise an impious heretic), had long preached that the speech of the muzhik was the expression of the most profound thought, to be compared for grandeur only with the words of the Gospels. If the Siberian peasant, Rasputin, was revered as a saint, it signified nothing but obeisance to the uncorrupted divine power dwelling in the people. By the recognition of Grisha's saintly life, the holiness of the people, of the peasantry, and thereby of the true Russian idea, was bound to be confirmed. If supreme wisdom and marvellous enlightenment were to be found in the talk of a simple Siberian peasant, what was left for Western civilization to do? And what an advantage it would be to be able, when a political decision had to be taken, to appeal to the will of a holy man from whose mouth God himself had spoken! Everyone who did not wish to be a rebel against his religion and his country would have at once to recognize as right any policy that had been approved and blessed by Grigori Efimovich.

These and many similar statements were made by Iliodor at the meeting, and his words were forcible, emphatic, and convincing as they had seldom been before. When he had finished his discourse he could see that all those present were affected by it, and were thoroughly convinced of Rasputin's importance.

As Iliodor returned to his place another cleric rose, the Priest Vostorgov; like all the rest he had been overwhelmed by Iliodor's speech and, in a confused fashion, he humbly expressed the thanks and admiration of the meeting. He assured Iliodor that the Committee was absolutely convinced by his arguments, and would make its future decisions in accordance with his wishes. He begged to add on his own account that, during a propaganda tour through the Tobolsk government at the time of the last elections, he himself had arrived at a conviction that they must attract specially gifted peasants for political work. He had submitted a detailed report to the Central Committee at the time, but it had evidently not been thought of sufficient value. Now he thanked the venerable gentlemen, the Archimandrite Feofan, Bishop Hermogen, and especially the highly esteemed priest Iliodor, for having returned to these ideas and given them the full weight of their support.

While Vostorgov was speaking Iliodor's face visibly changed colour, and everything seemed to be swimming before his eyes; as this stupid, garrulous priest endorsed his own arguments

Iliodor felt clearly that he was of exactly the opposite opinion, that he believed Grisha to be a hypocrite, a sham saint, a clod of a dirty peasant. What devil had driven him to speak against his own intuitions? As he looked at that blockhead of a Vostorgov consequentially agreeing with him, and bowing deferentially towards him, the monk-priest was seized with a fit of furious rage.

But at the same instant, another member of the Committee rose and intervened in the discussion of the case of Rasputin, the peasant from the Tobolsk government. The new speaker was a distinguished advocate, and a stout member of the Union, who had already done it many important services. He began, nevertheless, in a diffident and modest tone, for he was well aware of the difficulty and danger, after the speeches of Iliodor and Vostorgov, of not joining in the universal enthusiasm for Grigori Efimovich. He, however, felt it his duty to bring forward certain objections, and to warn the meeting of the danger of the project; but he did this in such a low and shrinking voice and with so many reservations, that his speech apparently passed almost unnoticed; only the "curser" followed his words with strained attention. As the shrewd and discreet advocate said that they ought seriously to consider whether this peasant would not later involve them in many difficulties, and whether they would not have cause to repent precipitate action in the affair, Iliodor drew a deep sigh of relief, as one saved. With each of the speaker's words his heart grew lighter and more at ease; he rejoiced that at last, in this unwholesome atmosphere of religious enthusiasm, the voice of reason had been heard, that one man had kept his head clear and given open utterance to his own secret fears.

"You expect advantage from this peasant Rasputin," the advocate had said warningly; "but I believe that in the final result he will do nothing but harm." Yes, that was the truth, the liberating truth at last! Iliodor rose to support the speaker cordially. But immediately he again fell under the spell of that devilish power which forced him to serve "the spirit of lies" to his own destruction, and not only not avert the fatality he clearly discerned, but even hasten it. With grim visage, Iliodor began to thunder at the unassuming advocate, reproaching him with "Western scepticism," "unpatriotic ideas," and "lack of understanding of the holy Russian people." In the last resort the world would be saved from ruin only by the holy Russian people, and not by accursed advocates, journalists, and all the rest of the Jews!

The meeting ended, as was inevitable, in a complete success. Father Feofan and Bishop Hermogen were radiant with joy, and Hermogen at once proceeded to work on the little Archimandrite, as the Empress's confessor, to bring the new starets to Tsarskoe Selo. Only Iliodor was unapproachable and angry, and his always alarming insolence that evening assumed even more unpleasant forms than usual.

CHAPTER V

THE FATEFUL IDYLL OF TSARSKOE SELO

"SUNSHINE" was the pet name, with its suggestion of sunny gaiety, that had been given to the young Princess Alix of Hesse before she became Empress of Russia, as the consort of Nikolai II. The name stuck to her, and her husband hardly ever called her anything else.

As soon as the Tsar had finished the burdensome business of State, he hastened to his Alix like a young husband very much in love, as if the moment to return to her and their peaceful and beloved home could not come too soon. He found the duties his position imposed upon him unpleasant and irksome; for hours he sat discontentedly over his papers, signed documents, studied ministerial reports, and made marginal notes on them; he endured the necessary audiences with boredom, and was overjoyed when they did not last too long. His official life was one long struggle with the mountain of documents on his desk, which swelled alarmingly, if he even once neglected to discharge his regular prescribed task.

Since his accession to the throne, day had succeeded day in an alternation between the unpleasant hours devoted to the business of Government and the pleasant hours of family life. The Tsaritsa, too, in all the long years of her marriage, had never been able to reconcile herself to the fact that she must be separated from her husband for a few hours. If Government business took longer than usual she became impatient and longed for his return. She almost always kept to her pale mauve boudoir, surrounded by a mass of flowers; she either lay reading on a couch, wrote letters in her rapid hand, occupied herself with needlework, or, in later years, talked with her friend Ania Vyrubova, and told her of her life with the Tsar. She talked of him and thought of him practically all the time, for, even in hours of

THE TSARITSA IN HER SITTING-ROOM

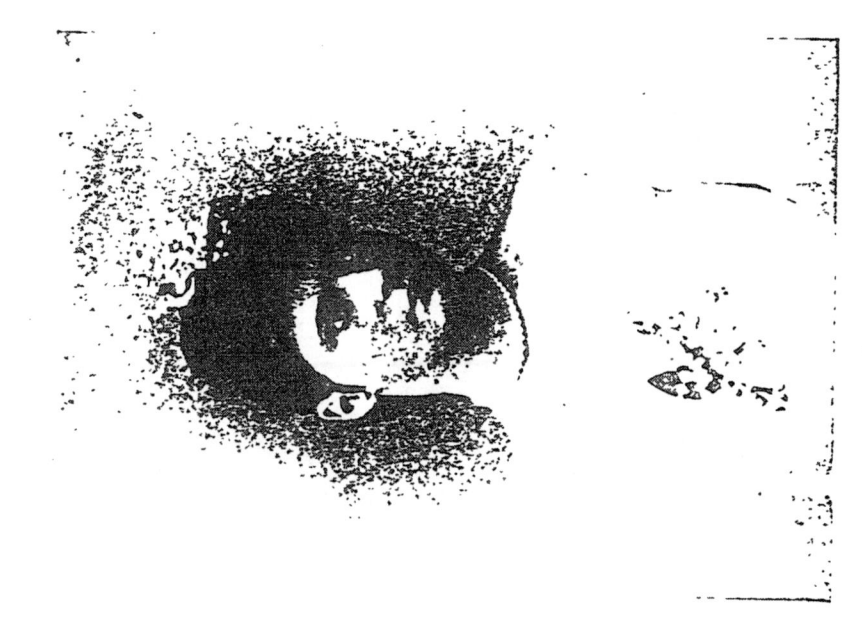

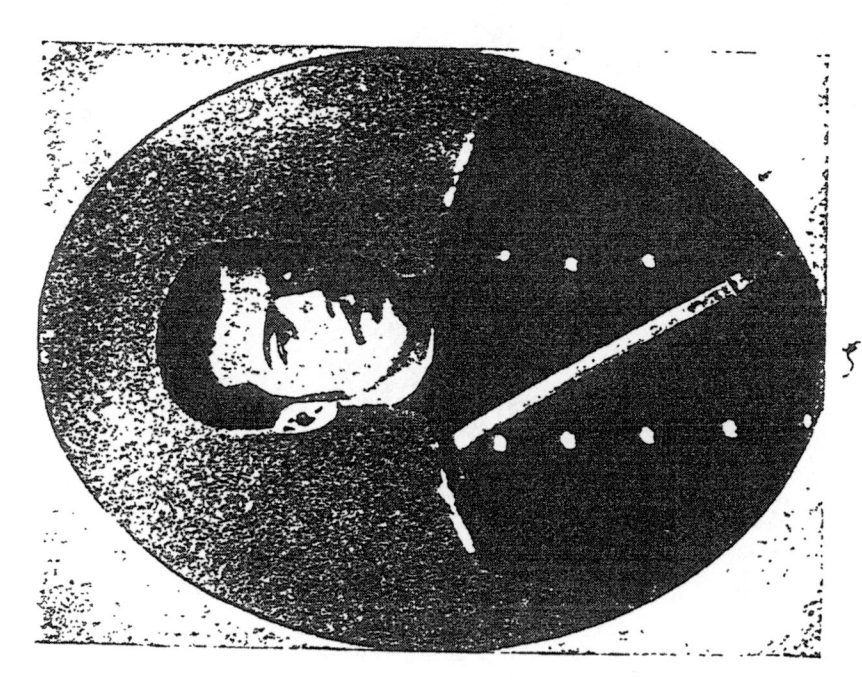

THE TSAR AND TSARITSA AT THE TIME OF THEIR MARRIAGE

absence, she wished to be with her husband in spirit at least.

Then when hurrying steps sounded in the corridor, and the crystals of the chandelier began to tinkle, she jumped up, as excited as a girl, the blood rising to her cheeks. The doors flew open, and the Tsaritsa, joyfully and with shining eyes, ran to meet her smiling husband. They would talk for hours, happy and care-free, about their children, their joint plans, excursions and walks, and all the thousand trifles that make up the conversation of two people in love with one another.

It sometimes happened that, while the Empress was receiving visitors, a slow whistle like the note of a bird was heard in the next room. Alexandra would rise, her face one burning blush, shyly remark that the Emperor was calling her, and, excusing herself to her guests, disappear into the adjoining room. She never failed to obey the call.

Every hour not spent together was a torment and a weariness. When the Tsar, after several years of marriage, was for the first time obliged to leave his wife for a considerable period, in order to visit the King of Italy at Racconigi, Alexandra shut herself up in her rooms and would admit no one, not even her children. She did not recover her spirits until his return, and her one complaint then was that the reunion took place in the presence of the whole Court, which prevented her from giving free rein to her happiness.

Only twice in the course of twenty-three years was the harmony of this marriage slightly disturbed by misunderstandings. The first time was when gossip reached the Emperor's ears that the Empress was not quite indifferent to the handsome Prince Orlov. There were many people at Court who never tired of insinuations of that kind, and the fact that General Orlov spent nearly every evening in the royal apartments, playing billiards for hours with the Emperor, gave fresh food for rumours. Even after lung trouble had sent Orlov suddenly off to Egypt, where he died soon after, it was for a long time impossible to silence these evil tongues.

Although the Tsar had never seriously doubted the loyalty of his wife, the Tsaritsa at one time became very jealous of her friend Ania, and believed that she had infringed on her most sacred wifely rights. Anna Vyrubova had been simple and honest enough to confess to her one day that a feeling of love for the Tsar was beginning to germinate in her heart, quite against her will. The confession, innocent though it was, turned the excitable Alexandra against her friend for a time, and even caused her to speak disparagingly of the "traitress" in family letters.

Such trifling misunderstandings, however, passed as quickly as they came, and could not permanently trouble the happiness of the two. Both the Tsar and the Tsaritsa quickly saw the folly of their suspicions, and their former harmony was completely restored.

Never, not even during these transient storms, had a single unkind word passed between husband and wife; they were always inspired by the tenderest consideration for one another, and avoided hurting each other even by a glance. From their marriage right up to the tragic end they shared, their love for each other showed no decline, and they lived together like a newly married couple.

This unclouded family happiness is seen most clearly in the diaries in which Nikolai used to make notes every night. Their pages tell of wonderful quiet hours, of the joy of watching the children grow up, and of gratitude for the "complete and boundless happiness" of his marriage. From the start the young imperial couple had withdrawn into the simplest and most modest surroundings possible, for they both loathed the magnificence of the great State apartments. From the date of their first visit Tsarskoe Selo became especially dear to the imperial pair, and they soon moved from the capital into permanent residence there. They sat together evening after evening, played with the children, or turned over illustrated books, magazines, and photograph albums. The Tsar grumbled every time his State duties kept him longer than usual away from his wife:

"It is a pity that business takes up so much time, when I so long to spend every hour with her."

"This forenoon I had to deal with reports again, but in the afternoon I walked with Alix in the garden. We cannot bear to be parted from one another."

"As I was busy in the forenoon I did not see Alix at all till lunch time. But in the afternoon we drove to Pavlovsk again and admired the beautiful sunset. In the evening, after tea, I read aloud to her for a time."

"I received Durnovo, Fredericks, Richter, and Avelan. Then I drove to the Academy of Sciences where the ceremonial annual meeting was being held. It was not interesting, but lasted not quite an hour, so that I was home again by two o'clock. I went with my dear little wife to the Islands; the evening was wonderful and the excursion very pleasant. We did not get home till half-past eleven."

In the first years of her marriage Alexandra used to intersperse the Tsar's jottings with notes and sentences, mostly expressions of love in English, which overflow with tenderness and heartfelt devotion.

"To-day I had a lot of free time," writes the Tsar, "as I had hardly any reports to read. We lunched and dined alone. I cannot describe how happy our life is alone together in beautiful Tsarskoe." The Tsaritsa adds in English: "Your little wife worships you."

"My happiness knows no bounds," remarks the Emperor another time. "It is only with reluctance that I leave Tsarskoe, so dear to us both. Here, for the first time since our marriage, we have been alone, and lived together quite undisturbed." And the Tsaritsa adds: "Never did I believe that there could be such utter happiness in this world, such a feeling of unity between two mortal beings. I LOVE YOU—these three words have my life in them."

For the most part the Emperor writes of State business quite superficially in his notebooks, in order to devote more time to the happy hours of his private life. A brief enumeration of the people to whom he has given audience is frequently followed by cries like:

"I am indescribably happy with Alix."

"It is inexpressibly delightful to be able to be together day and night in peace, undisturbed by anyone. We have our meals à deux in the corner room and go to bed early."

"I thank God daily with all my soul for the happiness He has given me. No man on earth could desire greater or fairer bliss."

When Alexandra was not sitting with her husband or Anna Vyrubova in her boudoir, she was sure to be found with the children. Her maternal solicitude was so great that she hated to leave the nursery, and often even received official visits there. On one occasion, when the head of the Court Chancery had urgent business to discuss with her and a number of documents to submit for her signature, the Empress received him holding the little Grand Duchess Olga on one arm and rocking the cradle of the new-born Tatiana with her other hand.

When at last, after years of fruitless hopes, a son was born, Alexandra took even more pains with him than over the earlier children; although she had an excellent and reliable nurse for the little Alexei in the person of Vishniakova, and although there were other nurses employed at Tsarskoe Selo, the Empress herself undertook every duty, however trifling: she bathed, dressed, and tended her son, taught him to speak his first words, and played with him for hours. In later years, as the children gradually grew up, Alexandra herself superintended their education; she bent with them over their books and exercises, helped them with the tasks set by the house tutors, and prepared them for their lessons with Fräulein Schneider, Mr. Gibbs, and M. Gilliard. She did needlework with her daughters and, while they were little, sewed dolls' clothes for them; later she loved to take part in the preparations for little domestic parties.

The Emperor also loved to play with his children, and he too spent much time in their company. He had one of the great marble halls at Tsarskoe Selo set aside as a playroom for them, and had a long parquet slide constructed there. Here Nikolai enjoyed himself with his daughters and, even in times of serious political unrest, he would spend an hour or two almost every day rushing down the smooth wooden slide with the children.

The sovereign's day generally began with a short walk after breakfast, followed by the reception of the regular visitors. As a rule, the Emperor summoned his ministers but seldom, and generally received their reports in writing. But almost every day there were some high officials or military dignitaries who had asked for an audience, and whom the Emperor could not refuse to receive. These conversations bored him horribly, and he was glad when one o'clock arrived, at which time he lunched in the company of the Empress and the officers on duty. This was usually followed by a long walk in the Park of Tsarskoe Selo, generally in Alix's company, but sometimes with his elder daughters; on these occasions they would pick flowers and lie on the grass. In the afternoon they often drove or made excursions by motor-boat; and the Emperor frequently took his gun with him and shot crows. Then at last came the hour at which the whole family assembled round the tea-table. Then work again, for the Tsar must spend an hour or two with the papers piled up on his desk. Dinner was at eight o'clock.

At nine o'clock, when dinner was over, the Tsaritsa went to the Tsesarevich's room to say evening prayers with him. On her return, and while the Tsar retired to his study for a little, she would often play duets with Ania, generally Beethoven or Tschaikovski's sonatas. The Emperor was frequently attracted by the sound of the music and would creep in on tiptoe to listen. He stood quietly behind the performers, only the delicate smell of the inevitable cigarette betraying his presence to them. If no official business remained the Emperor liked to sit in his wife's room and read aloud to her and Ania from the works of Tolstoi, Turgenev, Dostoevski, Gogol, or Chekhov until finally, about midnight, tea was served once more and the royal couple retired.

Life at Tsarskoe Selo was, as a rule, interrupted only twice a year by holidays: in winter the imperial family went to the Crimea for a few weeks, to their country house at Livadia, and in summer they almost always went on a cruise to the Finnish islands. On these holidays their life was even quieter than usual, for then State visits and official business practically ceased, and the Emperor could devote himself entirely to his family. At Livadia the day was spent in long walks in the quiet countryside. The Tsar had successfully prevented Livadia from being linked up with the rest of the world by a railway, because he did not wish to spoil the idyllic seclusion of this glorious district. The glittering white imperial castle lay amid rose-covered hills and slopes, with a magnificent distant view of the dark blue waters of the sea and the snow-covered mountain peaks. The imperial family would set out early in the morning, armed with provisions, for long excursions in the woods lasting all day. They would light a fire and cook the mushrooms they had gathered, and the imperial couple spent whole days of delicious idleness with their children.

At other times they took long rides or bathed. The Emperor loved all kinds of physical exercise; he was a splendid rower, walker, swimmer, cyclist, and tennis-player. Tennis, in particular, was one of his greatest pleasures, and he played it with passion. He could spend many hours a day on the courts, and he played as if it was the most important thing in the world. The loss of a game seriously upset him, which often put his partners, especially Anna Vyrubova, in a very awkward situation. He hated to be distracted by conversation during the game. The Tsar was also fond of shooting; his diaries are full of notes about the most trifling details of his shoots and the size of the bags.

Life in the Finnish islands was as peaceful as in the Crimea. They crossed the Gulf of Finland on the imperial yacht "Standard," and plunged into the maze of uninhabited rocky islands, where the days were spent in excursions into the woods, in rowing, bathing, and swimming. The family visited the charming wild spots in the little islands, arranged picnics, climbed about the rocks, and gathered berries. Meanwhile, the children played with the sailors who had been detailed for the purpose. In later years, when the Grand Duchesses were grown-up young ladies, innocent little flirtations developed between them and the elegant officers of the crew, on which the parents looked with good-natured smiles, and over which the girls were heartily chaffed. In the evenings they all sat on deck round the tea-table, while the Emperor puffed contentedly at his cigarette, told stories of his young days, or chatted about the trifling events of the day. Under the spell of this idyllic atmosphere he once exclaimed happily that he felt as if the whole party were one big family.

The quiet peace of life was broken only by the unwelcome appearance twice a week of a royal messenger, who brought the Emperor a mass of important documents which had to be dealt with. Then the sovereign was forced to spend a day at his desk, until State business was finished, and he was free to return to the bosom of his family again.

So the life of the Emperor and Empress, whether at Tsarskoe Selo, on their estate of Livadia, or in the Finnish islands, passed year after year in tranquil happiness. When the great Revolution broke out, and the Emperor was deposed and had to leave Tsarskoe Selo with his family, Alexandra wrote to her friend: "Dearest, how inexpressibly hard it is to leave here, to part from this dear house, now so desolate, our home in which we have spent twenty-three happy years."

And later in Tobolsk, with an uncertain and menacing fate before them, the one consolation of the imperial family, almost their one topic of conversation, was the remembrance of their indescribably happy life together. "The past is lost," writes the Empress to Anna Vyrubova from Tobolsk, "but I thank God for all that has happened, for the rich treasure of glorious memories of which no one can rob me."

For in the whole of the great Russian Empire there was perhaps no other woman who was more thankful for her lot, who regarded her quiet, almost middle-class life among her family as a greater happiness, than the Empress of Russia. To her the existence she had lived, in the narrowest surroundings, with her husband, their children, and her one faithful friend, Ania, was "quite the greatest happiness on earth. . . ."

* * * * *

And yet: in those twenty-three years of intimacy a terrible tragedy was slowly gathering over the heads of the royal couple, so wrapped up in love and family happiness. While the Tsar was impatiently waiting for the last of the wearisome visits and reports so that he could hasten back to the arms of his beloved Alix, while he was rushing down the slide with his children amid joyous laughter, or looking for mushrooms in the woods, or chattering cosily in the evenings about the trifling events of the day on the deck of his yacht, during all his games of tennis, his motor-boat excursions, and his shooting parties, the dark cloud that portended the storm in which he and his family were to be destroyed and the Russian Empire ruined, was slowly gathering. From the very beginning this "sunny happiness" bore in it, like a pestilence, the seed of inevitable catastrophe. Even the love of these two people, their absorption in each other that isolated them from the world, was overshadowed by a dark fatality: nay, perhaps the spirit of destruction lay more heavily, oppressively, and calamitously over this quiet, uneventful, petit-bourgeois idyll of wedlock than over anything else in their lives. Perhaps this perfect "freedom from care" was itself the disease, perhaps a cruel fate was pursuing its course deceptively, hiding corruption under the mask of happiness.

The realm of this innocent royal couple had long been advancing to ruin, almost imperceptibly, but surely, and the very essence of this Empire, the soul, life, and disposition of the nation, were already infected with disease when Nikolai ascended the throne.

The middle-class "family idyll" of Tsarskoe Selo was, from its first moment to its terrible end, involved in an endless chain of tragic accidents, war, peril, sickness, murder, and catastrophes; these people, in their apparent freedom from care, trembled with a ceaseless, tormenting fear that knew no end. From early youth, the continual terror of new menaces and dangers and fresh blows of fate plunged both Emperor and Empress into a kind of melancholy. The Emperor, always prone to superstition, had from the very beginning of his reign the crushing feeling that nothing that he undertook could be crowned with success, since he was born on the day of Job, the great sufferer. Moreover, a century before, the holy monk and prophet, Serafim of Saratov, had prophesied that, in the reign of the Tsar who would be ruling at the beginning of the twentieth century, evils of all kinds would befall the country: poverty, war, and rebellion. The Emperor Nikolai believed this prophecy, and faced every undertaking with suspicion, fear, and doubt.

The events of his early youth had also been such as to confirm this gloomy belief in an inevitable fate: his boyhood had been shadowed by the frightful end of his grandfather, the Emperor Alexander II, who was blown to pieces by a bomb. It was this murder by a nihilist that made Nikolai's father Tsar and himself Tsesarevich, so that his accession as heir to the throne was marked by a bloody outrage.

When, later, happiness in love seemed to beckon to the Tsesarevich, this too was immediately darkened by evil influences: the young Princess Alix of Hesse, whom it was his dearest wish to make his bride, displeased his mother from the beginning, and the old Empress did her best to prevent the betrothal. It was not until four years after the Princess's visit to Russia that, in the presence of the dying Emperor, his mother abandoned her opposition, and Alix was invited to the Crimea, where Alexander III, in his last illness, received her with all due ceremony as his daughter-in-law and the future Empress. But the young couple had no time to enjoy their happiness. The last weeks of their betrothal were spent in the oppressive atmosphere of a house in which the old Emperor lay dying over the rooms of the young couple. Then, when the inevitable happened, the two had to travel all over Russia with the coffin of the dead Emperor from one memorial service to another. "I had a long talk with Uncle Vladimir," wrote the Tsar in his diary, "about whether my wedding should be celebrated publicly or privately after the obsequies. Then came a royal messenger, and I dealt with official documents till evening. After the funeral service I went for a walk with Alix, but at half-past six the sad ceremony began, and the body of my dear father was carried to the church: the coffin was borne on a bier by Cossacks. This is the third time I have had to be present at a funeral service in this church. When we came back to the empty house, we absolutely broke down. God has afflicted us all with heavy trials."

After that the long journey began, and from every halting-place the young ruler has melancholy ceremonies to report: "We stopped at Borki and Kharkov, where a funeral service was held. . . ." "At Moscow we carried the coffin from the train to the hearse. On the way to the Kremlin we stopped ten times, a litany being sung before every church. The coffin was placed in the Archangel Cathedral; after the memorial service I prayed before the bones of the saints in the Uspenski Cathedral and in the Chudov Monastery. . . ." "At Obukhovo station we again

entered the train reserved for the mourners and arrived in St. Petersburg at ten. The reunion with the rest of the relations was a painful one; the weather was grey and it was thawing. . . ."
"To-day I had again to live through the sorrow and affliction which the 20th of October brought us. The service celebrated by the Archbishop began at half-past eleven, and after that my dear, never-to-be-forgotten father was blessed and committed to earth."

"Such was my entry into Russia," said Alix later. "Our marriage seemed to me a mere continuation of the masses for the dead, with this difference, that I now wore a white dress instead of a black!" The young Tsaritsa, from the outset of her stay in Russia, was a disliked and even detested stranger. Beginning with the Dowager Empress Maria Fedorovna, a strong feeling against "the German" spread through all Court circles, and this universal frigidity persisted even after Alix of Hesse became Empress of Russia. She did her best to win the sympathy of her mother-in-law and the Court; but all her attempts in this direction were wrecked on this prejudice as well as by her own shyness and awkwardness. She says herself, "The young Emperor was too much occupied with events to be able to devote himself to me, and from shyness, loneliness, and the multitude of impressions crowding on me I did not know which way to turn."

In addition to the Court of the young Emperor and Empress, a second Court soon formed itself round the Dowager Empress, the centre of waves of ill-will against Alexandra Fedorovna. The older Court ladies, with Princess Obolenski and Countess Vorontsov at their head, had always something to lay to the account of the young Empress, were always spreading fresh gossip against her, and did their best to embitter the life of that lonely and helpless young woman. Her letters of this period contain frequent complaints about her loneliness: "I feel quite alone and in despair." Once when she was driving with one of her ladies, a beggar came up to the carriage and held out his hand for alms; she gave him something and he smiled gratefully. "That is the first smile I've received in Russia," she remarked sadly to her companion.

From the coldness of Court circles the young wife fled to the only place where she felt secure and happy, to her husband and the intimacy of her home. But even here pure, untroubled happiness was denied her, for here the deepest grief of her life had its source: the Tsar passionately longed for a son, the Empire was expecting an heir to the throne, and the Empress bore one daughter after another. With increasing sorrow she had to bear the silent reproaches of her mother-in-law, the Court, and even the whole country, as if she had proved inadequate to her duties as Empress. It was only in the midst of the bloody disaster of the Russo-Japanese War that the longed-for event took place: on July 30th, 1904, Alexandra gave birth to a son. Transported with happiness, the Tsar wrote the same day in his journal:

"A great and unforgettable day, on which the grace of God has manifestly been vouchsafed to us. At a quarter past one Alix gave birth to a son, who at prayers received the name of Alexei. In the morning I received a report from Kokovtsov and a visit from the wounded officer of artillery, Klepikov, and then went to have lunch with Alix. Half an hour later the joyful event took place. I have no words in which to express my gratitude to God for this consolation in our heavy trials. Dear Alix is well. At five o'clock the children and I went to a thanksgiving service, at which the whole family had assembled. . . ."

From now onwards the life of the parents was entirely absorbed in their joy in—and alas! also in their anxiety for—their little son. The Tsesarevich developed into a charming, lovable boy with fair, curly hair, who was the delight of the Emperor and Empress and all about them. With ever-fresh happiness they watched his first movements, and his games, and listened to his first attempts at speech. But to their horror the parents discovered that their "only treasure," as the Emperor calls his son in his diary, the happy, laughing boy with the golden hair, had a painful and incurable disease. Any careless movement might be his death, for the eagerly expected and idolized Alexei suffered from hemophilia, that terrible disease in which the slightest injury may be fatal. Whenever he violently hit his foot or his arm an internal hemorrhage immediately occurred, accompanied by a bluish swelling and severe pains. Thus the life of the heir to the throne was, from the beginning, a series of torments for him and a source of continual fear for those about him.

The parents of the unhappy child tried, by giving him presents, to console him for his many privations, and to make him forget that the games which other children of his age enjoy were forbidden to him. His room was full of the most costly and expensive playthings, great railways, with dolls in the carriages as passengers, with barriers, stations, buildings, and signal-boxes, flashing engines and marvellous signalling apparatus, whole battalions of tin soldiers, models of towns with church towers and domes, floating models of ships, perfectly equipped factories with doll-workers, and mines in exact imitation of the real thing, with miners ascending and descending. All the toys were mechanically worked, and the little Prince had only to press a button to set the workers in motion, to drive the warships up and down the tank, to set the church bells ringing and the soldiers marching.

But what was the use of all these fine and perfect playthings? Alexei sat among them, watched by the faithful sailor Derevenko, who was ever on the alert to prevent the boy from making any dangerous movement with arm or leg. He never dared to run, jump, or romp like other children; at once came the voice: "Alexei, take care, *you* will hurt *yourself*."

It was wretched for the child to have to sit quiet all the time when he would have gladly given all his costly playthings for one day of free and unrestricted frolic. If he could just once, only once, be allowed to rush about to his heart's content without hearing Derevenko's warning voice: "Alexei, take care, be careful!"

Again and again the Tsesarevich would come to his mother with requests that she was obliged sorrowfully to refuse. "Give me a bicycle, Mama," he would plead, and the Tsaritsa had to answer, "Alexei, *you* know that cycling is too dangerous for *you*."

"I would like to learn to play tennis like my sisters."

"*You* know *you* are not allowed to play."

And the child would burst into tears and cry in despair: "Why am I not like other boys?"

Often it was impossible to check his natural impulses; the boy took a quick step or two, made a thoughtless movement, and the mischief was done. He began to bleed, and nothing would stop the bleeding. The best doctors of the capital attended the sick child and tried every means known to medical science. The Tsesarevich lay moaning pitifully, and his helpless parents had to look at the apparently inevitable approach of death. Despairing intercessory services were held in the chapel of Tsarskoe Selo and were continued until the miracle happened once again and the dying boy was saved.

But terrible as her son's malady in itself was for the Tsaritsa, she had besides a special reason for despair: she was perpetually tormented by the thought that she herself was to blame for the agonizing suffering of her child. For hemophilia was hereditary in her family, and one of her uncles, a younger brother, and two nephews had died of it. This mysterious disease, as a rule, attacks only males, so that the Empress herself had escaped, while transmitting it to her son.

As soon as the parents were certain of the disease of the heir to the throne they abandoned formal Court life altogether and withdrew into their intimate family circle. Henceforward, all their care was devoted to the sick boy. Whenever Alexei played, his parents saw everywhere a possibility of danger—death lurking behind every one of his playthings, ready suddenly and unexpectedly to pounce and snatch away their beloved son.

As a result of all this agitation the Empress fell ill of a serious nervous ailment, which manifested itself at first in stubborn, nervous abdominal pains and confined her to bed for a long time.

* * * * *

But while trouble was beginning to find a footing in the imperial family and to cast its shadow over the idyll of Tsarskoe Selo, there was looming up in the background the still more terrible spectre of the great catastrophe that was preparing in these "twenty-three happy years."

It began with the coronation festivities in Moscow: in the midst of the magnificent entertainments there occurred one of the most ghastly disasters in history. The young Emperor, in accordance with ancient custom, had made great preparations for a general "entertainment of the people" on the Khodinski

Field on the outskirts of Moscow. The people assembled in thousands from far and near to be for once the "guests of the Tsar." In joy and jubilation they crowded in increasing masses round the tables spread with good things, when suddenly the gay scene was transformed into a picture of horror. In order to level the field, some careless officials had had a big trench covered over with boards; under the weight of the crowd the boards gave way and thousands fell into the trench, while those behind pushed heedlessly on. Soon the whole of the huge trench was filled with human beings, trampling each other down in their desperate fight for life, a mass of people, mad with panic, rolling over each other. This festival to celebrate the Tsar's coronation exacted about three thousand victims, and the police were occupied for hours in disposing of the bodies with all possible speed.

In the popular memory the accession to the throne of Nikolai II was always associated with this catastrophe and, although the Tsar was not directly to blame for it, it sowed the first seeds of hatred against him. For the advisers of the young ruler concealed from him the full significance of what had happened and recommended that the remainder of the festivities should be proceeded with. In spite of the irresponsibility of this advice the young Emperor had not the courage to resist it, and so it came about that he danced with his wife at a Court ball, while outside the bodies of the victims were still unburied. This apparent indifference to an event that plunged the whole of Moscow into deepest mourning naturally produced an effect of heartlessness, even of provocative arrogance, and Nikolai was never afterwards "really loved" in Moscow.

Only a few weeks later another disaster happened at other festivities in honour of the new Tsar. At Kiev a decorated ship with three hundred persons on board sank before his eyes and only a few were saved. These ominous happenings at the time of his accession and coronation were the beginning of an almost unbroken series of bloody disasters; fresh misfortune dogged his steps in a hundred different forms and variations. As if subject to an inevitable curse, all Nikolai's enactments, however well meant they might be, turned out badly. The reason was, perhaps, that in his perpetual fear of fresh misfortunes, he had not the courage to act directly and energetically, but always, in Witte's phrase, "sought for by-paths, and on those by-paths arrived always at the same goal, a dirty puddle or a pool of blood." Unprejudiced witnesses, statesmen whose attitude towards him was in many respects critical, assure us that Nikolai was often animated by the best intentions and honestly tried to serve his country according to his lights. But the true picture of Russia under this rule is painted in striking words by Tolstoi in a letter to the Emperor, written in 1902, when he felt that death was near:

"I do not wish to die," he writes, "without having told you what I think of your activities up to the present, what, in my view, they have been, how much good your rule might bring to yourself and millions of human beings, and how much evil they will bring if you continue in the direction in which you are now going. One-third of Russia is in the state of so-called 'heightened defence,' that is to say, in a state of complete anarchy. The army of police, secret and public, is steadily growing; the prisons, places of exile, and penitentiaries in Siberia are filled to overflowing, not only with hundreds of thousands of common criminals, but also with political prisoners, with whom workers are now included. The censorship forbids everything with an arbitrariness greater than that which prevailed in the worst period of the 'forties. Religious persecutions have never been so frequent and cruel as they are to-day, and this state of affairs is daily growing worse. In the towns and the great industrial centres troops are massed, who are called out against the people, and armed with loaded muskets. In many places there has already been fratricidal bloodshed, and further bloodshed is preparing and will inevitably occur. As a result of all this inhuman administration the peasantry, those hundred million men on whom the power of Russia depends, become poorer every year, and famine is a regular and even normal phenomenon in our country. . . ."

This Tsar, who had desired to live in history as the apostle of world-peace, by his unstable and vacillating policy caused the two greatest wars of the twentieth century, or at least did very little to prevent them. In the war against Japan he was egged on by frivolous councillors, by ministers who wanted "a little victorious war" to distract attention from the intolerable domestic situation. The Emperor had to suffer a campaign which they thought could be treated as a "bagatelle," in which one defeat led to another, and in which the best regiments of Russia poured out their blood in Manchuria, and the proud battle fleet was annihilated in the Bay of Tsushima.

Before this disastrous war ended new troubles broke over Russia: civil war threatened, unrest and revolts occurred all over the country, and the throne seemed all at once seriously endangered. The impetus to these new horrors was given by a massacre that took place directly under the windows of the Emperor. Some hungry and discontented workers, led by the Priest Gapon, had marched to the Winter Palace to present a humble petition to the Tsar. The demonstrators carried ikons and pictures of the Emperor, and were animated by the most peaceful intentions. Nevertheless, the military commandant, without warning, received the procession with volleys of musketry, as a result of which hundreds wallowed in blood.

From this day forward a bitter anger against the Emperor prevailed, and earned him the evil name of "the Bloody." Rebellions increased; all over the vast Russian Empire there were risings among the masses, and soon the Imperial Palace was like a beleaguered fortress. Revolts and massacres followed each other in unbroken succession, in St. Petersburg and Moscow, in Warsaw, Kiev, and Odessa, in the Baltic Provinces, and in Kronstadt. Blood had flowed in streams before the Emperor's ministers succeeded in crushing the Revolution.

And more blood flowed after this was finally accomplished: the special tribunals inflicted death sentences in scores and hundreds, and punitive expeditions were fitted out that exterminated the population of whole villages in the rebellious provinces and razed their houses to the ground.

Henceforth, the imperial family, too, lived in perpetual fear of murderous attacks, bombs, and infernal machines. As the Empress, after one of those "care-free" sea-trips, took leave of her fellow voyagers, she was in the habit of saying: "It was lovely—

perhaps it is the last time." Not for a single moment could the royal couple be sure of their lives; any hour might mean death.

One minister after another fell a victim to assassination. On the eve of the Revolution Plehve, the Minister of the Interior, and seven of his retinue were blown to pieces by a bomb in Warsaw Station. A little later the Grand Duke Sergei Alexandrovich, the uncle of the Tsar and brother-in-law of the Tsaritsa, died by the hand of an assassin. He was Governor-General of Moscow, and as such, had made himself bitterly hated for his pitiless harshness and cruelty. His wife, the Grand Duchess Elisaveta Fedorovna, the Tsaritsa's sister, had foreseen the trouble, and had tried to prevent her husband from going out alone. But one day she heard the explosion of a bomb in the street, and, seized with terrible forebodings, had rushed out immediately, to see at her feet, covered with blood, the mutilated body of the murdered Grand Duke.

Elisaveta Fedorovna had loved her husband, in spite of his capricious and domineering character—he was often in a state bordering on mental derangement—and after his terrible end she retired for life to a convent near Moscow. With her beautiful, serious face she made people think of a Madonna in her nun's dress, and her slim, graceful figure under the flowing white veil was at once touching and fascinating. When she left the convent, on special occasions, and appeared at the Court at St. Petersburg she always aroused feelings of admiration and reverence, as if she, with her clear, innocent eyes, her regular features, and her delicate, almost floating walk, were the good angel of the imperial family.

Not long after the last a new catastrophe occurred in the immediate circle of the Tsar, which almost cost the life of one of his best counsellors, Stolypin, the Prime Minister. Stolypin was spending the summer on the so-called "Apothecaries' Island," not far from the capital, when his house was blown up by an infernal machine. Over forty people were killed or wounded by the explosion; the Prime Minister himself escaped by a miracle, but his daughter was crippled for life.

But fate had granted Stolypin only a brief respite: in 1911, at a gala performance in the theatre at Kiev, he was shot, under the eyes of the Emperor, by a young anarchist who had insinuated himself into the confidence of the secret police on the pretext of having discovered a conspiracy, and had in this way obtained entry to the theatre. The mortally wounded minister, falling back in his seat, had only time, before he expired, to look up to the imperial box and make the sign of the cross.

It was against this dark background of disasters of all kinds, war, rebellion, executions, and murders, that the "idyll of Tsarskoe Selo" so strangely stood out. Here, bathed in light, a picture of middle-class contentment was displayed: the Tsar playing billiards, the Tsaritsa gaily talking with her friend Ania, the children happily engaged in needlework, or performing little comedies and arranging house balls. And there, in the background, as it were, a land in devastation, towns treated to volleys of musketry, long trains of exiled prisoners on their way to Siberia, prisons, and the bodies of muzhiks and ministers riddled with bullets.

While in the room next to the Empress's a low entreating whistle was sounding, like the longing cry of a bird, in far Manchuria the groans of dying soldiers were mingling with the thunder of cannons. The Emperor Nikolai was calmly and safely playing tennis, and hardly ever missing a ball, while at the same moment his fleet with many thousands of brave sailors sank in Chinese seas.

The Emperor's continuing to live his untroubled life, shooting, walking, playing tennis, swimming, and rowing, in the midst of all these calamities, was bound to give an impression of frivolous provocation. A large part of the population was even inclined to ascribe this curious indifference of the Emperor in the face of disaster to cruelty and entire lack of feeling. Many of the courtiers, ministers, and ambassadors could cite concrete cases in which the Tsar displayed this queer lack of understanding of the sorrows and sufferings of his subjects in a peculiarly blatant form.

This characteristic showed itself for the first time on the occasion of the disaster on the Khodinski Field, when the young Emperor did not countermand the festivities, but was himself present at a ball. On May 14th, 1905, when the Russian fleet was annihilated at Tsushima, the Emperor received the news while he was playing tennis. He opened the dispatch, said: "What a terrible disaster," and, taking up his racquet, went on with the game. He showed the same calmness over the assassinations of Plehve and his uncle, and also, later, over the murder of Stolypin, of which he was actually an eye-witness.

His diaries, too, confirm the impression that the Emperor was completely lacking in any understanding of grave events. In his notes he merely touches on happenings of the greatest importance, disasters, and tragic fatalities; such things occupy no more space than remarks about quite trivial everyday matters. Among detailed accounts of the bags at shooting parties, of excursions and walks, the greatest events of his reign are referred to in passing. In particular, his notes on the course of the war with Japan are so scanty as to give the impression that he deliberately shirked dealing seriously with the subject. Here and there, it is true, the unfavourable news from the Far East depressed him; but he proceeds at once to happier subjects and tells of rides, of the weather, and of cosy evenings with his Alix. On the decisive day of Tsushima the Tsar writes: "Depressing and contradictory reports are arriving all the time about the unfortunate battle in the Bay of Tsushima. I heard three reports, then the two of us went for a walk. The weather was wonderful and warm. We had tea and dinner on the balcony. In the evening I gave audience to Bulygin and Trepov, who stayed a long time."

Even the Revolution left very few traces in the diaries; here and there he expresses his displeasure; he is particularly angry over the mutiny on the armoured cruiser "Potemkin"; he dismisses the massacre before the Winter Palace in a few indifferent words; but, otherwise, the reports of shooting parties and other expeditions continue to occupy most of the space.

Yet, in spite of everything, the reproach that Nikolai and Alexandra were cruelly unfeeling must, on closer consideration, be characterized as unjust. The apparently perfect, untroubled happiness of their family life, the "idyll of Tsarskoe Selo," that no external event could disturb, did not betoken a cynical provocation, an arrogant lack of understanding of the sufferings of their people, but rather a way of escape for two weak people, dogged by misfortune and harassed by perpetual fear, who tried to hide from fate in their narrow, secluded "happiness."

While Nikolai and Alexandra moved within this "magic circle" they were handsome, happy, good, and lovable people. The few who were admitted to their secluded home life admired the beauty of the Empress and the happy, natural glance of the Emperor, and spoke with sincere enthusiasm of the charming character of the couple. But anyone who caught sight of them outside this peaceful domesticity, who met them at receptions, festivities, or on other State occasions, and who was not dazzled by outward appearances, felt immediately that here were two shy, fearful, everlastingly embarrassed people.

Everyone had to admit that the slim figure and beautiful face of the Empress gave an impression of majesty, and that the Emperor had charming social manners and was amiable, although self-conscious; but they felt at the same time that Alexandra's upright carriage was forced and artificial and that Nikolai's courteous smile was unnatural and constrained. Paléologue, the French Ambassador at the Court of St. Petersburg, had frequent opportunity of observing the imperial couple at State functions. He reports that, in conversation, the Empress used to look fixedly into vacancy, her smile quickly became set, and her characteristic shy blush alternated with livid pallor. Her bluish lips were swollen, and the diamond ornaments on her breast rose and fell with her laboured breathing. "Until the end of dinner, which was very long, the poor woman was obviously struggling with hysteria. Her features suddenly relaxed when the Emperor rose to propose the toast." With this observation, Paléologue concludes his account.

Strangers could not help being immediately struck by her shyness and awkwardness, from which she had suffered as a young girl, and which she never succeeded in overcoming, even in later years. Alexander Taneev, the faithful and devoted Keeper of the Privy Purse, was amazed when, during his first interview with the young Tsaritsa, she confusedly bent down to pick up some papers he had inadvertently let fall. Even in conversation the Empress was shy and lacking in confidence; she often stuck in the middle of a sentence, began to stammer, and was unable to continue. This awkwardness earned her the contempt of the Court, and many people mockingly called her a "little German provincial," with a malicious allusion to the "petty Court" of Hesse, which was despised and looked down on in Russia.

Often, however, her embarrassment was thought to be due to pride and haughtiness. She was incapable of unconstrained friendliness, and the Court at once attributed this to coldness and arrogance. Some even denied her any beauty, and maintained that her figure was clumsy, her face uninteresting, and that their total impression of her left them quite indifferent. The frigid reception she met with everywhere must inevitably have increased her reserve and nervousness; she felt unhappy and lonely whenever she was obliged to leave her intimate home circle. Only with her family did she get rid of this oppressive nightmare; there she was gay, open-hearted, and friendly.

The character of the Tsar, too, although quite different from hers, yet showed similar traits: he, too, was fundamentally shy and constrained; he, too, hated all official functions and he, too, was credited with haughtiness and insincerity. Nikolai II, by the sudden death of his father, reached the throne while still young, and was consequently ill-prepared for his difficult position. Accordingly, in the first part of his reign, he relied entirely on the advice of experienced relations, and was largely influenced by his energetic and intelligent mother. Lacking all experience in State affairs, he was at first completely in the hands of his ministers, which was for the best in so far as these had been for many years the advisers and confidants of his father. But in the course of time, they all, one after the other, died either natural or violent deaths, and the young Tsar, for good or ill, had himself to choose his new ministers. But for this he lacked not only an inborn knowledge of men, but also all opportunity to become acquainted with useful men. His grandfather, Alexander II, was accustomed to frequent all circles, even private, by which means he made the acquaintance of a very large number of people, and he did not hesitate to appoint as a minister anyone whom he thought capable, without any regard to his previous rank. Nikolai II, on the other hand, held aloof from all social life, so that he was restricted to a very narrow field in his choice of advisers.

Moreover, the Emperor was lacking in strength of will, energy of character, and consciousness of aim: it was easy for anyone to talk him over, but no one could ever be sure that he would adhere to the decision he had made. It often happened that he apparently accepted a proposal of a minister with complete conviction, and then, a little later, gave an exactly opposite order. This characteristic was only too well known to his ministers, and they often had recourse to curious expedients in order to guard themselves against surprises. On one occasion the old Prime Minister Goremykin, on his return from an audience in which he had persuaded the Tsar to approve an important measure, gave orders that under no circumstances was he to be awakened before midday. He had correctly foreseen that the Tsar would send a contrary order the same night, and took this means to secure that no one would dare to bring him the new order, and that the desired measure would be put into force in the interval.

The Emperor had an avowed dislike of painful scenes and discussions, and, therefore, preferred to deal with unpleasant business in writing. The fact that he had decided to dismiss a minister did not prevent him from receiving the latter in the most friendly fashion, and then, immediately after, surprising him with a written order of dismissal. Inevitably, he gained a reputation for insincerity.

Meanwhile, as time went on, the circle of those trusted by the imperial couple became narrower and narrower. Even once intimate friends of the family were, one after the other, politely but firmly set aside; under Alexander III, Prince Obolenski had been on intimate terms with the imperial family, and was always invited to luncheon after he had made his report in the morning. The new imperial couple found this regular guest a nuisance, and the Tsar tried all sorts of subterfuges to evade the invitation. Finally he found the way out by postponing the Prince's report until the afternoon.

In the period immediately following his accession Nikolai was still very much under the influence of his relations, especially

"Uncle Misha," "Uncle Alexei," and "Sandro," the Grand Duke Alexander Mikhailovich. Soon, however, the Emperor broke off relations with this group and, for a time, fell even more strongly under the influence of another family group, composed of the Grand Dukes Nikolai and Peter Nikolaevich, generally called, for short, "the Nikolaevichi," on account of their common patronymic, and their wives, the two "Montenegrins," Militsa and Anastasia.

These beautiful and interesting women, daughters of Prince, afterwards King, Nikita of Montenegro, had contrived with great skill to insinuate themselves into the confidence of the Tsaritsa. They saw her helpless position in an entourage alien and hostile to her, and they overwhelmed her with proofs of love, devotion, and esteem. When the Empress was suffering from an abdominal complaint they made of this an opportunity to win her favour. They superseded her regular attendants, and themselves undertook to nurse her, and fulfilled all the duties connected with this task with admirable zeal. The reason for their attitude was, of course, only too transparent: to that time the "Montenegrins" had played an insignificant part at the Imperial Court, and they now saw a chance of winning an influential position through the Tsaritsa. In spite of this Alexandra met their ostentatiously paraded love and devotion with sincere gratitude. It was the "Montenegrins," too, who succeeded in satisfying the mystical tendencies of the Empress, and who introduced her to a series of "miracle-workers," "magicians," and "holy men." At first this common interest in the supernatural world strengthened the friendly relations between the three women; a little later, however, this very mysticism led to a complete break between them.

The Empress's precarious health helped further to curtail both official Court life and also intercourse with the other members of the family. At this time, this seclusion had already gone to such lengths that it was extremely difficult even for the Grand Dukes and Duchesses to obtain audience of the Emperor and Empress.

From then on Nikolai and Alexandra lived a lonely life in

their home at Tsarskoe Selo. Gradually the Tsaritsa became her husband's only confidante, and both official receptions and private visits of other relations became fewer and rarer.

Only one solitary person succeeded in breaking through the iron barrier that surrounded the imperial pair. This was Anna Alexandrovna Taneeva, who quickly gained the confidence of her mistress and soon became her only intimate friend. A year or two after "Ania's" first appearance at Court she was already, in a sense, regarded as belonging to the intimate family circle; the Empress called her "our big baby" and "our little daughter," and gave her her unreserved confidence about all her cares, worries, and doubts. Anna was the daughter of Taneev, the director of the Imperial Chancellery, a most distinguished and conscientious man, who had also a considerable reputation as a composer. She had been summoned to Tsarskoe Selo at the age of twenty-three, to take the place of Princess Orbeliani (one of the maids of honour, who had fallen ill), and had formed a warm friendship with the Empress during a cruise in the Finnish islands. When they parted after this holiday Alexandra cried happily: "I thank God for having at last sent me a true friend."

And Ania was in truth a real friend to her Empress up to her tragic end: Alexandra's last letters and her last words of love were for Ania, and Ania, too, up to the end, did everything humanly possible to serve, help, and support her royal friend. This woman, who enjoyed the unlimited trust and affection of the Empress, was a most unusual and original person, whose character, outlook, and bearing exquisitely fitted her for the idyll of Tsarskoe Selo. Amid a crowd of Court flunkeys, all trying to win personal advantages by flattery and intrigues, Ania remained the sincere friend who never sought her own ends. During the whole of her intimate intercourse with the imperial family she had no other thought or wish than to be allowed to sacrifice herself for Nikolai, Alexandra, and their children. She had no rank or official position at Court, and the material support given her by the Empress was ludicrously small. She herself had no private means, and her circumstances may be described as indigent. Occasionally the Tsaritsa succeeded in making her accept some worthless trinket or a dress, and her whole appearance was of a piece with this extreme modesty. "No royal favourite," remarks Paléologue, in amazement, "ever looked more unpretentious." She was rather stout, of coarse and ample build, with thick, shining hair, a fat neck, a pretty, innocent face with rosy, shining cheeks, large, strikingly clear, bright eyes, and full, fleshy lips. She was always very simply dressed, and with her worthless adornments had a provincial appearance. For some time after a railway accident of which she was one of the victims she was able to move about only on crutches, or was wheeled about in a bath-chair.

Anna Taneeva was for a short time unhappily married to a naval lieutenant called Vyrubov, but the marriage was dissolved in less than a year because Vyrubov was subject to severe nervous attacks, which at times degenerated into madness. This melancholy experience only strengthened her relations with the Tsaritsa, for, disappointed in her marriage, she attached herself all the more closely and devotedly to her imperial friend.

"The Vyrubova," as Ania was henceforward known to the whole of Russia, often passed for a dangerous intriguer, and foreign diplomatists, in particular, have more than once represented her in this light. There can be no doubt that Anna Vyrubova did engage in politics to a considerable extent, and influenced the fate of Russia in more than one respect. Her "intrigues," however, never served her own ends, but always those of the imperial couple.

After her separation from Lieutenant Vyrubov, Anna resumed possession of a modest cottage not far from the Palace of Tsarskoe Selo, which she had rented during her betrothal. Hardly a day passed on which she did not appear at the Palace, or receive a visit from the imperial family in her home. "Ania's little house" gradually became one of the imperial couple's favourite resorts, for there they were quite undisturbed and remote from burdensome official duties; there they could be entirely free and careless, and could cast aside all considerations of etiquette. Later on, the little house became a place of high political importance; for it was there that the Emperor and Empress met all the people whom they could not receive officially at the Palace. The cottage lay at the corner of Sredniaia Street and Tserkovnaia

Street, scarcely two hundred paces from the Palace, so that the Tsar and Tsaritsa could visit it on foot whenever they liked, without attracting attention.

Anna Vyrubova herself describes her home as primitive and rather uncomfortable. It had no foundations, and was therefore very cold; this was especially noticeable in winter, when an icy cold blast rose from the floor. "On my marriage the Empress gave me six chairs with covers embroidered by her own hands, as well as a tea-table and some water-colours. When their Majesties came to tea with me in the evenings, the Empress generally brought fruit and sweetmeats with her, and the Emperor sometimes brought a bottle of cherry brandy. We used to sit round the table with our legs drawn up so as to avoid contact with the cold floor. Their Majesties regarded my primitive way of life from the humorous side. Sitting before the blazing hearth we drank our tea and ate little toasted cracknels, handed round by my servant, Bertsik, a former valet of my late grandfather Tolstoi. I remember the Emperor once laughingly saying to me that, after such an evening, nothing but a hot bath would make him warm again."

The Vyrubova's modest way of living was the very thing that gave her special value in the eyes of the imperial couple. They felt that here, for the first time, they had met a really disinterested person, and they knew how to value this rare privilege. In time Ania became almost the only society of the imperial family, for even the number of the Court officials in attendance was always diminishing, since the suspicions of the Emperor perpetually demanded fresh victims.

* * * * *

What a melancholy spectacle the Court of Nikolai and Alexandra afforded, compared with the brilliant times of earlier sovereigns! Once the Russian Imperial Court, both by its magnificence and by its lively social and political life, could put many of the great European capitals in the shade; former Russian rulers were always surrounded by the most important statesmen, the most skilled diplomatists, and the shrewdest wire-pullers of the time; around the Emperor subtle intrigues were planned, clever political duels fought out, and bold *coups d'état* carried through. A gay profusion of busy figures had animated the capital: grand dukes and grand duchesses, the numerous princely uncles, aunts, and cousins of the sovereign, who exercised greater or less influence on the Emperor according to the nearness of the family relationship; the proud bearers of old noble names with their various ambitious interests; ministers, summoned to the Presence in their gold-laced Court dress, generals wearing their medals, dignitaries of the Church with gold crosses on their breasts, couriers and adjutants who brought important despatches and carried important despatches back again; a galaxy of Court ladies, princesses, and countesses, old and young, beautiful and ugly, in splendid toilettes adorned with glittering jewels.

At great receptions, State dinners, and rustling Court balls these formed the magnificent *décor*, and their figures had lent the Imperial Court of the past that colourful animation, those richly gleaming, characteristic hues which united the refinement, culture, and pulsing activity of European courts with the heavy, florid magnificence of Asiatic despotism.

Even under Alexander III, however, life had gradually become quieter; the colours faded, and the glitter grew dim. Alexander III passed most of the last years of his reign in the Palace of Gachina, outside St. Petersburg, or in the Crimea, and the Winter Palace became deserted. But, after the accession of Nikolai II, the last remnants of ceremonial Court life almost vanished. More and more seldom were important and striking figures to be seen at Court, and no one knew exactly whether they were all dead or whether they were just sitting at home because neither the new monarch nor his consort desired their society. A new generation of gifted young statesmen and diplomats was also lacking, since the ruler neither possessed the capacity for, nor felt the need of, attaching young and lively talents to his service.

The great contests of intriguing statesmen, which once the whole of Russia followed with breathless interest, became more and more rare, for the reign of Nikolai II offered no opportunity for an exciting war between really ambitious politicians. They retired and left the field to the insignificant stratagems of petty place-hunters.

The relatives of the imperial couple, too, the many grand-ducal uncles, aunts, and cousins, one after another, began to keep away from the Court; every year fewer covers were laid for the official reunions at the ceremonial family dinner, until at last the Emperor and his wife and children sat round the table alone. The family now met only at masses for the dead, when one or other of the grand dukes died, or was the victim of a conspiracy.

The Empress hated, loathed, and feared her ladies-in-waiting, the princesses and countesses, the ladies, old and young, ugly and attractive, in their magnificent toilettes and their glittering jewels. In her eyes they were all "false, wicked cats," every one of whom was ready to betray her, to intrigue against her, and to spread gossip about her.

Nikolai and Alexandra were afraid of everybody and mistrusted everybody. The Emperor felt that all those courtiers who bowed before him in slavish devotion were ready at any moment to betray him without scruple for the sake of their own selfish interests. This perpetual suspicion of the monarch was bound in time to give the Court a peculiar stamp: anyone with opinions and a will of his own immediately seemed to the Emperor suspicious, or at least troublesome, and was banished; only quite colourless people seemed safe and were tolerated in the entourage of the imperial family, which, in an ever-increasing degree, came to consist of uninteresting and insignificant shadow figures. But the few men whom the Emperor tolerated about him and trusted, gained ever greater influence over him, while the rest of the Court officials were reduced to complete insignificance. Thus the number who could be initiated into the private affairs of the family was very small: they included in all two or three trustworthy aides-de-camp, the old Minister of the Court, and the Governor of the Palace, men of delicate tact who, from fear of giving offence, refrained from any expression of opinion whatever. They never said "no" to anything, and their lack of judgment was so great that they could sincerely approve whatever the Tsar and Tsaritsa did. These "intimates" came and went on tiptoe and anxiously avoided ever bringing an unpleasant report in their portfolios. Their spirits were always equably gay; their favourite topic was the weather; and they inquired daily with devoted politeness after the same trifling matters as if everything in the world were arranged for the best.

This was not courtly hypocrisy, for they were men of much too simple and innocent minds ever to observe any injustice or evil anywhere. Of all the evil things that were enacted in Russia during their period of service they had really seen and heard nothing, so that they were spared the necessity of approaching the imperial couple with disturbing reports.

Right up to the day on which the revolutionary soldiers broke into the Palace and laid rough hands on the "imperial dreamers" in order to take them prisoners and, later, to execute them, the peace of the "idyll of Tsarskoe Selo" was protected by these faithful servants, whose feet trod softly and whose refined upbringing took care that Nikolai and Alexandra never became aware of the perilous illusoriness of their hot-house happiness.

Without this little circle of eternally optimistic courtiers the idyll of Tsarskoe Selo would never have been possible; but also, without these creatures, who never appeared with an unpleasant question or report, this idyll would hardly have led to such a fatal end for the Tsar and the Empire. These Fredericks, Voeikovs, Zablins, and Nilovs contributed not a little to the terrible collapse, the frightful end of the idyll of Tsarskoe Selo.

The most interesting of them was without doubt the Minister of the Court, Fredericks, a very distinguished old gentleman who had occupied his confidential post as long as anyone could remember. He was the best type of tactful person, a master of etiquette and Court formalities. His was the difficult office of arranging all the private affairs of the imperial family, fixing the appanages of the grand dukes and their wives, distributing presents, suppressing scandals, and paying debts. He had to look after the well-being of all the members of the imperial house, and thus had always to be initiated into the most intimate secrets of the family. The imperial couple were very fond of this handsome, elegant old man; they called him "our old man," and allowed him to address them as "mes enfants."

It is true that Count Fredericks had already become a little peculiar owing to his great age: his memory was no longer what it had been, and amusing stories were told about him in Court circles. On one occasion when Prince Orlov, the chief of the Military Chancery, was submitting a report to him, Count Fredericks suddenly interrupted him with the question: "What do you think, my dear Prince? I believe I haven't been shaved to-day." Orlov declared that he could not say, and went on with his report. Five minutes later Fredericks laid his hand on his shoulder and said: "Excuse me a moment, I haven't been shaved to-day." The Prince smiled and said it would perhaps be best to ask the valet. The old Count rang the bell and, when the servant appeared, asked him whether he had been shaved. The valet said he had.

Hardly had Orlov ended his report when Fredericks rose from his chair, crying: "I haven't been shaved yet. I must go to the barber." But on the way he fell asleep in his carriage, and the coachman elected to bring him home again unshaven.

Stories of this kind were told everywhere with the greatest gusto, but this in no way interfered with the universal popularity of the Minister of the Court. Only Count Witte, always malicious, declared bluntly that Fredericks was "abundantly lacking in ideas," and that his colleagues had to hammer his reports for the Emperor into him like a school task.

Voeikov, the son-in-law of Count Fredericks, was the Governor of the Palace. At the beginning the Tsaritsa did not care much for him; but later she changed her views.

A somewhat strange figure in the Emperor's entourage was the aide-de-camp, Admiral Nilov, a gruff old bear, who loved his wine; it was his custom to speak his mind plainly to everyone, even the Emperor; but as a matter of fact, his "truths" were sufficiently removed from the real truth never to give serious offence.

A curious part was played by the many other aides-de-camp, who watched each other jealously, and none of whom, with few exceptions, had any influence whatever. If anyone made a request to one of these officers he would reply: "I only open doors," or "I only play chess."

The financial position of all the aides-de-camp was very poor: they received salaries that hardly paid their tips, with the result that they often fell into the hands of moneylenders, speculated on the Exchange, and did their best to make use of their position at Court for their own financial advantage. But only one of them had any real influence, Zablin, who had contrived to acquire the Emperor's confidence to some extent.

Thus the imperial couple were entirely isolated by these colourless, devoted courtiers, as by an impenetrable wall, from the outer world, from the whole Russian Empire. "It is pitiable!" exclaimed Sazonov, the Minister for Foreign Affairs, on one occasion. "Little by little, a vacuum has formed round the imperial couple; no one can now approach them. With the exception of the official relations between the Emperor and his ministers, no voice from the outside world ever penetrates to the Palace."

* * * * *

While Court life proper was thus gradually dying out, an all the more lively activity was developing in the political salons of the capital; such salons, of which there had been a number in earlier days, ever since the time of Frau von Krüdener, began to spring up like mushrooms at St. Petersburg in the beginning of the twentieth century.

The busy activity of the Court having been driven away from the Palace of Tsarskoe Selo, which came to bear an ever greater resemblance to an enormous and magnificent sick-room, it was forced to lead an inglorious, miserable, ghost-like existence in the political salons. The intrigues, schemes, rivalries, and plans which, in the glitter of the Imperial Palace, had had a certain style and could sometimes dazzle by their very vastness, languished in these little salons. Here what in the vicinity of the Emperor had been "politics" on the grand scale, degenerated into petty repulsive busyness, into endless agitated chatter and unsavory speculation.

Since men of rank and importance seldom gained access to the sovereign, had practically no influence over him, and never were sure of his real intentions, the new political salons of St. Petersburg did not centre round them, but generally round people whose relations with the Court depended on their acquaintance with some subordinate Court official who, precisely because of his low position, could always have access to the Emperor. It was lackeys, doorkeepers, and other "dignitaries" of the kind whose friendship was now sought in political circles.

The fortunate man who could boast of relations with subordinate palace officials of this sort immediately became highly regarded, and a salon formed around him; politicians who aspired to ministerial rank thought it desirable to visit him, and also priests who wanted to be bishops, and contractors, bankers, and spies, whose business it was to secure trustworthy reports of the Emperor's doings. They all hoped to succeed through the intervention of a lackey or some other apparently insignificant Court official.

The busiest of these curious political circles was that of Prince Andronnikov. There innumerable people met daily to advance their own schemes by means of the excellent connection with Tsarskoe Selo enjoyed by the Prince. The Prince was often in a position to communicate to his friends the most secret decisions of the Emperor some hours before they were publicly announced, and thus do them very valuable service. Andronnikov was also able to advance requests of all kinds, and put through appointments and honours. Therefore, many a high functionary, officer, or prince of the Church regularly spent his mornings in the Andronnikov salon, until he had actually secured the desired promotion or decoration.

Andronnikov owed this remarkable influence over the decisions of the Emperor to a long-standing friendship with the Emperor's groom-of-the-chamber; in later years, he also came in touch with the Governor of the Palace; but the latter was never able to do him such valuable service as the groom-of-the-chamber. Through him he always knew what documents were lying on the Emperor's desk, and how Nikolai intended to decide this or that affair. The speculators and spies who frequented the salon based their enterprises and secret reports on these communications; Andronnikov's information was always very reliable, and the influence which the Prince, through the groom-of-the-chamber, exercised on the Emperor hardly ever failed of its effect.

There were times when even high dignitaries of the State like the War Ministers, Sukhomlinov and Belaev, princes of the Church like Bishop Varnava, and men who themselves were favourably regarded at Court, received their real information in the Andronnikov salon, for the reports of the groom-of-the-chamber were more trustworthy than anything that these important gentlemen learnt during their personal visits to Tsarskoe Selo. In addition to these distinguished visitors, many poor frightened Jews crowded the Prince's salon, hoping, through the agency of Andronnikov, to secure the repeal of an order of banishment, in which hope they were seldom disappointed.

But the chief customer for Andronnikov's reports was the Ministry of the Interior. It was this high department of State that financed the whole business of the salon. Prince Andronnikov came of an impoverished family and, though he possessed practically no property, was a notorious spendthrift. But the Ministry of the Interior thought it desirable to pay out a considerable sum to him every month in order to secure the information supplied by the groom-of-the-chamber. By subsidizing Andronnikov, the Ministry saved large sums which would have had to be spent in spying on the monarch. The Ministry was well aware that the Tsar never spoke openly and unreservedly to his ministers, and that, in consequence, they could never trust his utterances, but must always be prepared for painful surprises. Through the Andronnikov salon, however, the Minister received exact information of the mood and intentions of the Tsar, which report had secured his approval, and which aroused his displeasure. The groom-of-the-chamber delivered the information, and the intelligent and cunning Prince guessed all the rest worth knowing.

At the same time, through his alliance with Andronnikov, the Minister was also always *au fait* with what the very reverend lord bishops, the generals, and the politicians were after at the moment. The Prince betrayed to the Ministry the plans which these gentlemen entrusted to him for transmission to the groom-of-the-chamber, and thus its officials were in a position to form a clear and accurate picture of all the events of internal politics.

Prince Andronnikov had long been regarded as an interesting personality in political and social circles. His appearance was typical of the perpetually busy man, who is acquainted with everybody and always dashing about the town on important and secret missions, suddenly appearing here, there, and everywhere, and disappearing again, and whose whole life has a fascinating flavour of adventure. He always carried a large, bulging, bright yellow attaché case about with him, over the contents of which he dropped mysterious hints.

This attaché case in time became so famous that the police began to take an interest in its contents. On one occasion the Minister, Plehve, decided on a bold stroke: to have Andronnikov attacked and the case stolen. The plan succeeded, and an Okhrana official bore the yellow attaché case in triumph to the Minister. When he opened it Plehve found that it contained nothing but old newspapers.

But Andronnikov was more than a harmless poseur. He was a passionate intriguer, and took a fierce delight in setting ministers and bishops by the ears, originating libellous rumours, and breaking old friendships. He did this not so much for material advantage as, in Witte's opinion, "from a passionate love for the art of intrigue." With his malicious wit and his keen eye for the weaknesses of others, he was a very great danger to his opponents or the opponents of his friends. He could not only produce elegant and flattering little books in honour of ministers whom he favoured; he could publish equally elegant satirical pamphlets against his enemies, and contrived to slip these annihilatingly malicious "portraits" onto the desks of all the influential men in St. Petersburg.

In later years he acquired a paper of his own for the exercise of his literary activities. After that, whenever any of his enemies attempted to move, this journal immediately printed a leading article with remarks about the past life and the "true face" of the person in question, and these lines generally sufficed to make the unfortunate man a laughing-stock for the rest of his life.

In order to vent his spleen on various enemies of his, Andronnikov once published, in French, a book called *Contemporary Memoirs,* in which he discussed, with devastating irony, the activities and capacities of the different ministers, and which kept the whole of St. Petersburg society for weeks in a state of the greatest excitement. Even the members of the imperial house, the Dowager Empress and the grand dukes, were enormously diverted by these memoirs, and the groom-of-the-chamber took care that a copy reached the Emperor's desk.

But while the Prince's literary gifts made him a dangerous opponent, it was his friendship with the groom-of-the-chamber that made his influential patronage so coveted. His prestige rose higher and higher, and his social and political connections visibly increased in scope and importance. As he was a welcome guest of the grand dukes, Mr. Shervashidze, the Steward of the Household of the Dowager Empress, sought his favour, which led the aristocracy to take an interest in him. Every new minister, on taking office, was confidentially informed by the head of his department that his predecessor had cultivated good relations with Andronnikov, so he also took over the traditional friendship, and left it as a legacy to his successor. The remainder of the high officials of the department knew that the minister was in touch with Andronnikov, and they also courted his favours; the lesser officials had always been accustomed to imitate their superiors, so they displayed an exaggerated devotion to the Prince. Whenever he appeared in a ministry the "chinovniki" officiously leapt from their chairs, helped him out of his fur coat, and pulled off his snow-boots.

Only two men were bold enough to refuse to pay due respect to the Prince: Sukhomlinov, the Minister for War, who had once transacted certain land speculations in Bukhara and Khiva with Andronnikov and afterwards quarrelled with him, and Maklakov, the Minister of the Interior. The latter had actually once dared to reply to a telegram of greeting from Andronnikov without becoming politeness, and had even withdrawn the Prince's free railway-pass. Both ministers later felt the weight of Andronnikov's power, for the ruthless Prince contrived rapidly to ruin them one after the other, and even to have the unfortunate Sukhomlinov confined in the Fortress of SS. Peter and Paul.

After this no one had the courage to oppose Prince Andronnikov, and Beletski, the Chief of Police, could justly maintain that, in the decade preceding the Revolution, no important decision was taken in Russian policy without Andronnikov's somehow having a finger in the pie.

But the Andronnikov salon was not the only one; it had an important rival in the circle surrounding Burdukov, the Imperial Master of the Horse. This Burdukov was also attached to the Ministry of the Interior, and his title of Master of the Horse had nothing whatever to do with his real functions. His political strength lay in his friendship with the Tsar's two favourite aides-de-camp, General Zablin and Admiral Nilov. Through the instrumentality of these two men he, too, was able to supply his clients and the visitors to his salon with rapid and trustworthy reports from Tsarskoe Selo. He was in regular postal and telegraphic communication with his friends at Court, and the "old sea-bear," Admiral Nilov, not infrequently appeared at his banquets and drinking parties to partake of a bottle or two of good wine. Burdukov's followers, that circle of political and social fortune hunters, maintained that their patron's influence at Court was greater and more valuable than that of Andronnikov. Between the two salons and their chiefs a bitter war raged, which was carried on with all the weapons of intrigue, slander, and espionage.

But whichever of these rival salons was the more influential, no one ever doubted that the hospitality of the Burdukov salon was superior to that of the Andronnikov. The reason for this was that the cost of the Andronnikov salon was met by the Ministry of the Interior from its restricted resources which, although abundant, were not inexhaustible, while behind the Burdukov salon stood the truly lavish and far-seeing financier, Ignati Porfirievich Manus.

Manus was anything but mean, in which he was most desirably different from the narrow-minded bureaucrats of the Ministry of the Interior. Manus knew very well that the sums he invested in the Burdukov salon were advantageously laid out, and would repay him tenfold, nay, a hundredfold. By the help of Burdukov he was enabled to overtop his most dangerous and powerful competitor, Dimitri Rubinstein, the banker, a victory which meant the crown of a brilliant financial career.

Manus, a Jew who had risen from poor circumstances, had always contrived to use the political situation cleverly for his business purposes. After he had succeeded in some considerable speculations, he brought off his first really big transaction by allying himself with Prince Meshcherski, the fanatical champion of orthodox Pan-Slavism, and placing his fortune at the disposal of the Prince. With the help of Manus's Jewish money, Meshcherski, the reactionary and one-time friend of Dostoevski, was able to develop a lively anti-Semitic agitation in his *Grazhdanin*; Manus himself, under the pseudonym of Seleni, also wrote some ultra-nationalist articles for this paper. In this way Manus established excellent relations with the influential circles of the reaction and the nobility, and was soon regarded as the richest and most respected financier in St. Petersburg.

Like all really skilful financiers Manus, or the "yellow man," as he was called in St. Petersburg, liked to remain in the background; he was never concerned with the satisfaction of petty vanities, but always with great affairs, and he found it most satisfactory to shelter behind his protégé, Burdukov.

The chops and changes in the banker's operations often involved his executive in certain difficulties; thus Zablin once wrote despairingly to his principal: "You recently ordered me to stop abusing Bark, the Minister of Finance, and three days ago you even gave me strict orders to praise him. Now today, all of a sudden, I am to attack him again. I must ask you seriously to consider that it is somewhat difficult for me, after lauding a minister to the skies one day, to speak disparagingly of him the next."

Manus's commissions were rarely of a purely political character; they related generally to matters of business. What the financier wanted to obtain, by means of the Burdukov salon, was the grant of new concessions, building permits for factories, and food and army contracts.

During the Great War it was repeatedly asserted that Manus was in the employment of the German Secret Service, a suspicion entertained by the Minister Khvostov in particular. Although there was a fair amount of incriminating evidence against the banker, he went on with his work quite undisturbed, and hardly troubled about the accusations brought against him. The Burdukov salon, with its connections with Zablin and Nilov, afforded him such strong protection that right up to the outbreak of the

Revolution Manus never had to feel any serious alarm. Through this political circle which he financed and which served him, the "yellow man" was beyond the reach of his enemies and quite unassailable.

Of all these circles of adventurers, half-social, half-political, that were formed in St. Petersburg in the absence of a healthy Court life, the salon of the Baroness Rosen was particularly remarkable. While Prince Andronnikov proudly proclaimed to the world his relations with the Tsar's groom-of-the-chamber, and Burdukov made no secret of his friendship with Zablin and Nilov, the name of the personage who formed her connection with Tsarskoe Selo was never mentioned in the salon of the Baroness Rosen. No one knew whence the Baroness obtained her reliable reports; but there was no doubt that the channel existed, and that the information was nearly always correct. The discreet guests of the discreet hostess had long ago discovered that this was a carefully guarded secret, and they were satisfied if the "reliable source" delivered the reports and passed on their requests to Tsarskoe Selo. The Baroness Rosen, too, was in poor circumstances, but this did not prevent her from dressing with exquisite elegance and from giving most tasteful and sumptuous parties; her dinners sometimes surpassed in luxury even those of the "yellow man" in the Burdukov salon. There was some vague relationship between the Baroness and the beautiful Princess Dolgorukaia, a lady of Spanish origin, whose formal marriage with a Russian aristocrat had made it possible for her to carry through profitable transactions.

The curious Khvostov had tried more than once to fathom the secret of the Baroness Rosen and her life, and frequently visited her for this purpose. He met there, at intimate breakfasts, police spies and adventurers, including Rashevski, the notorious official of the Okhrana. At midday he found grand dukes and duchesses and some of his ministerial colleagues; while in the evening, in the same salon, he saw himself surrounded by actors, courtesans, and newspaper correspondents. A mysterious "engineer," who never appeared in person, paid alike for the breakfasts of the spies, the lunches of the grand dukes, and the dinners of the actors, courtesans, and journalists. But who this unknown "engineer" was, his real reason for paying for all this, and where he got the necessary money, neither Khvostov's own perspicacity nor the machinery at his disposal ever succeeded in discovering.

There was still another circle that pursued different, more general, and more dangerous aims. This was the Ignatiev salon, where all the adherents of poisonous national and religious intolerance and political reaction assembled, with the object of directing the decisions of the Emperor.

Count Alexander Pavlovich Ignatiev, a former ambassador to the Sublime Porte and afterwards a minister, had been the first to foresee, as early as the reign of Alexander III, the decay of Court life and the rise of the salon. As soon as the old Emperor retired to Gagchina, Count Ignatiev, with the aid of his energetic wife, began to hold "political receptions" thrice a week. These soon developed into the notorious "black Ignatiev salon" that for a time was regarded as the influential political centre of the capital. Ignatiev, during whose ministry the most loathsome reactionary persecutions took place, used his salon as an active social instrument for his propaganda, as the starting-point of a thousand intrigues, all aimed at influencing the Court of the Tsar, in its isolation from the rest of the world, in the desired direction. Here assembled fanatical clergy and politicians from the ranks of the reactionary "All Russian Union," diplomatists, soldiers, and would-be ministers, who all, like their host, clung to the idea of the conquest of Constantinople, and had already worked out detailed military plans for that purpose. The circle also included bankers and contractors, who hoped, by pushing themselves forward at the right moment, to create valuable connections, and to secure orders and contracts for the coming war. Finally, the Count's salon was also frequented by various officials of the ministries and the police, gloomy men, imbued with "holy nationalistic convictions," supporters of absolute autocracy and the banishment to Siberia of all political opponents.

The same subordinate Court officials who were called upon to carry out business for the Andronnikov, Burdukov, and Rosen salons, were also used by the Ignatiev salon for purely political activities: theirs was the historic rôle of bringing the intolerance and reaction of the "black salon" to the otherwise unapproachable ears of the Emperor.

In the early days, when the "black Count" was still vigorous and full of enterprise, the activities of his salon were of a serious nature, and exercised a fatal influence in many directions. But later, as the Count retired more and more from public life, and when he finally died, the political agitation of the Ignatiev salon increasingly degenerated into frivolous, tri-weekly gossiping. Not that the "black salon" under the direction of the old widowed Countess abated a jot of its reactionary ideas, its orthodox views, and its fierce intolerance; these had, however, since the Count's death, lost all serious significance. The same guests assembled as before, and carried on the same conversations; but the salon became more and more like a tea-party, at which bigoted old ladies gossiped with their spiritual pastors and with retired generals.

The older the hostess and her friends grew, the more apparent the endless garrulity of the circle became. Gradually, the political subjects of conversation, eternally the same, no longer sufficed, and they lapsed into that delight in mysticism and occultism which so often goes hand in hand with a reactionary temper. Thereafter, when the old ladies, generals, and clerics met thrice a week in the Countess's salon, they spent only a minute or two in assuring each other of their unchanged political and religious reactionariness, and by a tacit agreement, passed on to the subject of the "supernatural powers." With agreeable shivers running down their spines, they told each other till far into the night of "mystical experiences" and "revelations"; the guests of the "black salon" often found it difficult to tear themselves away, and went on endlessly talking in the doorway of the "secrets of the supernatural."

Soon everyone interested in the occult tried to gain admittance to Countess Ignatiev's circle. For in the meantime, the usual result of such associations of zealous drawing-room occultists had come about: when people assemble for the purpose of conjuring up the unseen in eternal chatter, the unseen does not long delay its appearance, and every day gives clearer signs. Thus, in the Countess's salon, the magic world of spirits manifested itself in all sorts of "signs" and "astral phenomena."

Ere long the credulous, but still ignorant, members of the circle found their "teachers"; "messengers" were sent to the house, "clairvoyants," "mystagogues," and "barefoot pilgrims," who possessed the power of interpreting and explaining the supernatural signs. These "enlightened men" were all alike regarded by the guests with the greatest veneration as saints, and from the salon of the old Countess most of them found their way into the drawing-rooms of the "Montenegrins." In this way one or another finally arrived at Tsarskoe Selo, and appeared there with a firmly established reputation as a miracle-worker and "emissary from God."

And, in proportion as the Tsar and Tsaritsa, on account of the illness of the little heir-apparent, fell more and more under the spell of such "saints" and "clairvoyants," in the same degree they came more and more deeply under the influence of the ideas, wishes, and interests cultivated in the "black salon" of the Countess Ignatiev. Thus the morbid distaste of the Emperor for the advice and society of important men, his suspicion of all sincere people, and his complete isolation from his whole Empire finally led to a state of affairs in which only the petty interests of a reactionary circle of old women and retired generals could influence his decisions.

* * * * *

From his earliest youth Nikolai II had accepted all the blows of fate with fatalistic resignation, in which a kind of humble religiosity gave him inner support. Later in life, too, both in his capacity as the ruler of an Empire tottering on its foundations, and as the father of a son plainly condemned to an agonizing death, he endeavoured to find refuge in the divine will. Evil, silent and mysterious, lay in wait for him everywhere, for which it was difficult to find any other explanation than that it was nothing else than a "divine ordinance." All attempts to resist it with the feeble strength of man were inevitably foredoomed to failure. "The Emperor believes in the decrees of fate," once declared one of his ministers. "If anything goes wrong, instead of kicking against it, he immediately thinks that God has willed it so, and abandons himself without resistance to the will of the Almighty."

Thus for the Tsar there was no other way of salvation to be found except in a firm faith in Providence, a humble acceptance of all adversity and perpetual prayer for the help of the Lord. When, through some heavy blow or some too impetuous movement, the bleeding started in Alexei's little body, and his face, pale as death and distorted with pain, was turned to the wall, the Emperor and Empress sought strength in prayer. They prayed, too, before every important political decision, and, whenever difficulties and dangers to the State arose, they were convinced that these could be overcome only by prayer. When, in the year 1905, the Emperor, after much hesitation, signed the ukase summoning the Imperial Duma, the Tsar and Tsaritsa knelt down, and prayed to God that this grave decision might be a blessing to the Empire.

The Palace of Tsarskoe Selo contained a chapel, a half-darkened room with heavy silken hangings, against one wall of which rose the gleaming ikonostas. It had beautiful carved wooden arm-chairs for the imperial couple, and a number of plainer ones for the imperial children and the Court ladies. But this magnificently appointed chapel did not quite satisfy the wishes of the Empress, who was inclined to solitude, and she had another place prepared for her own devotions. In the crypt of the "Fedorovski Sobor," * the church of the Life Guards, not far from the Alexander Palace at Tsarskoe Selo, the Empress had a subterranean chapel fitted up, and betook herself there when she wanted to pray undisturbed. She would lie for hours on the stone flags in the dim light of a few oil lamps.

But, as one disaster followed another, and one new menace after another raised its head, the Tsar and Tsaritsa gradually began to feel the inadequacy of the strict Orthodox faith. In their trouble and fear they could no longer find any real satisfaction in the sermons and masses of the Court priests, the choral singing, and the ever-repeated prayers to which Heaven returned no answer. Like many weak and despairing souls before them,

* Fedorovski Cathedral

THE FATEFUL IDYLL OF TSARSKOE SELO

they felt the need of coming into immediate touch with God, of seeing him directly face to face. The Orthodox Church, with its strict doctrines, was less suited than mysticism, whatever its kind, to satisfy this longing for a miracle.

The Empress, who had been brought up in the strict Protestant faith, and who, as a girl, had come for a time under the influence of the ideas of David Friedrich Strauss, became at once a zealous and fanatical adherent of Orthodoxy, after she became Empress of Russia and went over to the creed of Byzantium. Later she developed an increasing leaning towards mysticism, to which she afterwards succumbed completely. At this period she seems to have been very deeply influenced by a work of the fourteenth century dealing with mediation between God and man, and with the "friends of God," mortals especially endowed with grace. She firmly believed that men existed who could approach the Godhead through their fervent prayers, and who, therefore, though not themselves priests, could discharge the office of mediator between Heaven and earth better than any ordinary clergyman.

The Emperor was far from opposing these enthusiasms of his wife; he, too, as a young man, had inclined to religious mysticism, a characteristic he shared with his ancestor, Alexander I. This inclination had been encouraged in his father's house, for Alexander III had also been convinced of the miraculous power of man endowed with divine grace. At his father's Court the young heir-apparent had become acquainted with that strange figure, John of Kronstadt, who was regarded as a saint, not only by the simple people, but also by the old Emperor himself.

It is true that John of Kronstadt was a priest of the Orthodox Church; but, in the eyes of all Russia, he stood high above the rest of the clergy, for he was credited with the ability to perform miracles, foresee the future, and save the sick and suffering from their troubles. When he preached the people flocked in crowds to the church, and knelt before him in devotion. In grave situations, when important decisions had to be taken or a member of the family was ill, the Emperor Alexander used to summon the holy man to the Palace, and ask for his advice and help. His successor, Nikolai II, remembered all his life an early mass in the church at Orianda, at which John of Kronstadt preached to the old Emperor, then seriously ill, and the whole imperial family, and prayed with them. In short, abrupt sentences, that sounded almost like cries, John of Kronstadt implored that the mercy and blessing of Heaven might descend on the imperial house. Nikolai was convinced that here spoke a truly holy man, a messenger of God. After that mass the Emperor shared with his whole heart the conviction of the thousands of pilgrims who, year in and year out, in their pious belief in miracles, came in crowds to John of Kronstadt.

And, on that dark day when Alexander III was hourly awaiting death, Nikolai witnessed another scene that was never to vanish from his memory. On entering his father's sick-room he saw him lying on the bed, struggling for breath, while John of Kronstadt bent over him, holding the Emperor's head in his hands, and whispering the last words of earthly consolation in the ears of the dying monarch.

Moreover, the man who was entrusted with the education of the heir-apparent, the first and chief adviser of Alexander III, the Procurator of the Holy Synod and influential statesman, Pobedonostsev, friend and patron of Dostoevski, also believed in supernatural powers and phenomena that could influence existence on earth. He was not only convinced of the holiness of John of Kronstadt; his belief in miracles went so far that he once carried out in his house, with the assistance of high prelates, a formal exorcism of devils. Like Pobedonostsev, most of the other ministers of the Emperor Alexander believed in supernatural powers, miracles, and prophecies, so that the young heir-apparent was reinforced on all hands in his mystical emotions.

This already morbid mysticism of the new imperial couple was afterwards further increased by their intercourse with the Grand Dukes Nikolai and Peter Nikolaevich and their wives. Although these grand-ducal couples were mainly interested in utterly absurd and primitive "occult séances," with table-rapping, spirit conjuring, and other spiritualistic nonsense, nevertheless, at that time, the Emperor and Empress, in their desire to escape somehow from the torment and care of their life in the world, snatched at anything that seemed to be a bridge to the supernatural world. In their flight from the dark dangers of real life they abandoned themselves without reflection to the shallowest forms of occultism.

In the drawing-rooms of the "Nikolaevichi" and their wives all kinds of spiritualistic séances went on, and all sorts of prophets, clairvoyants, preachers, pilgrims, faith-healers, and miracle-workers tumbled over each other. The young Emperor and his wife came more and more under the influence of this circle, and, when later they both began to keep aloof from the Court and the rest of their relations, it was the "Nikolaevichi" who retained their confidence longest.

The Tsaritsa, it is true, later rejected spiritualism as practised in the houses of her relatives, and abhorred it as heathenish, since preoccupation with such things endangers true faith; nevertheless, her conviction of the existence of clairvoyants and mediators between Heaven and earth, men endowed with divine grace, remained unshaken to the end. This belief appeared to her to be not incompatible with the Orthodox doctrines. She continued to spend many hours in the subterranean chapel of Fedorovski Sobor, took communion, and followed all the ordinances of the Church; but she was always seeking for "miracle-workers" who would satisfy her primitive yearning for direct communication with the Godhead.

It was at the beginning of the century that the Empress met the first of the long series of the "miracle-workers of Tsarskoe Selo," the French "thaumaturge," Doctor Philippe, who started those curious séances which, by their amalgamation of high politics with magic and sorcery, must be accounted one of the strangest phenomena of the recent past. In them modern diplomacy joined hands with necromancy, the supreme business of State with magic spells, constitutional reforms with "miraculous bells" that sounded whenever the Emperor encountered an "evil person." At these séances the policy of all the Russias was jointly decided by ministers and magicians.

At this period the Empress was enduring great suffering on account of the hardly concealed contempt of her mother-in-law and the whole Court, and was being openly reproached in all quarters for not giving the Empire an heir, and thus fulfilling her duties as the mother of the country. In consequence, the poor woman gradually fell into a morbid condition of fear and nervousness, and was ripe for blind faith in anyone who professed to bring the fulfilment, by a "miracle," of her dearest wish. At this time, the year 1901, during a visit to France, she made the acquaintance of the quack doctor Philippe. He had made an appearance at the house of the Grand Duchess Militsa, then staying at Compiègne, and she introduced him to the Emperor and Empress. This "truly holy man" immediately made a favourable impression, and soon the imperial couple gave him their complete confidence.

Philippe had originally been a butcher's assistant, and his real name was Nizier-Vachot; and however inappropriate it may seem to his trade, he was of a dreamy disposition and spent night after night, with burning cheeks, devouring books on ghostly apparitions, magic, and mysticism, until finally his leaning to the supernatural led to his dismissal as a good-for-nothing, his master having no use for an assistant "who saw ghosts." This was the beginning of Nizier-Vachot's career as a miracle-worker, which was finally to land him in the Court of the Tsars. Almost immediately after his dismissal he set himself up in his native village, which was not far from Lyons, and started to practise miraculous cures. As generally happens in such cases, he was able to boast of a few successes, especially as he was endowed with certain hypnotic gifts. After he had failed in some cures, however, he attracted the attention of the authorities; they started a prosecution; but he was able to turn the political situation to his advantage by securing the support of the nationalists. A little later Count Muraviev-Amurski, the Russian military attaché in Paris, became one of his followers, and introduced him to the Grand Duchess Militsa Nikolaevna.

On his arrival in Russia, Doctor Philippe first played an important part in the drawing-room of the Grand Duke Nikolai Nikolaevich and then in the Imperial Court itself. Séances under his direction were held almost continuously, at which the Tsar sometimes, and the Tsaritsa more frequently, were present. Meanwhile, the "Montenegrins" were urging that the title of doctor should be granted to Philippe, a distinction to which he

THE FATEFUL IDYLL OF TSARSKOE SELO

attached great importance. Finally, they succeeded in inducing the Minister for War, Kuropatkin, to grant the French magician the title of military doctor and state counsellor, whereby the medical practice of the doctor seemed to be legally authorized.

The Empress hoped to be able to realize the fulfilment of her ardent desire through Philippe's miraculous power, and she begged the magician to entreat the mercy of God for her, so that the gift of an heir to the throne might be vouchsafed to her. Philippe transferred himself to the Palace of Tsarskoe Selo, and began a series of mystical conjurations through which the Empress was to be blessed with a son. A short time afterwards the glad news spread through the whole Court that the miracle had happened; the Empress ceased to hold official receptions, and put on loose garments. As she moved about in her dark velvet dress all the relations and Court ladies were able to observe with satisfaction that good grounds existed for joyful expectations. The Emperor radiated happiness and contentment, and the happy news spread over the whole Empire.

When the nine months at last came to an end all St. Petersburg awaited from day to day, from hour to hour, the traditional volleys of cannon from the Fortress of SS. Peter and Paul which, according to their number, would announce whether the newborn infant was a son or a daughter. The Empress had not left her rooms for several days, and had remained in bed; before her bedroom door the four Abyssinian guards, in their embroidered robes and white turbans, were stationed to prevent anyone from disturbing the Empress.

But day after day went by, and still the happy event did not take place. Finally, after some opposition, the Court doctor, Professor Ott, received permission to examine the Empress. To the general consternation it appeared that Alexandra was not pregnant at all. As the whole country had been expecting an heir it was naturally impossible to conceal this tragi-comic catastrophe permanently, and countless rumours were immediately flying all over Russia which were not calculated to increase the prestige of the Tsaritsa.

On the demand of the Governor of the Palace, Rashkovski, the representative of the Okhrana in Paris, made exhaustive inquiries there about Philippe's past, and ultimately drew up a most devastating report, which he personally submitted to the Minister Zipiagin. The Minister was sufficiently well acquainted with conditions at the Imperial Court to advise Rashkovski to throw his report into the fire. Rashkovski, however, did not take this wise counsel to heart, but submitted the document to the Tsar, which at once brought the imperial displeasure on his head. In spite of all disappointments and evil rumours, the Emperor and Empress maintained their faith in Doctor Philippe, and continued to bestow their favour on the miracle-worker. It was not until some time later that Philippe, loaded with gifts, was sent back to his native country.

On his departure he presented the Empress with a little bell, which he claimed would automatically begin to ring whenever a wicked person approached the imperial couple. He further left a prophecy that was to have great influence in the later course of events: he declared that God would soon send the Empress a new "friend," who would faithfully stand by her in all her troubles.

Soon after his return to France Philippe died, not least through grief over his dismissal, since, after the fine times at Tsarskoe Selo, he could not adjust himself to his simple home surroundings. His followers maintained that he was not dead, but that, after fulfilling his mission on earth, he had ascended to Heaven alive.

The Orthodox clergy had, from the beginning, mostly looked askance at the rise and influence of the foreign miracle-worker. When the Frenchman had departed they thought that the moment had come to bring the imperial couple once more under their own spell. The Court prelate, Father Feofan, who had been among the chief ones to deplore the Emperor's and Empress's estrangement from the Orthodox Church and their submission to the influence of this devilish Western European superstition, considered that it was time to bring the sovereigns back to the native belief in miracles. For this purpose he bethought himself of a genuine Russian miracle-worker, long dead, who, through criminal negligence alone, had not yet been canonized. This was the monk Serafim of Saratov, who had uttered portentous prophecies at the beginning of the nineteenth century. Father Feofan persuaded the Tsar to order the canonization of Serafim, and, by this pious act, to earn the gratitude of the heavenly powers. The Tsar, urged on by his wife, was at once all enthusiasm for this plan, and pushed on the canonization of Serafim with as much zeal as if it had been the most important State business.

There was much opposition to be overcome before the project could be realized. The most eminent and powerful pillars of Orthodoxy expressed themselves against it, in particular, Pobedonostsev, the Procurator of the Holy Synod. But, finally, those behind the Tsar carried the day, and even succeeded in overcoming Pobedonostsev's objections at an intimate breakfast party.

Thus, on July 30th, 1903, amid splendid ceremonies, the canonization of Serafim was carried out in the presence of the Emperor and Empress. On the eve of the day a gala banquet took place in honour of the Emperor, at which the higher clergy, a large number of State dignitaries, and numerous princes and officials were present; they had flocked to Saratov from all quarters on this occasion, on the correct assumption that their presence at the ceremony would be useful in their careers.

As the night advanced the strange red spots on the Tsaritsa's face, which always betokened excitement, became more and more noticeable. Her breast rose and fell spasmodically, and her eyes had a restless glitter. At midnight she left the table and went out into the garden. There she was awaited by some old priests and the most intimate of her ladies, who conducted her to the holy well by the bones of Serafim. This well was reputed to possess miraculous powers, and the sick, the halt, the blind, and the deaf, as well as sterile women, were many of them said to have found healing in its waters. The Empress had already been convinced of its efficacy by the evidence of her own eyes: on her arrival at Saratov she had been shown a number of peasants of both sexes, who had all formerly suffered from serious afflictions. But now the halt took part in the festival procession without crutches, the blind saw once more, the deaf heard, and the once sterile women carried children in their arms. Alexandra had resolved to test the power of this miraculous immersion.

On her way to the well, accompanied by three priests and her ladies-in-waiting, she first proceeded to the grave of Serafim, where she fell on her knees, and in long, silent prayer entreated the saint to be her advocate with God, that He might fulfil her longing and grant her a son. When her prayer was ended she went on to the sacred well accompanied by her ladies-in-waiting, the priests remaining to pray at the grave. She laid aside her glittering ornaments and her festive array, and in the light of the stars bathed her body in the beneficent waters.

And the miracle happened! In due time the Empress, to the jubilation of her husband and the whole country, gave birth to a son, Alexei.

The clergy were triumphant, since they attributed the happy event solely to the blessed and miraculous power of the saint of Saratov. The high officials and dignitaries who had flocked from all parts of the Empire for the canonization of Serafim were not disappointed in their expectations. They received distinctions, and rapidly advanced in their careers, for their Majesties were convinced that this canonization had been pleasing to God and, therefore, rewarded all who had taken part in it, since the Almighty had so richly rewarded them. A large picture of the sainted Serafim was hung in the Tsar's study, and the Tsar's faith in this patron saint was in future so strong that, during the war with Japan, he sent thousands of images of Serafim to the troops at the front. "The Japanese have shells," said a mordant witticism of the period; "our soldiers have pictures of the saints."

* * * * *

In spite of the ascendancy of Serafim, there were many in the Empress's entourage who believed that the merit for the birth of the heir-apparent should be attributed less to him than to another wonder-working personage. These people asserted that the nocturnal immersion in the holy well might perhaps have helped the miracle, but that in reality it had been brought about solely through the "holy fool," the afflicted peasant girl, Daria Ossipova. For immediately after the dismissal of Philippe, other "miracle-workers" and "mediators" appeared at the Imperial Court, of whom it was affirmed that they were able to fulfil the

Empress's wish through magical influences. Unlike the Frenchman, however, these miracle-workers were not cultured doctors and "drawing-room magicians," but belonged rather to the specific Russian type of "Iurodivye," "holy idiots." These were purely native phenomena, as old and highly respected as the Orthodox priests themselves.

Such "Iurodivye" were frequently to be met with in the villages; they were generally men (more seldom women) physically and mentally deficient and, in most cases, also afflicted with epilepsy. The people regarded the very simplicity of these village idiots as a special sign of God, and their "falling sickness" strengthened their reputation for sanctity. Among the intelligentsia, as well as among the peasants, a belief had long existed that the Lord found particular pleasure in deformed persons, deaf mutes, epileptics, and idiots, and that the spirit of God loved to reveal itself in the solecisms, meaningless sounds, wild cries, and convulsive movements of such creatures.

When one of these "Iurodivye," barefooted, dirty, and clad only in a torn smock, appeared in the village street, the peasants knelt before him, kissed the hem of his shirt, and listened absorbedly to his confused talk, so that they might interpret the will of God therefrom.

One of these "miraculous idiots" was brought to Tsarskoe Selo by persons who speculated skilfully on the mystical tendencies of the sovereigns. This was Mitia Koliaba, also called Mitia Kozelski, a simple cripple belonging to the district of the famous monastery of Optina Pustyn. He was bandy-legged, deformed, almost dumb, and had only two monstrous stumps for arms. He had to be led, as his sight was very weak; his hearing was rudimentary, and his speech mostly consisted of a few hideous sounds which he produced jerkily with painful efforts. When he was seized by an epileptic attack and began to cry out, his voice sounded now like a dismal whining, now like a hideous croaking, and finally degenerated into a terrifying and fearsome yowling and yelping. The repulsive impression made by these sounds was further increased by the crazy waving of his stumps, so that good nerves were needed to endure the presence of this idiot.

The peasants of his home district had at first merely given him food out of sympathy, without any idea that the animal noises he made could be interpreted as prophecies. It was the monks of Optina Pustyn, the monastery to which Dostoevski raised an immortal monument in his *Brothers Karamazov*, who first discovered Mitia Koliaba's wonderful capacities. Although they were not yet able to interpret the meanings of his cries and mutterings, they nevertheless immediately recognized that here was a "fool in Christ," a seer in an ecstasy of God. The key to interpret Mitia's oracles was later granted "by special illumination" to one of the "humbler brotherhood," Egorov, the sexton and psalm-singer. As he prayed before the ikon of St. Nicholas, the voice of the saint had revealed to him the secret meaning of Mitia's sounds, and had ordered him to put in writing the hitherto hidden method of interpretation of these prophecies. The wonderful voice added that the fool, Mitia Koliaba, was fated to have a great influence on the destiny of Russia.

After this the psalm-singer Egorov became the inseparable companion of the wonder-idiot and the interpreter of his oracles. Soon afterwards Mitia happened to prophesy to a distinguished lady that she would give birth to a son, which event actually came to pass. The fame of this incident penetrated to St. Petersburg and was generally discussed and marvelled at, especially in the salon of the pious Countess Ignatiev. Some of the members of this distinguished circle had the idea of bringing the holy fool to the Imperial Court, so that he might exercise his office there and, by his miraculous powers, help the Empress to produce a son. Prince Obolenski, who had an estate in the neighbourhood of Kozelsk, and who thus had personal experience of the activities of the idiot, at once undertook to bring him and his interpreter to Tsarskoe Selo.

One day, then, Mitia Koliaba and Egorov appeared in the drawing-room of the "Montenegrins," and after a friendly reception there were presented to the Emperor and Empress. Mitia was inspired and endowed with miraculous powers only during his epileptic fits; at other times he was an ordinary fool, who conducted himself in an unseemly fashion and whom no one could manage. This was the reason why he never acquired a really important position at Court, as the other miracle-workers easily contrived to do.

But when Mitia was suffering from one of the attacks that made him "clairvoyant," Egorov stood by him and by means of his "key," interpreted the screeching, mumbling, croaking, yowling, and yelping sounds that proceeded from the idiot's mouth, and the hideous waving of his stumps. In the presence of the Tsar, the Tsaritsa, and the Montenegrins questions were put to this imbecile as he writhed in convulsions, to which he replied with incomprehensible noises, foaming at the mouth. It was then Egorov's turn to interpret this prophesying; but to all questions about the prospective birth of an heir to the throne only evasive answers could be given: "It is still early days, it is still long before the birth, and Mitia cannot say whether it will be a girl or a boy. But he is praying unceasingly, and in course of time will give exact information." And, however often these curious séances were repeated, the fool and his companion could not be induced to give further details. It seemed that the miraculous idiot completely failed in this case, and the only result of the séances was that the Empress was driven to fits of hysterical weeping by Mitia's ear-piercing roars and frightful gesticulations.

In consequence, the "Iurodivye" was abandoned in disappointment, with all the more reason since, in the meantime, General Orlov had succeeded in finding a new miracle-worker on his estate, this time an imbecile woman called Daria Ossipova. When her attacks came on, this "holy fool" did not confine herself to prophecies; her shrieks in themselves had magical powers, and could give fecundity. Even in her home district, where she was in service on an estate, she had been able to "avert the evil eye" from the peasants, to bless women with children, cure hopeless invalids, and also to curse her enemies. The village honoured and feared her, for they looked on her as one of those real and genuine witches who had unfortunately almost all died out. When in the throes of an attack she had to be tied up with rope, for in a mad frenzy she struck out at everything within her reach. And in this state she did not merely utter unintelligible cries, like Mitia Koliaba, but quite understandable words of abuse and curses of the worst kind. Nevertheless, the people listened to her words with reverent attention, for was it not just when she conducted herself in this mad way that Heaven poured its grace into her and enabled her to prophesy and work miracles? It was at the very time that Daria Ossipova was brought to Tsarskoe Selo and terrified the poor Empress with her abominable curses that the "miracle" happened and the heir to the throne arrived. As the canonization of Serafim had also taken place shortly before, opinions were divided on whether the happy event should be attributed to Saint Serafim or to the "divine fool," Daria Ossipova.

The Empress had become so used to associating with all sorts of miracle-workers that very soon she did not confine herself to imploring them to fulfil her desire for a son, but, along with the Emperor, sought the aid of such magicians and miraculous idiots in State affairs also. Philippe had already been drawn into important political discussions, and later the Emperor used to ask Mitia Koliaba for his "advice" before he made a serious decision. During the war with Japan Mitia was more than once summoned to the Tsar's rooms, so that his stammering prayers might avert disaster from the army. Nikolai received him again in 1906; the fact is noted in his diary.

The strannik, Antoni, the successor of Daria Ossipova at Tsarskoe Selo, also functioned temporarily as a political magician and clairvoyant in the days of the first Duma. He was followed by ever fresh crowds of "pilgrims" and "penitents," who were all asked for their "inspired counsel" in political affairs.

Although in this way the native element gained an increasing predominance, the famous French "magician," Papus, the Paris gynecologist, Dr. Encausse, also played a certain part from time to time. He appeared in St. Petersburg for the first time in 1900, when he was mostly seen in the company of his friend Philippe. At the beginning of October 1905 Papus, after a longish absence, was again summoned to the capital to support the sovereign in the difficult position caused by the Revolution. The Tsar's advisers were not at that time unanimous about what course the Government should pursue, whether they should yield to the demands of the insurgents, or whether they should stand up to them and make no concessions. Papus, at a séance, conjured up the spirit of Alexander III, to whom the Tsar addressed a number of questions. Influenced not least by the information obtained at this séance, Nikolai II finally decided to sign the ukase summoning the Imperial Duma.

* * * * *

One of the most curious phenomena of the Russian Imperial Court, however, was the "doctor of Tibetan medicine," Badmaev, a singular personality who towered above the crowd of home-produced magicians and clairvoyants. All these other "thaumaturges," "miraculous idiots," and "mystagogues" were peculiar people only when in a state of "inspiration," when they were attacked by the "holy frenzy" that endowed them with supernatural insight.

The abilities of the Tibetan magician, Badmaev, on the contrary, were of a far higher kind: they did not depend on accidents, séances, inspirations, or attacks of disease, but were rooted in a "secret knowledge," established and studied for centuries, the ancient "sublime tradition of Tibetan wisdom." In his Mongolian home Badmaev had been initiated into the mysteries of the miraculous healing art and of magic, and this enabled him at all times to discern the hidden forces in the ordering of destiny and to bend them to his will. He passed at Court for one of the last of the "wise men of the East" and, therefore, met with more consideration and reverence than all the other "empirical" miracle-workers.

The political counsels and oracles of this Tibetan were very highly valued by the Tsar. Badmaev did not need to call up the ghost of Alexander III when grave problems of State had to be decided; he was himself a man of great political experience and knowledge of the world, familiar with all the subtleties of Asiatic diplomacy. In the counsels he gave the Tsar, ostensible magic was combined with real diplomatic shrewdness, for his eye grasped with unerring keenness not only the "inner light" of things, but also their real meaning and practical importance. Thus it was that, while all the other miracle-workers often failed and had to retire ingloriously one after the other, Badmaev was able to maintain his prestige and confidential position right up to the overthrow of the imperial regime. Unlike the long series of rival "prophets" and "miraculous idiots," the Tibetan magician in his white smock and high white cap remained a permanent figure of outstanding personal influence. There was a time in the history of Russian politics when not only the imperial couple but the ministers and administrative officials as well were entirely under the sway of Badmaev, and when many important measures were taken in accordance with the prescriptions of his "secret science."

This singular man belonged to Transbaikalia, and was the son of a Buriat; he had grown up on the steppes, then attended the grammar school at Irkutsk, and afterwards St. Petersburg University, where he studied the Chinese-Mongolian languages. It was at this time that he was converted to the Orthodox faith, and exchanged his Buriat christian name of Shamzaran for the Russian name, Petr Alexandrovich. The Emperor Alexander III himself acted as godfather, having thus early recognized the great abilities of the young man. This imperial sponsorship gave him the right of entry to the Court for life, and the rare favour of being allowed to write direct to the monarch.

In the year 1875, on the completion of his university career, he entered the civil service, and until 1893 held a regular post in the Ministry for Foreign Affairs; he was at the same time lecturer in Mongolian at St. Petersburg University. He was repeatedly entrusted with special commissions of a political nature, in cases where an exact knowledge of Eastern Asiatic conditions was required; there are frequent references to this in the diaries of Nikolai II. One such note reads: "After breakfast I discussed Mongolian affairs with Badmaev."

At the time of the Russo-Japanese War, Badmaev was entrusted with the mission of winning over the Mongolian tribal chiefs to the Russian cause; he was given two hundred thousand roubles for purposes of bribery. He discharged his task with great skill and remarkable success, although envious persons maintained that he had contrived to get on without bribes, and to divert the two hundred thousand roubles to his own pocket.

Shamzaran Badmaev affirmed that he had acquired an exact knowledge of the secret doctrines of "Tibetan magic" and medical science in his father's house, as this knowledge was an ancient tradition in his family. His elder brother Zaltin had also studied "Asiatic medicine," and had practised as a "Tibetan apothecary" in St. Petersburg since the sixties, but at that time his clientèle was very sparse. Petr Alexandrovich practised in his brother's shop, and it was through him that the business first began really to flourish. Very soon Petr Alexandrovich overtopped his elder brother and, when later he took over the management of it himself, this obscure little shop became a great "sanatorium." The fame of Badmaev's magical cures spread rapidly, and clients flocked to him from all classes of society, seeking to be cured in his sanatorium. His followers maintained that he could charm away the most stubborn troubles in a marvellous fashion, and that his curative treatment was particularly successful "in serious cases of stubborn nervous diseases, mental maladies, and disturbances of the female physiology."

The laboratory of the sanatorium was fitted up according to the rules of the "Tibetan magical art"; only the master himself had the entry to it, and there, in complete seclusion, with the aid of magic crucibles and mysterious formulæ, he prepared his various alchemic remedies, "infusions of asoka flowers," "nivrik powder," "Nienchen balsam," "black lotus essence," and "Tibetan elixir of life." He had established a whole pharmacopœia of his own of drugs, tinctures, and mixtures with mysterious, magical labels that were supposed to indicate the method of preparation to the initiated; but only the master himself was able to interpret these labels, and the invaders who took possession of his laboratory after the Revolution found themselves confronted with a chaos of incomprehensible names, perplexing memoranda, and useless apparatus to which they lacked any key.

But what completely distinguished Doctor Badmaev's sanatorium from all the other curative institutions in the world was its political character. Anyone who had once been a patient there, no matter for what reason, was immediately placed on the list of candidates for ministerial posts or other high positions in the State. The decoctions, potions, and powders brewed by Badmaev from the strange herbs of the steppes served not only to remove the physiological disorders of his patients, but also to give them an immediate claim to important State offices. For the Emperor had gradually got into the habit, not only of asking Badmaev's advice, but also of appointing high officials, as occasion arose, on his recommendation, of procuring them, as it were, from the Badmaev sanatorium.

The party affiliations and political views of every patient at his institution were carefully noted on his chart, and next to his name, between two mysterious Tibetan prescriptions, was often to be found a note such as "The right wing must be strengthened," which referred not to the lungs,* but to the Duma. Badmaev kept up an active correspondence with his patients after their treatment was over, in which, in addition to medical advice on, say, blood pressure or constipation, he also gave them political instructions.

In the course of time medicine and politics, ministerial appointments and "lotus essences," became more and more involved in each other, resulting in a fantastic political sorcery that had its origin in the Badmaev sanatorium, and that decided the destiny of all the Russias.

This quack doctor owed his great influence to the success of his medico-political treatment of the Tsar, for whom he had been able not only to cure an abdominal complaint, but also to solve technical administrative dilemmas. For the stomach trouble he prescribed a decoction of Tibetan herbs, surmised to be a mixture of henbane and hashish, the effects of which were marvellous; the political difficulties of the sovereign he treated with a suitable dose of diplomatic skill and statesmanlike insight, and here, too, the results were satisfactory. In consequence, Badmaev rose higher and higher in the esteem of the imperial couple, and all the attempts of his opponents to make things unpleasant for him, to overthrow him, or to set the police on him, were doomed to failure beforehand. The Minister Khvostov, who had tried in vain to take steps against him, had to recognize that the Tibetan's excellent relations with the imperial family made him practically unassailable.

Even in 1917, after the imperial regime had been overthrown,

* The Russian word "Krylo," wing, also means the lobe of the lung. (*Translators' note.*)

the power of this unique personality was proved; Badmaev was arrested and imprisoned by the Council of Sailors of the Baltic Squadron on his way to Finland with Madame Vyrubova and the adventurer Manasevich-Manuilov. But it was not long before his original and dignified bearing and his many successful cures won him the affection of the prison warders, and he was treated not as their prisoner, but as their friend.

The art of the Tibetan magician, however, failed in the very case in which it was most important to be successful: even he was unable to cure the malady of the little Tsesarevich; here his magical potions and formulæ had not the slightest effect. Grief and helpless despair continued as before to surround the sickbed of Alexei, until the day when Grigori Efimovich Rasputin first appeared at the bedside of the unfortunate boy.

CHAPTER VI

THE FRIEND

IT was the third day that Alexandra Fedorovna, Empress of Russia, had spent by the bedside of her sick son; with her hands convulsively clenched together she had been gazing hour after hour, her face motionless and despairing, at the suffering child. A week before, on that unlucky morning when the athletic sailor Derevenko had brought in, in his strong arms, the body of Alexei doubled up with pain and almost lifeless, she had fallen in a dead faint, overcome with unutterable grief.

How anxiously everyone around him had watched over Alesha since his last attack; what infinite care had been spent in protecting him from another accident! But in spite of all, it had happened once more! The little boy had been playing in the park with the son of his attendant, carefully watched by Derevenko and his nurse Vishniakova. But Alesha, jumping up suddenly, had made a careless, impetuous movement, and had fallen back, pale as death, into the arms of the sailor who had rushed up to him.

After they had laid him on his bed and tenderly undressed him, they saw those terrible blue swellings which were the signs of the internal hemorrhage so dangerous to his life. The child lay with one leg, cramped in agony, drawn up against his body, and his nose stood out sharply from his waxen, yellow face, like the nose of a corpse. The doctors called in by the Emperor in his despair had hurried to the Palace, examined the little patient, applied this and that remedy, held consultations, made fresh examinations, but in the end had to confess their impotence. The potions of the Tibetan magician, administered by the Empress, failed entirely. It was as if God intended to try to the uttermost the Empress of Russia, so envied by all the women in her realm: even Badmaev's magic herbs could not relieve the sufferings of the Tsesarevich! And Alexandra threw herself down by the sick-bed and implored God in fervid prayer to work a miracle, this once more, and save her son from death.

Day followed day, night followed night, and still it seemed that the Almighty was reluctant to let the miracle happen. Alexei's suffering increased and the pains grew worse and worse. At the outset there had been times when the boy had talked with his tutor, Gilliard, or with his governess, until the pain started afresh. But now there were no such intervals; the child cried and moaned unceasingly, and no one in the Palace dared to approach the sickroom.

From time to time Alesha sank into exhausted silence, and the anxiety of the agonized mother increased; she thought that now death would snatch her son at any moment. The Tsar frequently came into the sick-room to comfort his Alix. Once the boy felt a cool hand on his forehead; waking out of semiconsciousness he drew down his father's head with his little, emaciated hands and whispered in his ear in a soft, sighing voice: "Papa, if I die, let me be buried out there in the Park."

The Emperor, after freeing himself cautiously from the child's clinging arms, rushed to the door, and the Empress heard him burst into loud sobs.

Alexandra sat motionless by the bed, worn out by her long nursing, hopeless, but not yet resigned to fate. She had ceased to pray, convinced that God would no longer listen to her; she waited there with staring eyes, till twilight began to fall. Since Alexei's accident she had scarcely left the sick-room; she had not taken off her clothes or lain down. Her hair was unkempt and neglected; her beautiful face was hollow, pale, and twisted like the careworn face of an old woman; her inflamed eyes were lustreless and expressionless, as if she had wept too much to be able to shed another tear.

Suddenly someone knocked at the door, and then a second and a third time. As no one answered, the door opened almost noiselessly and Stana, the Grand Duchess Anastasia Nikolaevna, came in. In her torpor the Empress had remained unaware either of the knock or the entry, and she did not awaken from her apathetic reverie until she saw the flushed face of the Grand

Duchess close to her own. Then she heard the coaxing, caressing words such as only Stana and her sister, Militsa, knew how to use.

For a while the Empress listened in silence; then at last she again found relief in tears; her body relaxed and, sobbing, she flung her arms round Stana's neck. Stana stroked her, comforted her, kissed her, knelt at her feet, embraced her knees, laid her head in her lap. With a flood of soothing words, the Grand Duchess gradually managed to rouse the interest and attention of the Tsaritsa. She assured her that Alexei would soon be quite well again, and everything else would also take a turn for the better. The Tsaritsa herself would win the love of the people, and the malicious old Court ladies and ministers would sink in shame for their base intriguing; a time of wonderful happiness was coming for all Russia, such as she had never yet known.

Stana went on in rapid, excited whispers, jumping from one subject to another, to tell of the amazing Siberian peasant, the holy pilgrim, whom she and Militsa had met a few days before. He was a quite extraordinary man, far cleverer and endowed with far greater divine powers than even M. Philippe and Dr. Badmaev. Without blasphemy she might say that this peasant surpassed even John of Kronstadt in holiness; this opinion was not only that of herself and her sister; the sainted John had himself asserted it.

The Grand Duchess, in hurried words, then told how, the other day, at mass, John of Kronstadt, in the presence of the most distinguished ladies, the élite of the society of the capital, had publicly extolled the simple muzhik, Grigori Efimovich, as a man endowed with the grace of God. It had happened in this way: Father John had just finished the service; he had, as usual, preached marvellously and the church was filled to the doors. The most magnificent toilettes were to be seen, and many ladies had appeared in the long gloves "which are now coming into fashion." At the end of the mass the priest, with the sacraments in his hand, had uttered the usual words: "Approach in faith and in the fear of God." But, as all the ladies were pressing forward to receive the communion and the blessing of the saint, a strange thing happened! Stana was uncommonly grieved that she herself had not been present. She had intended to go to mass at Kronstadt that day; but at the last moment a visitor had come in and she had had to give up the idea.

But to continue: as the ladies crowded up to Father John, he stepped forward before the altar with shining eyes, raised his right hand, and cried in a powerful voice: "Stop! to-day we have a worthier among us who must partake first of the Holy Communion—the simple pilgrim who stands there in your midst." He indicated an ordinary muzhik at the back of the church, where the beggars and the blind and halt are accustomed to follow the mass. Startled, they all turned round to see the man pointed out by Father John. He was really an ordinary peasant in a common sheepskin coat, with heavy, greased boots, a pilgrim's staff in his hand, and a coarse bread-bag on his back. Nevertheless, the ladies, at least according to the account of Countess Ignatiev, from whom Stana had had all the details, did not fail to note what splendid eyes this peasant had, eyes such as they had never seen in any human head. But the most extraordinary thing was his behaviour. It might have been thought that being specially distinguished by Father John would have confused him; but the wonderful man did not even seem surprised, much less embarrassed; he had quietly stepped up to the ikonostas, taken the communion, and then had actually blessed the sainted Father John!

This incident naturally caused a great sensation in the salon of the Countess Ignatiev; inquiries were made about the strange pilgrim: where did he come from, and who was he? The Grand Duchess went on to tell the Tsaritsa how the Archimandrite Feofan had met him and talked with him in the corridor of the monastery hostel. Next day Feofan appeared in the salon and told of the impression the Siberian peasant had made both on himself and on Bishop Hermogen and the venerable monk Iliodor. But it was not only these princes of the Church who were enthusiastic over the piety, profound knowledge, and native wisdom of Rasputin; even quite sober, sceptical people, professors, advocates, officers, and officials who had met him at the meeting of the All-Russian Union were fascinated by him, and convinced of his sanctity.

Father Feofan had brought this amazing peasant to the Palace of the Grand Duchess Stana and her husband at Sergeevo, and Nikolai Nikolaevich had also liked him enormously. A deputation of the "true Russian people" had waited upon the Grand Duke, and begged him to have the new saint brought to Tsarskoe Selo and introduced to the imperial couple. They believed that from this peasant spoke "the voice of the Russian soil," the soul of the holy Russian people. And it had never been so necessary to listen to the voice of the people as now, when the "nefarious activities of the revolutionaries were imperilling the throne and the Orthodox Church." The Tsar and Tsaritsa were surrounded by false and untrustworthy courtiers, who were coquetting in their hearts with the pernicious ideas of the "Westerners"; therefore, it was all the more important that a true representative of the Russian people should for once make his voice heard at Court.

Stana herself thought that she could not but recommend this proposal to the Empress: the "true Russian people" were indeed the truest and most faithful pillars of the monarchy and, if they advocated any course to the Tsar, they undoubtedly acted solely in the interest of the throne and the dynasty. Nikolai and Alix were quite right to distrust their hypocritical entourage, who tried to conceal from them the nation's real interests. The peasant, Grigori Efimovich, was, however, a genuine Russian, and moreover, a sincere, Orthodox Christian; he knew the people, their objects and wishes, and he was bound to be in a better position than anyone else to advise the Emperor wisely on what was to be done to check the hateful anarchists.

But it was even more important that Grigori Rasputin was possessed of wonderful healing powers and could cure hopeless invalids. Stana was absolutely convinced of this, because a simple but respectable and God-fearing middle-class woman, the widow Bashmakova, had come to St. Petersburg to tell how Grigori Efimovich, before his arrival in the capital, had been honoured in his Siberian home as a saint and a miracle-worker, how mothers with sick children, and men and women with incurable diseases, had flocked to him and come away cured. The widow herself had given the whole of her not inconsiderable

THE FRIEND

fortune for charitable purposes, as a thank-offering for her cure by Father Grigori.

Besides, the personal impression Rasputin had made on Stana was overwhelming, and not only on her, but on her husband also; her sister and her brother-in-law had been convinced of his holiness immediately they met him. Since then Grigori Efimovich had been a regular visitor, not only at Stana's house, but also at that of Militsa and her husband, Peter Nikolaevich. Yesterday, when he had been at Stana's again, she had told him how ill the poor Tsesarevich was and how Alix was in despair over it. Whereupon, as Stana announced to the Empress, beaming with happiness and enthusiasm, the miracle-worker had answered: "Just tell the Empress not to weep any more. I will make her youngster well again! Once he is a soldier, he will have red cheeks again!"

For the first time in many days the Empress smiled. At first Alix had hardly listened, so sunk was she in grief and anxiety; but as Stana went on, she began to attend, at first only half-consciously, and at last she grasped what was being said: this peasant was trying to protect the Emperor, herself, and little Alexei from the attacks of the revolutionaries, to save Russia and the Orthodox Church, and to make her dear Alexei, her only son, well again! Slowly the colour returned to her pale, weary face, and life and light to her eyes. And when Stana began to imitate Rasputin's comical way of talking and to reproduce his own words with the peasant accent, she could not help smiling. Everything this peasant said about "making well," and "red cheeks" sounded so simple and sincere that Alexandra already felt drawn to him. She became possessed by a strong desire to meet this unique man, and decided to talk to the Emperor about it that very day.

Stana, noticing that she had succeeded in rousing the Empress from her grief and in awakening her interest in "Father Grigori," became enthusiastic. In impressive language she described Grigori's appearance, and especially his eyes and the wonderful look in them. She spoke of the compelling force that lay in his gaze, and that made you at once forget that you were talking to a common peasant. The Grand Duchess stopped clasping the Empress's knees, and accompanied her description with animated gestures; as she repeated his words she sketched in the air the form and attitudes of the new saint. Her vivid and spirited description, and the ecstatic faith that breathed from her, gradually carried the Empress away.

Meanwhile it had become dark in the sick-room, and only a faint glimmer of light came from the window.

"Do you remember, Alix," the Grand Duchess continued, "what Dr. Philippe said to you when he had to leave you all? He prophesied that God would send you a new friend to help and protect you. Believe me, Alix, this is he, this is the friend whom Philippe foretold. He will save Russia and make your son well again. God has sent him to you!"

As she stared into the dark room Alexandra imagined that she saw the new "friend" in the flesh before her eyes. He stepped up to the bed, and raised his hand over the sick child as if in blessing. "He will make your son well again," cried Stana, and her voice was now no longer soft, but loud and clear. The Empress also began to speak aloud:

"How good you are to me, Stana. You and Militsa are the only ones who are good to me."

And she pressed Stana's hand with the fervour and vehemence with which unhappy people express their love and gratitude.

The nurse came in to light the lamp, and the Tsar followed soon afterwards. They were both surprised at the change in the Empress: she was almost gay, and said she would dine downstairs again.

The Emperor, deeply moved, kissed Stana's hand. "She and Militsa," thought he, "are our only true friends among our relations. And yet people are always trying to make bad blood between us." The Emperor was continually being warned that the "Montenegrins" had a bad influence on the Tsaritsa, that they were uneducated, superstitious, and ill-bred—in a word, that, in spite of their education in the Smolny Convent, they had remained "peasants," as was only to be expected of the daughters of a peasant prince. Count Witte, in particular, with his everlasting nagging, was continually bringing forward fresh complaints and fresh warnings; he never tired of reiterating that

Stana's and Militsa's affection for the Empress was inspired by purely selfish motives. But he had known well enough what to think of all these intrigues. He knew enough of his courtiers and ministers, and despised them, wretched creatures whose one object was to insinuate themselves and drive out everyone else. Their objections to Stana and Militsa were nothing but slanders, in his opinion! And now that Stana had succeeded in cheering his beloved Alix the Emperor was firmer than ever in this opinion.

When Alexandra appeared at table, Anastasia began immediately to give the Emperor a lengthy account of the Siberian man of God, Grigori Efimovich. The three of them discussed the matter at length, and Alix permitted the Grand Duchess to repeat all that she had told her about the pilgrim. For the first time for days the imperial couple felt in a somewhat hopeful mood.

Even when the Tsaritsa hurried back to the sick-room and found the Tsesarevich still lying moaning, pale as death, with his legs drawn up against his body, she was, in spite of everything, more light-hearted and could now at least hope again that everything would ultimately turn out well. She went to the bedside and pondered long over the words that M. Philippe had spoken before he departed. Had the moment really come, and had God at last heard her fervent prayers and sent her a new helper, a new "friend"?

A day or two later Nikolai and Alexandra were sitting in the Emperor's study. It was almost nine o'clock in the evening, and Alix was impatiently counting the minutes; several times she went to the door to listen, thinking she heard footsteps, and ran to her husband's writing-table, crying excitedly, "He is coming." But no! the clock on the mantelpiece had already struck nine and the eagerly expected guest had not yet appeared. The Empress was seized with impatience and fear; her breath began to come in short gasps, and her cheeks displayed the dangerous red patches.

The Tsar, too, was nervous: he turned over the pile of documents and reports spread out on his table, and tried in vain to read them. They were reports of new risings, murderous attacks and mutinies, ukases to be signed proclaiming martial law in this or that part of the Empire. What trouble these new revolutionary ideas were causing! The Emperor was no longer able to finish his daily task in his usual working hours, but had to sit at his desk till far into the night.

This evening, however, he could not get on with his work at all. Although he was able to suppress his agitation in order not to make Alix uneasy, he was secretly very impatient at the long waiting. For he, like the Empress, had been deeply impressed by what he had heard of the peasant Grigori Efimovich. Although Father Grigori was a simple peasant, he had a way of being natural and sincere, of looking you straight and openly in the eyes, that was bound to prepossess you in his favour from the start; his shrewd talk had amazed Nikolai and Alix. As, in imagination, he passed in review his ministers, generals, and adjutants, he found among them no face that seemed to him so innocent, friendly, and kind as that of Grigori Rasputin. This simple peasant had said at once that he was prepared to help Alesha, and this undertaking had already calmed Alix surprisingly. If he would only come! Stana had promised to bring him in her carriage from Sergeevo to Tsarskoe Selo, so that he should have arrived by nine o'clock at the latest.

The Emperor rose and laid his hand on his wife's shoulder: "Don't worry, Sunshine," he said, "there is not the slightest reason to be nervous."

The most minute precautions had been taken to bring the Siberian miracle-worker unostentatiously to Tsarskoe Selo. If Father Grigori had come to the Palace in the ordinary way through the reception rooms, he would have had to pass through three controls, the Palace police, the convoy, and the combined police guards. He would, like everybody else who wanted an audience with the Emperor, have been stopped at least twenty times and questioned about the object of his visit. His name would have been entered in twenty different books. There would have been telephoning and inquiries of the Governor of the Palace, and even the answer of this supreme functionary would have had to pass through several hands before the visitor was admitted. And any one of these officials might raise "objections" and turn the visitor away.

For the Emperor and Empress were surrounded by a manifold cordon of spies in uniform and mufti; every step the imperial couple took was watched, spied on, and noted in twenty different registers. How often Alix had said gloomily to her husband: "We are prisoners here, Niki dear."

But this time all possible measures had been taken to prevent such vexatious delays. A side entrance at the back of the Palace was to be used to admit Rasputin into the royal apartments unobserved. This entrance led to a back stair which was generally closed, and there Maria Vishniakova, the faithful and trustworthy attendant of the Tsesarevich, was awaiting the arrival of Rasputin and would conduct him through the dark passage and up the staircase to the Tsar's rooms. He was to be brought to this side entrance under the protection of the Grand Duchess Stana, whose arrival would excite no particular surprise in the few guards stationed at the back of the Palace, as she was a frequent visitor at Tsarskoe Selo.

As the Tsar was once more about to explain to his wife all the reasons why she need not be anxious, the door opened unexpectedly, and Grigori Efimovich, the Siberian peasant, in long, black caftan, with his great beard and untidy hair, appeared in the Tsar's study. Vishniakova came in behind him. She had her hands folded over her stomach, as simple women do when they are astonished; with her wide-open eyes and her half-opened mouth, she was a picture of amazement. She was so carried away that she was apparently quite unconscious that she was in the presence of the Emperor and Empress.

As he entered Grigori Efimovich looked graciously round to his guide, noticed her amazed face, and cried with a grin: "Now then, my good soul, what are *you* gaping at?"

Shock at this mode of address recalled the nurse to a sense of where she was, and she was overcome with confusion; blushing to the roots of her hair, she rapidly made a deep curtsey and retired as fast as she could. But, while she was still in the doorway, she witnessed a scene that kept her rooted to where she stood: Grigori Efimovich went up to the imperial couple with a beaming smile and, without ceremony, embraced the all-powerful ruler of all the Russias and his consort, and gave them a smacking kiss!

* * * * *

In the Tsesarevich's nurseries another sleepless night was expected, a night full of grief and anxiety, and the necessary preparations had been made, when suddenly Grigori Efimovich came softly into the sick-room, followed by the Empress and Vishniakova. Alesha was lying in bed, pale as death, his little face twisted with pain, and his legs still drawn up stiffly against his breast. Even when Vishniakova went up to him and gently asked how he felt, the half-conscious boy made no movement, and only moaned slightly.

As soon as he entered Rasputin fell on his knees before the sacred ikons in the corner of the room, and prayed in a low voice; then he rose, went up to the child's bed, and, bending down, made the sign of the cross over him. Alesha opened his eyes and looked wonderingly at the queer stranger with the great beard, who smiled at him so seriously and yet so kindly. He even shrank a little under the gaze of this unknown man; but he immediately felt that the man certainly meant him no harm.

"Now, don't be afraid, Alesha, everything is all right again," said the stranger, in a pleasant and melodious voice that was kind and firm. To the feverish boy it was as if a divine voice spoke to him. "Look, Alesha," went on the stranger, stroking the child's whole body from head to foot, "look, I have driven all *your* horrid pains away. Nothing will hurt *you* any more, and to-morrow *you* will be well again. Then *you* will see what jolly games we'll have together!"

The awkwardly caressing movement of the big coarse hand gradually cheered the still rather frightened child, and he began to smile, while the stranger went on talking in a more and more urgent voice: "When I was as little as *you* I played the most wonderful games, which I'm sure *you* don't know; but I'll teach *you* them." And Grigori told the boy of the mad pranks he used to play at home, in his Siberian village, with the other peasant children. He spoke about the enormous size of Siberia: it was so large that no one had ever seen the end of it! And all this country belonged to Alesha's papa and mamma, and one day, when he was healthy, strong, and big, it would belong to him. It was full of huge forests and endless steppes, and the people there were quite different from the people in St. Petersburg.

The kind stranger sat down on the edge of the bed and took the child's hand in his big peasant's hands and stroked it. He promised Alesha that when he was well again, he would take him to Siberia and show him everything he himself had seen there. For he had seen everything, lands and men, that no one but himself had ever seen. The boy listened to these tales with growing attention; his eyes became bigger and bigger and began to shine. He had quite forgotten he was ill, and thought no more about his pains; his legs gradually relaxed, and he raised his body higher on the pillow into a sitting position, in order to get a better view of the face of the dark-bearded stranger.

The Empress, who had remained quietly in the background, rushed anxiously forward at this movement, fearing that the child might do himself a fresh injury by leaning on his arms. "Take care, Alesha," she cried apprehensively, "*you* know *you* must be careful."

"Leave me alone, Mama! I must listen," answered the child, and turning to Grigori Efimovich, he added with childish eagerness: "Please, please, tell me another story."

Rasputin smiled approvingly. "*You* are quite right, Alesha," he said in his friendly way, "nothing can hurt *you* now. Nothing will happen when I am with *you*."

And he told him more about Siberia, and then began to tell fairy tales. The child listened excitedly to the stories of the humpbacked horses, of the legless rider and the eyeless rider, of Alenushka and Ivanushka, of the unfaithful Tsarevna, who was turned into a white duck, the Tsesarevich Vassili and the beautiful princess Elena. Grigori Efimovich spoke of the life of the flowers of the vast Siberian steppes, where even the flowers and the old trees of the forest have a soul and can speak to each other. The animals, too, had a language, he said, and he himself as a child had learned to understand what the horses in the stable whispered to each other.

"Do *you* hear, Maria," said the child enthusiastically to his nurse, "I've always told *you* that the animals can speak. But *you* are so stupid and know nothing about it."

Vishniakova, who was herself fascinated by Rasputin's tales and had continued to gaze marvellingly at him, merely nodded assent.

"But we both know," said the Tsesarevich, smiling mysteriously at Grigori, "that the animals can speak! And *you* will tell me everything *you* heard from the horses, won't *you*?"

It was now very late, so Rasputin said smilingly: "To-morrow, Alesha. I'll tell *you* more to-morrow."

The Empress assured her son that the good little father would come back to-morrow evening for certain; but many reassuring words were necessary before the child resigned himself to hearing no more then. He no longer felt any pain, and would have preferred to listen all night to his new friend. After Grigori Efimovich had said good-bye and, while he was still in the doorway, Alexei shouted eagerly after him: "Come to-morrow for sure, little father. I will not go to sleep till *you* come." And even after the door had closed behind his visitor, the boy continued to gaze with a look of radiant happiness at the place where the good man with the big beard had disappeared.

"Who is he, Maria?" he asked Vishniakova at last.

"A holy pilgrim," she replied, herself still absent-minded and dreamy. "A holy man who will make *you* well again. God Himself has sent him to *your* papa and mama."

"A holy man," repeated the child, as his eyelids drooped, overcome by the need of sleep.

When Grigori Efimovich had left the sick-room, the Empress almost burst into tears of emotion and gratitude; she impetuously seized the hands of the peasant and kissed them.

But Rasputin made the sign of the cross over her, and said: "Believe in the power of my prayers, and *your* son will live."

* * * * *

Grigori returned next night and the following nights; the

clumsy Siberian peasant and the little son of the Tsar were soon excellent, indeed inseparable, friends. Alexei always waited impatiently when Father Grigori was coming, and often and often he eagerly begged his attendants to fetch Rasputin, so that he might tell him his lovely stories and fairy tales, sometimes merry, sometimes sad. On one of the first visits Alexei had rushed up to him beaming with joy, and then hurried into his father's study, crying: "Papa, papa, the new man has come again!"

This led to Rasputin's being generally referred to in the imperial family as "the new man," "novykh"; a little later the Tsar conferred the name of "Novykh" on him in an autograph letter.

On later occasions, when Rasputin came to the Palace by the dark back stairs, he first kissed the Tsar and Tsaritsa, and then they all sat down comfortably to listen to Grigori's tales of the life of the Siberian peasants and his own pilgrimages. On these evenings the Tsesarevich was allowed to stay up longer, and to sit on Rasputin's knee in his trailing pale blue silk dressing-gown.

"Rasputin succeeded in winning the love and trust of the imperial couple," said a high Court official once. "He was able to stimulate, encourage, cheer, rouse, comfort, and edify them. He often reduced them to tears, for he never minced matters and sometimes treated them very severely; but afterwards he told them merry jokes and droll stories, so that soon they could no longer be without his company."

The elder daughters of the Emperor, in particular, had always something secret to discuss with Grigori Efimovich whenever he came to the Palace. He became their most confidential adviser, and they initiated him into all their private affairs, of which, like other young girls, they had plenty. If one or the other of them liked an officer, they at once confided in the good Grigori and, even when he was away, they asked him for his "wise advice" in letters.

The Grand Duchess Olga, for example, who had fallen in love with an officer called Nikolai, wrote to Rasputin from Livadia:

"My dear precious friend,—It is very sad that it is so long since I have seen *you*. I am longing for *you* and often think of *you*. Where are *you* going to spend the Christmas holidays? Please write to me. I am always so happy when I get a letter from *you*.

"Do *you* remember what *you* said to me about that Nikolai? Ah, if *you* knew how difficult it is for me to follow *your* advice. Please forgive my weakness, my good friend. God grant that Mama will be better this winter, or I shall be very sad.

"I am very glad to be able to see Father Feofan from time to time. Not long ago I met him in the new Cathedral at Yalta. Our little private chapel is very pretty. *Au revoir*, my dear, precious friend, it is time for me to go to tea. Pray for *your* true and loving

"Olga."

Anastasia, the second daughter, also wrote several letters to Grigori Efimovich.

"My dear, precious, only friend," one of them begins. "How much I should like to see *you* again. *You* appeared to me to-day in a dream. I am always asking Mama when *you* will come, and I am happy even to be able to send *you* my greetings. I send *you* my warmest wishes for the New Year, and hope it will bring *you* health and happiness. I think of *you* always, my dear, because *you* are so good to me. I have not seen *you* for such a long time, but no evening passes without my thinking of *you*. I wish *you* the best of everything. Mama has promised that when *you* are here again, I shall see *you* at Ania's. This thought already brings happiness to

"*Your* Anastasia."

But naturally it was the little Tsesarevich who was most attached to his friend; the enigmatic personality of the Siberian peasant filled the boy's imagination. Soon, in cases of slight illness, if Rasputin merely spoke to Alexei on the telephone it was enough to cheer him up immediately and put him in a good humour. If he complained of a headache, say, one of his sisters rang up Rasputin, and then gave her brother the receiver. One of Rasputin's women friends describes one such telephone conversation which she overheard. She was visiting him when the telephone bell rang, Tsarskoe Selo speaking. Rasputin rose and went to the instrument.

"What's this?" he cried. "Alesha is not yet asleep? He has earache? Bring him to the telephone."

He made a sign to those present to keep quiet, and then spoke into the telephone:

"Now then, Aleshinka, what's the matter, why are *you* not asleep? *You* have pains? That is not true, there's nothing the matter with *you*. Go to bed at once and sleep. *Your* ear does not hurt *you* any longer, I tell *you*, it does not hurt *you* any more. Do *you* hear? Go to sleep."

A quarter of an hour later the Palace again rang up to say that the earache of the heir-apparent had stopped, and that he had already fallen asleep.

The whole imperial family loved and idolized Grigori Efimovich. Both parents and children soon called him "Little Father Grigori," "friend," and "starets." He was often present at the masses said by the Court chaplain, Father Vassiliev, in the crypt of the Fedorovski Sobor. The Tsaritsa and her children stood with the peasant Grigori before the ikonostas to receive the sacrament and exchange the kiss of peace; Rasputin kissed the Empress on the forehead, while she kissed his hand.

* * * * *

The diaries of the Emperor contain brief references to Rasputin's first visits to Tsarskoe Selo. They begin with the words: "I have made the acquaintance of a man of God, Grigori by name, from the Tobolsk government."

A little later he notes: "This evening we were in the Sergeevska and saw Grigori." A few months after this he again writes in the diary: "Grigori arrived at a quarter to seven; he brought a picture of Saint Simeon of Verkhoture, greeted the children, and talked with us until a quarter to eight." The note ends with the remark, "Militsa and Stana dined with us; we talked of Grigori the whole evening."

The visits of the starets to Tsarskoe Selo were not, however, allowed to continue undisturbed for long. Thanks to the secret espionage service the whole Court was soon aware of the appearance of the new miracle-worker, although he did come by the back stairs. For the agents of General Spiridovich had also kept their eyes on the back doors of the Palace, and had given their chief exact details of every one of Rasputin's visits. In a short time all the Court officials were in revolt against "this muzhik" who had had the audacity to "force his way into the imperial family," and all sorts of more or less dangerous intrigues against Grigori Efimovich were at once set on foot.

It must be confessed that Rasputin's behaviour was calculated to rouse disgust and indignation among the courtiers: not even in the Imperial Palace did he make the slightest change in his peasant ways; when anything displeased him he unceremoniously banged with his fists on the table, and generally behaved in the Tsar's presence as with an equal.

The first openly to attack Rasputin was the governess of the Tsar's daughters. The starets had got into the habit, on his evening visits, of going to the rooms of the young grand duchesses, who were generally in bed at that hour, to give them his blessing. Miss Tiucheva was scandalized by Grigori's visits, and succeeded in persuading the Emperor to forbid Rasputin to enter the girls' rooms.

M. Gilliard, too, the tutor of the heir-apparent, was not particularly impressed by his pupil's new friend, and tried in vain, when in the company of the Emperor and Empress, to bring the conversation round to Rasputin, so that he might express his disapproval. It seemed, however, as if there were a conspiracy between Nikolai, Alexandra, and the children, never to mention Rasputin before Gilliard; nay, the Empress had expressly forbidden the children to discuss Grigori Efimovich with the tutor. She had a feeling that this "pedantic Swiss" would never understand the true value and holiness of Rasputin, and she was obviously avoiding all painful discussion.

Meanwhile, a flood of gossip and scandal poured forth from the ladies of the Court, old and young: it was said that Rasputin, shortly after his first appearance at Tsarskoe Selo, had seduced and even raped the children's nurse, Vishniakova; she had complained to the Empress, but had been met with unbelief and been reproved in the bargain.

Soon there was a rumour that the Empress was making shirts for Rasputin with her own hands—for a good-for-nothing, dissolute peasant, who had had a very bad reputation in his home district on account of his vicious life! His very name was a proof of this, for "Rasputin" meant nothing but "the dirty one," "debauchee," or "ravisher of girls." This last assertion was reported to the Empress, who resolved to investigate the matter. She despatched a trustworthy person to Pokrovskoe to institute inquiries about Grigori Efimovich. There it was proved that the name Rasputin had nothing whatever to do with Grigori's way of life: the village of Pokrovskoe had originally been called "Podkino Rasputie," for which reason various families there had for centuries borne the name of Rasputin.

Fresh slanders and suspicions were called forth by the rapidly growing friendship between the starets and the Tibetan quack-doctor, Badmaev; they were frequently seen together, and the rumour went round that Rasputin treated the sick Tsesarevich with powders from Badmaev's laboratory. Some courtiers even said that they knew that Badmaev kept Rasputin informed of every improvement in the boy's condition, so that Grigori could hasten to Tsarskoe Selo, say his prayers, and in this way make it appear that he had brought the recovery about by a miracle.

The old and tactful Count Fredericks, as was his way in difficult situations, thought it best to know nothing at all of this affair which was causing such lively excitement in the Palace. When asked his opinion of Rasputin, he replied with a courteous smile that he had never even heard of a man of the name.

Of the aides-de-camp, only Admiral Nilov, the not always discreet "Court buffoon," openly attacked Rasputin, whose bluntness so far surpassed his own. However, when this led to an indignant reproof from the Emperor, he immediately retired and made friends with Grigori Efimovich with all speed. At a later period he tried once more to go over to the opposite side, this time also with no great success. The rest of the aides-de-camp did not dare to criticize the new saint; they all, Zablin, Loman, Prince Putianin, Maltsev, and the rest of them, though furious at the growing power of Rasputin, outwardly attempted to establish cordial and friendly relations. In this Captains Loman and Maltsev were most successful; they, in time, became the regular "postillions" between the Tsaritsa and her "friend."

Grigori's appearance at Court roused the greatest interest in the different political salons, and all the speculators, intriguers, place-hunters, and spies who frequented these circles developed a feverish activity. The Master of the Horse, Burdukov, with his unerring eye, was one of the first to recognize the importance of the change in the state of affairs at Tsarskoe Selo: it was no longer sufficient to gain the Emperor's ear through the intermediary of grooms-of-the-chamber and aides-de-camp; it would in future be far more important to be in the good graces of the all-powerful "little father" who was a "tsar above the Tsars."

How these men rejoiced to discover that this "tsar above the Tsars" took bribes, pocketed commissions, drank Madeira, and loved the society of beautiful women; that he liked to embrace society ladies, courtesans, and servant girls, and loved to stroke their bosoms! Burdukov's guests quickly contrived to exploit the "saint's" human weaknesses for their own purposes; the Baroness Rosen and her friend, the beautiful Princess Dolgorukaia, were particularly skilful at this game. Their salon was frequented by many women who could satisfy the most fastidious tastes and, besides, the "engineer" provided excellent wines. The result was that the Baroness's house became Grigori's favourite resort, where, over many a glass of Madeira, he would gossip with countesses and courtesans about what was happening at Court.

And, lastly, the success of the starets caused a veritable paroxysm of enthusiasm in the salon of Countess Ignatiev. Was it not there that Grigori Efimovich had first been recognized and appreciated? Had they not from the start believed in his sanctity? His acceptance at Tsarskoe Selo was thus a blazing personal triumph for the Ignatiev circle. These reactionary politicians who, even earlier, had found Rasputin's words shrewd, now designated his utterances as sublime and divine; women who had liked him before fell madly in love with him. Luncheon parties were arranged even more frequently, at which they talked of the

THE FRIEND

new miracles and splendid utterances of the starets, and strengthened each other's convictions that he was a newly risen saviour. With voluptuous rapture they abandoned themselves to the unusual experience of being visited by a real redeemer, drinking tea with him, and discussing the deepest things in Heaven and earth with him over a cigarette. This was reserved for St. Petersburg society alone; where else in the whole world would such a sensation have been possible?

Meanwhile, Rasputin's visits to the Imperial Palace had practically ceased; the Tsar, influenced by the growing scandal, finally thought it advisable that his and the Empress's meetings with Grigori Efimovich should be transferred to neutral ground; this was found when Ania Vyrubova moved into her cottage close to the Alexander Palace. Like her imperial friends, Anna had been convinced of the holiness of the starets the first time she met him, at the palace of the Grand Duchess Militsa. Her simple soul firmly believed that Grigori was an emissary of God, commissioned by Heaven to watch over the well-being of the royal house, and protect the Tsar and his son from all adversity. So she joyfully undertook the rôle of hostess, and arranged regular meetings at her house between Alexandra and Grigori Efimovich.

The Empress soon expressed a wish to know Rasputin's family, and bring them into touch with her own children. Matriona Rasputin, the eldest daughter of the starets, gives a charming and vivid picture of their first meeting at Ania's house:

"We drove to Tsarskoe Selo in one of the Court carriages; I still remember my feverish trembling when I entered Madame Vyrubova's house. The Tsaritsa had not yet arrived, so we sat down to wait on a soft sofa. The living-room was comfortably furnished; there were brackets everywhere with innumerable knick-knacks and engravings and photographs on the walls.

"Suddenly the door bell rang and, soon after, we heard the rustling of ladies' dresses. Berchik, Madame Vyrubova's favourite manservant, opened the door and the Tsaritsa came in, followed by her daughters. She greeted us with a kindly smile; we kissed her hand respectfully; and she sat down and asked us to do the same.

"The Grand Duchesses clustered round Varia and me, and vied with each other in asking us questions:

"'How old are you? What do you do? How do you like school?' they asked, and they spoke so quickly that my sister and I found it no easy matter to satisfy their curiosity.

"The Tsaritsa talked to my mother, and now and again glanced at me with her beautiful, infinitely sad eyes. I had a vague feeling that I must speak to her and, finally, taking my courage in both hands, I said: 'Mama' (we called the Tsaritsa Mama because we looked on her as the mother of all Russia), 'tell me, have you many servants'?

"The Tsaritsa replied laughingly: 'I have, my love!'"

Such meetings between the imperial family and Rasputin's were frequently repeated, and a regular friendship developed between the children.

In the meantime, however, Grigori Efimovich had some dangerous opponents to contend with—all the clairvoyants and miracle-workers who had previously been influential at Court and now saw their position threatened. Dr. Badmaev, the cleverest of them all, had immediately gone over to Rasputin's side, and formed a direct alliance with him: John of Kronstadt, too, for good or ill, had to stick to the starets, since he had been the first in St. Petersburg to recognize him as a holy man. However much he might have liked to do so, it would not have looked well for him, John the "seer," to confess that he had made a mistake, and that Grigori Efimovich was an impostor.

The lesser miracle-workers of the "iurodivye" class, however, were furious at the rise of Rasputin. Mitia Koliaba fell from one epileptic fit into another, screamed and howled, and waved his stumps angrily in the air and, in his language, which only the psalm-singer Egorov understood, called down all imaginable evils on the usurper. The half-crazy epileptic, Daria Ossipova, on the other hand, at once took a passionate interest in Rasputin, and persecuted him with shrieking declarations of love whenever she could get hold of him.

* * * * *

It was some years before Rasputin's power made itself felt outside the imperial family; at first the starets had been careful

THE TSARITSA HAVING TEA WITH RASPUTIN

RASPUTIN

THE ROOM IN WHICH THE ROYAL COUPLE RECEIVED RASPUTIN

not to exercise his by no means assured influence on the sovereign in any way that might excite remark. But, little by little, he began to interfere increasingly in State affairs, more particularly, however, in Church policy.

When the see of Tobolsk became vacant in 1911, Grigori succeeded in persuading the Tsar, regardless of the protests of the Synod, into appointing the simple and entirely uneducated monk Varnava as bishop of Tobolsk. Before he became a monk Varnava had been a mere gardener's boy in a monastery. Rasputin had been friendly with him in earlier days, and he took advantage of this opportunity to infuriate the learned and arrogant prelates by elevating the gardener's boy to a bishopric. For Grigori Efimovich, the simple and unlettered peasant, had never had any use for scholastic theology and its representatives; and it gave him enormous pleasure to be able to humiliate the Synod and all the princes of the Church by this coup.

Naturally, by acting in this way, he embroiled himself with the higher clergy and, at the same time, he also sacrificed the friendship of the "true Russian people" by setting himself sharply against their political aims. He declared at every opportunity that the sovereign must be honoured and loved by the lowest classes of the population, and that his power chiefly depended on these classes.

It is true that the "true Russian people" had themselves preached a similar doctrine when they admitted Rasputin to their membership; but, while the phrase about the "God-fearing people" was to them a mere phrase, Rasputin, a real peasant, took the idea quite seriously, a fact that was bound to bring him into definite opposition to his former supporters. When, on one occasion, someone said at a meeting of the "true Russian people" that the simple folk were an unreliable element in politics, and could easily be roused to rebellion, Rasputin burst out in a rage: "If that is true," he cried, "then the fault lies solely with those who cunningly keep the people in ignorance. Just think of the state of things in the country. There are neither hospitals nor schools, but instead public-houses innumerable! There we peasants are poisoned with spirits. You should sweep your own doorsteps rather than blame the simple people and the Jews.

You see very clearly the mote in your brother's eye; but you are blind to the beam in your own."

In consequence of such speeches and others like them, the reactionary clique, which had formerly given Rasputin their full support, withdrew it, and tried to overthrow him. So great was the influence of this group that Rasputin's position became very insecure. He felt this clearly and decided on an impressive step which, he thought, would forestall further hostilities. He reached for his wanderer's staff and set out on a pilgrimage to the holy places of Eastern Christendom, to Kiev, Constantinople, and Jerusalem. He proclaimed that he was undertaking this journey because evil men had sullied his purity, and he himself felt that he had not opposed the temptations of Satan with sufficient strength; to atone for this weakness he now designed to start on a great pilgrimage of penitence.

This decision raised him higher than ever in the esteem of the Emperor, and even more in that of the Empress; and, when he really started, Alexandra regarded it as a special proof of his pure and pious character. She was here experiencing exactly the same feeling as the simple peasants of Pokrovskoe had. The saint might get drunk and sin with all sorts of girls and women; but the explanation could always be found, if you only considered how the pious man, more than all others, was exposed to the wiles of the devil. When Rasputin, after a period of dissolute living, resumed his self-mortification, this seemed to confirm the assumption, and the peasants, like the Empress, said: "The holy man has won a great victory in the fight with the devil."

When grave rumours about Rasputin's private life first began to be heard at Court, and incontestable proofs of his debaucheries were laid before the Tsaritsa, it proved impossible to shake her firm conviction of the holiness of her "friend." When she was told that Grigori had kissed this or that woman, she would refer to the brotherly kisses of the first apostles; and the many reports about carousals and orgies were in her eyes either "calumniation of the holy man" or "temptations of the devil," from which Grigori would certainly emerge victorious. By his pilgrimage of penitence Rasputin proved in the clearest possible way that he had really succeeded in "escaping from the claws of Satan"; and, after his return from the Holy Land, he was welcomed by the Tsaritsa with the greatest love and reverence.

But soon a new danger threatened the starets. The Prime Minister, Kokovtsov, began to see a serious menace in Grigori's increasing power. Stolypin, his predecessor, had sometimes been annoyed about this "dissolute peasant," but had let the matter rest because he observed that the monarch did not receive his suggestions in a friendly spirit. But Kokovtsov had, from the first, taken a violent antipathy to Rasputin, and made up his mind to remove him from the capital at the earliest possible opportunity. As ex-Minister of Finance, he first tried bribery and offered the starets two hundred thousand roubles on condition that he would immediately retire for good to Pokrovskœ. To his utter amazement Rasputin flatly rejected this proposal, declaring that he was ready to disappear if "papa" himself so desired, but that he was not to be bought. Further exasperated by this reproof, the Prime Minister next addressed himself direct to the Tsar, and tried to explain to him that Rasputin was a common swindler against whom public opinion was already universally in revolt.

But the Tsar interrupted Kokovtsov with a contemptuous wave of his hand and asked with a smile: "So you attach importance to what the newspapers say."

"Yes, your Majesty," answered the Prime Minister; "I pay attention to the newspapers, especially when they vilify the person of the Emperor. But, in the present case, even the most loyal journals contain harsh criticisms."

The Tsar looked bored. "These critics are idiots," he said. "I know Rasputin."

Kokovtsov was at his wits' end; but he was bold enough once more to implore the Emperor, in the name of the dynasty, to permit Rasputin's dismissal from the capital. In the end the Emperor coldly declared: "I will tell him myself to go away and never come back."

The Tsar really asked Rasputin in the most considerate way to leave the capital for a time. Grigori Efimovich needed no persuasion, and made preparations for immediate departure. On bidding them good-bye he said to Nikolai and Alexandra: "I know that evil men are trying to rob me of your love. Do not listen to them. If you part from me you will lose your son and your crown in six months."

The Empress burst into tears and cried: "How can we part from *you*? Are *you* not our only protector, our best friend?"

With these words she fell on her knees and begged for his blessing.

* * * * *

It was autumn; the imperial family had, as often before, again gone to Poland, to Skiernevice, in the "Belovechkaia Pushcha," where the Emperor was in the habit of hunting the aurochs. At that time many of these rare animals were still to be found in the dense forests of that region.

In these lonely parts one day a fresh accident happened. The Tsesarevich had gone out in a boat on the marshes and, on his return, had leapt ashore too venturesomely; he slipped, struck his knee against a stone, and immediately started a severe internal hemorrhage. This became much worse when the Tsaritsa, after a temporary improvement, took him out for a drive. The jolting of the carriage caused the child the most terrible agony and, when they drew up at the door of the hunting lodge, Alexei had to be carried to his room more dead than alive.

The doctors diagnosed a swelling in the groin; one foot also swelled, and the invalid's temperature rose alarmingly. Alexei moaned and groaned continuously, and fought against an examination, as any touch on the injured parts caused him intolerable pain.

Symptoms of blood-poisoning appeared, and there was the greatest danger of fatal complications.

Intercessory services were already being held all day long over all Russia, and the parents scarcely dared to leave the sick-room. As the Empress was trying once again to soothe the moaning child she mentioned Grigori's name. The boy opened his eyes at once, looked at his mother, and passionately begged her to send for the "little father." Later in the evening, when the danger had further increased, the Empress secretly, without the knowledge of the doctors and the courtiers, made her friend Ania telegraph to Rasputin at Pokrovskoe, begging him to pray for the sick child. The same night brought that remarkable reply which seems to have made a profound impression on the Empress. Next morning the whole Court was anxiously assembled in the drawing-room to make inquiries about the Tsesarevich's health when Alexandra appeared with a strange, peaceful smile on her lips and said that, though the doctors had noticed no improvement, she herself was no longer at all anxious, because she had received a telegram from Father Grigori. This she produced and read aloud to the company. It ran: "God has lent an ear to *your* tears and prayers. Do not despond. *Your* son will live. The doctors must not worry him any more."

The Empress hastened to the sick-room and showed the telegram to her son. On hearing that Grigori had promised that he would recover, he showed obvious pleasure and became visibly calmer. A few hours later the fever abated and the little patient said he no longer felt any pain.

The doctors examined him again and observed that the swelling in the groin had gone down and that the crisis could be regarded as past. They declared that such a case was not uncommon, and that nature herself sometimes helped in situations before which medical art was powerless. But Alexandra, as she sat peacefully with her husband and Ania that evening, for the first time for a long while, maintained that Alexei's marvellous recovery was of course entirely due to Rasputin's intercession.

A few days later the heir-apparent was able to be moved to Tsarskoe Selo, and the Empress contrived that Rasputin should be once more recalled to the Court. She declared that his presence in the capital was indispensable in view of the health of the heir-apparent, who might at any moment have another accident, and Grigori Efimovich was the only person who could help him.

Several years passed, and it was during the War that another accident to Alexei led to Rasputin's being once more summoned as a saviour in time of need. After the Tsar had taken over the supreme command of the Russian forces he had often to stay at headquarters, first at Baranovichi and then at Mohilev. On one of these journeys he took the Tsesarevich, now a big boy, with him, although Rasputin had expressed strong disapproval of the plan from the beginning.

The royal train had hardly started when the boy, who had pressed his face against the carriage window, was suddenly attacked by a violent bleeding from the nose. The Court physician in attendance, Dr. Derevenko, tried all available remedies to stop the bleeding, without success. Orders had meantime been given for the train to turn back; but on arrival at Tsarskoe Selo the patient was already very weak.

The Empress, immediately she heard the news, sent Vyrubova to Rasputin and, soon after, he appeared in the Palace. He made the sign of the cross over the invalid, prayed for a while before the ikons, and then declared: "Give thanks to God. He has once more granted me *your* son's life."

The little Tsesarevich had become visibly easier as soon as Rasputin had appeared at his bedside; a few hours later there was a marked improvement in his condition, the fever abated, and the bleeding, which had been gradually diminishing, stopped altogether. Rasputin returned from Tsarskoe Selo in very good spirits, and told all his friends that, in future, the Tsar would think twice before disregarding his advice.

* * * * *

Since their accession to the throne all the decisions taken by the imperial couple had been strongly influenced by their anxiety about the heir; and, therefore, the influence of the man who had more than once been successful in saving the invalid in moments of despair naturally knew no limits. Whatever explanation the Court might have for Rasputin's marvellous cures, whether it was that his soothing presence alone had sufficed to aid in overcoming the crisis, or whether it was due merely to a fortuitous combination of circumstances, in any case the Empress was entirely convinced that God himself had performed a miracle on her son through the mediation of the holy man, Grigori Efimovich.

Just as earlier magicians had also contrived to acquire an influence on the conduct of politics, so it was not surprising that Rasputin's power at the Imperial Court soon ceased to be confined to private and religious matters, and that the Empress endeavoured to enlist the wisdom of this man, whom God had sent, in the interest of affairs of State. For she never for a moment lost faith in Grigori's divine inspiration, and was certain that the Almighty, in fulfilment of Philippe's prophecies, had sent him to them as their true counsellor and "friend."

Nor must those ideas be forgotten that at one time had moved the "Union of the True Russian People" to exploit Rasputin's personality for political purposes. The Tsaritsa also believed that Russia and the dynasty could be saved only by a really popular movement, and that the appearance of the simple peasant, Grigori Efimovich, was somehow mysteriously linked up with this.

The more markedly Rasputin's behaviour—his frank, unpolished manners, his blunt and often wounding speech—differed from the strict etiquette of the courtiers, the stronger became the belief of the Empress, who was sometimes afraid of her isolation in the "idyll," that in him she was dealing with a genuine representative of the people; she felt that, unlike all the other people who surrounded the Emperor and herself, the man was not seeking to hide the truth under smooth, polite formulas, but openly and sincerely expressed what he thought and felt. In her eyes Grigori Efimovich was sent by Heaven to make the voice of the Russian people heard above the cowardice of the Court flunkeys.

The Emperor himself was at first more prudent than his wife, and his attitude of reserve towards Rasputin did not melt immediately. The Empress was greatly troubled over this, and made it her most sacred duty to use all her influence to overcome her husband's distrust. She implored him to listen to the counsels of their "Friend," which came from God Himself, and endeavoured by all the means in her power to convince him that Rasputin, more than any other person, truly had his welfare at heart.

Later, during the War, when the Tsar was staying at headquarters, Alexandra never omitted to call attention in her letters to the holiness of Rasputin, and to beg Nikolai faithfully to follow their "Friend's" advice. On one occasion she wrote: *

* In these quotations from the Empress's letters, which were in English, and often very faulty English, the translators have followed the edition of the letters by Sir Bernard Pares, *Letters from the Tsaritsa to the Tsar, 1914–16.*

"In les *Amis de Dieu* one of the old men of God said that a country, where a man of God helps the Sovereign, will never be lost & its true—only one must listen, trust, and ask advice—not think He * does not know. God opens everything to Him, that is why people, who do not grasp His soul, so immensely admire His wonderful brain—ready to understand anything; & when He blesses an undertaking—it succeeds & if He advises people— one can be quiet that they are good—if they later on change that is already not His fault—but He will be less mistaken in people than we are—experience in life blessed by God."

Another time she tells her husband of a meeting with Grigori Efimovich:

"We dined yesterday at Ania's with our Friend. . . . He entreats you to be firm, to be the Master & not always to give in to *Trepov*—you know much better than that man (still let him lead you)—& why not our Friend who leads through God. Remember why I am disliked—shows it right to be firm & feared & you be the same, you a man—only believe more in our Friend (instead of Trepov). He lives for you & Russia. . . ."

"Believe our Friend's advice," says another letter. "Even the children notice how things don't come out well if we do not listen to Him & the contrary—good when listen. . . ." And again: "Lovy mine, be firm and trust our Friend's advice. . . . I wld. not write all this, were I not so affraid for you and yr. gentle kindness always ready to give in, when not backed up by poor old wify, Ania, and our Friend—therefore the untrue and bad hate our influence which is but for the good. . . ." Just a little more patience & deepest faith in the prayers & help of our Friend —then all will go well. I am fully convinced that great and beautiful times are coming for your reign & Russia."

The Empress even believed that Rasputin was able to control the forces of nature. In the autumn of 1915, when thick fogs were interfering with the movements of the Russian army, she wrote to her husband at headquarters: "Our Friend is always praying and thinking of the War—He says we are to tell him at once if there is anything particular—so she did about the fogg,

---

* The Tsaritsa always refers to Rasputin as He with a capital letter.

and He scolded for not having said it at once—says no more foggs will disturb."

And, in another letter, she again refers to the miraculous power of Rasputin's prayers: the ship "Vriag," in spite of a storm, had reached Glasgow from Gibraltar. Both vessel and crew were unharmed because Rasputin, in Tobolsk, prayed for them.

This infinite faith in the divine powers of the "Friend" also explains the importance Alexandra attached to certain small objects which had been blessed by him. She once, in a letter to headquarters, exhorted the Tsar without fail to pass the comb Rasputin gave him through his hair before an important council of ministers. She then repeated the advice by telegram: "I shall go to Church and place a candle before the ikon of the Mother of God, in order that God may support you. Do not forget Rasputin's comb."

The Emperor who, to begin with, had resisted the magic of this Siberian peasant, was bound, under the influence of his beloved Alix, gradually to fall more and more under his spell, especially as from his early youth he had been strongly inclined to mysticism and belief in heaven-sent "mediators." Thus, in the course of time, he, like his wife, became a convinced adherent of the starets. During a walk he once made the following confession to one of his aides-de-camp: "Whenever I am oppressed by any care, doubt, or worry, it is enough to talk five minutes with Grigori; I at once feel strong and calm again. He always says exactly what I need to hear, and the effect of his good words lasts for weeks. . . ."

Sometimes, it is true, his dependence on the "Friend" landed the Tsar in very awkward situations, especially when it was a question of carrying out Rasputin's wishes with regard to petitioners. Grigori soon acquired the habit of simply sending all the people who came to him with petitions direct to Tsarskoe Selo, with a letter of recommendation. In spite of his esteem for the starets, it was somewhat difficult for the Tsar to sanction without consideration all these requests from persons of the most varied ranks and classes.

In course of time the Tsar managed to persuade Grigori not

to send petitioners direct to him, except in very rare cases; but this still occurred occasionally, and involved the Emperor in many a painful dilemma, especially when Rasputin had brought his influence to bear on the Empress in favour of his protégé.

The Tsar's great esteem and reverence for Rasputin, the "saviour" of his son, is most clearly expressed in a statement made by Grigori himself to the monk-priest Iliodor: "Papa once took me by the shoulders, looked hard at me, and cried: 'Grigori, *you* are a Christ, *you* are a true Christ.' I smiled and he repeated once more: 'Yes, *you* are a Christ.' Another time, as we were sitting at table, Papa said: 'Grigori, *you* know how I love you! Please come to us every day, but do not use your influence on behalf of other people. It really distresses me not to be able to grant some of *your* requests.'"

An episode that took place at lunch at Tsarskoe Selo is also significant. The heir-apparent suddenly asked his father: "Papa, is Grigori Efimovich a saint?" The Emperor turned to the Court Chaplain, Father Vassiliev, who was present, and asked him to answer the Tsesarevich. The priest was in an awkward fix and gave an evasive reply which, on the whole, answered Alexei's question in the negative. The Emperor rose at once and broke off the conversation abruptly.

Rasputin's political views and his methods of putting them into practice were in complete harmony with his peasant character and, in this sense, he really did represent popular opinion at Court. He always remained entirely a simple muzhik, felt with his fellow-muzhiks, and understood the wishes and ideas of the common people.

This was shown clearly whenever a decision had to be made between war and peace: Grigori Efimovich hated war, as the common people hate it, because he, like them, knew that it is the lowest class that has to bear the main burden and sacrifice of war. In the year 1912, when the Grand Duke Nikolai Nikolaevich, largely under the influence of his Montenegrin wife, was doing his utmost to induce the Tsar to intervene in the Balkan conflict, it was Rasputin who earnestly implored the sovereign to abstain from this adventure.

"Think what will become of *you* and *your* people," he appealed to the Emperor. "*Your* grandfather helped Bulgaria to shake off the Turkish yoke, and how did they repay their saviour, little Mother Russia? Will our fathers, who shed their blood for these treacherous Tatars, bless their sons, if *you* send them on this campaign? Suppose we are victorious! What then? They say we must help our Slav brothers. But was not Cain the brother of Abel?"

This speech made a strong impression on the Emperor, and was not the least of the reasons for his decision not to participate in the Balkan War.

When the World War was imminent in 1914 it was again Rasputin who put the views of the muzhiks forcefully before the Emperor. But this time, unfortunately, the starets was unable to bring direct personal influence to bear, since he was lying in hospital at Tiumen, having received a severe knife wound from a woman.

Nevertheless, as soon as he heard that war was once again threatening, he sent an urgent telegram to the Emperor, exhorting him to preserve peace at any price, since it was absurd, for the sake of the susceptibilities of Serbia, to unloose a world struggle, the consequences of which were incalculable. In after years Grigori maintained, at every opportunity, that he would have been able to stop the war if he had not been lying on a sickbed at the time.

Right up to his death, Rasputin never ceased from emphasizing his profound aversion for war and the necessity of concluding peace with all speed. Paléologue gives an account of a very remarkable conversation about the war which he once had with the starets.

"In short, jerky sentences," says the Ambassador, "Rasputin drew a pathetic picture of the sufferings the war was inflicting on the Russian people:

"'We have too many dead, too many wounded, too many ruins, too many tears! Think of the unhappy men who will never return, and remember that every one of them leaves five, six, or even ten behind to mourn him. I know villages, big villages, where all the inhabitants lament their dead. And the men who come back from the war, Lord God, what are they like? Cripples, one-armed, blind! It is terrible! For more than twenty years grief will be our sole harvest from the Russian soil. . . . And you know, if the people suffer too much, things will be bad, they may be terrible! In many cases things have gone so far that there is talk of a Republic. You should tell all this to the Emperor.'"

And in the course of a conversation with Prince Yusupov, his future assassin, Grigori Efimovich said: "We have had enough of war and bloodshed! It is high time to put an end to this mischief! Why? Are not the Germans also our brothers? Christ said we should love our enemies; but what kind of love is this? Papa won't give in, and even Mama is pig-headed on the point; plainly some one or other is giving them bad advice again! The blame for the war rests with the Emperor. A whole lifetime of prayer will not suffice to atone for it. If it had not been that damned woman who ran a knife into me, I should have been on the spot and prevented it from ever coming to bloodshed. In my absence your accursed Sazonovs and the rest of them spoilt everything!"

To him, as to the mass of the people, the aims of Russian war policy were alien and incomprehensible; he knew that the muzhik took the field reluctantly and only because forced by compulsory military service. His clear-sightedness was so great that he once proclaimed, with the mien of a prophet, that the blood shed in this war would take a frightful revenge, not only on the generals and diplomats, but even on the Tsar himself.

"Russia," he cried, "entered on this war against the will of God. Woe to those who still refuse to see this. In order to hear the voice of God we have only to listen humbly; but the mighty are swollen with pride, think themselves very clever, and despise the simple-minded, until the day comes when the punishment of God descends on them like a flash of lightning!

"Christ is indignant at all the complaints that rise to him from the soil of Russia. The generals, of course, think nothing of driving a few thousand muzhiks, more or less, to their death; that does not stop them eating, drinking, and making money. Alas! the blood of the sacrifice will not only reach them, it will bespatter the Tsar too, since the Tsar is the father of the muzhiks. I say unto you: the vengeance of God will be terrible."

Since he had not succeeded in preventing the war, he bent all his energies on stopping or at least postponing various injustices, unimportant in themselves, but particularly oppressive for the people. Thus he did everything in his power to oppose the calling up of the second reserve class, which was composed of the older peasants, by quite rightly pointing out that it was not practicable to leave the land uncultivated. The incompetent generals, with their crazy idea that victory depended solely on calling up the greatest possible numbers, wanted to throw the last man into the front, without any regard to the needs of agriculture, although the army then with the colours was short of arms and munitions. Rasputin besieged the Empress with objections to this plan, and she at once wrote to her husband at G.H.Q.: "Please my Angel, make N[ikolai Nikolaevich] see with your eyes—don't give in to any of the 2nd class being taken—put it off as long as only possible—they have to work in the fields, fabrics,* on steamers, etc. . . . please listen to His advise when spoken so gravely & wh. gave Him sleepless nights—our faults & we shall all have to pay for it!"

On another occasion also Rasputin interfered energetically in the arrangements of the army command, this time without success. He warned the Tsar against the great offensive in Galicia in the spring of 1915, on the ground that the time was not yet ripe for taking the aggressive, and that the attack would end in disaster. But Nikolai Nikolaevich, the commander-in-chief, succeeded in enforcing his will: the complete failure of the Russian spring offensive and the crushing defeat of Gorlice subsequently proved the justice of Rasputin's objections.

In the summer of 1916, again, Grigori Efimovich advised against pushing Brussilov's great offensive too far, and held that this attack had already fulfilled its purpose of relieving the menaced Italian forces, and that now Russia could quietly wait for the inevitable collapse, which must occur sooner or later, of the Germans and Austrians.

"Our Friend is much put out," wrote the Tsaritsa to her hus-

---

*The Tsaritsa, throughout these letters, uses the word "fabric" for factory. The Russian word for factory is *fabrika*.—(*Translators' note.*)

band on September 24th, 1916, "that Brussilov has not listened to your order to stop the advance. . . . Now He says again useless losses!"

Rasputin particularly loved to use his influence to remove slight injustices that caused ill-feeling among the people: "He begged me to tell you," wrote the Empress to her husband, "that it is not clear about the stamp money, the simple people cannot understand, we have enough coins & this may create disagreeablenesses. . . . I send you two stamps (money) fr. our Friend to show you that already one of them is false. People are very discontented—such wee papers flie away, in the darkness they cheat the *cabmen* & its not a good thing—He entreats you to have it stopped at once. . . ."

"Gr. is rather disturbed about the 'meat' stories," reports Alexandra in another letter. "One of the ministers, he thought, ought to send for a few of the chief merchants and explain it to them that it is wrong at such a grave moment, during war to heighten the prizes & make them feel ashamed of themselves. . . ."

The sound common-sense with which Grigori Efimovich spoke against premature celebrations of victory is most refreshing: he was opposed to the Tsar's making a triumphal entry into the captured town of Lemberg, saying the end of the war would be time enough for this; as it happened, the Russians were driven out of Lemberg again a few months later, and the enemy once more advanced far into Russian territory.

The continual falling off in the food supplies of the country also caused him great anxiety. He again and again called for energetic measures against the food profiteers, and finally worked out a rationing scheme on undeniably reasonable principles:

"He would propose," runs one of the Empress's letters, "3 days no other trains should go except those with flour butter and sugar—its even more necessary than meat or amunition just now. He counts that with 40 old soldiers one could load in an hour a train, send one after the other, but not all to one place, but to *Petrograd*—Moscow—and stop some waggons at different places, and have them by degrees brought on—If passenger trains only very few would be allowed and instead of all 4 classes these days hang on waggons with flour or butter fr. Siberia. The lines are less filled there coming towards the west and discontentment will be intense, if the things don't move. People will scream and say it is impossible, frighten you, if it can be done and 'will hark' as He says—but its necessary and tho' a risk, essential."

But Rasputin gave the strongest proof of his influence when he succeeded in depriving of his command his former protector and afterwards deadly enemy, the commander-in-chief, Nikolai Nikolaevich. The Grand Duke, in whose house Grigori had at first been welcomed with open arms, soon recognized that this "repulsive muzhik" would endanger his position, and afterwards tried by all means in his power to turn the Emperor against Rasputin. His wife and her sister also abandoned the starets; but this merely led to a complete rupture of relations between the imperial couple and Rasputin's original discoverers. Rasputin was perfectly aware of all this, and began to hate the Grand Duke fanatically, especially after Nikolai Nikolaevich, at the beginning of the war, replied to a telegram in which Grigori had announced his arrival at the front with the words: "You come, and I will have you hanged." After this Grigori took every opportunity of inciting the Empress and the Emperor against the Grand Duke.

With the great defeats of the summer of 1915 the starets succeeded in implanting in the Empress the conviction that, at this critical juncture, the Tsar must himself assume the supreme command of the army. Although all the ministers expressed themselves against this plan, and although Nikolai himself long hesitated to humiliate his uncle by degrading him in this way, Grigori finally succeeded in having the Grand Duke removed from his post as generalissimo and transferred to the most remote theatre of war, the Caucasian front.

* * * * *

For a long time the advice of the "Friend" had been asked in every important appointment. Soon no one could hope for a ministerial post unless he had previously submitted to an examination by Rasputin and passed creditably; and a minister who had incurred Grigori's displeasure seldom retained his position for long. The one exception was Sazonov, who, although Grigori had long hated him, managed to maintain himself in office for several years in spite of this.

The method by which Rasputin, the "peasant chancellor," convinced himself of the eligibility of the various candidates for their posts was most curious. He never thought of making minute investigations into their political record, as all the Court officials and the Emperor himself were in the habit of doing; he did not ask how the person in question stood with the various members of the imperial house; for his primitive mind a look at the candidate sufficed. For example, when a new Chief of the Police was to be appointed, Rasputin sent for the person in question or visited him, looked him attentively in the eyes for a few minutes, and the examination was at an end.

The circumstance that a powerful and influential man was engaging in politics without troubling in the slightest about the ordinary principles of politics and diplomacy gave rise to a most peculiar state of affairs, unique in history. The most refined devices and intrigues of statesmanship were impotent before this muzhik, who made his decisions emotionally, not from subtle tactical and diplomatic considerations, but according to the mood of the moment.

Of course, in this way he raised to dignity and office a large number of corrupt and incompetent men; but it appears at least doubtful whether the Emperor, had his influence been removed, would have made a better choice. It is certain that the ministers whom Rasputin overthrew richly deserved their fate, and that he himself was the first to acknowledge an error and make amends for it.

It is also certain that his not infrequent interventions in the administration of justice were always to the advantage of the accused or condemned, and never to their disadvantage. There is not a single case on record in which Rasputin, unlike almost all Russians in positions of power, sent a personal enemy to prison or had him banished to Siberia, although he had abundant opportunity to do so. On the contrary, everyone who could convince him that he had suffered injustice at the hands of the law was sure of his help and support. When the old Minister of War, Sukhomlinov, was impeached and imprisoned, merely because a scapegoat was required for the military reverses, Rasputin did his best to get his former enemy released. In this connection a letter from Alexandra to the Tsar is characteristic:

"Then our Friend said 'General Sukhomlinov should be set free, so that he should not die in jail, otherwise things will not be smooth. One should never fear to release prisoners, to restore sinners to a life of righteousness—prisoners until they reach jail become through their sufferings in the eyes of God—nobler than we'—more or less His words. Every, even vilest sinner, has moments where the soul rises and is purified through their fearful suffering—then the hand must be reached out to save them before they are relost by bitterness and despair."

For anyone who had once been his friend he was always ready to use his utmost influence, even with the Emperor. One day, when the Tsar had expressed his dissatisfaction with the Prime Minister, Stürmer, a protégé of Rasputin's, the latter immediately sent him the following stern and laconic telegram: "Hands off the old man, I tell *you*." But he also reprimanded his own favourites with equal sternness, when he had cause to be displeased with them. This same Stürmer, whom he had defended so resolutely against the Emperor, had soon after to listen to downright abuse from Rasputin's own mouth. The Prime Minister had dared to postpone the immediate execution of an order from the Empress, whereupon her Friend shouted to him, as if he were a little schoolboy: "*You* must not act against Mama's wishes, or I shall at once abandon *you* and then *it will be all up with you*. Behave accordingly then." Then, pointing to the discomfited Stürmer, he remarked contemptuously to his secretary, who came hurrying up: "He tried to defy me, but I will break his neck if he doesn't obey."

Towards ministers who did not owe their posts to his influence there was no limit to the overbearingness he might display. The first time he encountered the minister Maklakov he ignored him entirely at the outset; then haughtily beckoned him with his crooked forefinger, saying, "Come here, *you!*" Maklakov, in his amazement, actually moved a step or two in Rasputin's direction, whereupon the latter burst out: "Pay attention to what I tell *you*. It will not be long before we make a good man of *you*, one pleasing to God. And now," he concluded, turning his back on the minister, "now, *you* can go."

Most remarkable, too, was the incident of Rasputin's expedition to "examine the soul" of a prospective minister. It occurred just before Stolypin's assassination, when the "true Russian people" were intending to make Alexander Nikolaevich Khvostov, the Governor of Nizhni-Novgorod, Minister of the Interior. A great Court hunt took place at this time, and every member of the "True Russian Union" who took part in it, used the opportunity to present Khvostov's personality to the Emperor in the most favorable light. The Emperor finally began to busy himself seriously over Khvostov's appointment, but decided first to entrust the "Friend" with the mission of obtaining further particulars about the candidate.

Rasputin at once proceeded to Nizhni-Novgorod and appeared one day in the office of the unsuspecting Governor.

"Here I am," he said simply. "Papa has sent me to examine *your* soul, as we are thinking of making *you* Minister of the Interior perhaps."

At these words from the peasant standing before him in his clumsy boots and dirty sheepskin, fat Khvostov, all-powerful Governor of Nizhni-Novgorod, burst into peals of laughter. He never thought of taking this muzhik's speech seriously, and treated the whole thing as a mad joke. Grigori Efimovich was much offended at being met with such contempt, and, turning away without a word, he seized his knotted stick and left the palace. But at midday, immediately before he left the town, he turned up again, opened Khvostov's door for one instant, and called out in a threatening and malicious tone: "I have dealt with *you* all right. I've wired a report about *you* to Tsarskoe Selo."

At first the Governor again laughed heartily; but soon a faint apprehension crept over him that there might be some reason for taking his visitor's strange speeches seriously. He sent for the postmaster and ordered him to produce Grigori Efimovich's telegram. Imagine his feelings an hour later when he had the text of this telegram in his hands.

"Anna Vyrubova, Tsarskoe Selo," it ran: "Tell Mama that the grace of the Lord is in Khvostov, but that for the time being there is still something lacking."

The Governor's fat face turned yellow, and his eyes like round marbles rolled with horror. What the peasant had said was true, then, and he might have been a minister! A few days later Khvostov hurried to St. Petersburg with a bundle of documents, and asked for an audience with the Tsar, on "urgent administrative business." He was received, but at once noticed that the Emperor's mood was anything but gracious. He was dismissed as soon as he had explained his quite insignificant business.

After this Khvostov made every effort to meet Grigori Efimovich as often as possible, and on these occasions he treated the starets with exquisite courtesy and devotion; he would have kissed his hand in public. But some years had to pass before he had a chance of becoming intimate with Rasputin. It was at a drinking party. On meeting the Tsar soon after this Rasputin said that he had had an opportunity of examining Khvostov's soul afresh, and found that it had improved. A few days later the fat Governor at last became Minister of the Interior.

The Prime Minister, Boris Stürmer, the successor of the aged Goremykin, also owed his appointment to the patronage of the "Friend." "This old chap," declared Grigori, when Stürmer was mentioned to him as a possible candidate, "has wanted to be a minister for a long time. When I was still staying on the English Prospekt, he and his wife visited me, and asked me to make him a minister. Well, to be sure, he is quite a good creature, and things will be fixed up."

Whereupon the starets met Boris Stürmer at the flat of a little actress, "examined his soul," and, on this examination's proving satisfactory, recommended his appointment to the Emperor. It was made immediately.

Stürmer's period of office marked the zenith of Rasputin's political influence. The new Prime Minister obeyed every one of his orders unconditionally. Stürmer met the "peasant Chancellor" secretly at least once a week to receive his instructions. The setting of these meetings must have been most romantic, for they took place at night in the Fortress of SS. Peter and Paul, to which Rasputin had the entry through one of his disciples, the daughter of Nikitin, the Governor of the Fortress. The beautiful Lydia Nikitina was an ardent admirer of the starets, and she called for him at his flat in the evening, and drove him to the Fortress. In her white maidenly room secret councils lasting till daybreak took place between Rasputin and Stürmer, at which all important orders, enactments, and appointments were exhaustively discussed.

It was not long before Stürmer disappointed expectations; he proved to be extraordinarily ambitious and vain, while his abilities left much to be desired. His every thought and wish were set on being president of the coming great peace conference, and in fancy he already saw his name in the history books of future generations alongside those of Nesselrode, Metternich, and Bismarck. But his capacities were out of all proportion to his lofty ambitions, with the result that the Emperor and his "Friend" soon became disappointed with him and removed him from office.

In the meantime Grigori Efimovich had taken a particular fancy to Protopopov, the Vice-President of the Duma, whose acquaintance he had made in his friend Badmaev's "sanatorium." Protopopov was a likable man of attractive social manners; but he was in an advanced stage of general paralysis. On account of this disease he alternated between states of excessive excitement and complete apathy. Occasionally he could fascinate everyone about him with his dazzling wit and brilliant *mots*, while at other times he was unfit for the most elementary mental work. For many years he had been a regular patient at the institute of the Tibetan, who had long ago marked him out for a high position in the State.

Grigori Efimovich met Protopopov in one of his good moments, and at once made up his mind that this charming and clever man must take over the Ministry of the Interior. The Tsar at first refused to make the appointment, because Protopopov belonged to the left wing of the Duma, and the most persistent effort on the part of Rasputin and the Tsaritsa was necessary to make Nikolai abandon his opposition and appoint Protopopov.

Even at the last moment an argument arose, and Rasputin had

to go to Tsarskoe Selo in person in order to put things right for his protégé. He returned to St. Petersburg in triumph, and the account he gave of the affair in the salon of his admirer, Madame Golovina, shows better than anything else the curious relations that existed between the imperial couple and their "Friend" who, in their eyes, was no longer merely the saviour of the sick heir-apparent, but also an indispensable, confidential adviser in the most momentous affairs of State.

"I have put everything in trim again," cried Rasputin with a smile of satisfaction, dropping into a chair. "I had only to go myself. The first person I ran into at the Palace was Ania. She could only groan and lament, that was all she could do. 'Things are all wrong,' cries she, 'he refuses to do it, only *you* can help, Grigori Efimovich.'

"Well, I went straight in. I saw at once that Mama was angry and defiant, while Papa was striding up and down the room whistling. But, after I had bullied them both a little, they soon saw reason! I had only to threaten that I would go back to Siberia and abandon them and their child to disaster, and they immediately gave in to me in everything. 'The man who turns his back on God,' said I, 'looks the devil in the face!' Somebody or other has been persuading them that this and that is wrong; what do they all know about it? Nothing at all. If they would only listen to me. I know that Protopopov is a good creature and believes in God. That is all that matters."

But that same evening he said to his secretary: "We were wrong about fat old Khvostov; he is a duffer, although a duffer of the Right! I tell you that all the men of the Right are blockheads. So we have now decided for the Left and made Protopopov a minister."

Then he looked proudly at his coarse, peasant fist, shook it vigorously, and cried: "Between these fingers I hold the Russian Empire!"

CHAPTER VII

THE PENITENTIAL JOURNEY OF THE GREAT SINNER

AS the Empress sat in her reception room of an afternoon, either alone or with her friend Ania, she would often take from the drawer of her escritoire the notes the "Friend" had made on his penitential pilgrimage to the holy places. They were jotted down on many crumpled sheets of paper, large and small, torn from a cheap notebook, in the big, clumsy peasant writing, every letter of which seemed to have been stuck on to the paper separately. The lines in their confused mass were some long, some short, some straight, and some sloping steeply; they looked as if one word had been piled on top of the other.

The slips themselves, too, were stained, covered with ink spots, creased, and eaten into by damp at the edges, for the pilgrim had preserved them in his dirty bread sack through all his wanderings, along with the innumerable trifles of his daily needs.

The Empress sat at her writing-table, and arranged these dirty slips with her delicate, carefully tended fingers. She pored over the confused characters, and read the papers again and again, until their meaning became clear and comprehensible to her. Then she made a fair copy of them in her album.

Here and there she corrected gross misspellings and altered unusual or awkward constructions, coarse words, and other clumsinesses; but for the most part she left the text exactly as the peasant had scribbled it down. For the oftener the Tsaritsa read Rasputin's words, the stronger became her feeling that she had never found anything more beautiful or more edifying than these "thoughts" of Grigori the pilgrim.

Never once had her imperial dignity given her such buoyant self-confidence as now. She was filled with the certainty that what she was doing was far loftier than anything she had ever

PENITENTIAL JOURNEY OF THE GREAT SINNER

accomplished in the discharge of her worldly duties as Empress of Russia. Grigori Efimovich, her God-sent "Friend," stood high above all earthly powers; he had jotted down these "thoughts" for the edification of his Empress; and it seemed to Alexandra that she was writing sentences originally dictated by God himself.

Could greater grace have been vouchsafed to any human being, even to the Empress of Russia herself, than the right to be the first to make a fair copy of the divinely inspired words of the sainted Grigori Efimovich? Alexandra devoted herself to her task with joy and enthusiasm, dipped her diamond-studded pen into the magnificent ink-well, and as she transferred her divine "Friend's" account of his journeyings to her morocco-bound album, the characteristic red patches appeared on her cheeks, and her breath came in short gasps.

Thoughts on My Pilgrimage
In the Kievo-Pecherskaia Lavra *

"I have arrived at the holy Lavra of Kiev from St. Petersburg, and I call St. Petersburg the world. But the world is full of trivial thoughts, while here in the monastery are calm and peace. When the picture of the Mother of God descends, when the anthem rings out, heart and soul are lost, and the trivial is forgotten.

"I also went to the caves, and saw simplicity there; there is neither gold nor silver, and the martyrs of God sleep in simple wooden coffins. And I thought how superfluity only oppresses us and evokes weariness in us: God has blessed these wonderful caves; his hand hollowed them out of the rock, and there the holy men hid from their enemies.

"Even now the holy man has many enemies, for brother fights against brother, and no one will leave another in peace. In earlier days, in the time of the martyrs, true believers were oppressed by strangers and the heathen; but now we ourselves torment one another, now priest persecutes priest, and sons, fathers. Thus is fulfilled the word of God about the approach of the end.

"And Job saw in the caves, how his cell was small and narrow,

* *Lavra* means "monastery."

but he was happy, calm, and patient in the midst of his tribulations. If we too would take refuge with our spirit in simplicity, and pray to God in a narrow cell, then we might be partakers of the Lord.

At Sea

"What shall I say about the peace of the ocean? As I put forth from Odessa, a wonderful quietude at once surrounded me, my soul rejoiced in the sea and slumbered softly. I saw how the little waves glittered, and I desired to seek no further. When I rose in the morning, the waves spoke to me, and their movement refreshed my heart. And as the sun slowly rises from the sea, in its light the soul of man forgets all sorrow, and understands the book and the wisdom of life. The sea makes us forget the trivial; it compels us to think of many things, and our thoughts come of themselves, without effort and difficulty. The sea is without bounds; but human wisdom too knows no limit.

"It is most beautiful when the sun is just about to sink its rays into the sea. It disappears behind the mountains, twilight comes on, and a marvellous peace broods over the waters. The voices of birds are dumb; but man remembers his childhood, compares this quietness with the noise of the world, and talks softly to himself.

"And then, after no shrub and no leaf has been visible for a long time, a shore appears, and man rejoices afresh in the nature of God and praises the Creator, who has made all these things.

"When the waves rise higher, the soul is uneasy; man loses his clear consciousness, and paces helplessly round the ship as in a fog. But the same sickness attacks us on land also, only we know nothing about it, for there the same wave lifts us, but we do not see it. But at sea all mark the sickness, while on shore it remains concealed. For the devil tempts our soul, but conscience is a great wave, and even if there were no waves on the sea, still the waves rise and fall in us.

In Constantinople

"What can I, with my poor human understanding, say of the splendid and marvellous Cathedral of Saint Sophia? Like a cloud on the horizon is this Cathedral. Woe unto us that God's wrath at our pride was so great that He surrendered this shrine to the unbelieving Turk! May the Lord hear my prayer and restore to us this Church, so that it may be his Ark!

"In this Cathedral is also to be seen the pulpit of St. John the Evangelist, and also the bones of St. Efim and the pillar to which the Saviour was chained. We stand on the spot where St. John once preached, and it is as if we still hear his voice.

"In Constantinople there is also a church where St. Andrew, who, out of love for the Saviour, played the madman, had a vision of the Mother of God. I went to the place; but saw only a little bit of wall, some ruins and a garden, by which a Greek church stands. My heart was moved when I thought how the Mother of God protected Her faithful servants. To-day, Her one anxiety is still to comfort us and grant us Her grace. She appears to the good and to the sinful, She hears all our prayers, knows our sorrows, and prays for us before the throne of God.

"In Constantinople there is also a column which was brought from Rome; it weighs a thousand *pud*. All this is a great marvel, and I can only write very little about it.

On the Journey through the Mediterranean

"We came to Mitylene. It is a little town where the Apostle Paul preached and kindled the flame of faith in the souls of the thirty martyrs. It lies very prettily by the sea, on a hill above the water. May God lead us by his ways! The farther we come, the more often do we arrive at places where the soul can be saved. It is plain that the Russian does not in vain save his kopeks to visit these holy places.

"I have encountered many people, and, especially in the third class, have met true Christian women, who read the Holy Scriptures day and night, so that it is a real joy. There are also Bulgarians who truly believe in the Kingdom of God and love the Lord Jesus. I have convinced myself that the Turks wear much the same clothes as the Christians and the Jews. I believe that even for them the words of God will be fulfilled, and that then, in spite of the apparent difference in clothing, there will be only one single Orthodox Church.

"Smyrna lies on the Asiatic coast at the head of a large gulf. It has some very beautiful Greek churches, including one on the spot where the woman of Samaria, after her talk with James, began to believe in the Saviour. Then there is also a church on the place where the Mother of God preached; there, too, repose the bones of St. George.

"Not far from Smyrna are the ruins of the town of Ephesus; there the Apostle John lived, there he finished his Gospel, and, therefore, the sea beats the more strongly against the shore, to awaken life from its sleep. Not far from Ephesus is the island of Chios, where St. Isidor died a martyr's death in the third century.

"We crossed the Mediterranean, and our steamer stopped nowhere else. God! How the Apostles kindled the flame of faith and made innumerable disciples everywhere on these coasts! But the Greeks were too proud of their philosophy, and so God punished them by transferring power to the Turks.

"The Greek bishops can all read and write, and can conduct divine service excellently; the services here are very ceremonious. But poverty in spirit is a higher thing. The bishop, who is not of the poor in spirit, weeps when he does not receive a cross; but who bears the cross in himself is fair even in his simple robe and enjoys the love of the people. Why do so many people to-day fall away into strange faiths? Because the spirit no longer lives in the Church—there are many letters and the Temple is empty. Many bishops are afraid of being confounded with simple monks; but the monks are lazy and wax fat in their cloisters.

"The town of Rhodes is full of splendid gardens, in which flowers and trees are in bloom in the middle of February. Great are the mercies of God in this place!

"The town of Tripolis lies on the sea, and is surrounded by mountains; indeed, it is nothing but a fortress like our Fortress of SS. Peter and Paul. Beirut too lies on the coast, all covered with verdure. It was there that St. George slew the dragon, and on the spot there is now a Turkish mosque. The lake is overgrown with grass. It is a misfortune when God punishes Christianity with his wrath.

"Jaffa is the town where the Prophet Elias lived. On the hill where he used to pray stands a monastery, and I have also visited the place where the fire descended from Heaven.

In Jerusalem

"I have reached the end of my journeying, and have arrived in the Holy City of Jerusalem. After passing from the great waves of the sea into the earthly paradise of peace, I first of all held a divine service. I cannot describe my joy, for ink is powerless in the face of so much happiness.

"It is true that many sad thoughts also come over me when I see how people here go about in strange clothes which recall old times. Here, in these churches, the Saviour Himself shed tears!

"What am I to say about the minutes as I approached the tomb of our Lord Jesus Christ? I felt that this tomb is a tomb of love; before it the heart is spiritualized, and we see before us all the people we love, and they too feel happy and at peace in that moment, no matter where they may be. God, Thou Thyself shalt rise from the depths of sin, for eternity lives in Thee!

"I have also been to Golgotha; on the spot where the Mother of God wept as Her Son was nailed to the Cross, now stands the Church of the Resurrection. My God, we will sin no more, save us by Thy Passion!

"We were taken to the palace of the Patriarch, where our feet were washed. We all had tears in our eyes at being shown in so wise a way that man must be humble. May God teach us humility and make us his pupils!

"We saw the house of Judas and the house of Pilate, which are not far from one another. Then, amid a great crowd, we went to the vault of the holy Mother of God, kissed the tomb, and sang joyfully. We saw plainly before us the scene enacted here when the might of Heaven took to itself the pure body of the Virgin. Joseph is also buried in the same vault, as it is written in the Scriptures: 'Here rests a marvellous old man.' Great old man, pray to God for us!

"Next we went to the Garden of Gethsemane, in which the Saviour groaned and prayed before His death. We unworthy ones greeted this place, and bowed in devotion at the thought that our Lord Jesus Christ here shed tears of blood. God save us, and have pity upon us in Thine heart! Then we saw the stones on which the disciples slept until Christ came to awaken them. But we sleep eternally in sin—awaken us, Lord God!

"Oh! the mercy of the holy Easter festival! How yearningly believers await the great procession of the Cross. Thousands of peoples and nationalities assemble here waiting for the holy light; all around stand Turkish troops and kavasses.

"Then comes the great moment; the Patriarch takes off his robes, draws on a shirt, and approaches the Holy Sepulchre. With tears in their eyes the crowd wait until he returns with the burning candles. Then all are happy and joyful, and light their candles at the holy light, and take them back to their houses. God, give me a good memory, so that I may never forget this moment!

"How wonderful it is to be on sacred ground, what a believer a man would be here, even if he stayed only a few months! Of course, it is impossible to see everything even in a year, if we are lazy, for God does not give ear to the lazy, even if they live for centuries. The holy shrine loves fear.

"Wine is very cheap here, and is drunk freely because it costs almost nothing. We went to the river Jordan, bathed in its waters, and saw the desert to which the Egyptian Mary fled for refuge. At the place where the Saviour was baptized we all descended to the water and thought of the remission of sins. Many ran trembling to the banks of the Jordan in order to win the remission of all their sins. God, cleanse us in the waters of Thy river Jordan!

"We also saw the Dead Sea. The punishment of God rests upon it, and we were seized with fear and terror at the sight of it. There is only water to be seen, not a beast, insect, or fish; we saw all this and wept. In the Jordan desert is also the spring of the Prophet Isaiah; but the kavass did not take us there, as he was cross with us.

"On a high mountain in this place, where Satan tried to tempt the Lord, now rises a marvellous monastery, where you are also shown the stone on which the Devil stood. We meditated on the suffering of the Saviour; but now spirits are sold at the place. Cunning Satan knows how to seduce the faithful! On the way we also passed a great oak tree; there Abraham welcomed the Saviour with bread and salt. We bowed before the tree, kissed it, and held a service before it. Half the trunk is rotted away, but God performed a miracle, so that after thousands of years some parts of the tree are still green and flourishing.

"According to Turkish stories, there is a remnant of Noah's Ark on the shore at Jaffa. This Ark is a symbol of the salvation of Christianity, and for us too the words of Noah are fulfilled. The true faith is our salvation, and everyone who listens to the call of the Saviour will find redemption.

"In Bethlehem there is a large church with many pulpits and various conveniences for other nationalities, but no provision whatever is made for us Russians. But before the manger where the Saviour lay we forgot our fatigue and everything disagreeable. We kissed the holy manger, and in our joy could hardly believe that God had been so gracious as to allow us to see the place where Christ was born.

"We were also shown the pit in which the Innocents were slain at Herod's command. We thought with horror of this evil deed and burst into tears. What must the mothers have felt when the soldiers took away their children and murdered them! Envy and malice are still ever in our hearts, and the truth awaits the rising of the sun like a grain of sand in an autumn night.

"Everywhere in the holy places we found many peoples; they are clever; but not strong in faith and love. We must be very friendly to them, and direct their souls to love and Heaven; then God will save them also. We must give an example of love, then we shall again be Christians, as in the first years after the death of the Saviour, and our mission will serve Good and not gold. These foreign people understand very well when we speak to them, and our words are marvellously reflected in them. But of course you must know the language and the ways of a people in order to be able to talk to them about God, for as a bell without silver has a discordant sound, so too the words of a preacher may do much harm if he lacks the proper experience.

"The greatest thing in the world is love, and only through love can we find the way to Heaven. A morsel of bread is often more important and precious to men than a great ship!

"The steamers are full of the faithful; each of them bears spiritual force in a corner of his heart. When he gets home he will talk about Jerusalem, and then the fear of God will awaken in the hearts of the children, and they will learn to love their Tsar and their home.

"More attention must also be paid to the pilgrims; travelling should be cheaper, and things should be so arranged that pilgrims are provided with a meal once a day, and boiling water for making tea is supplied free of charge. At present they are treated like cattle and shut up in hundreds in the hold of the ships; thus they have to endure many discomforts for the sake of the holy shrines. It is easy, of course, for the rich, for they have plenty of money and live in beautiful rooms. The authorities should take an interest in the poor pilgrims, for it is their faith that upholds the Empire.

"For this reason it is necessary that hostels should be built for the poor people, in which they can live like brothers. The simple pilgrim pays homage to the holy shrine, and then, full of faith, returns to his village and proclaims the truth to the people there. His simple talk awakens love for God in his home district also; the young people listen to his words and feel love and piety growing in their hearts.

"I also saw the Easter festival of the Catholics in Jerusalem, which was celebrated a week before ours. But this festival was not to be compared with that of the Orthodox Church. The Catholics did not look at all joyful, while at ours all the world, even the beasts, rejoiced on that day. Oh! we Orthodox believers are happy, and our faith is more beautiful than any other. The faces of the Catholics were gloomy even during the Easter festival, and so I think that their souls also do not truly rejoice.

"I do not want to compare the two religions with each other and condemn the Catholics, but I feel that in Russia everybody is happy when the church bells ring and when the holy springtime blossoms for us all. . . ."

CHAPTER VIII

STAIRCASE NOTES

AS Rasputin's political and social influence grew, his flat became the centre of manifold and multifarious interests.

While he was still living on the Nevski Prospekt, in the lodging rented for him by his disciple, Bashmakova, and even afterwards, when he stayed in the Kirochnaia, the authorities did not pay much attention to his house. But in later years, after the starets had, with amazing swiftness, become a personage of supreme importance, his house was not only thronged by visitors, but also carefully watched by the police.

The police had kept an eye on his quarters on the English Prospect, where he was living at the beginning of the war; but his new flat in the Gorokhovaia was under particularly strict surveillance, for the new Prime Minister, Stürmer, had informed Globichev, the chief of the Secret Service, that Rasputin must be guarded as closely as a member of the imperial family. "This is the express wish of the Emperor and Empress," added Stürmer, and it was not surprising, therefore, that "64 Gorokhovaia" was hereafter besieged by secret service men.

In the concierge's lodge and on the staircase—amid a steamy cloud of indefinable smells, in which the sourish odour of cabbage soup and rancid butter sometimes predominated, and sometimes the smell of hot sheep's cheese—lounged, day in, day out, four or five—or even ten or twenty—badly dressed men; their old-fashioned collars and ties, as well as their studiously inconspicuous bearing, proclaimed them detectives a mile away. The other people living in the house and Rasputin's frequent visitors knew every one of these agents, and had ceased to take any special notice of them; many, as the result of some chance conversation, were even on a friendly footing with them. The officials, for their part, gave up the attempt to conceal their profession from the regular habitués of the house, and, when one of them came through the gate and hurried up the steps, they did not stir from their easy, sleepy posture.

Sometimes one of the other people in the house made a break in the monotonous existence of the police on the staircase: the sempstress Katia would come out of Flat 31, or Mr. Neustein from the floor above would come down and talk to the agents. Occasionally Utilia, the masseuse, or another woman from the neighbourhood, would turn up, and then time passed quickly and comfortably round the steaming, dirty, tin samovar, in the lodge of Yuravleva, the concierge's wife. Katia, Utilia, the masseuse, and she would gossip about the starets, and give the latest news of him; other women would want to know exactly how the holy man lived, and the police were thus able to perform some part of their tedious duty in friendly chat with the women. The sempstress, Katia, and Utilia had much that was singular and interesting to impart about Rasputin, for it often happened that this darling of the fine ladies would weary of the society of grand duchesses, countesses, and beautiful actresses, and would knock at Katia's door, or send for Utilia, to keep him company for the night.

The porter's wife also knew a great deal about the peculiarities of the holy man. When, late at night, he came home drunk from a carousal, and Katia had refused to let him in and Utilia was not available, Grigori Efimovich would embrace the porter's wife, smother her with kisses, and press her with importunities which she modestly declined to describe any further.

The gatekeepers, in particular, through their peep-hole, noticed many things that escaped the detectives; and they received a salary from the police to report everything that occurred. Thus they could not only indulge in their love of gossip, but also take pride in having done their duty to the authorities. The sempstress and the masseuse, moreover, were all the more ready to report their experiences, as these reached the highest dignitaries of the Empire, through the police reports, and they thus acquired an unlooked-for importance.

Mr. Neustein often came out of his flat and drew the agents into conversation. He had very little to tell, in fact; but he had a way peculiarly his own of speaking in obscure hints, behind which a deeper meaning might well be hidden. The detectives did not think themselves called upon to decide whether this was really so: they took down every utterance of Mr. Neustein word for word; their superiors could decide what was to be made of these strange insinuations!

Thus, for example, one note runs: "24th January. Neustein, who lives on the same stair, said to us in passing: 'Your patron will soon be sent to Tsarskoe Selo, to light all the church candles there.'"

But it seldom happened that the activities of the agents had to be confined to noting conversations with Mr. Neustein. Innumerable visitors were generally entering or leaving the house, and the spies had no easy task in keeping up with the record of their names. If a new visitor came through the gate they did everything they could not to seem like detectives. For this purpose they would stage impromptu little comedies, hurry up the stairs as if they themselves were visiting the starets, or come down in careless groups, and remain standing before the house, absorbed in innocent conversation. But, as soon as the visitor passed through Rasputin's door, an excited whispering and a mysterious questioning began on the staircase: one spy asked the other if he knew the new guest; they all put their heads together and combined to give the fullest possible report. Pencils and notebooks flew out of pockets, and the stranger was described in the greatest detail: his hat, his clothes, the colour of his hair, and whether he carried an umbrella or a parcel. The parcels were particularly important, and every agent made it a point of honour to discover their contents. Their reports to their superior officers swarm with notes about parcels, baskets, etc.:

"10th January. Anastasia Shapovalenkova, the wife of a doctor, has given Rasputin a carpet."

"23rd January. An unknown clergyman brought fish for Rasputin."

"28th January. Councillor von Bok brought Rasputin a case of wine."

"21st February. Nikolai Glazov visited Rasputin to-day, and brought a parcel containing several bottles of wine."

"14th March. Simanovich, Rasputin's secretary, came with a box containing six bottles of wine, caviare, and cheese."

"14th June. The Inspector of the National School of Tsarskoe Selo appeared here to-day with a basket of wine."

When several visitors turned up at the same time, it was the detectives' job to overhear as much as possible of the conversation between them. Every one of their sentences, even though only half-heard and misunderstood, was faithfully noted in their reports, whether it had any meaning or not. They kept a sharp look-out for the words and facial expressions with which Dunia, Rasputin's maid, received the visitors; Dunia's friendly or unfriendly attitude as she showed them out also made it possible to draw inferences about how they had been received by the starets.

The spies devoted themselves with praiseworthy diligence to their difficult task of throwing the fullest possible light on the life and personality of unknown people during their brief passage from the house door to the door of Rasputin's flat. They noted down every imaginable trifle in the utmost detail, trying, by the enumeration of the greatest possible number of unimportant external features, to capture the incomprehensible and mysterious lives of perfect strangers. Sometimes they were lucky and succeeded in entering in a conversation with the unknown. Many petitioners were garrulous, especially after they left the starets, either with joy over the granting of a petition or with wrath at a refusal. On these occasions the reports would run:

"3rd November. An unknown woman visited Rasputin in order to try to prevent her husband, a lieutenant at present in hospital, from being transferred from St. Petersburg. When she left she gave an account, in the concierge's lodge, of the strange way in which Rasputin had received her: 'A servant opened the door to me and showed me into a room, where Rasputin, whom I had never seen before, appeared immediately. He told me at once to take off my things. I complied with his wish, and went with him into an adjoining room. He hardly listened to my request; but kept on touching my face and breast and asking me to kiss him. Then he wrote a note but did not give it to me, saying that he was displeased with me and bidding me come back next day.'"

"3rd December. Madame Leikart visited Rasputin for the first time to-day, to ask him to intervene on her husband's behalf. Rasputin proposed that she should kiss him; she refused, however, and departed. Then the mistress of Senator Mamontov arrived; Rasputin asked her to return at 1 a. m."

"29th January. The wife of Colonel Tatarinov visited Rasputin, and afterwards told the detectives that the starets embraced and kissed a young girl in her presence; she found the incident so painful that she has decided never to visit Rasputin again."

"18th January. The Greek lady, Madame Karavia, and her daughter tried to secure an audience with Rasputin. On the way down the two ladies burst into abuse of him, called him a cursed peasant, and said they had been present when Rasputin caused a great scandal by his appearance at the Villa Rode wearing only a shirt. They also said that a young person had appeared at Tsarskoe Selo who would soon put Rasputin in the shade."

"30th January. The priest from the church on the Lublianka, accompanied by an unknown man, visited Rasputin to-day. The priest was intervening in some affair for this unknown man, and asked Rasputin to make a personal visit to the Minister of the Interior and Senator Beletski: Rasputin, however, refused, and merely wrote a letter. As they went away the priest was making fun of Rasputin, because he found it so difficult to put pen to paper."

"5th February. When Sofia Karavia left Rasputin's flat she said to the detectives: 'He is in a bad humour, although he has just carried out a good stroke of business. He has arranged some matter or other for Rubinstein, the banker, who has given him fifty thousand roubles in return.' Rasputin also promised Karavia herself that he would use his influence on her behalf with the minister Shakhovskoi."

"7th February. Popermann, the merchant, came to see Rasputin to-day, and as soon as he came in he asked what was the matter with the miraculous monk. Neustein, who lives on the same staircase, also asked if it were true that an officer had beaten Rasputin at the station."

* * * * *

Whenever a messenger arrived from Tsarskoe Selo or one of the ministries or banks it was a happy moment for the detectives. The messenger was stopped on the stairs before he had time to ring the bell. The spies then inquired in an impressive, confidential, and urgent manner where he came from, who had sent him, at what time he left the house of his superior, and what message he brought. Afterwards they carefully opened the envelope in the concierge's lodge and noted the contents in their books; the letter was then skilfully gummed up again and the messenger at last permitted to ring the bell of Rasputin's flat.

When the messenger, after discharging his errand, once more appeared on the staircase, he was immediately besieged by the detectives. They ran down the steps with him, accompanied him through the courtyard to the street, and excitedly tried to discover who had received him in the flat and taken the document from him. If Rasputin had attended to the matter himself, they questioned the messenger exhaustively about his expression as he read the letter, and they also wanted to know what he had said, and whether there were any other people in the room. If the messenger was carrying a written answer this was opened straightway in the concierge's lodge and then returned to him.

The postmen knew their duty, for they had been ordered by their superior officers to allow all letters or telegrams addressed to Rasputin to be examined in the concierge's lodge, before they reached their destination. But Rasputin's own servants also used to stop for a moment when their master sent them out on an errand, and tell the police agents what the business was. If they were taking a letter or a telegram to the post office they first gave it to the spies, who made a copy of it. Their notebooks are full of reports about Rasputin's correspondence; his peculiar telegrams, in particular, partly composed of biblical texts and partly of dry business information, were minutely recorded:

"1st January. Rasputin sent a telegram to the village elder of Pokrovskoe in the Tobolsk Government: 'Have secured the concession for you to have the forest. You may proceed to cut as soon as you receive the permit.' "

"10th January. Rasputin sent the following telegram: 'Anna Vyrubova, Tsarskoe Selo. Although not with you in person am present in the spirit and send an angel to console and comfort you.' "

"13th January. Rasputin sent the following telegram to Vyrubova at Tsarskoe Selo: 'God himself allows me to proclaim the true joy. The way to truth will always be with my children. I do not know whether I shall live to see it.' "

"18th February. Rasputin despatched the following telegram: 'Vyrubova, Tsarskoe Selo. Tell Madame Golovina to come to see me to-morrow at 3 o'clock.' "

"30th March. Rasputin sent the following telegram to Moscow: 'Princess Tenisheva. I rejoice at your frankness. Kisses to my dear one.' "

"Rasputin also telegraphed to Elena Dianumova: 'My darling, am with you in spirit, kiss you.' "

"12th May. Rasputin telegraphed to the Governor of Tobolsk: 'For the last three months a suspicious person has been living in my village of Pokrovskoe. Send your answer to Vyrubova at Tsarskoe Selo.' "

"11th October. Rasputin telegraphed to Varnava: 'Mind the spy.' "

Rasputin's servants, stimulated by copious bribes, gave the detectives the most exact information possible about what went on inside the flat. If conferences of some length or parties were taking place in Rasputin's room, the housemaid, Dunia, would slip softly out into the passage, where she was immediately surrounded and questioned. Often there were very curious things to report, which made the poor spies gasp with amazement. Such moments richly made up for their long and tedious hours of fruitless waiting; and they greedily noted down the maid's reports of the shameless and disorderly scenes enacted in the flat:

"16th January. During the visit of the Pistolkors family, Rasputin took the prostitute Gregubova on his knee and murmured something to himself."

"In the night of 17th to 18th January Maria Gill, the wife of a Captain in the 145th Regiment, slept at Rasputin's."

"26th January. This evening a ball took place at Rasputin's in honour of some persons who had been released from prison, at which behaviour was very indecorous. The guests sang and danced till morning."

"16th March. About 1 a. m. eight men and women called on Rasputin and stayed till three. The whole company sang and danced; when they were all drunk, they left the house accompanied by Rasputin."

"3rd April. About 1 a. m. Rasputin brought an unknown woman back to the house; she spent the night with him."

"11th May. Rasputin brought a prostitute back to the flat and locked her in his room; the servants, however, afterwards let her out."

"On the night of 25th to 26th November Varvarova, the actress, slept at Rasputin's."

The detectives did not, however, always succeed in giving such a clear and unequivocal account of the meaning and significance of what went on in Rasputin's flat. The maid was frequently unable to get into touch with them, or else she knew nothing definite about the visitors' objects. Then there was nothing for the police to do but to make an exact note of the time of every visitor's arrival and departure:

"8th February. Madame Soloviev arrived at 10, Maria Golovina at 10.10, and the Princess Tatiana Shakhovskaia at 11.50; the last went away again fifty minutes later. At 12 precisely Rasputin received his private secretary, Simanovich; at 12.10 the wife of Staff-Captain Sandetski arrived and left in ten minutes; at 12 o'clock the singer Derevenski also appeared; at 12.20 Laptinskaia left, and at 12.40 an unknown man in uniform arrived in a motor to fetch Rasputin.

"At 1.35 Privy Councillor and Senator Mamontov called, and at 1.40 Basilevskaia accompanied by Gar; both ladies remained an hour and a half with Rasputin. At 2 o'clock Simanovich called with a man in uniform, but departed again at the end of twenty minutes. Then an officer's wife came and stopped twenty-five minutes; at 3.30 Simanovich turned up for the third time and stayed for half an hour; at 4.10 Knirsche came with some bottles of wine; at 5 o'clock Mesdames Turovich and Chervinskaia, at 5.10 Madame Soloviev, and at 6.20 Simanovich arrived for the fourth time. At 6.45 Reshetnikov came; at 7.20 an unknown lady; at 9.30 Dobrovolskaia, at 10 Katarina Bermann; at 10.10 Madame Turovich and her husband, and 11.10 Knirsche. At 11.15 five more people turned up, so that twenty-five people altogether were assembled in Rasputin's flat."

"9th February. The guests departed at 3 a. m. At 9.45 Anna Vyrubova called; at 10.25 Dobrovolskaia; at 10.50 the Golovin ladies, and at 11 Maria Gar. Dobrovolskaia remained for three hours, ten minutes, Gar only two hours. At 11.40 Manuilov and Ossipenko turned up with an unknown official in military car No. 5064, and stayed for thirty minutes. At 12 Dobrovolski called and stayed an hour and forty-five minutes; at 12.30 Bishop Varnava and Bishop Augustin arrived in a motor (No. 127); they both remained forty minutes with Rasputin."

"10th February. At midnight yesterday a man, apparently Manuilov, called on Rasputin, but soon left. At 11 a. m. Vishniakova came with an unknown lady, but was not admitted. At 11.40 Maria Golovina called and at 11.45 the maid of honour, Lydia Nikitina. At 12.40 Gar came with a lady, and at 1.20 Madame Soloviev, also accompanied by an unknown lady. At 2 o'clock Rasputin sent for motor No. 224 and departed in it at 2.10 with Maria Golovina."

* * * * *

The detectives thought it especially important to make exact notes of the movements of the wonder-monk himself, his appearance, his moods, and his talk. Rasputin frequently appeared in the hall in untidy house clothes, and visited the concierge's wife or Katia, the sempstress; on these occasions his powerful figure wandering about the house at the urge of sensual desire had something of a great wild beast about it. The agents of course confined themselves to sober statements of this kind:

"9th May. Rasputin sent the concierge's wife for the masseuse, but she refused to come. He then went himself to Katia, the sempstress, who lives in the house, and asked her to 'keep him company.' The sempstress refused, she had no costume, but

Rasputin said, 'Come to me next week and I will give *you* fifty roubles.'"

"2nd June. Rasputin sent the porter's wife to fetch the masseuse, Utilia, but she was not at home. Whereupon he betook himself to the sempstress Katia in Flat 31. He was apparently refused admittance, for he came down the stairs again, and asked the porter's wife to kiss him. She, however, disengaged herself from his embrace, and rang his flat bell, whereupon the servant appeared and put Rasputin to bed."

When Grigori Efimovich left his flat, either to go to church or to the baths, or when a car came to the door to take him to the Villa Rode or to Tsarskoe Selo, he was dressed in a decent and festive manner, and wore a long, black caftan, costly furs, snow-boots, and a beaver cap. At such times he seemed like a dignified "barin" to the detectives, and they would almost have felt sincere respect for him if his wrinkled, weather-tanned face had not always betrayed the peasant.

As the flat door opened and Rasputin's powerful figure appeared in the hall, a wave of excitement passed over the waiting, shabbily dressed crowd; they would bow, lift their hats, and many would hurry up to him and wish him a friendly and familiar "Good-morning."

He replied to their greeting cordially and with an indulgent smile. He knew them all, and had been accustomed for years to encounter them on the staircase or in the concierge's lodge, whenever he entered or left the house. He could also distinguish clearly between the various spies, of which there were several sets: the agents in the pay of Globichev, the Chief of the Okhrana, the officials of the police department of Colonel Komisarov, those of the Court Agency of General Spiridovich, and, in addition, the special confidential agents of the Prime Minister, the Minister of the Interior, the large banks, the stockbrokers, and the foreign ambassadors. As all of these people distrusted one another, they tried to keep informed of Rasputin's life and business through a secret service of their own.

Grigori Efimovich was flattered by this multifarious attention devoted to his person. Not only did this horde of detectives ensure his safety, it also made him more conscious of his own significance and importance. A self-satisfied smirk passed over his lips whenever he thought how sincerely concerned all Russia was over his life, and what large sums of money were regularly expended to protect him.

Of course, the other side of this surveillance was not hidden from his sound peasant mind, and he was well aware that he was not only protected, but also a prisoner, and could hardly take any step without the important Government offices and personages in the whole of St. Petersburg knowing all about it next day.

But this twofold activity of the police officials who, on the one hand, watched over his safety, and on the other hand, spied on him, in the latter case always trying to get the better of each other, no longer troubled Rasputin, and did not even cause him to impose any particular restraint on himself before them. He showed himself to them exactly as he was, and displayed the undisturbed, frank candour which had won him the confidence of his sovereigns, the hate and fear of his enemies, and the devoted love of his women worshippers. He had no objection to all the gentlemen and ladies of the Court, the ministers, superintendents of police, and bank directors knowing exactly how often he came home drunk in a week, or when a fine lady or a little sewing-woman spent the night with him.

His friends at police headquarters and in the ministries often retailed to him the agents' reports, without his showing any particular interest; but frequently, if he found that they had given unnecessary details or misunderstood things, he would get rather angry, take the spy in question to task, and abuse him with a few strong peasant oaths and, in the end, ask him in a conciliatory tone to refrain from such reports in future.

The detectives, with their mechanical devotion to duty, gave full details of such reprimands:

"14th January. At 4.30 p. m. Rasputin drove to Tsarskoe Selo with Rubinstein, the banker, and two ladies. To the agent who accompanied them he remarked in a displeased tone: 'One of you reported to your superiors that I took a lady on my knee. It is not proper for you to report things like that. It is your duty to protect me, not to spread gossip of that kind about me.'"

But apart from such little misunderstandings Rasputin was

on very friendly terms with the men who watched over him. Often, it is true, he took a childish pleasure in evading their surveillance; he would slip quietly out of his flat with a sly smile on his lips, hurry down the back stairs with great strides at a moment when they were unguarded, and throw himself into a passing droshky. When he succeeded in playing this trick he would, on his return, chaff the detective he had fooled and tell him all sorts of hair-raising tales about where he had been, what misdeeds he had been guilty of, and what important business he had dispatched, without their knowing anything at all about it. "What would the ladies at Court," he would cry with good-humoured mockery, "the worthy ministers and bank directors, not give to discover where I have been to-day and what I have done."

Occasionally, however, he took pity on the everlasting, devouring curiosity of his spies, and of his own free will gave them a true account of what they had failed to learn. In the course of time he came to feel sincere confidence in Major-General Globichev's agents in particular; they were allowed to accompany him to church or to the baths in the morning and, on the way, he often discussed very important political or private affairs with them. He was pleased with the devotion they displayed, for he felt with sure instinct that they were not only doing their duty in trying to win his confidence, but that they also found real and sincere pleasure in his society. These poor, badly paid little officials were often royally entertained by Rasputin's conversation, when he cracked his strange and often coarse jokes, or retailed to them the gossip of the Court and high society.

Of course, this personal attachment did not prevent the spies from reporting matters which he had expressly asked them to suppress. They promised to respect his wishes; and they reported not only the things that were to be concealed, but also the fact that Rasputin had asked them to be discreet. But, in spite of everything, they were very friendly to each other: the detectives liked their Grigori Efimovich and Grigori Efimovich liked his detectives, his special favourites being Terekhov, Svistunov, Popov, and Ivanov.

* * * * *

STAIRCASE NOTES

While, at the beginning, Rasputin had talked to the detectives only on the way to church or to the baths or in chance encounters, but kept his flat closed against their prying eyes, he later felt such confidence in them that he sometimes even admitted them to his rooms. This fact acquired very great importance on the occasion of his name-day in 1916: Colonel Komisarov had strictly enjoined on his agents that they must gain admittance into the flat whatever happened, and make a detailed report of everything that took place. For police headquarters expected that presents would arrive from the "highest personages," and hoped to be able to draw certain inferences from this fact.

Very early in the morning of the great day the detectives were already pacing anxiously up and down the hall, racking their brains to find a means of getting into the flat. After some time, Rasputin appeared on the staircase with his little niece Aniushka. He was in good humour, suffered the company of a number of detectives on the way to early mass, and talked to them in the friendliest possible fashion. On arriving at Rasputin's door after the service, the detectives officiously set about helping little Aniushka off with her coat, Rasputin looking on indulgently. In this way several of them, to the keen envy of their colleagues, stepped over the threshold into the hall.

Rasputin was absolutely overwhelmed with pleasant messages that forenoon. Hardly had he entered when his family, beaming with joy, rushed up to show him the beautiful and costly presents that had arrived in his absence. Immediately after, the telephone bell rang: it was Anna Vyrubova to wish her "revered Father" every happiness and say that she was coming to see him immediately. Almost at the same moment a telegraph messenger brought a telegram of warmest congratulations from the Emperor and Empress.

All these joyful greetings coming together made Rasputin uncommonly happy and pleased. His eyes shone, for he felt himself to be more loved and honoured than ever. He turned to the agents with a friendly smile, and invited them to drink a glass of Madeira to his health, stay for a little, make themselves at home, and enjoy themselves with him.

The detectives required no second invitation. They drank

Rasputin's wine with respectful gratitude, and admired his presents; nor did they fail surreptitiously to write down as exact a description of them as possible in their notebooks. There were all sorts of objects made of gold and silver, carpets, table cutlery and silver, jewellery for Rasputin's wife and daughters, beautiful furniture, pictures, wines, cakes, and other delicacies; each gift was accompanied by the card of the donor. With mild astonishment the police saw the cards of their own superiors, Colonel Komisarov, General Globichev, various ministers and other high dignitaries, alongside those of distinguished ladies, actresses, bankers, diplomats, and financiers.

Pencils became feverishly active, even more so when a great number of visitors arrived, and the festive breakfast began. Speeches were made in which the importance of Rasputin for the welfare of Russia was extolled in the highest terms; Rasputin himself beamed with contentment and drank to every new arrival, until finally, towards evening, he collapsed, exhausted by his great strain. However, after a few hours' rest, he continued the festivities on a more intimate scale, until at last not a single one of the participators in the party was sober.

The police spies had been drawn into the universal transports and, encouraged by Rasputin, had diligently applied themselves to the wine. Soon, however, they had to resume their official duties, this time not as spies on, but as protectors of, Rasputin. Towards morning two men forced their way into the house with revolvers drawn and declared that their wives were spending the night with the starets, and that they had come to avenge this dishonour. The agents had to rush to warn Rasputin and the two ladies, detain the intruders for a little, get the ladies safely down the back stairs, and then prove to the furious husbands that Rasputin was alone in his rooms.

But such special occasions were not always necessary to secure the detectives admittance to Rasputin's rooms. Often it happened merely because Grigori Efimovich was bored. Then he himself would invite the agents to keep him company, and would converse with them on every possible topic, even on matters of supreme political importance.

One of these conversations was so momentous that the chief

of police, on reading the report of it, became rigid with amazement, and, when he had recovered somewhat from his bewilderment, rushed off to inform the Minister.

Rasputin had returned home drunk in the early morning, staggered into his flat, and tried to sleep off his debauch. But he had a violent headache and could not sleep, so he came out into the hall again, and invited the detectives to have tea with him. Agreeably surprised, they followed him and took their places round the steaming samovar. For a time Rasputin sat silent and meditative, resting his head, heavy with wine, on his hand. At last one of the detectives said: "Grigori Efimovich, why are you so melancholy? What are you thinking about?"

"They have told me," answered Rasputin, staring uneasily in front of him, "that I must consider what is to happen about the Imperial Duma. I don't know what to do. What do you think?"

The agent to whom Rasputin addressed this unexpected question replied evasively: "I have no right to think, Grigori Efimovich, I might very easily get myself into trouble with my superior officers."

Rasputin ruminated for a few minutes longer, then turned suddenly to the spy and growled: "Do you know what? I shall send the Tsar to the Duma, to open it in person. If he goes and addresses the deputies himself, they will not dare to make bad speeches."

The arrival of this report at police headquarters acted like a bomb, for it coincided with the announcement of the amazing decision of the Tsar, in defiance of all custom, to open the Duma in person. The plan the starets had conceived under the influence of a headache after a night's carousal had caused the sovereign to take a step of supreme political importance.

But it was only very occasionally, of course, that the detectives' reports were as important as this. Generally, they were confined to trifling statements about when Grigori Efimovich rose, who visited him, when he left the house, and in what state he returned in the early morning, drunk or sober, accompanied by women or alone.

Under date of December 24th the detectives noted: "About 7 p.m. Ossipenko, the secretary of the Metropolitan Pitirim, called on Rasputin; about an hour later came princess Shakhovskaia, Alexandra von Pistolkors, and an unknown officer in a car, in which they all went off together. At eight a car stopped before Rasputin's house with the Countess Olga Kreuz and the daughter of State Councillor Golovin. Golovina went up to Rasputin's flat and immediately came down again accompanied by the peasant woman, Laptinskaia; whereupon they all drove off to the Alexander-Nevski Convent."

"7th February. Vyrubova came in a Court motor-car, and went off with Rasputin's secretary."

Not infrequently big parties in motor-cars drew up before the house in the Gorokhovaia to take Rasputin to a banquet at the Villa Rode, at Donon's or the gipsies', or in a private house. On these occasions Grigori generally came gaily through the hall with his boon companions, while the secret agents, silently pressed against the wall, carefully noted down the names of all those taking part in the outing.

As soon as the company had left the house the spies rushed to the door and signalled to the car stationed inconspicuously at the opposite corner of the street, the driver of which was in the service of the police. This taxi came along as if by chance towards the company as they strolled down the street, and nothing was more natural than for Rasputin and his friends to take the car which had come up so opportunely.

Meanwhile a second car had pulled up at number 64; a few detectives quickly sprang into it, and it proceeded to follow Rasputin's car at some distance. As soon as Rasputin and his friends alighted and entered a house, the agents usually succeeded in getting in touch quickly with the concierge of the building. In restaurants and other public places waiters or gipsies were sounded and induced by money and fair words to leave the room quietly from time to time, and give the spies an exact account of what was happening inside, who was with Rasputin, what was eaten and drunk, and the subjects of conversation.

Under date of December 14th we find this note:

"On the night of 13th to 14th December Rasputin, accompanied by the twenty-eight year old wife of the hereditary honorary burgess, Yazininski, left 11 Fuhrstadt Street about 2 a. m., in a car for the restaurant 'Villa Rode' in Novaia Derevna. He was refused admittance on account of the lateness of the hour; but he began to hammer on the doors and wrenched the bell off. He gave five roubles to the police officer on guard, not to annoy him. Then he went off with his companion to the Mazalski gipsy choir at Number 49 and remained there till 10 a. m. The pair, in a very tipsy state, then proceeded to Madame Yazininskaia's flat, from which Rasputin did not return home till midday. In the evening he drove to Tsarskoe Selo."

"17th December. Princess Dolgorukaia's car came for Rasputin to-day, and he proceeded to a private room in the Hotel Astoria. There he was immediately joined by General Kleigels, former governor of St. Petersburg, with whom Rasputin remained till 6 a. m."

"20th December. Rasputin, accompanied by Ossipenko, the secretary of the Metropolitan Pitirim, visited the honorary burgess, Knirsche, in Sand Street; later a gipsy choir and two hampers of wine were sent for from the 'Villa Rode.' About 2 a. m. Rasputin could be seen through the window dancing."

"5th January. Rasputin, Ossipenko, Dunia, the maidservant, and Müller went off in droshkies to Müller's flat, taking a hamper of wine with them."

"13th January. To-day Rasputin, accompanied by Ivanitskaia, an unknown officer, and two ladies, visited the widow of State Councillor Mitinski, at 14 Ligovskaia. At 5 o'clock he left with the officer and Madame Ivanitskaia, and returned to his own flat. Ivanitskaia was somewhat merry, put on Rasputin's coat, and later left with the officer, still wearing it. Rasputin then went off in a car sent by Popermann to the Hotel Europe, where a drinking party was taking place. The guests present were Popermann, Kovariski, a law student, Tatishev, the director of the International Bank, and two unknown ladies."

"21st January. Rasputin went to visit Knirsche in Sand Street with Maria Gar, one of his followers, and then proceeded alone to 36 Basseina, the house of the actress Lerma, the mistress of the Secretary of the Council of Ministers, Manuilov. Besides

Manuilov, Stürmer, the Prime Minister, was also present."

"29th January. This evening Rasputin was with Filipov at the Restaurant Donon."

"11th March. At 10.15 we noticed Rasputin on the Gorokhovaia and followed him to the house of a prostitute, the converted Jewess Gregubova; from there he went on to a bathing establishment."

"21st March. Rasputin drove with Nikolai Glazov to the big Nord Hotel to the courtesan Eugenia Terekhova, where he stayed for two hours."

"15th April. Rasputin, with his friend, the Abbot Martian from Tiumen, called on the honorary burgess, Pestrikov, at 45 Ligovskaia. As Pestrikov was not at home, he took part in a drinking party which Pestrikov's son was giving to some students. A musician struck up, and there was singing and Rasputin danced with a maidservant."

Sometimes, when the strange doorkeepers proved inaccessible, the secret agents' zeal for duty went so far that they climbed up the houses in which Rasputin was visiting, and tried to peer through the windows. There they sometimes saw very curious and mysterious happenings which they were unable to explain, as, for example:

"14th May. Yesterday at 5 p.m. Rasputin went to the house of Belkovski and Tsesareva, at 15 Little Arl Street. About 10 o'clock it was observed that the windows of the flat were not lit up; but the agents of the secret service were able to note that one of the women passed through a brightly lighted room and then looked into a dark one, in which some men were sitting. Later we saw Rasputin, evidently scenting danger, rush out of the room, seize his hat and stick, and run down to the street. A few paces behind him came two men, and we heard one of them say: 'There he is running.' Then the two men returned to the house again. Rasputin sprang into a passing taxi and drove, standing up all the way, to the Liteni Prospekt, looking round all the time to see if he were being followed."

* * * * *

The daily reports of the spies always close with a description of Rasputin's home-comings. When the chauffeur of the car that set him down in the early hours of the morning before the door of the house in the Gorokhovaia had given his report, the detectives followed Rasputin up the stairs to the door of his flat, partly to help him in his intoxicated state, and partly to hear what he had to say. The pencils moved for the last time that day, and the home-coming of the holy man was described in the notebooks:

"14th October. Rasputin came home drunk at 1 a. m., insulted the concierge's wife, and reproached her with taking a bribe of twenty-five roubles from a minister. Then he remarked: 'He tried to bury me, but now I will bury him.'"

"6th November. Rasputin was at Popermann's, the merchant from Samara's flat, and came back drunk five hours later, kissing Popermann when he said good-bye. As he went up to his flat he inquired if there were any visitors for him. On hearing that there were two ladies he asked: 'Are they pretty? Very pretty? That's good. I need pretty ones.' About 7 o'clock he left the house, and gave the concierge's wife ten roubles; he seemed to be dead with sleep."

"14th November. Rasputin came home in an intoxicated state with Tatiana Shakhovskaia, but left again immediately with her, and did not come back again till about 2 a. m., very drunk."

"23rd November. Rasputin came home at 5 a. m. blind drunk."

"3rd December. Rasputin came home drunk at 3 a. m."

"7th December. Rasputin came home early about 7 o'clock; he was pretty drunk."

"12th December. Rasputin came back with Varvarova at 9.50 a.m.; he must have spent the night with her."

"2nd January. Rasputin came home drunk at 1 a. m."

"8th January. Rasputin came home from a visit to Nordmann, the Secretary of the Chancellery of the Order, about 3 a.m., accompanied by three ladies. The ladies stayed with him for two hours."

"14th January. Rasputin came home at 7 a.m.; he was dead drunk. He had Ossipenko and an unknown man with him. He smashed a pane of glass in the house door; apparently he had had one fall already, for his nose was swollen."

"18th January. Rasputin came home at 7.30 a.m. with two men and a woman; he was dead drunk, and sang songs on the public street. The unknown persons accompanied him up to his flat and then departed."

"22nd January. Rasputin returned at 5 a.m. with Ossipenko, an unknown man, and a woman; he was dead drunk."

"26th May. Rasputin came home in the motor-car of the merchant Mandel with the prostitute Gregubova. He was blind drunk, kissed Gregubova passionately, and stroked her cheeks. After she had gone he sent the concierge's wife for Katia, the sempstress, who lives in the same house, but she was not at home."

In the course of time great bundles of records of this kind piled up on the desks of the Okhrana, the police, and the ministries. Reports continued to pour in steadily about when Rasputin rose, who visited him, in whose company he left the house, in what condition he came home, and what had been observed on the short passage between the house door and the door of the flat, on the way to the baths, to church, or to some strange house.

Police headquarters then endeavoured, with these reports, to reconstruct the form of this rich, many-coloured, and contradictory life; but, since the mysterious figure of Grigori Efimovich inevitably remained incomprehensible, not only to the perspicacity of the spies, but also to the brains of their chiefs, a most curious silhouette, built up on minute but always futile observations, was thus created.

And yet, in spite of all its deficiencies, the picture, imperfect, distorted, and unreal, that emerges from the reports of the police agents, is the only authentic portrait of the starets in existence.

The collection of the police reports on Rasputin therefore became a great treasure, and was passed from hand to hand: ministers, grand dukes, princesses, foreign ambassadors, stockbrokers, and Court officials applied for it, and thought themselves lucky to be able to study these "staircase notes" for a day or two.

CHAPTER IX

FATHER GRIGORI RECEIVES

RASPUTIN usually got up at six o'clock in the morning and went straightway to early mass at Afonskoe Podvorie. He returned with a crowd of his followers, who accompanied him into the dining-room. There breakfast was ready and he drank tea with the wholemeal rusks of which he was particularly fond. In addition to these regular guests whom Rasputin brought back from morning service, petitioners of various kinds used to arrive about 8 o'clock.

The best time to find Rasputin was about ten o'clock in the morning. However boisterous the previous night might have been, and however urgent the visits he had to pay in the forenoon, he was nearly always in his flat at about ten o'clock, awaiting the daily call from Tsarskoe Selo.

If the telephone bell rang at this hour Dunia, the maid, a distant relative of the starets, at once hurried to the telephone, cried: "This is number 646/46," and asked rather crossly who was speaking; but, on hearing that it was Tsarskoe Selo, she answered in a much more polite and obliging tone that she would call Grigori Efimovich immediately. She then shouted through the door of Rasputin's business room: "Anna Alexandrovna on the telephone."

Rasputin hurried up and his brief replies could be heard: "What do you say? Why, what's the matter, my dear soul? I have people with me, but there! I will come."

His mood for the rest of the morning depended very largely on the nature of his conversation with Anna Vyrubova. Moreover, this "ten o'clock talk" was also an important moment for the guests waiting in the ante-room. Almost as soon as ten o'clock struck Colonel Komisarov, Prince Andronnikov, Rubinstein the banker, the confidential agent of Burdukov, the Master of the

Imperial Horse, and a whole crowd of politicians and wire-pullers were in the habit, one after another, of calling on the starets, all in the hope of catching some indiscreet reference to the conversation with Tsarskoe Selo.

These "ten o'clock visitors" usually stayed only a few minutes, just long enough to learn what they considered necessary; then they took leave, rushed down the stairs, and threw themselves into their cars, in order to give their various partners the quickest possible information about the subject of their conversation with Grigori Efimovich.

At the same hour the ante-room was already full of petitioners and visitors, who took their places on the little benches or gaily upholstered chairs. They waited patiently, often hours at a time, for an audience with the starets. Often the stream of visitors flowed into Rasputin's ante-room from 8 o'clock in the morning till late in the evening. There were days on which callers were so numerous that many had to wait on the staircase for their turn; on holidays the crowd was particularly large. Rasputin's daughter relates that on such days the whole street was often full of people. Cars and carriages stood everywhere, and visitors of the poorer classes flocked in long queues. On such days the other people living in the house counted several hundred visitors.

The universally known fact that Rasputin was in high favour at Court, and that, in consequence, he exercised great influence on the supreme dignitaries of Church and State, made him seem "all-powerful" in the eyes of numerous officials, officers, adventurers, brokers, and politicians, as well as of all who were at odds with the secular or clerical authorities. People told each other far and wide that Rasputin's sovereignty over Russia was more far-reaching than that of the Tsar himself, since only Rasputin was able to enforce his will. Many people gave him the title of "Tsar above the Tsars," to which, in accordance with the usage of the peasants, only very great and holy personages are entitled.

Not only did Rasputin enjoy the reputation of possessing unlimited power, he was also regarded as a holy man who had extraordinary mystic faculties. Wonderful tales were told of how the starets could look into every man's soul, foresee the future, and heal the sick by a glance of his eyes or a touch of his hands.

People said that they knew of many such cases, in which Rasputin, like Christ, had performed miracles. Not only did the peasants, men and women, who had followed the starets to the capital, firmly believe in his divinity; wide circles in St. Petersburg society had also become accustomed to regarding this clumsy, simple peasant from Pokrovskoe as the newly arisen Lord. For many mystically inclined people in St. Petersburg had turned to the doctrines of the Khlysty several decades earlier, and from time to time, with the greatest secrecy, quiet communities, the so-called "ships," of a purely sectarian character, had been formed in the most distinguished society of the capital. So the ground was well prepared for Rasputin's appearance as a new saviour. His fame had, of course, spread surreptitiously, for secrecy is one of the articles of faith of the Khlysty sect; but this mysteriousness had further enhanced the prestige and importance of the wonderful man. Men and women of all ages and classes, princesses as well as their maidservants, went to Father Grigori, and thrilled in expectation of the solemn moment when they would be allowed to kneel and beg for the blessing of God who had once again become man.

* * * * *

With the same rapidity with which the report of Rasputin's divinity had spread, another secret also passed from mouth to mouth, till everyone interested knew of it, the secret that Rasputin was prepared to carry out various transactions, arrange releases from military service, get sentences of imprisonment quashed, or dispose of the granting of concessions; and the exact sum of money or the quality and price of the presents in return for which the help of the starets could be purchased was also known.

And, while it was being whispered in prosperous circles that Rasputin was open to bribes, the poorer classes quietly spread the consoling rumour that, although Grigori Efimovich did take presents for his services, he by no means made such gifts a necessary condition of his assistance. If, after submitting their petition, well-to-do peasants, rich widows, successful financiers, or persons anxious for ministerial rank put money on the table, Rasputin, without scruple or embarrassment, stuffed it into the wide pockets of his velvet breeches; but he was just as obliging, kind, and ready to help if a petitioner came to him with empty hands and empty pockets. Perhaps he showed even more kindness and benevolence to the poor than to the rich; at any rate, the way in which he received their gifts seemed to prove that he set more store by a trifling gift from a poor man than by a great present from a wealthy one. When a successful speculator handed him over a sum of money, no matter how large, Grigori Efimovich hardly thanked him, and treated him with haughty arrogance, or even with marked insolence; on the other hand, he would accept with demonstrative pleasure the gifts of those simple people who, though often feeling the pinch of need, would show their gratitude to him by some trifle, a bottle of wine, a cheese, or an image of the Holy Mother of God. On such occasions he would frequently summon Dunia, his secretary Simanovich, or his daughter Matriona, and say to them: "Look what a splendid present this dear fellow has given me! Truly a noble giver!" Rasputin, with delicate natural tact, knew how to treat the poorest of the poor so that they left him feeling that their gifts had absolutely delighted the holy father.

But not only did the starets willingly use his influence on behalf of poor people without asking anything in return; he had also to receive every day a crowd of petitioners who expected gifts of money from him. This expectation was seldom disappointed. Grigori Efimovich gave readily, quickly, and generously, without requiring to be told a long and pitiful tale of misfortune. He had scarcely received a bundle of banknotes for negotiating a concession or securing a release from military service, and stuffed them carelessly in his pocket without counting them, than he pulled them out again and gave them to poor petitioners; a mother who wanted to visit a sick son in a distant province, but had not the necessary money, a father who was too poor to send his children to school, a sick person who needed money for the doctor. Not infrequently Rasputin, in the course of the day, gave away all the money he had got from his rich business friends in the morning—in contrast to those high dignitaries of the Empire who were wont to be indignant at Rasputin's venality, but themselves extorted money, without ever giving a kopek away again for disinterested objects.

The sums that flowed steadily into Rasputin's pockets were of course large enough to leave plenty over for himself, although his assistants and his business friends consistently robbed and deceived him. For, in spite of his peasant shrewdness, Grigori Efimovich was essentially a naïve and trusting person, and did not like to calculate. What was left from his daily incomings, after deduction for losses through theft and charity, he used for his own needs or put in the drawer of his writing table, where he was gradually accumulating a dowry for his daughter Matriona. The son of his friend Soloviev had asked for Matriona's hand, and the starets prided himself on making the best possible financial provision for the future of the young couple.

He himself could not manage money, and spent it as easily as he got it; he complained more than once that he had "hands like sieves." But, on the whole, he spent very little on himself and his family: his flat was simple, and furnished with no special luxury; he ate and drank profusely, it is true, but this was mostly covered by presents from friends, especially from his women adorers. His wife and children never gave up their simple peasant life, although they, too, frequently received gifts.

Under these circumstances the bundle of banknotes in the drawer of the writing table kept on growing, and Rasputin himself took a childish pleasure in this. With simple pride he used to show his visitors how his daughter's dowry was growing bigger and bigger; on the very night he met his death he remarked how pleased he was that his future son-in-law would not be disappointed in the dowry.

Besides the one class of suppliants who came to Rasputin with gold and gifts, and the other who came to receive them, there was still a third group of visitors. These were the women and girls who came to beg for the protection and advocacy of the starets to ensure the welfare, the career, or the business interests of someone closely connected with them, and who offered in return not gold, but their charming smiles, their glances which promised so much, and their moist lips. Every one of these women had heard that no gift, however costly, could dispose the starets to help so readily as feminine charm. If he liked the smile or the passionate and seductive pose of a suppliant who offered herself as a gift, he always accepted this gift with joy and happiness, and spared no pains to carry out the wishes of his petitioners. In such cases he set in movement the highest authorities, ministers, and even the Tsar and Tsaritsa in person, although his protégée might be only a peasant or a simple servant girl.

But there were also women who called on Rasputin to ask him to do something, and who resisted his covetous glances, either because their love was already given to another man and they wished to keep themselves pure for him, or else because they found nothing attractive about this elderly, dirty peasant with his unkempt beard and his filthy finger-nails. Then Grigori Efimovich would give vent to his disappointment and wrath and sometimes be violent and rude; but he immediately became the good holy father again, and used all his influence and connections for these women too. For love, like every other gift, was very welcome to Rasputin, but it was not made a condition of his assistance.

Actually it seldom happened that such suppliants met Rasputin's advances with a refusal. Many of them even proudly boasted that the holy man had honoured them with his love. For at this time it was the supreme object of the desirous, but at the same time reverent, longing of many women and girls of all classes of society in St. Petersburg and the provinces to be admitted into the mysterious "holy of holies," as the starets' most intimate circle was called. On one occasion, when a novice refused to accede to Rasputin's desires, one of his most enthusiastic disciples, a married woman, asked her in amazement: "Why do you not want to belong to him? How can one refuse anything to a saint?"

The young lady replied indignantly: "Does a saint need sinful love? What sort of saintliness is that?"

"He makes everything that comes near him holy," was the reply of his disciple.

"And would you be ready to accede to his desires?"

"Of course. I have already belonged to him, and I am proud and happy to have done so."

"But you are married! What does your husband say to it?"

"He considers it a very great honour. If Rasputin desires a

woman we all think it a blessing and a distinction, our husbands as well as ourselves."

Women found in Grigori Efimovich the fulfilment of two desires which had hitherto seemed irreconcilable, religious salvation and the satisfaction of carnal appetites. The old Orthodox priest of their parish had promised them the fulfilment of their yearning for purity and spiritual peace, on condition that they led a stainless, pure, and virtuous life here below; but this demand was in terrible antagonism with the desires of their sinful bodies and ardent lips. The way to God required renunciation of sensual joy; the way of sensual joy, on the other hand, led away from God.

Then Father Grigori appeared, and to all the women, tormented by the painful dissension between soul and body, preached his new doctrine that sin was not the way to damnation, but rather the quickest and surest way to salvation; and the discord between soul and body, between religious and sensual release, was thus resolved. As in the eyes of his disciples Rasputin was a reincarnation of the Lord, intercourse with him, in particular, could not possibly be a sin; and these women found for the first time in their lives a pure happiness, untroubled by the gnawings of conscience, in the arms of Rasputin, the "holy satyr."

* * * * *

Many of Rasputin's women petitioners showed by their hesitating manner, as soon as they came in, and their shy, nervous attitude as they waited, that this was their first appearance, while others entered with the unembarrassed assurance of daily visitors. The very way in which the maid received them made this division into groups quite clear. Only those women visitors whom Dunia knew the starets would admit to his private rooms, were permitted to take off their coats in the ante-room. Anyone who had crossed the threshold of the dining-room or the bedroom was, in Dunia's eyes, a member of Grigori Efimovich's intimate circle, and, as such, enjoyed various little privileges; their outdoor clothes, for example, had a regular place reserved for them on the pegs.

The members of the "most intimate circle" did not have to

pass through the general waiting-room at all when they called on Rasputin. They could come and go by the back staircase, the way to which led through the narrow little kitchen, which was always blocked up with boxes and hampers. Those waiting in the ante-room only caught sight of these disciples when one of them came out of one door and disappeared through another, or when one stopped a moment in the ante-room to look for somebody.

These mysterious appearances of Rasputin's most intimate female followers afforded the other women, as they waited in the ante-room, food for all sorts of wonderful imaginings. To them, the women who enjoyed the exalted right of admittance to the "Holy of Holies" were beings set apart, and the strangest stories were whispered about them.

Chief of them was the faithful, indefatigable servant of Rasputin, the nun, Akulina Nikichkina, a quiet, amiable woman in the garb of a nursing sister. She was of robust, somewhat coarse build, had simple, peasant features which were, however, almost beautiful in their homely regularity, and a clear, intelligent, and steady gaze. Among Rasputin's immediate circle she was known as "the holy one" on account of her serenity, in which not the slightest trace of passion remained. If she came out of the inner rooms for a moment the conversation of the gossiping women in the ante-room was silenced, and all looked at her in reverent amazement. For it was well known that, of all Rasputin's followers, she was most faithfully devoted to him, had followed him everywhere, and blindly obeyed all his wishes. Nothing, not even the increasingly dissolute life of the starets, could shake her faith in him and his divinity.

Akulina had led a peaceful life of contemplation with her fellow nuns in the convent of Saint Tikhon in Okhtoi, deep in the forests of the Urals, until, shortly after she had taken her vows, she was attacked by a strange and terrible disease. During her fervent prayers before the image of the Saviour in her cell she had become subject to a feverish ecstasy followed by severe convulsions, and these attacks occurred at ever shorter intervals. Soon the other nuns when they met whispered to each other with trembling horror the sad certainty that the devil had entered into poor Sister Akulina.

One evening, just as Akulina, after praying before the image of the Saviour, had again fallen into convulsions and tremors, a strange pilgrim knocked at the gate of the convent. Grigori Efimovich, then a wanderer in the Urals, entered and asked for a night's lodging. As soon as he heard the wild shrieking of the nun and learned from the other sisters that Akulina was possessed by the devil, he asked to be taken to her cell, and remained there alone with her for a considerable time, in an endeavour to drive the Evil One out of her by special prayers and spiritual exercises.

When, with pale face and shining eyes, he left the cell again, he was able to tell the anxiously waiting nuns that God had aided him in his struggle, and allowed him to banish Satan for ever from Akulina's body. Soon after the young nun also came out of the cell, released and well again, her eyes beaming with happiness.

This, the first miracle wrought by the saintly Father Grigori, the re-arisen saviour from Pokrovskoe, was reverently noted in the annals of the Okhtoi convent; and Sister Akulina, with the consent of her Superior, devoted herself for the rest of her existence to the one august task of consecrating her life to the man who had saved her, and spreading the fame of his holiness throughout the world.

All the visitors knew the nun and almost all loved her, for she not infrequently received petitions and did various errands for the starets. Her pretty soprano voice was often heard singing the song "Strannik" at the common table of the women disciples, with Rasputin's pleasant voice in accompaniment. Her singing was sympathetic but melancholy, especially when, at the end of the folksong, she began to sing hymns.

Another lady in the circle was Olga Vladimirovna Lokhtina, the wife of State Councillor Lokhtin. She had had a terrible adventure with the truculent monk Iliodor, who tried to seduce her when she was visiting the monastery at Tsarytsin, and, failing in his design, declared to his numerous admirers that an evil spirit had entered into Madame Lokhtina. The overwrought disciples of Iliodor rushed at the poor woman, tore the clothes off her back, and bound her feet to a cart, which immediately went off at a gallop. Some peasants hastened up and released her at the last moment; but she suffered a severe nervous shock, which led to mental derangement.

She made Rasputin's acquaintance through old Madame Golovina, and he tried to cure her, and, for a time, seemed to have succeeded. But soon her madness took another form, religious worship of the starets himself. If she met Grigori Efimovich she fell on her knees before him, and proclaimed him her Christ and Saviour. She was imbued with the belief that Rasputin was the reincarnate God, and tried to convince everybody that his every touch was sanctifying. Moreover, she boasted that she had shared Rasputin's love, and told everyone of her happiness: "What a saint does is holy, what he touches is blessed, what he loves attains the holiness of Heaven. Believe me, my sisters, the body of anyone who surrenders herself to this God becomes itself divine by contact with him."

She would often cross her hands and bow her head and, if anyone talked loudly, she looked at her in displeasure and said: "In Father Rasputin's house it is as if one were in Church. Peace must reign here."

Olga Vladimirovna had been a faithful child of the Orthodox Church; but, in consequence of her fanatical worship of Rasputin, the priesthood had damned her as a heretic and an apostate. But all the wrongs she had to suffer for her faith in Father Grigori could not shake her confidence in the slightest. She revered him as divine, and herself led the life of a martyr, sleeping on bare boards with a block of wood for a pillow.

An elderly lady accompanied by a charming young girl was also frequently to be seen in Rasputin's waiting-room: in the dim eyes of the mother, as in the daughter's dreamy gaze, lay an expression of heartfelt, absolute devotion. Madame Golovina, the widow of State Councillor Golovin, like her simply dressed, fair-haired daughter Maria, was one of Rasputin's closest and most devoted followers. They were relations of Anna Vyrubova, and Munia, the pet name of the daughter, was the avowed favourite of the starets. She had idolized a young aristocrat and, when he died, had fallen into a state of melancholy. A chance meeting with Grigori Efimovich convinced the young girl that this man had been sent by God to comfort her, and from that time forward she devoted her whole life to his service and soon fell entirely under his influence. Whenever she saw him her whole body began to tremble, her cheeks flushed, and her eyes glittered strangely. The mother shared this boundless faith in the holiness of Rasputin, and nearly always accompanied her daughter to his house.

Another frequent visitor was the wife of a colonel, an opera singer with a beautiful voice. Her husband knew of her relations with the starets, but made no objection, being convinced that intercourse with the holy man could only be of benefit to his wife. The singer often rang up Rasputin, and sang him one of his favourite songs through the telephone. On such an occasion Grigori called his women friends together, let them listen in turns, and asked the singer to sing the gipsy ballad "Troika" or the song "Barinia." Sometimes he even danced holding the ear-piece.

Among the women of Rasputin's regular circle, besides those whom he had cured of sickness or comforted in some deep grief, were also to be found others who were devoured by restless sensual passion, and who sought release from their sinful lusts. Had not Grigori Efimovich overcome sin through the "mysterious death" and reached the "supreme passionlessness of a saint"? He himself had frequently said to his disciples: "God has granted me freedom from passion; I touch a woman, and it is as if I touched a bit of wood. I have no desires, and the spirit of passionless calm passes from me to the women with me, so that they, too, become pure and holy."

To these followers of Rasputin belonged particularly a tall young girl called Masha, wearing the uniform of a high-school pupil, who attracted general attention as she passed through the waiting-room on account of her unusual bearing and her strange, repulsive face. It was angular and almost as white as chalk, with a blunt chin like an animal's, a low, protruding forehead, and grey, sullen eyes. She wore her dull, colourless hair coiled in heavy ringlets, and a tuft was always falling over her eyes, causing her to shake her head impatiently: with an almost animal movement of her pointed tongue she would lick the thick, bright red lips of her half-opened mouth, and then disappear, yawning widely, through the nearest door. Vishniakova, the nurse of the Tsesarevich, was a more sympathetic figure; she was also one of Rasputin's intimate friends, and had submitted herself to the starets in the conviction that by so doing she would drive the devil of sensuality from her body. The same impulse moved two society ladies, Princess Dolgorukaia and Princess Shakhovskaia, the latter a woman with magnificent dark eyes, in the uniform of a sister of charity; both had left their homes and children for the sake of Rasputin.

Even Rasputin's own family, his wife and daughters, were convinced of his power to banish the devil of sensual desire. Praskovia Fedorovna bore her husband's infidelities calmly, patiently, and unreproachfully, for in her simple mind Grigori Efimovich had been entrusted by God with a higher mission, and his debaucheries, therefore, served a holy purpose. She felt profound reverence for him, and served him like a faithful and devoted servant. His two daughters, Matriona and Varia, were also united to their father by reverence and admiration, and firmly believed in his divine mission. Matriona, the elder, in particular, zealously spread the fame of the starets, and very often took part in the meetings of the women in Rasputin's dining-room. In her diary may be found notes belonging to a later period which show her belief in, and love for, her father.

"For the first time," she writes, in 1918, "I again felt the near presence of my dear father, who has been dead for over a year now. We can no longer hear his words from his own mouth, but we feel distinctly that he is with us. I myself have seen him in a dream, and Olga Vladimirovna Lokhtina has similar visions. Yesterday she was talking of my father's teaching, and it was as if his own spirit were speaking from her mouth. Since then I love Olga Vladimirovna more than ever; she told me that she had been in the Gorokhovaia in St. Petersburg, visited the courtyard of my father's house, and felt his spirit living in her."

Besides his two daughters, Rasputin also possessed a son, Mitia; he was a somewhat childish lad, who laughed continually in a strange way, and blinked at everybody. Otherwise he was good-natured and infinitely attached to his father, who was also very fond of him just for his very deficiencies. The starets succeeded, during the war, in getting his son the post of orderly on the Empress's hospital train, thus removing him from the dangers of serving in the lines.

As a consequence of the great reverence in which Rasputin was held by his family, a cordial feeling of patriarchal harmony had long existed between him and them. They recognized but one task, to care for him and make his life as pleasant as possible, while he, too, was tenderly anxious about their welfare. Regard for his family was not the least of the motives that induced him to accept bribes and presents on every hand; if he was invited to a banquet he always came home with his pockets full, and presented his wife and daughters with all sorts of dainties, which afforded him particular pleasure.

Thus Rasputin was surrounded by a ring of people who did everything to serve and protect him, and, as far as possible, to relieve him of the cares and responsibilities of everyday life. At the same time his women disciples, distinguished princesses and Court ladies as well as simple peasant women, and the members of his family were also his zealous apostles who never tired of proclaiming his saintliness.

* * * * *

Rasputin, when not calling at Tsarskoe Selo or on the most powerful people in the Empire in St. Petersburg, or when not negotiating with financiers in his business room, spent most of his time among his women disciples in the big dining-room. Whenever he returned home his first steps always took him into this "Holy of Holies," where the women were already impatiently awaiting him. They gathered there for the whole day, sitting round the great flower-decked, richly spread table, talking about their wonderful experiences with Grigori Efimovich, and trying to interpret the hidden meaning of his sayings.

Even if he had been away for only half an hour, the same scene of enthusiastic welcome was invariably enacted when the door opened and he rejoined them; the women jumped up from their seats, hurried up to their "holy father," surrounded him, and caressed him, until he raised his right hand, palm outward, to his forehead, blessed each one of them, and pressed a fatherly kiss on her hair. They swooned with happiness and, overpowered by his blessing, staggered back to their chairs round the table.

Grigori Efimovich would then sink comfortably into the place reserved for him, reach out to the piled-up eatables, and, in the intervals, talk unctuously of God and salvation. His admirers were accustomed to his habit of suddenly jumping from edifying subjects to the latest naughty story from Prince Andronnikov's store. Munching contentedly, he would favour them with the gossip of high society in St. Petersburg, chat about that old imbecile Protopopov's relations with a nurse, tell them the latest news from headquarters, and suddenly plunge into the high political secrets of Tsarskoe Selo. Often the face of a boy would appear at the door, laughing queerly and winking at the assembly. If a new member of the circle took fright, and asked who it was, Rasputin replied good-humouredly: "That is my son Mitia. He is not quite all there. He thinks everything a joke and laughs all day long."

While the starets chatted on every conceivable subject, told funny stories, and, in the intervals, ate and drank steadily, he would call one or another of his disciples, take her head in his lap, tease and caress her, and then suddenly begin preaching again in an unctuous tone.

The enraptured women at this curious Round Table reached out when he reached out, ate when he ate, and sipped their wine whenever he raised a brimming glass to his mouth. They listened with the same reverence to his talk of God and the way of salvation, and to the often extremely coarse stories told him by Andronnikov. To the members of the Round Table both his sermons on redemption and his gossip about the Court were equally manifestations of a sublime and blessed spirit.

The persons assembled in the waiting-room could only guess at what was happening in the "Holy of Holies" from the sounds that penetrated to them occasionally or from a fleeting glimpse through the door. But to the women who waited there, yearning for the appearance of the starets, the time did not seem long. They listened reverently to the noises from the adjoining room, and tried to discover what the holy man was talking about, what he was doing, and what sort of mood he was in. One or two of them had already, in a lucky hour, been admitted to the "Holy of Holies," and they related their experiences to the others. Sometimes, too, Dunia appeared in the ante-room, and had to give a detailed account of what was happening in the inner rooms. For although she played the part of servant in the ante-room, and helped the guests off with their furs, Dunia was held in great honour and regard by the women disciples. When she came in the ladies leapt from their chairs, offered her their seats, and were eager to be allowed to relieve her of her household work. So Dunia was able to listen to the talk of the starets at her leisure, and then go out, and, as a consolation and comfort to the crowd for their long, passive waiting, communicate to them one or another of Rasputin's utterances; for example, how the starets, as he was eating fish and cheese, had said to his disciples: "You believe that I pollute you; I do not pollute you, I rather purify you." Or else how he had emptied a glass of Madeira, taken a girl on his knees and softly stroked her hair, while he talked of the chastening power of contrition: "Only by humble repentance can we attain to redemption! Man must sin in order that he may have something to repent of. If God sends us a temptation, we must yield to it voluntarily and without resistance, so then we may afterwards do penance in utter contrition."

Then he let his head fall reflectively on the shoulder of the favoured pupil, and closed his eyes, only to raise himself again and begin to speak once more: "The first word of the Saviour was 'Repent.' How can we repent if we have not first sinned?"

Then Father Grigori had risen from his seat and gone into the adjoining business room, where the representative of Rubinstein, the banker, was waiting to see him on important business. His words had made a great impression on his faithful women worshippers; they sat round the table with heads bowed, absorbed in profound reflection.

On another occasion Rasputin, who had come straight home from a banquet, sat for some time in melancholy silence, and, at last, in a queerly changed voice, which had something distant and detached about it, declared that he had only five more years to spend among his faithful followers; after that he must leave them all, even his family, and retire into the deepest isolation. The disciples listened to this speech of their master, and they all felt very sad. They sat round the table, as if rapt, with white, troubled faces, until the countenance of the starets cleared, and his mouth again twitched in the slight smile they loved so much. He reached for the fish and the wine, and the women went on eating and drinking as before.

It was always a very happy moment for the waiting crowd in the ante-room when one of those living in the house opened the door of the "Holy of Holies" for a moment, and afforded them a glimpse into the mysterious room. They could at least see a small part of what was going on in the dining-room, and hear the voices of the disciples and even the talk of the starets himself, as he preached, told stories, or asked for wine. They stared through the door with curious eyes, and tried to take in as much of the picture as they could, one end of the great sideboard against the wall, a bit of the bronze lamp with its great glass shade, and under it the middle of the richly decked table with its load of food, on which they divined rather than saw baskets full of flowers, wine bottles, plates of fried fish, glasses of preserves, and tea. Near the window was a rocking-chair, and behind the table the clothes of some visitors could be discerned against the high back of the oak chair; in occasional lucky moments the starets himself could be glimpsed, or at least a bit of him, a sleeve, the hem of his kaftan, the toe of a boot, or his big hand swinging out in a broad gesture.

Unimportant though all this may have been, it was enough to send the excited and greedy imaginations of the waiting crowd on far flights. For long after the door was shut again everything that they had seen and heard was passionately discussed.

* * * * *

But discussion died before the excitement when the strong grip of Rasputin's hand pressed heavily on the handle, the door opened wide, and the powerful and patriarchal figure of the starets appeared in the doorway. The monotonous murmuring became silent, giving way to the clatter of chairs pushed back, and the rustling of people rising from their seats. The fine ladies put their hands quickly to their hats to tidy stray locks of hair, the peasant women pulled at their kerchiefs; the Government officials jumped up and smoothed down their frock coats; the leaders of peasant deputations unfolded their crackling petitions; the officers instinctively assumed a rigid attitude and rattled their spurs; the representatives of the banks opened their portfolios, and took out various documents; the messengers and servants held their letters ready in their outstretched hands. Women pushed through the crowd, fell on their knees before Rasputin, and crossed themselves again and again.

The starets stood motionless for a few seconds in the middle of the room. His rumpled clothes were witness of the fact that a girl had just been sitting on his knee; his lips were still moist with wine and kisses; his eyes had a strange, joyful light in them, and happy dimples played about his mouth.

A moment later these last traces of the banquet disappeared, and the waiting crowd saw before them Father Grigori, the all-powerful miracle-worker, the pious man of God. His lean frame was firmly planted in the heavy, high peasant boots, and he inspected all present, one by one, with a stern glance. The representative of Manus, the banker, had an urgent message to deliver and thought himself entitled to push up to the starets. But Rasputin turned from him with a haughty movement towards two girls in sailor suits, hardly more than children, who stood curtseying and crossing themselves shyly. Their cheeks had a dark flush as they made their petition in thin, childish voices; Grigori Efimovich bent down to them kindly.

"Well, well, my doves," he growled, when he understood what they wanted, "you need help in your education? Have you no one who could assist you—scarcely enough to eat—well, wait, just wait a moment."

Troubled and thoughtful, he gazed in front of him for a moment, gave the girl some rouble notes, and then called to Dunia to bring him writing materials. But suddenly he became impatient and turned to the bystanders, saying: "Have none of you a pen and a sheet of paper?"

Manus's representative seized the opportunity to get near him again, and offered him his receipt book and a pen. Then he tried once again in a rapid rush of words to give the great man his message. But the starets again ignored him, took the receipt book, turned his back on the messenger, and began to trace a name and address in clumsy characters on the back of a form: "Vladimir Nikolaevich Voeikov, Tsarskoe Selo." Beneath this he scratched a cross, and under that, the letters "Kh.V.", the sign for "Christ is risen," and then, with many pauses and breaks, wrote the following: "My dear and valued friend, do it for me. Grigori." He carefully folded the note, handed it to the two sisters, made the sign of the cross over their girlishly parted hair, gave them his hand to kiss, and then turned to an old careworn-looking peasant.

The peasant began to explain at length that he had come from the Saratov Government at the request of a peasant, Gavrila Shishkin by name, and begged the venerable Father Grigori Efimovich to use his influence with the Tsar in order to secure a pardon for Shishkin, who had been condemned to a term of imprisonment for fraud. Whereupon the old man untied the girdle of his shirt, drew from next his skin a large sheet of newspaper, unfolded it carefully, and took out two hundred and fifty roubles in notes. After a brief statement that Gavrila Shishkin would be very happy if the starets would accept this sum as a sign of his gratitude, the peasant handed the bundle of notes along with the petition to Rasputin who, after a rapid glance at them, slipped both into his trousers pocket.

"Go home in peace," said the starets kindly, "and tell Gavrila Shishkin that I will discuss his case with little Papa." Then he made the sign of the cross over the peasant, blessed him, and turned to Eugenia Terekhova, a society lady, who advanced with an ingratiating smile.

She, too, held in her gloved hands a beautifully written petition, asking that she be granted a contract for underclothing for the Ministry of War.

"*You* will do me this favour, won't *you*, Father Grigori?" she remarked roguishly.

"Yes, yes, my dear, I will do it." He stroked her breast, and smiled at her, while she kissed his hands, offered her beautiful brow for him to make the sign of the cross on, and took her leave with a radiant and triumphant look.

An officer in uniform, bald, with a gold pince-nez on his nose, stepped forward and announced himself as Sub-Lieutenant Maksakov; but before he had a chance of making his request, a civilian pushed him aside. The latter was shabbily dressed, and kept on turning a very worn and greasy hat in his hands; he interrupted the bald-headed officer, and began at once, in an excited voice and a mass of confused verbiage, to put an extremely complicated case to the starets. Occasionally he seemed to lose the thread completely and began the whole story over again. Finally only one fact emerged clearly from his talk, that he, a teacher in a village school, had been the victim of a grave injustice at the hands of his director, and that he wished Rasputin to give him a letter of introduction to the Minister of Education.

Grigori Efimovich wrinkled his brow and replied in a vexed tone: "I don't hold with this education! But there, for my part, very good, I will write the letter of introduction for *you*. Just wait a moment. . . ."

He turned to the bald-headed officer; he, however, asked for a private interview.

Rasputin threw a rapid glance towards the corner, where a pretty brunette, her eyes red with weeping, was leaning timidly against the wall; begged the officer to have patience for a moment, and turned to the strange lady.

She held a letter of introduction from a Moscow friend of Rasputin in her shaking hands, which were covered with common thread gloves; this letter stated that her name was Maria Alexeevna, and begged Grigori Efimovich to assist her in getting her husband's sentence of administrative banishment repealed.

The starets put a few friendly questions to the lady, took her hand in his, stroked it in a fatherly way, and said in a soothing tone that he would be able to arrange everything. Then he asked her to wait in the little room until he had disposed of all the other petitioners. He himself conducted her to the door of the room, opened it, and ushered her in. He came back immediately to the waiting-room and talked apart with the officer in a low voice. At this moment a messenger appeared with a magnificent basket of roses and a dozen silk shirts of various colours. Rasputin called Dunia and bade her take these gifts, a present from a lady of high degree, and put them away carefully.

At this point a man called Dolina pushed up to the starets and submitted to him a request that he use his influence to have Russian citizenship granted to a German merchant, who would show his gratitude liberally for the service. Rasputin gave a little nod of assent, and immediately bent down to an old woman in a coarse skin coat and a round hat, who complained that she was the widow of a poor official, was quite destitute, and did not know what to do. The starets at once put his hand in his wide trousers pocket, drew out the newspaper containing the two hundred and fifty roubles he had just received from the peasant Shishkin, and handed the whole bundle to the woman with a careless gesture. Then he made the sign of the cross over her and went on with his business.

But innumerable hands, seeking gifts, were stretched out towards him from all sides, the bony, rough hands of old men, little children's hands, toil-worn hands belonging to women workers and maidservants, the white, well-cared-for hands of beautiful women that told of better days.

Grigori Efimovich looked at these hands, and his gaze wandered up the arms of each in turn till it reached the eyes, in which he could read the misery of poverty, despairing entreaty, and little, timid hopes. His hand went again to his pocket, and searched distractedly for money in it; when he was sure that he had no more on him he whispered something to Dunia, who hurriedly disappeared behind the door of the study. A young man appeared at once with a sheaf of banknotes; Rasputin took the money from his hand and went from one petitioner to another, distributing considerable sums among them; then he made the sign of the cross over them and dismissed them.

Two men next addressed the starets, one of whom he had known for a long time: he was a certain Pogan, an agent, who lived on small commissions. Pogan introduced his companion as Mendel Neumann, an engineer, who desired a reprieve from his Majesty the Emperor from a sentence of eight months' imprisonment for a military offence. After a brief discussion in low tones of the material terms of Rasputin's intervention, he declared that he was willing to bring Mendel Neumann's petition personally to the notice of the Tsar.

At this moment the outer door opened and a tall, slim girl with beautiful dreamy eyes came in. When she saw the starets she flew up to him and kissed his hand. Some of the women present recognized the new visitor, and whispered excitedly to each other that she was the daughter of a grand duke. Rasputin greeted the beautiful newcomer with obvious pleasure, and clasped her in his arms, while she began to chatter gaily, telling him how well she had been since he had taught her to see the world with other eyes. "I have always said to *you*," remarked the starets in a dignified and cordial tone, "that everything depends on the way *you* look at the world. *You* have only to put faith in my words, and all will be well."

Meanwhile a little elderly man with sparse grey hair popped up and introduced himself as an attendant at one of the bathing establishments that Rasputin often frequented. Grigori Efimovich received the bath attendant very kindly, clapped him benevolently on the shoulder, and went straight off to the study to settle the business. A few minutes later, with a few friendly words, he handed him a letter of recommendation to the Prefect, which ran: "My dearest friend, please excuse me. Help the poor bath attendant. Grigori."

The women disciples belonging to the intimate circle had been looking on with interest at all these happenings from the door of the dining-room. They were heartily sorry for their holy starets, thus spending himself self-sacrificingly for the good of the people, and sparing himself no effort. Sometimes it actually happened that this endless business was too much for Rasputin's strength; he had to run into the dining-room for a few minutes, throw himself into a chair, and, wiping the sweat from his brow, complain how fatiguing this rush was. Then one of his disciples usually went anxiously up to him, kissed him, and expressed her willingness to deal with the petitioners for a while.

Meanwhile, the telephone rang almost unceasingly. Rasputin's niece was in charge of it; she made notes, answered questions, and sometimes called Sister Akulina, Anna Vyrubova, or Rasputin himself to the instrument. And the bell of the flat kept ringing, and new visitors and fresh messengers with presents continued to appear.

But again Grigori Efimovich took his place among the suppliants and listened to their complaints until Dunia came up to him and reminded him of Maria Alexeevna, the pretty woman waiting in the little room, whom he seemed to have forgotten completely in the rush of business. Smiling happily and slyly, he hurried into the little room to promise the poor woman his help in releasing her husband from Siberia.

* * * * *

Hardly had the starets left the ante-room than the solemn hush among the waiting crowds ceased, and the former noisy confusion of talk began again—chiefly about the little room where Grigori Efimovich was closeted with the shy Maria Alexeevna. All sorts of curious legends were afloat about the purpose of this room and what went on there. The women put their heads together and whispered to each other; many of them had a peculiar smile on their lips. They knew the secrets of the little room from their own experience on previous occasions, and could imagine what was happening to pretty, timid Maria Alexeevna at that moment. They recalled the day on which they had first found themselves alone there with the starets; and they discussed excitedly the modest furniture, the iron camp-bed with its fox-skin cover, a gift from Anna Vyrubova, the ikons adorned with ribbons and the lamps burning before them, the pictures of the Tsar and Tsaritsa, and the scriptural texts on the walls.

When Rasputin was closeted with a woman in his little room, no one, not even one of his intimates, was allowed to enter; only if a telephone call came from Tsarskoe Selo was Dunia permitted to knock softly at the door. For in this little room took place the "initiation" of the novices into the new doctrine of "redemption from sin," and here it was decided which of the women was to become a permanent member of the circle of "intimates."

Many a young girl had left this mysterious room with a happy, radiant face; but there were also many women who rushed out suddenly, with their dress disarranged and crumpled, weeping and deeply insulted, or trembling with fury, and raging and shrieking so that they had to be removed with the assistance of the detectives lurking on the staircase. Not every petitioner was able to understand and value properly the "holy rite of redemption through sin"; in many of them the "devil of pride" was too strong to let them take the "way of humiliation."

It had even happened that agitated women had gone to the police and complained that Rasputin had raped them. In such cases the Chief of Police, Beletski, would have a record made and copies sent to all official departments interested, and also to some privileged private persons. Those who received a record of this kind read it with a quiet smirk, and thought of that "damned holy man," Grigori Efimovich, with a mixture of comfortable prurience and sincere envy. Quite clearly, no one seriously thought of taking legal proceedings against the all-powerful starets on account of accusations of this kind.

All this was well known to the women who daily assembled in Rasputin's waiting-room. So, when a little later the timid Maria Alexeevna emerged from the little room looking more sad and frightened than before, many eyes examined her intently, in order to guess her fate from her appearance. A few minutes afterwards the starets also appeared in the ante-room again; his hair, untidy and rumpled, clung to his temples and, breathing heavily, he went up to a group of three peasants and received their complaints about the inhuman conduct of an estate-owner. Two nuns from Verkhoture begged and received his blessing; a stout gentleman, a banker from Kiev, accompanied by his servant, asked for a private interview; the messenger of Baron Ginsburg handed over a considerable sum of money, and got a receipt for it; the sculptor, Aronson, who was working on a bust of Rasputin, discussed his next sitting; and so Grigori Efimovich resumed the business of giving audience.

Then two very pretty ladies came in, both wearing elegant fur coats, one dark, the other fair with blue eyes. They were friends, and had arrived from Moscow about a week before, to claim the starets' assistance in their affairs. At their entry Rasputin's women housemates and disciples became agitated and hostile. For days the mysterious attitude of these two strangers had made them furious, because these pretty women, by their "devilish resistance," had occasionally upset the holy father completely. The poor starets had drunk and raved for nights together in order to forget the annoyance and vexation these "haughty devils" had caused him.

Sister Akulina, in particular, was in a boiling rage against these Moscow women who were abusing Rasputin's feelings in this frivolous way. Once, when the starets had remained out the whole night immediately after the arrival of the two ladies, Akulina next morning asked Lenochka Dianumova, one of them, whether he had spent the night with her; but Lenochka had furiously denied it. The idea that women existed who could refuse themselves to the holy father, outraged the disciples, especially Sister Akulina, as Rasputin obviously set great store by the attachment of these two ladies. In wonder, disgust, mockery, and contempt, Rasputin's women worshippers told each other that Lenochka Dianumova had visited the starets in Moscow to save her German mother from the threat of banishment from Kiev, and that he had immediately become passionately interested in her. At their first meeting he gave her the pet name of "Frantik" (Fop), and kissed her and, after he left Moscow, had sent her several affectionate telegrams.

Soon after this Lenochka appeared in St. Petersburg and had made the starets angry on her first visit by expressing a wish to bring a male acquaintance of her friend to the flat. Rasputin thought that Frantik had come from Moscow accompanied by a lover, whom she now wished to introduce to him.

"*You* are a fine one!" he shrieked in a fury. "*You* have brought your swain from Moscow with *you*. *You* could not bear to be parted from him! *You* come to beg me a favour and bring your swain with *you!* I will do nothing for you, you can go! I have enough women to love and fondle me in St. Petersburg. I do not need you."

Then he ran to the telephone and began to speak in a voice shaking with excitement: "Darling, are *you* free? I am coming to *you. You* are pleased? Yes? I'll be with *you* immediately."

He hung up the receiver, looked triumphantly at his two prudish visitors, and remarked angrily: "You see, I need no Moscow ladies. I like the St. Petersburg ones better!"

Nevertheless, next morning he rang up Lenochka Dianumova in the most friendly fashion, begged her pardon, and asked her to come and see him again very soon. Since then Frantik had been a frequent guest in the Gorokhovaia, and had brought with her her friend Lella, who needed Rasputin's help in a complicated family lawsuit. He had received the two ladies most amiably, and had asked both of them separately to come into his little room; but they had always contrived skilfully to evade his wishes.

The disciples got more and more nervous, feeling that the society of these haughty Moscow women could only bring the starets annoyance and disappointment. One or two of them had tried several times to warn him, and cure him of his strange passion; but he had vigorously forbidden any interference, and had once even refused an invitation to Tsarskoe Selo for the sake of these lovely ladies.

The two friends managed in a masterly style, by means of half-concessions, to hold out hopes and to put off the starets, without ever satisfying his real desires. Obviously, their aim was to secure his support but to refuse him the *quid pro quo*. Grigori Efimovich became more and more energetic, and had even sought out these "women possessed by the devil of pride" at night in their hotel. But in vain did he preach to them of human love and its blessing, and tell them that without love the soul is dark and God turns the light of his countenance from men; love is the commandment of the Lord, and must be obeyed like the other commandments, in order to avoid falling into the power of the devil.

Days and nights passed in this way, and still Rasputin did not succeed in reaching his goal. He paced up and down the dining-room in agitation, his eyes were angry, his face seemed distorted; he drank wine and carried on like a wild beast. When all his usual means of bending women to his will had failed, he finally called on Lenochka at one A. M., accompanied by the

Minister whose assistance she required. "Open the door, darling," he cried, "I have brought the Minister with me, and we can settle the whole business in a few minutes."

But the diabolical obstinacy of the Moscow ladies went to such lengths that they kept their door locked against Grigori Efimovich and the Minister, so that both had to retire with their purpose unaccomplished. To deaden his disappointment, the starets with his high-placed companion proceeded to a dance club, spent the night in the company of the gipsy girls, and did not get home till ten next morning, in time for the telephone conversation with Tsarskoe Selo.

That day, as he stood in the waiting-room dealing with the various suppliants, heavy-headed, weary after his night's debauch, and in a bad temper, the two Moscow ladies came in, gay and unembarrassed as if nothing had happened. The starets was seized by a fit of unbridled fury and excitement. He led the ladies through the ante-room to his little room, rushed into the dining-room, and came back at once with a bottle of wine in his hand. He was very pale and a dark fire burned in his eyes. Some of the disciples had hurried up to Lenochka and Lella, and almost implored them to abandon their resistance, and not to torment the holy father any longer. Rasputin poured the wine into tea-glasses and ordered all the company to drink. "I love these ladies from Moscow," he cried. "I love them, although they torment me. For their sakes I boozed all last night, for they have set my heart aflame!"

He returned to the ante-room, and found there two clerics with great golden crosses on their breasts. He addressed them à propos of nothing, and told them he had been gadding about all night. "I was with a beautiful gipsy girl, who kept singing the song 'I am going to my love.' What say *you* to that, Reverend?"

One of the two clerics dropped his eyes and said in a singing voice: "Holy Father, it was the angels of Heaven who sang to *you*."

Rasputin smiled: "I tell *you* it was a pretty young gipsy girl."

"No," replied the priest with an obsequious smile, "I am convinced it was angels from Paradise."

Rasputin turned on his heel with a smirk, and went up to an attractive young Polish woman, his intention being to take her into his little room. He caressed her casually, but immediately turned to the two Moscow ladies again; perceiving their coldness, he rushed madly into the dining-room, where he ramped about furiously. A violent crash was heard like china smashing. Dunia, terrified, hurried after him, while all the rest of the company hardly dared to breathe.

Grigori Efimovich reappeared, looking savage, as if he would have liked to destroy everything that crossed his path. Munia Golovina stood petrified, and gazed at her holy starets with an expression of extreme terror; she, like the other worshippers, seemed at that moment to fear Rasputin as she would have feared the wrath of God. At this critical moment the telephone bell rang, and Aniushka announced that the Tsaritsa requested Rasputin to come to see her. This gave a new turn to the situation: Princess Shakhovskaia said that Rasputin absolutely must have a little fresh air before going to Tsarskoe Selo, and she proposed a short sleigh ride.

"I will go if the Moscow ladies will come too," said Grigori Efimovich defiantly, like a spoilt child.

Lenochka and Lella agreed; Dunia hurried downstairs to order a sleigh, and a few minutes later the company set out. The starets in fur coat and beaver cap strode through the anteroom and nodded kindly to the petitioners still waiting: "Have a little patience, dear friends, I'll be back immediately; but I have to attend to an important matter."

And all the women, officers, clerics, peasants, and financiers who had not yet transacted their business actually waited for Rasputin's return. He appeared again about half an hour later, and at once resumed his dealings with the petitioners and their affairs.

* * * * *

Almost every day when Rasputin was engaged with his ladies and suppliants, the door bell would ring and an elegantly dressed gentleman enter, whose appearance was curiously different from the rest of the crowd thronging the ante-room. This was Manasevich-Manuilov, an official of the Ministry of the Interior, a man rather under middle height, dressed with the slightly exaggerated elegance often to be seen in little men. It seemed as though he tried to make up for the insignificance of his appearance by paying particular attention to his clothes. His suits were made of the finest materials by the best tailors in St. Petersburg; his hair and hands were unusually well cared for, he always looked as if he had just been shaved, and fragrant powder subdued the greasy shine of his skin to a pleasant dim lustre. Whatever the time of day might be, he always gave the impression that he had just left the hairdresser's and was about to pay a very important call on a minister or a distinguished lady. The expression of his face, his walk, the movements of his hands and arms, the intonations of his voice, were all in complete harmony with the too careful toilettes; all had the same studied correctness.

Manasevich-Manuilov was a regular visitor of Rasputin's; he would often call at the house several times a day. No one else was so sure of being received, and there was no other visitor to whom the starets would listen so willingly and interestedly. Manuilov was aware of his privileged position, but to all appearances made no particular use of it; however often he appeared in a day he never permitted himself the slightest carelessness in the observance of external forms, and nothing in his demeanour betrayed the intimacy existing between him and the starets. However urgent his business, or however dissatisfied he felt, not the slightest sign of it was apparent; he always preserved an attitude of calm composure and conscious dignity. His face beamed with the same amiable and winning smile; but this gaiety never overstepped the bounds of a certain distant reserve or degenerated into obtrusive joviality. The whole appearance of Manasevich-Manuilov, from his faultless dress to the equally faultless play of his features, was the very model of a cultivated and well-bred society man.

But behind this correct appearance was concealed one of the boldest and most unscrupulous rascals of the time, whose whole life was a series of infamies, impostures, blackmail, and shady business.

The son of a Jewish merchant of Gurevich, he had contrived

when still a boy to attract the interest of old Prince Meshcherski. That one-time friend of Dostoevski, the influential politician and editor of the reactionary review *Grazhdanin*, as he grew older, took increasing pleasure in pretty, girlish-looking boys, a fact which young Manuilov soon managed to exploit for his own advantage. Prince Meshcherski befriended the promising lad, and preferred him to all his other "spiritual sons"; he had him dressed by the best tailors, gave him a generous allowance of pocket-money, and procured him the entry to the best society in St. Petersburg.

Ere long, however, young Manuilov felt a keen desire to use his latent talents in other directions as well, and soon succeeded in winning the confidence of the St. Petersburg secret police. On their behalf he journeyed to Paris, not to the *ville lumière* of the rich young men of St. Petersburg, but to the centre of the anti-Tsarist revolutionary movement. There he spied with such success that his superior officers expressed their very great admiration for his talents, and he rapidly became the right hand of Rashkovski, the chief representative of the Okhrana in Paris.

His career as a spy was as adventurous as it was successful. In Paris he managed to obtain a sight of the secret documents of the Prefecture of Police; in Rome he got on the track of a conspiracy against Russia; in London and the Hague he contrived to get in touch with the members of Japanese military missions and discover their secrets; but his master stroke was made during the Russo-Japanese War, when he succeeded in deciphering the Japanese code and, by its aid, read the secret despatches of several Japanese embassies in Europe. He organized the Russian counter-espionage service in Vienna, Stockholm, and Antwerp, got possession of the diplomatic correspondence between the accredited representatives of the neutral powers in St. Petersburg and their respective governments on the subject of their negotiations with Japan and, by bribing an employee of the embassy in Madrid, obtained the German code and thereby successfully organized a secret surveillance of the Baltic Fleet. As a reward for his activities he was decorated on this occasion with the Persian Orders of the Sun and the Lion, the Order of Vladimir IV, and the Spanish Order of Isabella.

Meanwhile, he also busied himself with espionage of various kinds in internal politics, and here, too, he attained considerable success. Thus the secret archives of Count Witte fell into his hands, which enabled him, by handing over these compromising documents to the Opposition, to deprive this statesman of his office. Soon after this he sold important Russian State papers to Burtsev, the revolutionary, who started an anti-Russian campaign in America on the strength of them. Manuilov had also entered into relations with the monk Gapon, once, under the mask of a convinced revolutionary, in order to induce him to take violent action against the Government, an attempt that led to the events of "bloody Sunday" before the Winter Palace, and another time in order to have Gapon assassinated at the request of the Government.

In addition to this important State business he by no means disdained small private enterprises: he promised to provide exiled Jews with residential permits in return for large sums of money, which undertakings he did not carry out; he mulcted several people of considerable amounts on the delusive hope of releasing them from military service, and here and there set Jewish pogroms on foot for his own private purposes.

On this occasion Manuilov, too sure of his omnipotence and perhaps also egged on by his indomitably adventurous spirit, went too far and was on the verge of a criminal investigation which threatened to become a great scandal. But even here he was able to escape the fate hanging over him, for one day the advocate entrusted with the investigation received a laconic order to drop the case. A little later Manuilov was again playing a great part, and managed to blackmail the rich Colonel Meksasudi for large sums.

St. Petersburg society was well aware of this man's dark past —and present; but knew far too much about his power and the danger of his influence to treat him with anything but the utmost politeness and devotion. He himself was thoroughly imbued with the consciousness of his influence, and allowed it to appear to the outer world by his self-assured and dignified bearing.

When he came into Rasputin's waiting-room, he would draw

off his gloves at the door, hand his hat, coat, and silver-handled walking-stick to the maid with an easy gesture, bow a courteous greeting to all, and approach the starets with an elegant swaying walk.

At Manasevich-Manuilov's entrance Rasputin would leave any unlucky petitioner who might be putting his appeal to him and, forgetting him in a second, rush to meet the new visitor with his big, uncontrolled movements, embracing him with boisterous heartiness, and kissing him on both cheeks.

When Manuilov had freed himself with indulgent superiority from the arms of the holy father, the two of them would generally pace up and down the ante-room for a few minutes before going into the office with its crowd of commission agents, while Manuilov hastily told the starets the news which had brought him. The gathering in the waiting-room had frequent opportunity to observe the eager, low-voiced conversations between Rasputin and Manuilov; the latter took the starets by the arm with an elegant, careless gesture, and whispered to him in an undertone. The suppliants could catch only a word here and there, and had to content themselves with watching their expressions; but even this, quite apart from the subject of the unheard conversation, in itself produced a very peculiar effect. Manuilov's whole appearance, his confident, careless smile, his way of simply taking the revered miracle-man by the arm, were all strangely different from the humble behaviour of the other people in this room.

And in conversation with him the starets also seemed to undergo a queer change; as the annoyed suppliants, in whom Rasputin no longer displayed the faintest interest, saw the two men pacing up and down, side by side, it seemed as if suddenly everything that had lent the face of the starets its air of monastic goodness and fatherliness fell away like a mask; before their eyes appeared all at once the brutal face of a cunning peasant broker; even the beard which had previously made him so dignified and pious-looking was transformed at such moments into the waving reddish beard of a horse-coper. Confused by this incomprehensible sorcery, the suppliants stared helplessly at Grigori Efimovich. Not until Manuilov let go the arm of the holy father, and he could once more attend to his flock with his kind and fatherly glance and his right hand raised in blessing, did the hellish spell vanish that for a few moments had obscured their faith in the divinity of Rasputin.

Manuilov was better acquainted than almost anyone else with all the weaknesses of the holy man; he was as well informed as only a man can be about his partner in somewhat shady business. Perhaps he was the only person who had not fallen under the personal fascination of Rasputin, for feelings like reverence, humility, or bewitchment were entirely foreign to the experienced Manuilov. The indissoluble tie between him and Grigori Efimovich was sober business considerations, the knowledge that the starets was an important factor in his own commercial speculations.

In the days before he entered Rasputin's service he had been one of his bitterest opponents, for previously it had seemed to him advisable to insinuate himself into the confidence of Rasputin's enemy, the influential General Bogdanovich, by a campaign against the miracle-worker. However, during a sleepless night, he came to the conclusion that it would be better to change sides, especially as the then Minister of the Interior, Maklakov, had just come out energetically in favour of the starets. From that moment Manasevich-Manuilov became one of Rasputin's most zealous and devoted adherents, and immediately betrayed to him the intrigues of the circle of which General Bogdanovich was the centre.

This change of attitude very soon proved useful for his career: the Empress learned of his conversion and was not sparing in her recognition. Manuilov advanced rapidly and finally became secretary to the Prime Minister. It befell in this way. Rasputin made the closer acquaintance of Boris Stürmer through the intermediacy of Manasevich-Manuilov. The latter arranged a meeting between the two at the flat of his mistress, Lerma-Orlova, the actress, at which Grigori Efimovich was to decide whether Stürmer was a suitable candidate for the post of Prime Minister.

The meeting took place in somewhat dramatic circumstances: Manuilov, who was passionately in love with Lerma, had that very day caught his lady straying, and discovered that she had deceived him with Pets, a riding-master. He was mad with jealousy and rage, and was on the point of beating his beloved when the bell rang and Stürmer was announced; a few minutes later the starets also appeared.

Now Manuilov's whole future depended on this conversation between Rasputin and Stürmer, for Stürmer had made him great promises in the event of his becoming Prime Minister. So poor Manuilov was torn intolerably between his personal feelings and considerations of State interests and his future career. He ran from one room to the other, comforting and propitiating the howling Lerma in one, and advocating the candidature of Stürmer in the other.

However, this historic meeting finally ended to the satisfaction of all concerned. Rasputin had carried away a favourable impression of Stürmer, and had actually kissed him at parting; Stürmer was beside himself with joy, embraced Manuilov, and promised him that in future he would treat him like a son and give him any post he liked. Manuilov's amorous difficulty also ended happily, for his prospective advancement to be secretary to the new Prime Minister impressed the little actress, and she decided that she preferred to let the riding-master go. Furthermore, Manuilov got into touch with Beletski, denounced Pets for having engaged in the sale of horses to the enemy, and succeeded in having his rival put in prison. While the latter sat in jail and waited for his innocence to be proved, Manuilov was able to enjoy undisturbed the love of his lady. At the same time he was increasingly overwhelmed with requests from bankers and business men, and loaded with bribes; he also secured entry to the most distinguished society, even that of the diplomatic representatives of the foreign great powers.

Rasputin had no illusions about Manuilov's motives in coming over to his side; he knew the past of the secretary and his character, and was only too well aware that his service was due solely to practical considerations. But, with his peasant artfulness, he also recognized that no adherence resulting from personal admiration and esteem is so firm and reliable as one that depends entirely on sober business considerations. Since Manuilov derived his power and influence from the power and influence of

Rasputin, the latter could rely on his devotion with an easy mind.

Nor was it hidden from the starets that Manuilov had not severed his former relations with the secret police, but that, on the contrary, he had been charged by Beletski with the special function of keeping the police informed of all the political and financial plans of the starets. The secretary himself had made no secret to Grigori Efimovich about the mission he had been entrusted with; but the starets contrived to profit by his friend's connection wtih the Okhrana, for he had easily induced Manuilov in turn to inform him of the secret designs and plans of the police. In these circumstances Grigori Efimovich was quite indifferent to the fact that Manasevich-Manuilov from time to time sent exhaustive reports about him to Beletski.

He did not even trouble to conceal from Manuilov anything he did or neglected to do; Manuilov had the entry to Rasputin's flat at all times of the day and night; and all the pigeon-holes in his desk were open to him. Manuilov made use of this unreserved confidence on the part of his holy friend by appearing at his house at all hours, interfering in the business of the waiting crowd in the ante-room, and taking part in almost all the affairs transacted in the office.

While Grigori Efimovich was conferring with Manuilov in the ante-room, the door of the office would frequently open, and a dark, middle-aged man with a pronounced Jewish cast of countenance would appear in the doorway, bowing friendly and respectful greetings. This was Simanovich, Rasputin's first private secretary, who sometimes came to summon one of the waiting crowd into the office, and sometimes to go up and ask the starets a question in a low voice.

Whenever the door opened the crowd in the ante-room had a fleeting glimpse of the office. Several men, close together, sat round the table; some of them were bent over documents and notebooks, apparently busied in making important notes, while others talked excitedly together with vehement gesticulations. Almost all were shabbily dressed, two or three wore Russian shirts and looked like little commercial employees, the rest were typical representatives of the lower Jewish financial world of

St. Petersburg, with their ugly little eyes and reddish goatees.

With his back against the enormous desk, on which mountains of opened and unopened letters and telegrams lay in a confused jumble, stood Dobrovolski, Rasputin's second private secretary, calling out something from time to time to the men sitting round the table. Whereupon they would almost simultaneously bury their noses in their notebooks and enter Dobrovolski's information.

This picture of a crowd of excited figures with notebooks, round a man who called out names and figures, was strongly reminiscent of a bucket-shop, and in a certain sense this is a really apt description of Rasputin's office. For his various friends and secretaries, by using his connections and influence, had contrived to establish a flourishing business establishment there. Besides the four secretaries proper, who relieved each other at regular intervals, and of whom Simanovich, at one time a diamond-cutter, and Dobrovolski, a former national school inspector, had won Rasputin's special confidence, a whole staff of brokers and agents of all kinds functioned there.

The fact that almost all the influential men in Russia daily assembled, either in person or through accredited representatives, in the waiting-room of the miracle-worker made it possible to carry out on the spot, without any bureaucratic delays, big commercial business, the granting of concessions, stock exchange transactions, and political wire-pulling. People arrived in the morning with their business, explained it to the head of the house himself or to the competent secretary, and waited for the appearance of Rubinstein, the banker, Bishop Varnava, one of the ministers, the Tsar's adjutant-general, or the influential "mother of the Church," Countess Ignatiev. The secretaries attended to the rest, and usually the desired document was ready by the afternoon, and the petitioner could leave the house of the starets with everything nicely settled.

In that Russia where all business, whatever its nature, and however well it might be bolstered up by patronage and bribes, had to go on a weary and complicated way through a thousand official departments, Rasputin's office was distinguished by its functioning with undreamt-of rapidity. So it is easy to understand that this undertaking flourished as no other business in Russia, and that the number of its clients steadily increased.

The starets himself troubled very little about the technical details; the real manipulation he left entirely to his secretaries. In this way he was enabled to preserve to the full his peasant primitiveness. He treated the most complicated case, which must in reality have been far beyond his scope, with a naïve and original peasant good sense, without allowing himself to be confused by incomprehensible details, and in this way was successful: the most cunning and subtle stock exchange operators were powerless before the sound instinct and the gaze, unconfused by expert knowledge, of the wonder-worker of Pokrovskoe, who, with an unerring instinct, recognized the important points of every transaction, however difficult, and stuck to them with the utmost tenacity.

Just as he wrote with a few clumsy strokes of the pen those letters of introduction by the aid of which the recipients penetrated to Tsarskoe Selo itself, in the same way he dealt with great financial affairs, in a clumsy, primitive, but successful fashion. He hardly ever wrote more than a few words to the personages whose help he needed: "My dearest friend, do it. Grigori." These homely lines, surmounted by a simple sign of the cross, worked like magic: they were enough to make bank directors and ministers carry out apparently impossible demands. In the course of time he evolved an even simpler and more convenient method: in his leisure time he composed a supply of these stereotyped letters, "My dear friend, do it," so that in business hours he had only to fill in the addresses. Often he even neglected to do this, and left it to the person concerned, armed with this blank introduction, to call on whomever he liked.

A young girl who once visited Rasputin, and was summoned by him into the little room, left a description of the procedure followed by the starets in distributing letters to petitioners. During their conversation he was called into the waiting-room and, returning immediately, looked in vain for a ready-made letter of introduction. He excused himself, saying: "I must write a letter quickly: there is a man for whom I must settle some business."

He then seized a pen and began to write unwieldily, muttering each word aloud. As if he were guiding the pen in another person's hand, he laboriously scratched a few uneven characters, as though sticking each letter on to the paper.

"I hate writing," he said, breaking off, and embracing the girl. "Oh, how I hate writing! It is quite different with the living word: there you can express your thoughts more easily. But this is only a scribble, nothing but a scribble. Look, this is all I have written: 'My dearest friend. Be good enough to see to this. Grigori.'"

"But why do you not write the address?" asked the young lady.

He smiled absent-mindedly. "What for? The man himself will know which minister he needs. It's all the same to me. I write 'My dearest friend,' and that's enough. I always write like that."

Later, when the press of business in Rasputin's office assumed even greater proportions, he frequently distributed a bundle of ready-made letters of this kind to Simanovich and Dobrovolski. In consequence, the two secretaries immediately took on great importance in the eyes of the brokers and speculators waiting in the ante-room. Simanovich, in particular, enjoyed the greatest esteem: when he appeared at the door of the office backs bent low, and he met the most submissive glances from many uneasy little eyes.

If the starets himself was not present one could thus confidently address oneself to his representatives, Simanovich or Dobrovolski: they, too, took bribes and valuable presents with equal unconstraint, and they had in their pocket-books a sufficient supply of letters of recommendation signed by Rasputin.

Grigori Efimovich freely permitted his secretaries to transact profitable business from time to time in his name, and to slip the proceeds into their own pockets. To Simanovich, in particular, he was sincerely attached, and seldom refused him a request. Their friendship dated back to the time when Rasputin was a wandering pilgrim. It was in 1900, in Kazan station, that Grigori Efimovich first became friendly with the diamond-cutter, and their relations were further strengthened at a second meeting in Kiev, where Simanovich was still keeping a little jeweller's shop.

Born in the ghetto of a little town in South Russia, Simanovich learnt the jeweller's craft and began to lend out his savings at a high rate of interest. He had a hard life until the Russo-Japanese War gave him the opportunity for an ingenious marauding campaign. Armed with a trunk full of playing-cards, he betook himself to the seat of war and established a travelling gaming-table there. As he had not neglected to familiarize himself with all the niceties of card-sharping, he returned from Manchuria a rich man, to carry on his earlier trading in diamonds and also his moneylending business and his gambling enterprises in European Russia. As a moneylender he soon became one of the chief props of young aristocrats in need of money in St. Petersburg and Moscow. In the capital he resumed his former friendly relations with Rasputin, for he saw immediately how valuable the starets' influence could be for his own business affairs. Moreover, he had urgent need of a powerful protector, for the police were well aware of his objectionable undertakings, and had more than once been on the point of expelling him from the capital. As Rasputin's secretary he was safe from this danger.

Grigori Efimovich not only valued Simanovich for his business efficiency, but he also loved him as a man, in consequence of which the one-time diamond-cutter came to exercise a considerable personal influence over him. Simanovich used this not only for his business, but also to further the interests of the Jewish cause, and to secure the repeal of several oppressive laws directed against his race. How much Father Grigori, the Russian peasant, sectarian, and proclaimer of a new Gospel, loved the little, uneducated, homely Jew may be gauged by the fact that he once honoured him with his photograph with an inscription: "To the best of all the Jews."

Perhaps it was just the lack of education and the primitive cunning of Simanovich that particularly attracted Rasputin to him, for in these qualities he must have felt the Jew's kinship to himself. He did not need to stand on ceremony or put on company manners with Simanovich, but could be open and at his ease.

Grigori Efimovich had become so accustomed to confidential intercourse with his first secretary that he used to discuss the most important affairs with him, and once even took this little Jewish usurer with him to Tsarskoe Selo. On this historic day Simanovich's son was able with justifiable pride to tell his neighbours: "Papa has been summoned to Tsarskoe Selo to-day with Grigori Efimovich, to consult with the Tsar about the opening of the Duma."

In addition to Manasevich-Manuilov, Simanovich, and Dobrovolski, still another strange individual was to be encountered daily at Rasputin's flat, a certain Mikhail Otsupa-Snarski, who nearly always accompanied the starets on his visits to women, places of entertainment, and other orgies. He was always in readiness in the starets' rooms to perform such aide-de-camp's duties, although he fulfilled no particular function of his own. Introduced to Rasputin by Manuilov, Snarski, like Manuilov himself, Simanovich, Dobrovolski, and all the other faithful followers, was in the service of the secret police, but he was at the same time a faithful servant of Rasputin. He and his patron Manuilov had, through their connection with the Okhrana, succeeded in saving the starets from many unpleasantnesses and dangers. On one occasion Khvostov and his assistant Beletski made a plan to entrap the starets and have him beaten, with the object of winning laurels by releasing him at the last moment, and posing as having rescued him from a position of great peril. For this purpose, Snarski, whose flat was opposite Rasputin's, was to invite him to a drinking party and deliver him up to disguised police agents when he left the house drunk. Snarski accepted the commission and the money to carry it out, but at once informed Rasputin of the plot. Then the three of them, Manuilov, Snarski, and the starets, stayed comfortably in Rasputin's flat, and over their merrymaking with women and wine looked on mockingly while Khvostov and Beletski, with their band of rescuers, met in Snarski's house according to plan, and had to retire again in a rage over the failure of their plot.

During the morning receptions the door would frequently open to admit Ossipenko, the secretary of the Metropolitan Pitirim, who came to wait on the starets. Pitirim, that high clerical dignitary, as far as possible avoided public meetings with Rasputin, for fear of causing scandal and offence by intercourse with one so detested in clerical circles. He regularly sent his secretary in his stead, and in time the latter became so accustomed to representing the prince of the Church that his gestures and speech gradually assumed a peculiar kind of unctuous dignity.

Ossipenko was thrown rather off his balance by the alien deportment imposed upon him, and he behaved as if he himself were the Metropolitan. The Chief of Police, Beletski, had a disastrous experience of this in his own person, for when he tried to enlist Ossipenko in his espionage service by a gift of three hundred roubles, the secretary pocketed the money with a dignified gesture, and never wasted a moment on the business itself.

* * * * *

The guests in the waiting-room gradually dispersed; one by one the brokers and speculators left the office, with their documents under their arms, some alone, some talking in groups. The secretaries, assistants, and adjutants of the starets reached for their leather coats, hats, and furs, stuffed their portfolios under their arms, and took their leave. Meanwhile, in the dining-room, the women disciples were taking a touching farewell of their holy father, whom they would not see again till next morning. He embraced them one by one, kissed them on the mouth, and distributed little bits of wholemeal rusks among them, which they carefully wrapped in silk handkerchiefs and put in their pockets. Some of them whispered softly to Dunia, and asked her to give them some soiled linen of Rasputin's to wash, the dirtiest and most perspiration-stained she could find. The maid disappeared, and returned with the desired bundles of dirty linen, which she distributed. Then they all took their leave and departed by the back stairs.

CHAPTER X

IN THE HOLY OF HOLIES

"I FOLLOWED the maid through the door on the right," relates Vera Alexandrovna Shukovskaia, "and found myself in a long, narrow room with a single window; Dunia then departed, closing the door carefully behind her.

"I inspected my surroundings. Against the wall, close to the door, stood a bed, the bulging mattress covered by a shabby, bright-coloured silk coverlet; next to it, against the same wall, was a wash-stand, and near it a lady's escritoire, with a cheap writing-case, some penholders, dirty pens, and pencils; there was also a gold watch lying there, with the imperial arms on the case. In the middle of the room stood a table and two chairs and, in front of the window, a lady's walnut toilet table with a looking-glass, on which lay two opened telegrams and some letters. In this corner of the room there was not a single ikon to be seen; but by the window stood a big photograph of the altar of the Cathedral of Saint Isaac, hung with ribbons of various colours. I could not help remembering that it is also the custom of the Khlysty to place their ikons, adorned with ribbons, by the window.

"Soon I heard Rasputin's quick step, the door opened, and he came in. He brought up a chair, sat down opposite me, took my legs between his knees, and, bending forward, asked: 'What good things have *you* to say to me?'

"'There is not much that is good in life,' I answered. He laughed and I saw his white peasant's teeth, which reminded one of an animal's fangs.

"'That's *your* opinion, is it? Is anything going wrong with *you?*'

"He stroked my face and added: 'Listen to what I am going to say to *you*. Do *you* know the psalm: "From my youth up the lusts of the flesh have tormented me; Lord Jesus Christ, do not condemn me therefor"? Do *you* know it?' He blinked, and let his eyes glide over me in a rapid, fleeting glance, which flamed up in an instant, then died away.

"'I know it very well,' I replied, without catching his drift.

"'No, just wait a little,' he interrupted, pressing my knees more firmly. 'I will explain to *you* how everything stands. I tell *you* that people may sin up to the age of thirty; but then it *is* time to turn to God, do *you* see? And when *you* have once learned to surrender *your* thoughts completely to God, *you* may sin again, for that is a sin of a special kind—do *you* follow? And as far as sin generally is concerned, *you* can be freed from it again by repentance. Only repent of everything, then everything is good again. Look here, go to Communion next week, will *you*?'

"'No, I will not,' I replied.

"He became restive, bent his head down quite close to me, stroked my shoulders and hands, and said: 'Stop, stop! Not so fast. I will explain everything. Words alone, my little soul, *you* will of course not understand; *you* must be convinced by deeds. Only come to me often, little honey bee, love me and then *you* will understand everything. Love is the most important thing. From the loved one every word is clear; but so long as I am a stranger to *you* I may say what I like, and it will only go in at one ear and out at the other. Perhaps someone has told *you* something already? Or have *you* already several admirers?'

"I leant back involuntarily, since he had pressed too close to me and was literally clinging to me. Suddenly he kissed me rapidly on the corner of the mouth; but he did this so simply and as a matter of course that it was impossible for me to object.

"'Why do *you* trouble with all these people?' he whispered, with his eyes almost closed. 'Come to me, send them all to the devil; then I will explain all life to *you*.'

"Dunia appeared to call him to the telephone; a few minutes later he returned and sat down opposite me again, pressing my knees firmly in his as before.

"'Well, and what else have *you* to say to me, my angel?' A sharp flash shot from his eyes, he bent over me and whispered hurriedly: 'Now I shall not let *you* go again. Once *you* have come to me *you* will not escape again! Understand clearly, I will do nothing to *you*, only come, my juicy cherry.' He gnashed his teeth.

" 'Why shouldn't I come?' I answered gaily.

" 'What is *your* telephone number?' And, stretching in front of me, he seized a pencil and a piece of paper, and shoved both towards me. While I wrote he bent over me, squeezed my shoulders, and whispered in my ear with hot breath: 'Well, and what more have *you* to say to me?'

"I indignantly pushed his hand away. 'I came to you so that you could give me advice. You know well, don't you, where truth is and where sin is?'

"He looked at me searchingly. 'Do *you* know it?'

" 'No, I have no idea.'

"Rasputin smiled slightly, bent forward, and spoke rapidly: 'It is all due to *your* reading too many books; in them, the books, there is often no meaning; they only make the soul uneasy. *You* see, I have another friend, who reads so much, a very special person; perhaps *you* know her, Militsa Nikolaevna, the Grand Duchess. She has read through all the wisdom of the books; but she has not found what she seeks. We have talked a great deal together; she has a good brain; but she can find no peace. The first thing is love, then peace comes also. If *you* go on as *you* are doing, *you* will never find peace. She also asked about sin, and she also did not understand. . . .'

" 'And you understand?' I asked. He wrinkled his brow and looked me steadily in the eyes.

" 'If *you* wish to know, only he commits a sin who seeks sin. But in him who merely passes through it, sin has no part. If *you* like, I will show it all to *you*: go next week to Communion, and then come to me; while *you* still have Paradise in *your* soul, I will show *you* sin, so that *you* will not be able to stand on *your* feet!'

" 'I don't believe that,' I said, incredulously; but I felt very queer; like a magician he whispered with voluptuously open mouth: 'Do *you* want me to show *you*?'

"He looked at me, and all at once his eyes again became kind, friendly, and passionless. In an unexpectedly gentle voice he asked me: 'Why do *you* look at me like that, my darling?'

"Pulling my head towards him, he kissed me with priestly dignity, and said softly: 'Oh, my love. . . .'

"I looked at him in confusion. Had it all been a dream, that lustful whisper of 'Do *you* want me to show *you*'? Now, there sat before me a simple, honest peasant, with a thick, dark beard and a meek look in his light eyes.

"I stood up, saying: 'I must go.'

" 'But see here, my dear, only come again,' said he, rising and embracing me closely. 'If *you* are bored, ring me up. When will *you* come, you little darling?'

" 'I am engaged until Saturday,' I replied. He said eagerly: 'Good, good, come on Saturday evening at ten o'clock. Will that suit *you*?'

" 'Why such a late hour?'

"He wrinkled his brows: 'Well, come earlier, come at half past nine, but be sure to come, as I shall expect *you*. *You* like me, don't *you*, so come. Will *you* come?'

"It was a habit of his to repeat the last word twice.

" 'I will come,' and with these words I departed."

* * * * *

"On Saturday evening I rang the bell of Rasputin's flat at the appointed time. Dunia, the maid, opened the door, and said in a very unfriendly way that Grigori Efimovich was not at home.

" 'That is impossible,' I replied; 'he told me himself to come at this time.'

"Dunia inspected me with an oblique, distrustful glance, but showed me into the ante-room, where all the pegs were already hung with beautiful furs. As on my first visit, she did not let me take off my things here, but ushered me into the empty reception room. I sat down at the window. I was annoyed and cross. Dunia disappeared several times when a bell rang, and then brought in a hissing copper samovar, which was so heavy that she bent under the weight of it.

" 'Ah, a samovar too,' I thought. 'As enormous as those the peasants have at home.'

"The door leading to the ante-room opened and Rasputin came in with rapid steps. He wore a blue shirt, plush trousers, and brightly polished boots.

"'*You* have come then, my little soul,' he said, coming up to me. He put his arm round my shoulders and bent to kiss me, but I drew myself away.

"'Grigori Efimovich,' I said angrily, 'please inform your servants when you invite anyone to see you.'

"Rasputin exerted himself to restore me to good humour. 'Now, don't be angry, my little soul, I have told her often enough already, the tiresome creature, not to cheek my guests. This time I did not definitely tell her that *you* were coming, but forgive me, my darling!' He kissed me and drew me into the ante-room. "Let us go to them," he urged, as he helped me off with my things; suddenly he looked at me meditatively, and said: 'But perhaps it will be better if *you* remain alone, else *you* will run away from me in the end, if *you* see them in there.'

"'If I want to run away I will do it without that,' I retorted. 'At the worst it can only be a little uncomfortable, since I am not acquainted with your ladies.'

"Rasputin shook his head impatiently. 'If I am acquainted with *you* that's enough. Let us go, my little soul.' Putting his arm round me he led me into the dining-room, stepped up to the table, and said: 'See, I am bringing her to you; she is fond of me. . . .'

"I greeted them and sat down in an empty seat at the lower end of the table. Rasputin sat beside me. My embarrassment gradually grew less, and I began to look attentively at this extraordinary company.

"There were about ten ladies present, and among them a solitary young man in a morning coat, whose gloomy air showed that he was anxious about something. Near him, buried in an arm-chair, sat a young, pregnant woman with her coat open; her face was curiously pale, and her big, light-blue eyes gazed at Rasputin with devotion and worship. They were Mr. and Mrs. von Pistolkors, as I learned later from some remarks thrown out; the husband had come because he did not wish to leave his wife alone. Near Alexandra von Pistolkors sat old Madame

Golovina; her pale, faded face affected me pleasantly by its calm distinction. She acted as hostess, did the honours, and kept a general conversation going.

"Not far from her, at Rasputin's right, sat a beautiful, but no longer young, lady, magnificently dressed; near the young man sat a somewhat corpulent, melancholy woman in an ill-fitting grey dress. She looked as if she had just stopped weeping; her eyes were red, and red patches burned on her cheeks. She was the proprietress of one of the best-known private girls' schools, an old and devoted friend of Grigori Efimovich, who looked on him as a helper, adviser, and friend, and took no step without his blessing. At the moment, it is true, she, like old Madame Golovina, was more in the mood to see his defects, among which his too free intercourse with women obviously came first.

"Near her sat a big, sumptuous lady of uncertain age, elegantly dressed in deep mourning; like the lady in grey, she was silent all the time.

"Her neighbour interested me from the first; she was a big, full, fair-haired woman, not beautiful, and most tastefully dressed, but striking on account of her bright-red, very sensual mouth and her excitedly flashing eyes. In her face there was something equivocal, deceptive, and at the same time seductive. Faces like this may be found both among self-sacrificing heroines and also among women full of desire and depravity, who abandon themselves to vice as quietly and naturally as other women take a bath and then go to sleep in a very soft bed. It was Madame Anna Vyrubova.

"Munia Golovina, who was sitting beside her, looked at me with her gentle, blinking, pale-blue eyes longer and more frequently than the other guests. She wore a thin, light-grey silk dress and a little white hat with violets; she looked small and delicate; her movements were uncertain, and her voice very quiet. In her every look, her every word, was such meekness, touching devotion, and complete submission to Rasputin's will that involuntarily I asked myself: 'What has he done to deserve this?'

"When I looked at Munia's neighbour, for a second or two

I was unable to take my eyes from her face. Dark, almost yellowish, with great elongated black eyes, she seemed lifeless, and yet attractive with her expression of secret sorrow. Her complexion was unnaturally pale, which made her thin red lips stand out more sharply from her face. She sat there quiet and uninterested, her hands buried in an ermine muff. It was the Grand Duchess Militsa Nikolaevna, 'the Montenegrin.'

"When I seated myself Rasputin proceeded to entertain me by pushing one dish after another towards me. The table was laden with an untidy confusion of food, magnificent tarts and bowls of fruit alongside heaps of peppermint cakes and big coarse cracknels. There was jam in smeary glasses and a grey earthenware dish full of black bread and gherkins. In front of Rasputin stood a bright-coloured, deep plate of boiled eggs and a bottle of wine.

" 'Drink your tea now, drink your tea,' said Rasputin, and pushed forward the plate with the eggs. Immediately all the ladies, with their eyes sparkling, stretched their hands towards him.

" 'Father, an egg, please.'

"The expression of morbidly impatient desire in the eyes of the pregnant lady was particularly noticeable. I looked at them with amazement, almost with terror; it all seemed so extraordinary to me.

"Rasputin bent down to the table, seized a handful of eggs, shelled them, and laid one in each of the outstretched hands. Afterwards he turned to me and said, 'Will *you* also have an egg?'

"I refused on the plea that I was not hungry; they all looked at me in amazement, and then lowered their eyes. 'Well, well,' said Rasputin quickly, and turned round again.

"Anna Vyrubova now came up to him and handed him two pickled gherkins on a slice of black bread. Rasputin crossed himself and began to eat, biting alternately at the bread and the gherkins. He ate always with his fingers; even with fish he disdained the use of a knife and fork. I was not yet accustomed to his peculiar way of merely giving his hands a wipe with the table-cloth after eating, and then proceeding to stroke his neighbour, and I felt a feeling of nausea when he tried to do it to me; I leant back and hid my hands in my muff.

" 'Yes,' said he, munching gherkins, 'she was with me the other day, we talked much about the faith, but I could not convince her. . . .'

" 'Of what?' I asked.

" 'Of what?' he quickly repeated. 'Well *you* do not go to church—is that allowed then? I tell *you*, go to church, go to communion! Why don't *you* go?'

" 'You love the clergy then?'

"Rasputin smiled: 'Well, I cannot exactly swear that I love them particularly; but there are believers even among them. You cannot go through life without the Church. In time everyone comes to it, to the Church—do *you* understand?'

"At this point old Madame Golovina joined in the conversation. 'It is an excellent thing,' she remarked benevolently, 'that you feel drawn to Grigori Efimovich. He can tell you much. Come to him if only for a week, and everything will all at once become clear to you.'

" 'Hardly, hardly, not so fast as that,' rejoined Rasputin. 'I might try for three years at least before I did anything with her. She is a hard nut! But I am glad she has come to me, for I feel a sweetness in the heart coming to me from her, and know from that that she is a good and genuine child; for, whenever anyone comes to me and I feel this sweetness, I know it is a good person. When I feel emptiness in my heart it means that I have to do with someone bad. But I desire to talk with *you*,' Rasputin concluded, caressing my back and shoulders. 'Everything is well, I tell *you*, everything will be well.'

"At this point Mara came into the room; she wore a bright-red dress with a magnificent silk sash of the same colour, and her hair was carefully tied. Everybody held out their hands to welcome her: 'Mara, Marochka, good day.' Then Matriona Rasputin sat down in the place of honour next to old Madame Golovina.

" 'How fine it is to-day,' I said, blinking, as the setting sun lit up the table.

"Rasputin bent over me: 'The sun has come out from behind the clouds for *your* sake, because *you* strive after good, because *your* soul is good. It is always so, *you* know: the sun shines on all who have faith. If it looks down on a house it brings some special gift to all the people in it, and if *you* begin to be troubled about *your* faith then faith immediately shines like the sun. Go to church, I tell *you*.' With this somewhat irrelevant advice he ended his obscure talk, which everyone had listened to with close attention.

" 'Does everything then depend on the Church?' I asked.

"Rasputin excitedly pushed his glass away and cried: 'Yes, how can *you* get on without the Church? Listen to what I am going to say, do *you* understand? I will tell *you* something about Crazy Olga, who is soon coming here. She loved God, *you* see, and conscientiously lived in accordance with religion and went to church. But the way is narrow and she missed it, *you* understand? She broke away, along with Iliodor; but I am sorry about her. *You* will see for *yourself* what sort of clothes she comes here in, the mad bitch! She believes, poor creature, that she does me a favour with her devilish craze. I feel it in my heart: before I have finished drinking my glass of tea she will be here.'

"And actually, as if to confirm his words, a violent uproar was heard in the hall. I turned towards the half-opened door, and saw a figure on the threshold staggering in, improbably bright, broad, pale pink, puffy, dishevelled, absurd. In a high, piercing voice she shrieked in the manner of an epileptic: 'Chr-i-st is ri-s-en!'

" 'There, *you* see Olga, now *you* will have an experience," said Rasputin gloomily.

"At first I could distinguish nothing, and had only a vague impression of a white ball of tousled goat-skin that flew past me. The new arrival had flung herself down by Rasputin's chair, and continued her cries with her head leaning against the edge of the chair. It was a most painful sensation when I saw something emerging at my feet that looked like the neck of an animal covered with thick yellow wool. Then Madame Lokhtina raised herself a little, handed Rasputin a chocolate cake, and cried, this time in somewhat more human tones: 'See, I have brought something for *you,* white outside, black inside.'

"Rasputin who, from her first appearance, had sat frowning with his back to her, now turned round, took the cake, pushed it carelessly on to the table, and said curtly: 'Now that will do, let me be, stop it now, Satan.'

Madame Lokhtina jumped up precipitately, took his head in her hands from behind, and covered it with wild kisses, shouting all the time in a quick, stammering voice: 'Oh my dearest . . . vessel of blessing. . . . Ah, *you* lovely beard. . . . *You* delicious hair . . . me, the martyr. . . . *You* precious pearl . . . *you* precious stone . . . *you* my adored one . . . my God . . . my beloved!'

"Rasputin struggled desperately and growled, half-suffocated: 'Away! Satan! Away, *you* devil, *you* monster! That's enough, more than enough. Ah *you*——.' What followed was a string of the filthiest abuse. Finally he tore her hands from his neck, pushed her into a corner with all his force, and shrieked, crimson, dishevelled, and breathless with anger: '*You* always put me in a sinful rage, *you* accursed abomination, *you* sickening . . .!'

"Madame Lokhtina, breathing heavily, dragged herself to the divan and sank on to it. Gesticulating with her arms, which were enveloped in bright-coloured draperies, she stormed on: 'And yet *you* are mine, and I have lain with *you.* I have lain with *you.* Oh, my life! It belongs to *you;* now for the first time I see how beautiful it is. *You* are my God! I belong to *you* and to no other. Whoever may come between us, *you* are mine and I am *yours.* However many women *you* take, no one can rob me of *you. You* are mine! Say, say, that *you* cannot suffer me! And yet I know that *you* love me, that you lo-o-ve me!'

"'I hate *you, you* bitch,' replied Rasputin, quick and decidedly. 'I tell *you,* I hate *you,* and I do not love *you.* The devil is in *you.* I'd like to kill *you.* I'd like to smash *your* jaw.'

"'But I am happy, happy, and *you* love me,' cried Madame Lokhtina, still in the same position, bobbing up and down and waving her gay frills and ribbons. The broken springs of the divan creaked beneath her weight. 'Soon I will lie with *you* again.'

IN THE HOLY OF HOLIES

"Suddenly she ran up to Rasputin again and, with fierce, voluptuous cries, seized his head in her hands and began to kiss it madly.

"'*You* devil!' growled Rasputin, furiously. Another push, she fell against the wall, but jumped up again, and stood shouting: 'Now, strike me! Strike me, strike me!'

"Her voice rose higher and higher, and there was such uncanny frenzy in her shrieks that everybody felt afraid.

"Then she bent her head, and tried to kiss the place on her breast where Rasputin had struck her; when she saw that this was impossible, she jumped up again, ran round and filled the air with loud, greedy, crazy kisses. She pressed her hands to her breast and then kissed them, writhing all the while in voluptuous ecstasy. Finally she became a little calmer, lay down on the sofa, and covered herself with her draperies.

"Now I was able to distinguish the details of her strange attire, which made her look like an Indian goddess. She was hung all over with finely pleated skirts of all colours; her violent movements made them flare out, and encircle her like gigantic wings. Then the long veils threaded with bright ribbons also unfolded on both sides of her face. On her head she wore a Siberian wolfskin cap, once the property of Rasputin; the upper part of her body was clad in a red Russian shirt of Rasputin's, from which little bags hung on straps. These little bags also contained objects which had once belonged to Rasputin, dried remnants of food and several pairs of his gloves. Strings of rosaries of different colours dangled from her neck and jingled at every movement; her feet were stuck into old broken boots, which also had once been worn by Rasputin. Her face was covered with a double thickness of veiling, so I could see only her delicate, sad, and beautiful mouth.

"'Go-od, Go-o-od, Thine is the power!' she cried suddenly in the midst of a general silence.

"Rasputin, who had again begun to drink his tea, turned to her. 'My God, this time I'll soon lose patience. I'll crack *your* skull in with something, *you* raving mare! *You* have poisoned my heart, damn *you!* If only *you* would perish, if only I need never see *you* again.'

" 'Why do you insult her like that?' I asked indignantly, and immediately all eyes were turned on me.

"Rasputin reverted to his usual friendly tone, patted me on the shoulder, and said: 'Just think *yourself*, my dear soul, how can I help insulting her since she has deserted the Church; and not only has she fallen away herself; but she is also trying to lead Munia astray, the wretch!'

" 'But you yourself have said that all must be forgiven,' I remarked.

" 'What's that I hear? Who is talking so cleverly?' cried Olga Lokhtina, throwing back her veil, and looking at me searchingly with her big, dark-grey, still beautiful eyes. 'Who is she? A new one? Come here, quick, quick. On *your* knees, on *your* knees with *you*, and kiss my hand.' Stamping with impatience, she stretched out her hands and waved them around.

" 'I have not the slightest desire to kneel at present,' I said. 'But I will gladly kiss your hands, even without your ordering me to.'

" 'A stupid creature, I see,' cried Madame Lokhtina. 'Clever talk from a blockhead.'

" 'Will *you* be quiet, *you* beribboned Satan!' growled Rasputin angrily. 'Don't drive me too far, *you* devil. It is *you yourself* who are stupid.'

"I interposed again. 'Stop insulting her,' I said impatiently.

"The ladies round the table were silent as before; their faces had gone strangely red; their eyes seemed veiled, and their breath came more quickly and jerkily. Dark patches appeared on old Madame Golovina's face.

"Rasputin turned to me curiously: "Why do *you* defend her?'

" 'I am sorry for her,' I answered.

" 'I reject the sympathy of men,' cried Madame Lokhtina. 'I am alone, but I am stro-o-ng! Day by day I utter the one cry; but people are deaf and blind.'

"All of a sudden old Madame Golovina turned to Madame Lokhtina. 'I cannot understand,' she said, 'why you deliberately make Grigori Efimovich angry. Don't you see for yourself how unpleasant all this is for him?'

"Then Madame Vyrubova rose from her seat, went up to

Madame Lokhtina, and, kneeling before her, took her hand and kissed it.

"'Have *you* seen it at last?' said Madame Lokhtina, very quickly. But she began at once to shout again: 'Do not forget that my hand must not be touched. Kiss it, kiss it, but do not dare to handle it.' Then she fell into a silence as sudden as her outburst, dropped her head, pushed back her veil a little, and began to inspect the guests sitting at the table.

"'I do not see my servant. Where is she, why does she not come? On *your* knees, on *your* knees, and kiss my hand!'

"Munia Golovina rose and, as Madame Vyrubova went back to her seat, went up to Madame Lokhtina and, kneeling down, kissed her hand respectfully.

"'Just wait, *you* heathen,' cried Rasputin. 'Am I never to be free of *you, you* carrion? As for you two,' turning to Munia and Madame Vyrubova, 'just you humiliate yourselves once more before Olga! I swear by God you shall never cross my threshold again; I shall throw you both out at the door, and her along with you, damn you! As for *you,* you crows' carrion, I'll find a knout for *you.* . . .'

"'God lo-o-oves the tru-u-th!' shrieked Madame Lokhtina.

"'There's no truth in *you, you* spawn of hell!' snarled Rasputin. Munia came back to her place with tears in her eyes and a very flushed face.

"'*You* will learn to know me yet, *you* unwashed fool,' threatened Rasputin once more.

"Old Madame Golovina, whose face had gradually become covered with red patches, asked timidly: 'Grigori Efimovich, why do you scold Marushka so?'

"'Why does she not listen to me, why does she commit a sin? She kisses Olga's hands and obeys the witch. Did I not say to her straight: "Do not dare to give Olga anything at all"? She gets nothing from me, the crazy creature.'

"'Am I then to sit hungry?' cried Madame Lokhtina. Suddenly her tone became quieter, and she went on in a reasonable voice: 'Am I to have nothing to eat to-day again? I ate nothing yesterday; I have no money, I gave the last to the chauffeur to-day because he drove me so nicely. I was afraid of being late, and after all I arrived last, though I wanted to be the first to greet *you*. And now I have nothing, nothing, nothing. To-day is Atonement Sunday; people come and beg their friends for forgiveness—one gives a tip; but I have nothing, nothing at all. I am hungry myself; I have eaten nothing for two days. I should love something to eat. . . .' And this was said in an extremely plaintive tone.

"'Serves *you* right, *you* carrion,' said Rasputin placidly.

"Munia rose, filled a plate with the soup which stood before Rasputin in a queer-shaped dish that reminded one of a washtub, and took it to Madame Lokhtina.

"'Munia, will *you* obey or not? Do not dare to give her anything,' said Rasputin, and added a brief but expressive term of opprobrium. Munia, however, took no notice, but pulled a round table up to the divan and placed the soup on it.

"'Why is that there?' asked Madame Lokhtina, pointing to a basket of hyacinths on the window-sill. 'My flowers used to stand there, and my apples and oranges. My bowl used to stand there; they have eaten everything up, thrown everything away, the vile creatures!'

"Munia silently lifted the heavy basket of hyacinths from the window, and with difficulty placed it on the floor in a corner, her delicate shoulders bent with the strain. Rasputin turned round:

"'There, what is going to happen,' he cried, 'if this cursed bitch takes Munia away from me? God Almighty, if only some one would drive this horrible woman from the town. I would fall on my knees in gratitude!'

"Old Madame Golovina turned a troubled face to Munia: 'Marushka, what are *you* doing; why do *you* anger Grigori Efimovich?'

"'Mama, please let me alone, say no more about it,' whispered Munia almost inaudibly.

"'Can't *you* do all *you* wish?' cried Madame Lokhtina, at once getting furious. Then she cried louder and more desperately: 'Take a pen and paper quickly, write, and one, two, three, I fly, I fly, away! away! They will turn me out, turn me out, drag me away, drag me away, and I shall suffer anguish for *you*. Blows, chains, fetters, prison, death, all for *you!* But then I will come back, to *you*, to *you*, under *your* roof, for *you* are mine, *you* love me, my precious darling, my bearded one, my God, my all! Only write, write.'

" 'And then everyone would say that I had driven *you* out of the town and that *you* had gone crazy because of me. I won't have that,' said Rasputin gloomily. 'The women have worried me enough without that on *your* account, *you* bitch! What am I to do with such a mad woman? *You've* long been loathsome to me, *you* abomination!'

" 'God suffers no betrayal, never! Rejoice ye over His resurrection!' Madame Lokhtina began shrieking crazily again, jumped on to the groaning divan, and moved her arms up and down like wings.

"The melancholy lady in grey got up, went slowly past Madame Lokhtina, took a glass of tea from the little table near the window, and returned to her seat in the same way. Madame Lokhtina rose from the divan, tore the covering from her face, and cried to Rasputin frenziedly: 'Carry me off, beat me! Insult me as *you* like, spit at me. But do not permit them to pollute my path. They must not pass by *your* holy sister. When I am with *you* they must be silent and listen. And now I will lie with *you*, I will lie with *you* immediately. . . .'

" 'Just try it, *you* bitch,' answered Rasputin in a threatening tone, rising and assuming a defensive position. 'Just touch me, and I'll smash *you* against the wall until *your* own mother won't know *you*.'

" 'I can't understand,' said Madame Golovina again, 'why you deliberately try to infuriate our Grigori Efimovich.'

"Madame Lokhtina drew herself up and briefly replied in a contemptuous tone: '*Tiens, je trouve votre façon de parler assez drôle, Madame, vous vous adressez à une personne sans la nommer*. . . .'

"Old Madame Golovina was embarrassed and replied in the same tone of studied politeness: '*Mille excuses, chère Olga Vasilievna, je n'avais aucune intention de vous offenser.*'

" '*O! de grâce, point d'excuses!*' replied Madame Lokhtina simply and quietly, like a real woman of the world; but she immediately began again to crow like a cock and to blow kisses through the air to Rasputin, who was pacing up and down the room. He stopped by me, pointed to Madame Lokhtina, and said in a tone of sincere sympathy: 'There, ask her *yourself* why she plays such a fool's comedy and slanders me besides, as if I had given her my blessing on it.'

" 'Who then, if not *you*,' cried Madame Lokhtina piercingly. Then she began to dance, waved her arms, and sang: "My God and Saviour! Sing ye all his praise, fall down on your faces!" Suddenly she noticed that her veils had slipped back, and that we were looking at her; she covered herself up again closely, and nodding slyly at us, said, 'Did you see anything?'

" 'Well, do as *you* like,' said Rasputin, gesticulating wildly. 'What I'd really like to do would be to wring her neck, she's such a nuisance to me, the horror! If only she would get out of my sight! I hate the carrion and her devilish masquerade! She is mad, that's all there is to it!'

"The telephone bell rang. Rasputin answered, and the usual conversation began: 'Yes—yes, I have visitors; well, I am drinking tea at the moment. Will *you* come to-morrow?' He chatted in this way for some time with the unknown lady. Then he sat down more quickly than usual, and began to eat soup with the wooden spoon from the dish in front of him; some of the ladies ate with him. Dunia brought in an enormous casserole, and set it on the little table against the wall.

" 'Have some soup,' said Rasputin to me, but I declined. 'Very well, now tell me,' he went on, wiping his moustache with his hand, '*you* think that we should not curse anybody?'

" 'Certainly I do,' I replied.

" 'Good. I agree; but how can I help cursing Olga when she behaves in this way? What else is there to do when she is the cause of their all beginning to call me Christ?'

" 'Not Christ, but God,' cried Madame Lokhtina. '*You* are the living God of Sabaoth, the living God.'

" 'There, *you* see! *You* speak to the raving lunatic,' sighed Rasputin.

" 'Ask her why she thinks *you* God,' I said.

" 'Rasputin made an impatient gesture: 'My dear soul, I

asked her that long ago! If *you* like, ask her *yourself*. She will reply at once: "On account of my good deeds."'

"'Does one only have to do good then,' I remarked, 'to be taken for a God?'

"'*You* have a try to bring her to reason, the fool,' said Rasputin quickly. 'Can anyone talk to her at all? I tried to explain everything to her, but it is quite useless.'

"'And what did she answer?'

"Rasputin made a resigned gesture with his hand. 'I asked her: "Does a God sleep with a woman then? Has a God children?" But she always gave the same answer: "Don't try any subterfuge, *you* can't conceal it, for I know that *you* are the God of Sabaoth."'

"'The li-iv-ing Go-o-d, Glory be to Thee unto eternity,' sang Madame Lokhtina. 'You all sit in Sodom and see it not. I alone cry to you in the sweat of my brow; but you have hearts of wood and will not hear.'

"'Oh, what shall I do with the monster?' Rasputin rose from his chair, but all the ladies at once stretched out their hands with: 'Father, calm yourself.'

"The telephone bell rang, and Rasputin went to answer it. Dunia, the maid, came in, cleared the plates, then turned to Miss Golovina, and said: 'Munia, take the dishes to the kitchen.'

"Munia quickly rose and obediently took the dirty dishes.

"'What do you mean by being so offensive, addressing people so unbecomingly?' cried old Madame Golovina indignantly. 'You can surely call my daughter by her Christian name and patronymic, as is customary!'

"'Don't, Mama, why . . .' whispered Munia in a low voice when she came back.

"'God loves work,' announced Madame Lokhtina.

"'Well, nothing special, I have visitors with me—I am drinking tea,' sounded from the telephone.

"Madame Lokhtina suddenly calmed down, slipped quietly from the sofa, and went into the bedroom; Rasputin, who was coming back from the telephone, signed to Munia to follow her. With quick, cat-like movements Munia threaded her way behind the ladies on the divan, and crept cautiously after Madame Lokhtina, who suddenly stopped at the door of the bedroom, turned, and said haughtily to Munia: 'What do *you* want, spying on me?'

"She spoke so proudly and imperiously that for a moment you completely forgot her crazy costume and her whole behaviour. Even Rasputin was a little perplexed, and his voice sounded different when he said: 'She is not following *you*, she is only going to arrange my shirts'

"'I am not interested in new things,' remarked Madame Lokhtina contemptuously 'I will have *yours*, *yours*. I'll take it off *your* body. If I want to, I'll take it, and *you* will give it to me. But I must see to something there.'

"She rushed into the bedroom and Maria whisked in after her with long steps, almost leaping like an animal. Rasputin ran across the room and disappeared behind the door, which he shut after him. Immediately a furious uproar arose, something fell to the ground and smashed, then the sound of blows on something soft was heard, all drowned by inhuman howling and screeching. The cries became more and more desperate; at last a door banged, heavy steps sounded in the hall, and Madame Lokhtina came running into the dining-room, dishevelled and with her veil torn. She was shouting something unintelligible, and making convulsive movements with her hands.

"At the same instant Rasputin came out of the bedroom, breathing heavily, with his face red and bathed in sweat. Munia glided past him like a fish; she was holding something in her hand, and pushed behind the ladies again and sat down by her mother, breathing quickly. When Madame Lokhtina caught sight of her she ran towards the table, but stopped suddenly before she got there and threatened Munia with both hands. 'Muck! dirt! *you* monster. If *you* loved him *you'd* be bound to know that he can't use such State trash, but only a priceless watch with rubies, diamonds, emeralds, and amber! Like one I saw on the Nevski Prospekt. He shall have it, he shall have it. But hand over that one. Hand it over! It must be trampled to powder, trampled to dust, and thrown on the dung-heap or the ash-bin. Oh, *you* don't love him, *you* wretch, and *you* want to quarrel with me!' Munia quickly passed a small object from one hand to the other. It was Rasputin's gold watch with the imperial arms, a present from the Tsar. For a few minutes nothing was heard but shrieking and howling, cursing, and indecent abuse. Rasputin and Madame Lokhtina talked at the same time and shouted each other down, deadening and destroying all thought. The ladies, on the other hand, sat quietly and correctly as before. Their faces merely became a little paler or redder than usual, as the case might be.

"Madame Lokhtina surrendered first, and retreated before Rasputin's attack to the divan, on which she flung herself in the silence of complete exhaustion. Rasputin sat down, breathing heavily, and wiped the sweat streaming down his face with the sleeve of his pale-blue Russian shirt. Silence reigned for a few moments, then old Madame Golovina turned to Madame Lokhtina, and said in a trembling voice: 'Is it not unscrupulous of you, Olga Vladimirovna? When you are not here we sit quietly and listen to Grigori Efimovich. But as soon as you appear there is nothing but quarreling and shouting—it's all your fault. We cannot even hear Grigori Efimovich's voice.'

"'And which of you has done anything for him, may I ask?' cried Madame Lokhtina furiously. 'Which of you glorifies his name? Who loves him more than I do? Who gives her life for him?' She began again kissing her finger-tips, throwing kisses to Rasputin, and whispering her crazy, indecent, but almost unintelligible endearments and avowals.

"Munia Golovina brought in a dish of fried fish, and handed it round, serving Madame Lokhtina first. She became suddenly quiet, took some fish, and said in a stern tone to Munia: '*You* know that *you* are guilty, Munia. Beg my pardon immediately.'

"Munia, with her shy smile, at once set the dish down on the table, went up to Madame Lokhtina again, and, kneeling at her feet, kissed her outstretched hand and bowed to the ground.

"'Marushka,' whispered her mother bewilderedly, "why do *you* do it? Why do *you* anger Grigori Efimovich?'

"Munia grew pale, shook her little head, and whispered gently as usual: 'There, now, Mama, don't bother, don't say anything about it. . . .'

"Rasputin said nothing, and Munia went on helping everybody to fish from the dish in front of her.

"Madame Lokhtina had covered her face and leant sideways, as if she were looking at something on the divan; finally she cried with a peal of triumphant laughter: 'Now I see it all! I see, there sits the white one, nothing to me, nothing to *you*, and under the protection of her honourable and prudent husband she has stolen. . . .'

"The young man in the morning coat got very red and answered sharply: 'I beg you to leave my wife's name out of the conversation.'

" 'Be silent, miserable man!' cried Madame Lokhtina, threateningly. 'How can *you* have the effrontery to speak to me in that tone?'

"Old Madame Golovina remarked again: 'You yourself are the one who prevents us from listening to Grigori Efimovich.'

"Madame Lokhtina made no reply, because at that moment, for some reason, the little table against the wall overturned with the tureen of soup on it. This caused a great uproar, everybody started, and the pregnant lady, in particular, trembled all over, and looked distractedly round her, pale as death. Munia ran for the maid, a queer confusion arose, but everybody remained in their places while the spilt fish-soup ran quickly in a little yellow trickle over the floor. Madame Lokhtina quietly rose, crept up to Rasputin, and seizing his head, began to kiss him, crying all the time: 'I have lain with *you*, I have lain with *you*. . . .'

"He pushed her away for a moment, but she came back again, stood behind him in such a position that he could not reach her with his fists, and asked him to give her a glass of wine.

" '*You'll* get nothing,' he said curtly and decidedly. 'If only I were free of *you*, curse *you*,' he went on crossly, 'if only *you* would go to *your* Iliodor, the son of a dog. *You* left the Church together. I'm damned if I can see the slightest sense in what Olga and Iliodor are doing. He severed himself from the Church, and thinks me a villain, a rascal, a libertine, and a seducer, while Olga lets him lead her astray into apostasy, and yet looks on me as the God of Sabaoth. If you were to strike me dead, I can make nothing of it.'

" 'Does Iliodor not love *you?*' cried Madame Lokhtina. 'He loves *you,* he loves *you,* oh, how he loves *you.* . . . But to me *you* are God, my bliss, and my world.'

"Rasputin beckoned with his hand. Dunia came up and whispered something to him, indicating the bedroom with her eyes. He rose quickly and went into the bedroom through the hall. Madame Lokhtina immediately rushed to the table as fast as her enormous boots would let her, seized the glass out of which Rasputin had drunk, filled it with wine, climbed on to the divan, stretched her hands out towards the farther corner of the room, and stood for some seconds with bowed head before the empty corner like a priestess celebrating a mystery. A tense, oppressive, unpleasant stillness reigned in the room. Finally Madame Lokhtina stirred again, raised the glass to her lips, slowly drank the wine, and then fell forward on the divan, where she lay with her arms outstretched and her face covered.

"Old Madame Golovina gave a loud sigh and said to Munia: why did *you* bring me here to-day? I shall be ill again.' She turned to me and said: 'If you had only seen what happened here yesterday morning. They had to restore me with bay-cherry drops, and even to-day my whole body is trembling. I simply can't remain indifferent to the sight of all these things.'

" 'Mama, stop,' whispered Munia uneasily.

" 'Why does Olga Vladimirovna behave so queerly?" I inquired.

"Munia's blinking eyes gazed at some point in the distance; with a peculiar expression of devout admiration she answered softly and happily: 'One has only to understand her.'

" 'No, no', replied her mother quickly, 'I gave that up long ago.' She pointed to the bright red spots on her cheeks, and added with slight bitterness: 'Just look what I am like! I don't want to make myself out better than I am, and I am not being a hypocrite, but all this agitates me incredibly. I have known Grigori Efimovich for four years, and I love him unreservedly. I love Olga Vladimirovna too; but her behaviour is quite incomprehensible to me and I cannot approve of her way of going on.'

"'When I am silent the stones will speak,' cried Madame Lokhtina, who had suddenly come to herself again, clapping her hands. Then she got down from the divan, and crept to the door of the bedroom, through which Rasputin's hoarse murmur and a woman's laughter could be heard. She bent forward and greedily pressed her face to a crack in the creaking door.

"'Don't come in, don't come in,' cried Rasputin crossly, and planted himself in the entrance.

"Madame Lokhtina laughed wildly, and beat with her fists on the door, crying: 'Take another, take another! Only take her in, hide her under the bed, under the bedclothes! But *you* belong to me, and I will resign *you* to no one, no one, no one! *You* may sleep with the whole world for all I care, but *you* are mine, mine!'

"She ran away from the door, and whirled round and round, and then, feeling giddy, collapsed on the divan again, muttering something to herself.

"A movement began at the table. I turned round, and saw the pregnant lady rise slowly and go up to the divan with her hands stretched out before her like a sleepwalker. Her wide-open eyes stared fixedly at Madame Lokhtina, and her dry lips were twisted. But she did not reach the divan; her husband jumped up quickly, overtook her in a few strides, and dragged her by force into the hall in spite of all her struggles and resistance. The conversation which had developed at the table suddenly ceased; silence again took possession of the room.

"It was impossible to look on indifferently any longer. The pregnant lady, by her actions, had merely expressed what had been for some time clear to the minds of all present, that they must either depart or shriek, fall into convulsions, and smash things. Madame Vyrubova rose first, and went to the bedroom; the Grand Duchess Militsa Nikolaevna and her young companion followed. The Grand Duchess turned towards the hall; but suddenly Maria Golovina rushed out of the bedroom and threw her arms round her neck. The Grand Duchess bent down, and Maria kissed her passionately, her neck, her hair, her lips, and her eyes, then she embraced her, and drew her out of the room.

"I was impatient for Rasputin to come back in order that I might say good-bye and depart. When at last he rushed in from the hall I rose, said good-bye to the others, and turned to him: 'I am going Grigori Efimovich. *Au revoir!*'

"He came up to me quickly and, taking me by the shoulders, looked deep into my eyes and said in concern: 'Are *you* going already, darling? Well, when will *you* come again? I have taken a great fancy to *you*.'

"I remarked that he might ring me up, and a wild laugh was heard. Madame Lokhtina was writhing on the sofa and crying madly: 'I must see that! He, the God of Sabaoth, is to call up a girl on the telephone!'

"'That's enough,' I said and almost ran into the hall. Rasputin hurried after me, put his arms round me, and pressing me against him, asked uneasily: 'Tell me, have *you* only seen bad things here, or have *you* perhaps also found some good?'

"'I don't know,' I answered, and tried to free myself. But he would not let me go and whispered in my ear: 'And will *you* come back or not?'

"Madame Vyrubova and the Grand Duchess came out of the bedroom in their outdoor clothes. They went up to Rasputin and held up their faces to him, saying, '*Au revoir*, Father.'

"'Farewell, farewell,' said Rasputin, making the sign of the cross over them both and kissing them. Madame Vyrubova took his hand, pressed it with a low moan to her hot face, and kissed it with boundless devotion. Her eyes sparkled with an unnatural light and her whole body trembled.

* * * * *

"I took advantage of an unguarded moment and slipped through the kitchen to the back landing. Slowly, absorbed in amazed reflection over the events of the evening, I went down the darkening staircase. Suddenly I felt someone touch my fur coat gently and heard a woman's low voice: 'Do you come from him?'

"I turned round in surprise and, in the dim semi-darkness saw a little female figure crouching on the top step of the stairs. She stretched out her hand and held fast to my dress.

"'Why do you go to him?' she asked in a feeble, sad, meek voice.

"'I'm not quite sure myself,' I answered evasively. The stranger rose and came close up to me.

"'You do not belong to his regular circle, I know that,' she whispered urgently, and tried to see the expression of my face. Her cold, little hand slipped into my muff and clasped my finger-tips. 'For Christ's sake listen to me. I shall lose my reason if I don't talk to somebody.' She pulled me down the steps, past the concierge's lodge, and out into the street. We went through a house that had a passageway through it, then along an empty lane, through a low gate, and finally halted by a house door covered with oilcloth. The unknown woman knocked loudly, the door opened, and a young girl in a white dress looked out and said something in Polish. Unresistingly I let myself be led into a room which smelt of earth, withered leaves, moss, and orange blossoms. Obviously we were in the back part of a flower-shop, for there were bowls full of half-withered rhododendrons standing about, and bits of coloured paper, heaps of moss, and baskets of flowering hyacinths lay in the corners.

"'I must tell you everything,' whispered the stranger, sitting down on a box and pulling me towards her. 'Listen to me for God's sake. You are so young, so happy—listen to me. . . .'

"Then she pulled her veil closer, and her shoulders in her thin marten fur coat shivered. She turned away without saying anything, then drew a deep breath and asked quickly: 'Are you a stranger?'

"'Yes, I do not live in St. Petersburg.'

"'I, too, came from distant parts, and now I do not know what is to happen, what will become of my life. Why ever did she send me to him? However could I have believed her? I am not a young girl, I am thirty-two. Why did I believe her when she said he knew everything and could discover my secret, that my sorrows would all be over if only I spoke to him?'

"She bent forward quickly and asked in a whisper: 'Did he send you to Holy Communion?'

"I nodded.

"'And did you go?'

"'No.'

"The stranger turned as if tortured with pain. 'Ah, you were clever. But I? I was always religious, I believed in God and Christ. Why did I seek salvation in him?'

"Crouched forward, she whispered thickly through her veil: 'Did he also tell you to go to Holy Communion, and then come back to him, cleansed from all sin, and with the body of the Lord in you? I did it, and visited him in the evening after the Holy Sacrament, as he ordered. But Christ did not protect me, probably because I sought Him in a wrong way.'

"She stopped and breathed heavily. Drops of water were falling softly from somewhere, and behind the dull leaves of a sad wintry palm a tiny lamp burned dimly; there was a grave-like smell of earth and hyacinths. . . . .

"'No, no, I must tell you everything. I went to him out of curiosity, impudent and vulgar curiosity, with the body of the Lord in me. And he winked shamelessly at me, as if he were asking whether I knew what he wanted from me. He was waiting for me alone in his best clothes, seized me, pulled me into the bedroom, and tore off my dress as we went. I felt his hot, burning breath on my neck. Do you know the corner near the window in which an ikon hangs? He forced me to kneel down there and whispered in my ear: "Let us pray." He stood behind me and began to bow, saying: "Saint Simeon of Verkhoture, have mercy on my sins."

"'Then he asked me, gnashing his teeth: "Did you go to Holy Communion as I ordered you?" The next moment he was nothing but savage, animal desire. . . . And I did not kill him, I did not spit in his face! The last thing I remember is his tearing off my underclothing, then I lost consciousness. . . . I awoke and found myself lying on the ground torn and defiled. He stood over me shamelessly naked. When he saw that I had opened my eyes he said with the laugh you know, a word—I will not repeat it. He bent over me, lifted me up, and laid me on the bed, saying, "But do not sleep, for Christ's sake." Christ, he actually dared to say His name at that moment. I don't know now how it happened, but I began to howl and shriek and strike out at him.

"'Someone came running up, they dressed me, pushed me down the stairs and into a droshky. The driver drove about for a long time and at last asked where he was to take me to. I did not know, I had forgotten. We stopped near a lamp. An officer who was passing spoke to me, took his place beside me, and told the driver to go on. Then I again remember no more. . . .

" 'Next day when I woke it was evening, I was lying on a strange bed. He had not touched me, he gave me tea, gave me time to wash, and got a bath ready. Now I wander round and think: "Where now? What is to happen?" For I believed in Christ—do I still believe in Him? I do not know, and I come to Rasputin's home every day to ask him why he did it to me. Why did he defile and destroy the holiest in me? I had taken the body of the Lord before I went to him. Now I do not know what to do, I cannot go away, and day after day I wander helplessly through the town. . . . .'

"After she had finished her story I did my best to calm and comfort her, and at last succeeded to some extent. Then I said good-bye and went home, still stupefied by all I had seen and heard that night.

"I left St. Petersburg next morning and went back to my home. I did not see Rasputin again for two years. . . ."

CHAPTER XI

THE DANCING STARETS

NOTHING made Rasputin so happy as dancing. It was to him the most perfect expression of his inner life, as important as breathing, eating, drinking, or any other elemental human activity. Everything for which the speech of the muzhik was inadequate, his emotions, impulses, and intuitions, received in the dance their most powerful and liberating form, and the movements of the dancer expressed the incomprehensible yearning for the infinite, the immemorial melancholy, as well as the exultant, primitive joy of the creature in being alive.

Among the Russian peasants the dance is not yet degraded to a form of social entertainment; it has remained a rite of primitive religious activity, which in many respects assumes the character of prayer. Whenever his courage threatens to fail, the Siberian peasant begins either to pray or to dance. No special hour and no special occasion are necessary for either the one form of religious ecstasy or the other. The songs, too, to which he dances, are not uncommonly church hymns; but even the melancholy or childishly exultant folk-songs have always something solemn and devotional about them: the Slav song is often a chanted prayer, the dance of the Russian peasant an expression of humble piety.

When Rasputin, in his Siberian village, in the course of a sermon on the redemption of man from sin, suddenly jumped up, stamped with his feet on the floor, and began to dance, his village disciples saw nothing strange in this, and certainly nothing inconsistent with his dignity: the "dancing starets," the saint who preached and then, when words were no longer adequate, continued his sermon in dance, was a comprehensible and natural phenomenon, nothing more than the spontaneous cry of joy at a happy event, or the wail of lament at an unexpected grief.

In the Siberian "izbas," the cabins where men and women, old and young, sat together on rough benches round a long table, it happened every day that one or another of them, seized by an inexplicable emotion, suddenly sprang up from the bench and began to dance in the middle of the room, either alone or with others, overcome at the same time by a like feeling. As soon as their excitement had died away in the dance they would return quietly to their places, and none of those present would be in the least surprised at this sudden outburst.

Rasputin retained all his home customs almost unchanged in the capital, and, as he sat at breakfast surrounded by his women disciples, talking unctuously about God and the "mysterious resurrection," he would begin to hum softly to himself. Several voices round the table at once joined in his song, until it swelled to a loud chorus, and the starets leapt from his seat and the next moment was flying through the room as light as a feather.

For in dancing his strong figure seemed to lose all its heaviness; the artistes of the imperial ballet had more than once envied him his light and winged feet. With a swaying movement of his body he approached one of the women, and with seductive, caressing, beckoning movements of his hands invited her to join him. He circled round her, crept up to her on his toes, his dancing fingers glided along her body, and the piercing glance of his eyes fell on her now from this side, now from that. She felt his swaying body nearer and nearer to hers, and his flushed face closer and closer to her face.

Finally the woman he had invited rose slowly as in a dream. Unresistingly she followed his lure, waved her lace handkerchief in her raised hand, and began to revolve in time to the singing and the stamping boots. The ecstasy of the dancing starets and his partner communicated itself immediately to the rest of the company.

But the woman whom he had chosen for his partner and found worthy to celebrate the sacred rite of the dance, even during their whirlings had the feeling of partaking of those mystical influences of which the starets had so often preached. As the stamping of the dancing saint became ever more passionate, fast and furious, the cheeks of his partner flamed with crimson; her eyes gradually grew dim, the eyelids grew heavier and heavier, and finally dropped. In the end Rasputin took the tottering, half-fainting woman in his great, strong peasant's arms, and carried her back to her seat. Anyone who was present at this scene for the first time might have thought that here was a satyr bearing off his fainting victim; but the women disciples saw it all as a solemn mystic rite; and they surrounded their fortunate sister and heaped tender attentions upon her; they kissed, stroked, and caressed her hair and her limbs, for the body of this "chosen one" was holy, and to them Rasputin, even in dancing, was a preacher, a saint, and a redeemer.

The men friends and followers of the starets, as well as the business men and politicians who gave drinking parties in his honour, generally provided music on these occasions and, whenever possible, a gipsy choir; for it was known that neither the finest food nor the oldest wine could make the holy man so happy and enthusiastic as song, music, and dancing. Anyone who had sung for him was sure of his goodwill and protection, and was thereafter numbered among his friends. Many a stroke of business had been carried through, and many an important appointment made, because the petitioner was the owner of a beautiful and melodious voice, which set the starets dancing.

Fat A. N. Khvostov owed his appointment as Minister of the Interior to a chance of this kind: Rasputin met him one evening at the "Villa Rode," where Khvostov, in his Chamberlain's uniform, was enjoying himself with some friends. Grigori Efimovich was not satisfied with the singing of the gipsy choir; he thought that the basses were too weak and, finally, he said to Khvostov: "Brother, go and help them to sing. *You* are fat and can make a lot of noise!"

Khvostov needed no second invitation, as he was already a little tipsy. He leapt on to the stage in full Court dress and made his thundering bass resound. Rasputin was charmed, clapped his applause, and shouted that Khvostov was a splendid fellow.

A few days later the fat Chamberlain was unexpectedly appointed Minister of the Interior, which made Purishkevich, a deputy of the Duma, exclaim that, under the present regime, the Ministers would have to pass an examination not in political science but in gipsy music.

Rasputin loved most the gipsy choirs, those bodies of from twenty to thirty-five men and women who, in accordance with the Russian custom, placed themselves in a semicircle round the guests and, under the direction of the "precentor" or the "precentress," struck up in turn songs passionate, melancholy, or gay. This gipsy music always had a peculiarly exhilarating effect on Rasputin, and he could be enticed anywhere at any hour of the day or night by the promise of a gipsy choir. He would often carouse and dance till the early hours of the morning, listening to gipsy music; on such occasions his true nature, the goodness as well as the baseness of his soul, his melancholy as well as his joy, reached an ecstatic climax; then he was at once preacher and brawler, redeemer and debauchee.

Rasputin's favourite resort in St. Petersburg was the cabaret called the "Villa Rode." The proprietors always kept in readiness for Rasputin's parties a little annex somewhat apart from the main building, where they could amuse themselves as they liked, unperceived by the rest of the guests, and where it was possible to keep a careful surveillance over all those present.

The starets' visits were announced beforehand by telephone, so that, when he arrived with his following, he found the table decorated with flowers and spread with attractive dishes, especially the fish and sweetmeats of which he was so fond. In one corner of the room the gipsy choir stood in readiness, and the waiters had provided an ample supply of Madeira. Rasputin sat down with a motley company the like of which could have been found nowhere else in the world. The starets himself, in a Russian shirt of cornflower blue or bright-red silk, drank steadily, clapped his hands in time to the gipsy singing, or jumped up and danced, immediately afterwards tossing down greedily a few glasses of wine. Suddenly he would quote scripture, or turn to one or another of the guests, look at him with dull, drunken eyes, and say: "Do *you* know what *you* are thinking of, my friend? I know." On these occasions he was hardly ever wrong;

it was as if the wine and the gipsy music had heightened his instinctive faculties to clairvoyance.

Often again, he would gaze into vacancy, as if some distant picture held him in a spell, and then he would tell in a melancholy tone of Siberia, his little village, his farm, and the scented flowers on the banks of the Tura. In a kind of amorous rapture he recalled the horses in his stable at Pokrovskoe, which he had not seen for so long. Suddenly he began to give an unseemly description of the sexual life of horses, as he had observed it as a child in his father's stable. With a coarse air he pulled one of the distinguished ladies towards him and whispered roughly, threateningly, "Come, my lovely mare:" Then he fell to praising again the beauty of the steppes and the dignity and value of farm work, and held up his rough, horny hands for all the company to see. In a proud voice, not without arrogance, he cried: "Look at my hands. Their horniness comes from hard work!"

Frequently he would turn provocatively to one of the fine gentlemen with diamonds in his shirt-front, or to one of the society ladies in a very décolleté dress, saying: "Yes, yes, my dears, I know you, I can read your souls. You are all much too pampered and also much too artful. These fine clothes and arts of yours are useless and pernicious. Men must learn to humble themselves! You must be simpler, far, far simpler, only then will God come nearer to you. Follow me in summer to Pokrovskoe, to the great freedom of Siberia. We will catch fish and work in the fields, and then you will really learn to understand God."

The drunken peasant must have made a curious impression upon the distinguished ladies and gentlemen as, sitting at a table covered with heavy silver and delicate china, he waved his coarse, knotted hands in the air and proclaimed, amid his ceaseless potations, that farm work and fishing were pleasing in the sight of God.

Still another peculiarity of the starets must have struck the guests as singular: he had a habit, while he drank, sang, and danced, of distributing to the ladies he wished to please, and also to the gipsy singers, the servants and waitresses, little notes, on which he had written extremely naïve, banal, and generally muddled maxims like: "Go not from the way of love, for love is your mother," or "I gladden you with the light of love, and I live thereby. God send your soul humility and the joy of beneficent love."

On one occasion, as he was handing a maxim of this kind to a lady, he noticed that her maid was watching him. He immediately composed a note for her, which read: "God loves work and your honesty is known to all."

Simple though those "wise sayings" of the starets, inspired by wine and song, might be, his female admirers found a profound hidden meaning in every one of them. The elegant ladies preserved these hardly decipherable "love letters" of Rasputin's in costly caskets, and the maidservants hid them in their bosoms beneath their bodices, and took them out every day to kiss them fervently; the more obscure their meaning, the more precious these strange notes seemed to Rasputin's female admirers.

The ecstasy of the holy man, however, did not always exhaust itself in harmless quotations from the Bible, sermons on the joys of the stable, or these naïve and nonsensical scribblings: his elevated mood often rose to a real Siberian drunkenness, to a wild transport of joy, or an outburst of desperate, raving madness.

More than once a banquet that had begun quite peacefully degenerated into an orgy of debauchery, and Grigori Efimovich would lose all control, and finally cause a terrible public scandal. Every occurrence of this kind was exaggerated and broadcast everywhere by the enemies of the starets, for in society, as well as in Court circles, in the Government, and the Duma, there were influential groups to whom every opportunity to attack Rasputin was most welcome.

The imperial couple, on the contrary, were painfully affected by every disagreeable rumour connected with him, especially as attacks on Rasputin were always at bottom directed against the Tsar and the Tsaritsa. The result was that the few people who had access to the imperial couple tried to prevent any scandal from coming to their ears. Careful precautions were also taken, especially while Beletski was Director of Police, to restrict as far as possible expeditions of Rasputin's likely to have serious consequences, and to persuade the starets himself not to hold his parties in public places of entertainment. As these efforts were not always successful, and Grigori Efimovich even took a particular pleasure in evading the surveillance of the police, the authorities had arranged that secluded rooms, from which not so much as a sound could penetrate to the public, should be assigned to him in his favourite restaurants. However, it was sometimes impossible to avoid a fracas, when Grigori Efimovich, after singing and dancing with the gipsies, staggered about the corridors in a state of extreme intoxication.

While the dignitaries devoted to the Tsar did everything to avoid scandal, other persons and authorities, hostile to the starets, left no stone unturned deliberately to cause such scandals and exploit the public indignation for their own ends. More than once drinking parties were arranged in the "Villa Rode" or the "Donon" in St. Petersburg, or in the "Yar" in Moscow, for the sole purpose of rousing public anger and compromising the starets. It was well known that Rasputin, who, in a sober state, kept a fair check on his utterances, became garrulous when drinking and listening to the gipsies.

On these occasions he would sometimes reveal the intimacies of Tsarskoe Selo, proclaim that the Tsaritsa Alexandrovna Fedorovna was a "second Katharine," and that it was she, not the good-natured, honest weakling, Nikolai, who really ruled Russia. When he was tipsy Rasputin was easily persuaded to talk to ministers on the telephone in the presence of his boon companions, and, in this way, to make indiscreet statements. Every word that the naïve and intoxicated Rasputin uttered in this irresponsible state, suitably embellished, was next day broadcast by his enemies all over the capital. This mean trick of making a man drunk and then exposing his indiscreet remarks, for a long time had not the success desired by its promoters: the Tsaritsa, and even the Tsar, who were both well aware of the primitive and simple good nature of their Grigori Efimovich, refused to believe the gossip, however circumstantial, about Rasputin's alleged insulting remarks against the imperial house. They were faithful to their friend, although his enemies saw to it that these artificially arranged scandals should not come to an end.

Thus on one occasion a serious collision occurred in the "Villa Rode" between the starets and Obrasov, a young officer in the Guards, which ended in Obrasov's boxing Rasputin's ears. As a result of this the police closed the "Villa Rode" for some time in order to prevent the repetition of such incidents. Of course, a detailed report was immediately drawn up and sent to the Tsar; he, however, put it aside unread.

Even on his journeys to Pokrovskoe the starets was dogged by spies, who gave detailed accounts of all he did and left undone in his home, and often enough contrived to make great scandals out of quite harmless incidents.

Thus on June 24th, 1915, the spies reported as follows: "Rasputin had a number of visitors to-day in his house at Pokrovskoe. He was drunk, put on the gramophone, danced, and then told his admirers that he had enabled three hundred Baptists to escape punishment, and should have been paid a thousand roubles by each of them; he had, in fact, received only five thousand roubles altogether. He also boasted that it was he who, during his last visit to the Tsar, secured the postponement of the calling up of the older reservists until after the harvest."

An incident that took place on the steamer between Tiumen and Pokrovskoe served as the pretext for a violent attack by his enemies. While the starets was going to his village accompanied by his friend, the Abbot Martian from the monastery of Tiumen, he made friends with some newly called-up soldiers, imbibed too freely, and finally caused a riotous scene.

The secret agents gave a full account of all that happened:

"9th August. Rasputin, on leaving the monastery, went on board the steamer, which left for Pokrovskoe at 11 o'clock. About 1 p. m. he left his cabin in a drunken condition and went up to some soldiers going to Tobolsk. He began to talk to them, gave them twenty-five roubles, ordered them to sing, and then went back to his cabin; a few minutes later, however, he appeared on deck again and gave the soldiers a further hundred roubles. The singing was then resumed, Rasputin joining in. About 1 o'clock he conducted all the ten soldiers to the second class, bade them be seated, and wanted to treat them to lunch; the captain, however, forbade this.

"After some time Rasputin came on deck again, told the soldiers to form a circle, placed himself in the middle, and sang songs with them. He was in excellent spirits, gave the soldiers another twenty-five roubles, and betook himself to his cabin again.

"He came back in twenty minutes drunker than ever, went to the third class, and began a dispute with a man from Tiumen; he then got involved in a discussion with a merchant, Mikhalev, also belonging to Tiumen, and began to express himself unfavourably about the activities of the Bishop of Tobolsk. Later, meeting the waiter, he insulted him, called him a rascal, and accused him of stealing three thousand roubles from him.

"After this incident Rasputin returned to his cabin, remained standing by the open window, laid his head on the table, and let the passengers stare at him. Hostile cries were heard from the crowd, such as: 'Cut his beard off! Shave him!' At the request of the detectives the cabin window was closed; two hours later Rasputin fell down and lay in a drunken stupor until the steamer arrived at Pokrovskoe. The detectives asked the captain to let them have a few sailors to help take Rasputin ashore. Four men dragged the drunkard on to the landing stage, where his daughters met him, put him in a cart, and took him home."

"10th August. At ten A. M. Rasputin came out of his house and questioned the detectives about what had happened the previous day. He said he was astounded that he had become insensible so quickly, as he had only drunk three bottles of wine."

The starets' enemies magnified this comparatively harmless occurrence into a tremendous affair, about which a mountain of documents was compiled. The police drew up a report, and sent it to the Governor, Stankevich; the Governor passed the document on to Prince Shcherbatov, then Minister of the Interior, and he referred it to A. A. Khvostov, the Minister of Justice. The last declared that the matter was outside his competence, and that it belonged to the Ministry of the Interior. Prince Shcherbatov, who was obviously at a loss what to do, submitted it to Goremykin, the Prime Minister, and from him it passed to A. N. Khvostov, the new Minister of the Interior. Finally Anna Vyrubova and Beletski succeeded in hushing up the whole affair, as well as the scandalous happenings at the Yar Restaurant at Moscow which had taken place in the interval.

This new affair had looked very threatening for Rasputin, and the greatest skill was required to prevent unpleasant complications. In the autumn of 1915 Rasputin went to Moscow to pray at the tomb of the Patriarch Hermogen, and a number of pretended friends invited him to the Yar Restaurant. Among those present were some journalists, who were expressly brought in as witnesses of the expected scandal, as well as several young ladies from the highest social circles.

Supper began about midnight, wine flowed abundantly, and an orchestra excited the starets to dance. Heated with wine Rasputin began to talk about his influence, his popularity, and his amorous adventures in St. Petersburg; in this connection he also dropped some remarks about the imperial couple which, however harmless in intention they may have been, were at once used against him by his enemies. He said that the Tsaritsa called him "Christ" and followed all his advice blindly; that he had often had to help her out of difficulties, and that the imperial apartments were always open to him.

After supper a chorus of women appeared, and Rasputin, as usual, immediately entered into conversation with the girls. He told them, too, of his friendly relations with the royal family, and took off and showed them his waistcoat, embroidered with flowers by the Empress's own hands.

At this moment, doubtless, recollections of the orgies of the "people of God" invaded his wine-clouded mind, for he did not stop at his waistcoat but, before anyone could prevent him, he had thrown off his clothes and, standing stark naked in the middle of the room, sang hymns and danced.

Meanwhile, the police authorities had been informed, and the Prefect, Adrianov, appeared in person. Next day this terrible scandal was being discussed all over Russia, and no time was lost in submitting an exact account to the Tsar.

* * * * *

Rasputin's trips to Moscow were nearly always marked by

some great nocturnal entertainment, which more than once threatened to take a dangerous turn, for Moscow was the real centre of the intrigues and plots against the imperial couple and their favourite.

Grigori Efimovich was very fond of taking one of his new women disciples with him to these entertainments, so that we have two lively descriptions of the starets' carousals from such novices, in which the strange figure of the "dancing starets" stands out most vividly. In Moscow it was Elena Dianumova who was allowed to accompany Rasputin.

"The telephone bell rang," she narrates. "I heard a familiar singing voice. 'Good-morning, Frantik, good-day, my darling, I have come to Moscow to *you*, and am speaking from the station. From there I am going to the Reshetnikovs'; come there to lunch. I want to see *you*, I am longing for *you*.'

"Naturally I was very curious to meet Rasputin again; Madame Reshetnikov worshipped all clerical celebrities and, whenever any one of them was in Moscow, he stayed with her. She had been enthusiastic over John of Kronstadt, Iliodor, and Varnava, besides Rasputin.

"About one o'clock I called at her flat; a monk received me at the door, and two saintly ladies dressed in black were sitting in the waiting-room. I requested that Rasputin should be informed of my arrival; but at that moment he appeared in the doorway, and began to embrace me and kiss me in his customary way. He looked ill; his face had become long and narrow and traversed with deep wrinkles; but the eyes were unchanged, and gazed at me as penetratingly as ever.

"He took me to a room with heavy old furniture; a monk came in at the same time. It was Varnava, as I learned later. He made the sign of the cross over me, asked my name, and said: '*You* are called Elena? Then *you* had *your* name-day recently. Make an offering to my church, a carpet or something of the kind.'

"Rasputin listened to this conversation disapprovingly and cried suddenly: 'Frantik, come with me to the dining-room; they are expecting us there.'

"We went to the adjoining room, where an old lady of about eighty was sitting behind a table, surrounded by other equally old ladies. One of them, by whom I took my place, was Varnava's sister; opposite me sat a young officer, a Grusian, who had been detailed to watch over Rasputin. Next to Varnava sat a merchant's wife, a young woman, with big diamonds in her ears; she gazed amorously at him all the time, and laughed loudly at his jokes. Rasputin himself was silent, while Varnava talked incessantly.

"Towards the end of the meal Rasputin turned to me: 'I shall come to supper with *you*, and bring him with me,' he said, pointing to the officer. The ladies protested: 'Little father Grigori Efimovich, *you* are like the sun in the clouds! Hardly have *you* appeared when *you* vanish again. We have not seen *you* properly yet.'

" 'No,' replied Rasputin, 'I will return to you. Now I must go to my Frantik.'

" 'You have only to show him a beautiful woman,' remarked Varnava maliciously, 'and you will see no more of him.' These words annoyed Rasputin very much, and he threw an angry glance at Varnava.

"In the ante-room Grigori Efimovich said to me: 'Did *you* hear Varnava's remark? He is jealous of me. I don't like that sly dog.'

"I hurried home as fast as I could, bought food and Madeira at Eliseev's, ordered fish dishes from a restaurant, and rang up a few of my acquaintances to ask if they would like to see Rasputin. About seven o'clock he turned up with his aide-de-camp. He was very gay, joked incessantly, his conversation as usual jumping from one subject to another, and he often indulged in incomprehensible allusions. He studied everyone present attentively, and his eyes seemed to bore through them. He treated Varnava particularly sharply, and said to me: 'It is nice at *your* house, here my soul is glad. *You* have no secret designs, and so I love *you*. But he, did *you* hear him? He does not love me, oh, how little he loves me.'

"His gaze remained fixed for some time on Mr. E. and his wife. This Mr. E. had once been engaged to me; but no one knew about it; we had both married since, and were very happy in our marriages. Nevertheless, Rasputin suddenly said to me, indicating Mr. E.: 'You once loved each other, but nothing came of it. It is better so, for you do not suit each other and his present wife is the right one for him.'

"I was amazed at his wonderful clairvoyance, for it could hardly have been possible for him to have heard anything about our engagement, which we ourselves had almost forgotten.

"When supper was over Rasputin all at once asked me to send for the gipsies, and would not be put off. Mr. E., noting my awkward situation, proposed that we should go to the gipsies instead, to which Rasputin agreed. The party broke up at once, and transferred itself to the Yar Restaurant.

"There Rasputin was at once recognized, and the proprietor, fearing a scandal such as had already occurred there, immediately communicated with the Prefect, who dispatched two officials to the restaurant. They arrived in the shortest possible time, came to our room, and asked to be allowed to remain, on the ground that they had to protect Rasputin against possible attacks; soon afterwards several police officers in plain clothes appeared with the same object.

"Meanwhile the gipsy choir with the famous singer, Nastia Polakova, had come on the stage; Rasputin began to feel happy and ordered fruit, coffee, cakes, and champagne.

"It was incredible how much Rasputin could drink. Anybody else would rapidly have fallen down insensible, but with him the only signs were that his eyes grew brighter, his face paler, and his wrinkles deeper.

"'Now then,' he shouted suddenly, 'begin to sing, children!' Behind the screen which cut off our room two guitars began to twang and the voices of the gipsy girls were heard; Rasputin sat in silence and listened with bowed head. 'Nastia,' he declared at the end, '*you* sing so beautifully that it grips the heart.'

"Then all at once he jumped up and joined in the singing in his full, clear voice. 'And now, Nastia,' he called, 'we'll drink a glass. I love gipsy songs, and when I hear them my heart exults with joy.'

"Nastia gave him curt, unfriendly answers, and looked at him darkly. That struck me very much, and I asked one of the party why the gipsies were hostile to Rasputin; in reply I was told that there had been a great scandal during one of the starets' recent visits, which had had most unpleasant consequences for the choir.

"I felt an involuntary twinge of fear lest there should again be painful scenes, and I regretted having visited a public place of entertainment in Rasputin's company. I thought of getting up and going away quietly, but somehow I was already infected by the general atmosphere and stayed.

"'Now sing my favourite song, the "Troika,"' cried Rasputin, jumping up. He was pale, and stood before us with half-shut eyes; with his hair falling over his forehead he began to beat time with both hands: 'I go, I go to her, to my love.'

"His voice was full of fire and passion, and his tones stamped themselves deeply on my memory. What elemental strength lay hidden in this man!

"Our party had meanwhile noticeably increased: every moment acquaintances were rung up and asked to come along; and other guests in the restaurant came up and asked to be allowed to join us. When the rich factory-owner, K., and his wife learned that I was there, they begged me to introduce them to the starets; some Englishwomen who had come to Russia with a military mission implored to be allowed to see Rasputin; when they had received permission they sat down quietly in a corner, and after that never once took their eyes off him. When our number had swelled to about thirty someone proposed that we should go to the 'Strelna,' so we set out. One of the party wanted to pay the bill; but the waiter replied that the Prefect's officers had already arranged everything.

"At the 'Strelna' a big, reserved room was assigned to us, the windows of which looked out on the Winter Garden. The public soon discovered that Rasputin was with our party and people climbed up the palm trees in the Winter Garden in order to look in at the windows. The wine was flowing freely at our table, and Rasputin also ordered a number of bottles of champagne for the choir.

"The gipsies paid their reckoning with a great song of praise: 'We drink to the health of dear Grisha.' They gradually got drunk too, and began to recite various pieces, only to break off immediately and burst into peals of laughter.

"Rasputin was now in his element: while a Russian dance was being played he whirled wildly and impetuously through the room, his black hair and his great beard flying from one side to the other. His feet, in their heavy top-boots, moved with amazing lightness, and it seemed as if the wine had multiplied his powers. From time to time he burst into wild cries, seized one of the gipsies, and danced with her.

"Meanwhile two officers had come into the room, to whom no one paid any attention at first. One of them sat down beside me, looked at the dancing Grigori Efimovich, and remarked: 'What do people really find in this creature? It's a disgrace! A drunken peasant dances, and everyone looks at him as if he were a saint. What has come to the women that they cling to him so?' He followed Rasputin's every movement with a look full of hate.

"Dawn was beginning to appear and the restaurant had to close. We all rose and prepared to depart; it appeared that here, too, the Prefect's officers had paid the bill.

"We now proceeded to another restaurant some way from the town, where we settled in a lilac arbour in the big garden. After the stuffy atmosphere of the 'Strelna' the warm spring air was doubly pleasant, especially when the sun rose and the birds began to sing.

"'How splendid! What heavenly beauty!' said Rasputin, sitting down and ordering black coffee, tea, and liqueurs.

"The two unknown officers had come with us, and were whispering to each other. At last this struck the police agents, and they made discreet inquiries about these two gentlemen. When they discovered that no one knew them, they requested the officers to leave. They protested, a dispute arose, and suddenly a shot was heard.

"A terrible panic began, more shots were fired, shrieks were heard, some ladies had fits of hysteria, everybody pushed towards the exit, someone seized me by the hand and hauled me into a motor-car; Rasputin was sitting near me and at first refused to come away. Everything happened like a flash of lightning, and I had no clear idea of what had taken place. Then the car flew off as fast as the wind, shots and shrieks still ringing in my ears.

"Naturally, we were all very much agitated. Rasputin was the first to recover his composure and remarked thoughtfully: 'My enemies do not love me.' Then he relapsed into a heavy silence.

"We were driven to Mr. E.'s flat, where we learned that the officers had been arrested, and had confessed that they had intended to attack and maltreat Rasputin.

"Rasputin's face had, in the interval, become quite yellow, either through agitation or alcohol, and he looked several years older. Soon an unexpected episode occurred with the wife of K., the factory-owner, who had asked the starets why he did not drive the Jews out of Russia.

"'*You* should be ashamed to talk like that,' Rasputin rebuked her. 'The Jews are as good people as we are. I am sure that each of you knows an honest Jew, even if he is only a dentist!'

"Then he explained to Mrs. K. that he must speak to her, and left the room with her for a quarter of an hour. When they returned Mrs. K. said in a changed voice: 'How clever *you* are. I never thought to have to do with such an intelligent man. I took *you* for an adventurer!'

"Rasputin looked at her with a sad air, and said, 'I would rather have been maltreated by the officers than have had to listen to such words from a woman's mouth.'

"At this point the aide-de-camp joined in the conversation and began to defend Rasputin, whereupon the lady burst into tears, said that they were insulting a helpless woman, and departed.

"Shortly after this I also withdrew and sought my own flat, which was not far away. I fell on the divan half-dead, and was immediately asleep; but an hour later I was roused by the persistent ringing of the telephone. It was the Grusian officer, asking if Rasputin was by any chance with me. He told me that they had put the starets to sleep on the sofa in the little room, but that he had suddenly gone out. After this the telephone rang every moment and ever new people inquired about Rasputin's whereabouts. According to the statement of the Grusian, the police were already alarmed, and search parties were looking for Grigori Efimovich all over the town.

"About one o'clock my flat bell rang, and I heard Rasputin's voice in the hall asking if I were ready to go out.

"'Where have *you* been?' I asked through the door. 'They're searching all Moscow for *you*, and the whole of the police have turned out!'

"He laughed and said: 'Isn't it all the same to *you* where I've been? I have brought a new lady with me; if *you* wish I will introduce *you* to her. She is good.'

"I was not yet dressed, and I flatly refused to receive a strange lady, whereupon she said good-bye to Rasputin, and went away. So that I was unable to learn where he had spent the rest of the night.

"I rang up the aide-de-camp and told him that Rasputin had turned up at my flat, and he hurried round immediately. Then we all three went off to see the wife of General K., in whose elegant drawing-room a large company was assembled. On our appearance the doors of a beautiful dining-room were opened, and we were invited to lunch at a richly spread table, with flowers, porcelain, and old silver. The ladies wore thin spring dresses. One place was empty, as a Polish countess was expected, who wished to make Rasputin's acquaintance.

"Finally this lady arrived wearing a grey dress and a heavy string of pearls about her neck. Rasputin went to meet her, and looked at her keenly in his usual manner, at which she swayed, began to tremble, and had to be led away to a bedroom. As it was announced during lunch that the Countess felt better, Rasputin went up to her, stroked her, and spoke soothingly to her. But the lady immediately had a new attack and cried that she could not face those eyes that looked into the very depths of the soul.

"When Rasputin returned to the rest of the party the ladies begged for an autographed photograph; but he declared that he did not possess a single likeness of himself. I remembered an acquaintance of mine who had recently opened a photographic studio, so I rang him up, and told him I was bringing the starets to him.

"Accompanied by the aide-de-camp we then betook ourselves to the studio, where I was at once struck by the unusually large number of women assistants; later I learned that these were ladies who wished to see Rasputin under this disguise.

"My friend made several exposures, and Rasputin insisted on being photographed with me: 'I want to be in a picture with *you*, Frantik,' he declared. I had foreseen this and given the necessary instructions to the photographer, so that he only pretended to take us without putting a plate in the camera.

"On our way back from the studio, Rasputin sat down beside me and began to speak very cordially: 'I annoyed *you* in St. Petersburg,' he said, 'forgive me. I spoke badly to *you*; but I am only a simple peasant, and what is in my heart comes at once to my tongue.'

"He took off his hat and let his hair wave in the wind. 'May God punish me,' he cried, crossing himself, 'if *you* ever hear another evil word from me. *You* are better than all others, for *you* are a simple nature. Tell me if *you* have any wish and I will do everything for *you*.'

"As I remained silent and refused to speak of my case at that moment, he said: 'Perhaps *you* need money? Would *you* like a million? I am about to transact a big affair for which I shall get a lot of money.'

"'But I do not require any money from *you*, Grigori Efimovich,' I remarked with a smile.

"'As *you* think best; but I should be happy to be able to do something for *you*. *You* are a good creature, Frantik, and my soul is at peace in *your* company.'

"When we returned to the General's wife, two of the Prefect's officers were waiting for us. Rasputin kissed all those present, begged me to come back to St. Petersburg, and then went off to the station, accompanied by the two officials, whence he started at once for the capital."

* * * * *

Vera Alexandrovna Shukovskaia accompanied the starets to one of these parties in St. Petersburg; her description gives a good idea of their strange atmosphere, in which drunken orgies were mixed up with grave decisions of high clerical policy:

"'Come with me to-night, we'll dance and drink,' Rasputin said to me one day.

"'Where?' I asked.

"'At the house of my friends. Do *you* consent? It will be very jolly.'

"'All right,' I said. 'I'll come.'

"'That's splendid,' he cried joyfully. 'Come about six o'clock.'

"When I went back to his house I found him in the waiting-room surrounded by four men and a lady; they were obviously Caucasians. Rasputin himself was ready to go out. . . . They were all talking promiscuously in loud voices, and I could not quite understand what it was all about. The words 'concession' and 'stock exchange' occurred several times, and pressure was to be put on certain people. Rasputin deprecated this, gesticulating with hands and walking-stick, and murmured his eternal 'All right, I'll do it, come to-morrow, I have no time now.'

"'Ah, darling, *you* have kept your word and have come, thank *you*.' He took my arm and went down the stairs with me. When we reached the street I saw an elegant motor-car waiting for us. The chauffeur, a soldier, gave Rasputin a military salute; we got in quickly and drove off.

"In a little while the car stopped before a high house.

"'It should be here,' said Rasputin. 'Darling, ask the porter if the P.'s live here.'

"I looked at him in amazement: 'But you said they were friends of yours, and you do not even know where they live?'

"The porter hurried up, and led us to the second floor, where he rang the bell. The door was opened by a fat little woman who shouted with joy at the sight of us. 'Father, dear Father,' she cried, and embraced Rasputin. In the hall a tall, thin man came up and welcomed the starets, and finally we reached the dining-room which, it seemed, also served as a reception-room, for, in addition to the richly spread dining-table, sofas tastelessly upholstered in gaudy red plush were ranged along the walls. They were occupied by several young men of indeterminate appearance, who rose respectfully as we came in.

"The hostess winked slyly at me and, turning to Rasputin, said: '*You've* got a new sweetheart, I see.'

"Grigori Efimovich laughed heartily, flung his arm round me, and said gaily: 'One does not interfere with another! Oh, how frightfully I love this one!' With these words he drew me on to the sofa, pulled the table in front of me, and said, still laughing: 'Now *you* will not run away from me!'

"Suddenly I heard a soft, singing voice: 'Christ bless you!' I looked round; in the corner, under the ikons, a little old man in a coarse pilgrim's garment was kneeling.

"'Ah, Vassia,' cried Rasputin to him. 'How are you?' The little man made no answer.

"Rasputin muttered something to himself: the host appeared in the doorway with bottles of wine in his hands, placed them on the table, and said: 'Be good enough, dear Father, to drink this port until *your* favourite wine arrives.'

"'Give me some,' muttered Rasputin, and pushed forward his glass. Then he took a gulp and handed the glass to me: 'Drink, my darling,' said he. 'People may say it is a sin as much as they like; to hell with sin!' And he emptied one glass after another.

"'The cursed rascals,' he broke out suddenly, 'are always wanting something; but they do not understand what is the chief thing.' He had another drink.

"'And what is the chief thing?' I inquired.

"Rasputin bent over me: 'The Church should know that,' he whispered, blinking at me slyly.

"'The Church? That should mean the Synod?' I asked teasingly.

"'Well, *you* have made a fine discovery! The devil take *your* Synod! If only it weren't for this war, God Almighty, one could do everything! Drink,' he cried, and poured some wine into my mouth by force. 'Drink, *you* can drink splendidly. Come here,' he called to the young men. 'Everybody is to get tipsy with me. Come!'

"The whole company came up and looked greedily at the wine glasses. At this moment the host came in and brought two other bottles, Madeira this time, Rasputin's favourite wine. At the same moment the hostess also appeared with a big dish of fried bream.

" 'That is good,' cried Rasputin delightedly, and began to eat. He ate the fish with his hands, put big lumps on my plate, and stroked me with half-wiped, greasy fingers.

"The host sat down opposite Rasputin, and seized an unoccupied moment to ask: 'When do *you* intend to visit Pitirim in the Caucasus?'

" 'I am going at Easter, at Easter,' answered Rasputin quickly, and drank a glass of wine. 'Pitirim is a good fellow who will find his way about. There is brawling and strife on his account now. Pitirim belongs to us.'

" 'He is a sly fox, however, you have to be careful,' rejoined the host. 'Pitirim will be stricter with the Consistory.'

"Rasputin would not listen, clapped him on the shoulder, and cried: 'Ho! Music! Look alive! Where is the champagne? Fall to . . .'

"In the twinkling of an eye two balalaika players appeared. At the first notes of a real Russian dancing song Rasputin leapt into the middle of the room.

" 'Drink to the last drop,
  Only lose not your head!'

sang Rasputin. 'Drink, my little bee.' He tossed the wine down at a gulp, flung his glass on to the floor, and whirled round the room in a wild dance, cheering and shouting. That was a dance! In his mauve silk shirt, with a red girdle round his waist, and in high, polished boots, drunk and happy, he danced in rapturous transport, shrieking wildly.

"The uproar, clinking of glasses, and the strains of the instruments made me giddy; everything whirled madly before my eyes. Rasputin shoved aside everything that came in his way, and in a twinkling the middle of the room was empty. Then he seized me, pulled me over the table into the middle of the room, and cried: 'Dance!' Carried away by his fierceness, I whirled with him; the dance became more and more boisterous, until at last I dropped into a chair, almost fainting. I saw Rasputin's flushed face as in a mist. Whistling and stamping he struck into the song:

" 'Lady, lady, gracious lady,
Give me your little hands!'

Then he sat down on the sofa breathing heavily.

" 'Well, I've danced my fill this time,' he said; 'but it is not to be compared with our dancing in Siberia. All day we fell trees, such trees. Three men could not get their arms round them. And when evening comes we make a fire in the snow and sing and dance till midnight. That's a life for you, I tell *you*.'

"The room was unbearably hot. One of the half-drunken youths was sitting on the floor, the others were still playing on their instruments. Suddenly Rasputin thumped on the table again and pointed to his empty glass; it was at once refilled. As he drank the host asked him humbly: 'What is your view about the Church Assembly? When will it be convoked?'

"Rasputin stared at him, and mumbled thickly: '*You* see, the war . . . as soon as we are free. We are always ready, Russia will not remain without Patriarchs. Only we must send the war to the devil.'

" 'What about the Consistory?'

"He would not leave Rasputin in peace; but the latter jumped up again and clapped his hands, crying: 'The devil take the Consistory!'

" 'Lady, lady, gracious lady . . .

And as for Pitirim, the son of a dog, we'll make him Metropolitan!'

"The youth sitting on the floor crawled on all fours behind the wildly dancing Rasputin: the strings clanged; like a madman Grigori Efimovich whirled round the room. His greedy eyes stared at me: 'To-day *you* will not run away from me; *you* must stay with me.

" 'Lady, lady, gracious lady . . .

Synod, Pitirim, to the devil!'

"At the door I tore myself free. I said I would come back immediately. In the hall I found my furs with difficulty and agitation and departed hastily. Behind me echoed the sound of the song and Rasputin's words: 'Pitirim, the dog, shall be Metropolitan!'"

CHAPTER XII

THE REVOLT AGAINST THE HOLY DEVIL

AT first, hatred of Rasputin had merely smouldered in the intrigues of courtiers and ministers; then it shot into flames of prurient gossip, and spread in ugly rumour until it blazed up in the virtuousness of a prim governess, who protested against the intrusion of this "disgusting peasant" into the chamber of the Emperor's daughters. Later, the hostility reasserted itself in the form of patriotism and loyalty to the Emperor: "true Russians" puffed out their chests and warned the Emperor of the fatal danger of his intercourse with Grigori Efimovich.

Zealous governors, chiefs of police, and ministers vied with each other in laying before the Tsar reports of the dissipations, orgies, and scandalous conduct of the imperial favourite. Well-meaning relatives, grand dukes and grand duchesses, appeared at Court with serious faces, and even the sister of the Empress hastened to warn her before it was too late.

But all these attacks on the power of the diabolical peasant proved vain. The Emperor regarded the intrigues of the courtiers and ministers as an expression of petty jealousy; it seemed beneath his dignity to pay any attention to such gossip. It might be the business of newspaper reporters to concern themselves with rumours; but he, the ruler of all the Russias, was not interested in such things. The prim governess's objection to the visits of the starets was nothing but "impudent presumption," and was punished by dismissal from the imperial service.

If one of the "faithful" appeared at an audience with a face full of trouble to warn Nikolai against Rasputin, he was met with the answer: "But, my dear fellow, you are taking too black a view! Don't be at all uneasy, I know quite well what to make of Rasputin."

The reports of the ministers, governors, and directors of police were skimmed in haste and irritation, and thrown into the wastepaper basket. What further significance had they? For had not Grigori himself said that his enemies had allied themselves with the devil in order to lay snares for him? Was it surprising that the holy man did not always succeed in overcoming all his tribulations in a moment, and that he sometimes had to struggle long and hard to free himself from the claws of Satan?

All the relatives, Nikolai Nikolaevich and his brother, Anastasia and Militsa, who once had been untiring in their assertions of Rasputin's saintliness, now appeared and implored the Emperor to banish this horrible muzhik. But had not the Tsar meanwhile had ample opportunity to convince himself of the self-seeking and untrustworthiness of all these relatives? Had they not supported Grigori merely because they thought to make him their tool? But now, when he had proved himself to be a true "friend" of the imperial couple, they found him irksome and were trying to dislodge him again.

Elisaveta Fedorovna also came to prejudice her imperial sister against Rasputin. She was the only one whose intentions were honest, for was she not a nun, almost an angel? But what did she know of the world and its failings? Was she not led astray by malicious slanders into blindly believing all the evil people told her about Rasputin? Alix and Nikolai, however, were acquainted with the world, and knew that the pure man is always persecuted and slandered. So Alexandra was able to say to her beloved sister in a calm, superior tone: "Believe me, my dearest, you are misled. A saint is always reviled."

And the warnings of the "true Russian people"? What could the Emperor think of their words? Was it not they whose patriotic hearts had first burst into a flame of enthusiasm for Rasputin? Were not they the very people who had first proclaimed that the voice of the Russian people spoke directly from the mouth of the peasant? And now they abused him because he had disappointed their ambitious hopes! Yes, Grigori Efimovich was truly "the voice of the people," and the unkempt beard, the peasant kaftan, the knotted staff, and the greased top-boots were more than the trappings of imposture for which the "true Russian people" had taken them. His peasant beard really grew on him in this unkempt fashion, his wide trousers were as natural as if he had come into the world with them, and his knotted staff and top-boots had, as it were, grown on him. He was the genuine muzhik that the sovereign saw and felt, and neither intrigues nor slanders could persuade him against the truth of these signs.

A disinterested person could understand only too easily why the "true Russian people" had repented of their enthusiasm for Grigori Efimovich, and why they now hated and loathed him. For years they had been babbling of the "genuine peasant" who must come to preserve the throne; the genuine peasant had come, and he did not mince his words. He banged on the table when the chatter of the "friends of the people," generals, politicians, advocates, and priests, did not please him, and, at every difference of opinion, unconcernedly made the "voice of the people" heard with perfect clearness.

If ambitious generals, in their swashbuckling way, talked of Pan-Slav ideas, and politicians and advocates eagerly seconded them, and priests blessed their designs because a new war would offer great possibilities to "true Russian" generals, politicians, advocates, and priests, Grigori Efimovich became very disagreeable and stormed, vituperated, and cursed blasphemously: "We peasants do not want war. It is you damned townsmen who want to shed the blood of the country people to further your own schemes."

But there were also a number of others, whose profound dislike of Grigori Efimovich was based on purely personal grounds: many of them had been sharply rebuffed by Rasputin; when they waited on the all-powerful "friend" with a request that he should find a ministerial position for them in the near future, Grigori Efimovich answered insolently: "*You* surely don't expect me to make a horse a minister?"

Painfully unpleasant incidents of this kind had happened not infrequently, especially if the petitioner, confident of his position and abilities, had behaved with self-assurance; while, on the other hand, Rasputin had almost over-night raised to the highest offices of State other people who had come to him simply and modestly.

But what won him most enemies was his artlessness and the

casual manner in which he was accustomed to speak of his influence at Court. His way of saying: "Certainly, I can manage everything with 'Him' and 'Her'" made much bad blood, for it wounded the heart of every ambitious place-hunter. There must be something wrong with the world when theological graduates, trained strategists, and tried administrative officials achieved nothing while this ignorant lout of a muzhik could brag of his omnipotence? There were people whose grandfathers had served at Court and who now, in spite of the greatest exertions, could hardly obtain a few moments' audience. If you wanted to obtain anything from the Emperor, you had first to sue for the favour of this arrogant peasant, and even then you ran the risk of being met with remarks like: "I cannot make every simpleton a bishop!"

It was no wonder that wounded dignity and mortified ambition were everywhere up in arms against Rasputin. Even people, otherwise kindly and guileless, like gentle Father Feofan, could not help a feeling of irritated envy when they saw the unceremonious way in which Grigori Efimovich dealt with them, and it was not surprising that they began to be wroth with him.

* * * * *

This very Father Feofan, the man of child-like spirit, was one of the first to give rein to his wrath against Rasputin. Who would ever have thought that the little peasant preacher would have had such a rapid and successful career at Court and far outsoar his early patrons? For even the heart of a truly holy man like Father Feofan was subject to attacks of jealousy. His jealous hatred of Grigori blazed up as rapidly as his earlier enthusiasm for the starets had done; and, with the same uncritical attitude which once made him see a new Saviour in the Siberian peasant, he now pointed to the coarse dissipations of this peasant as an infallible sign of his alliance with the devil.

Father Feofan once again took the way he had taken before when he had proclaimed Grisha's holiness. He went to Bishop Hermogen of Saratov, to Iliodor, to the "true Russian people," and to the Grand Duke Nikolai Nikolaevich, and told them all that Rasputin was nothing but an incarnation of Antichrist.

The good-natured Bishop of Saratov had little use for apocalyptic extravagances; he had never thought Grisha a saint, and he was as little inclined to think him a devil. He listened in his usual manner, sitting comfortably on a sofa, to the fanatical adjurations of the little Archimandrite, and finally remarked, quietly and meditatively: "A profligate scamp, this Grisha!" Whereupon he immediately began to discuss the practical and political side of the case, and to consider how Rasputin could be overthrown with the help of the "true Russian people."

Finally, Feofan and Hermogen agreed that every effort must be made to get rid of the troublesome starets; from now on they raised their voices openly and unreservedly against Rasputin, and took every opportunity to be unpleasant to him. On the monk-priest Iliodor, however, the hellish curse still rested, which forced him against his better judgment to support Grigori Efimovich. While the feeble old Feofan stormed against Grisha in his weak voice, the redoubtable "great curser" had, as before, to follow Rasputin humbly and reverently like an acolyte.

And yet he knew better than anyone the full diabolical depravity of Grigori. Neither Feofan, praying eternally before his little oil-lamp, nor Hermogen, immersed in problems of clerical policy, had witnessed Rasputin's sinful conduct with his own eyes, as Iliodor had done. The envy and hate of the monk-priest were nourished on personal, vivid, and incontestable evidence.

On one occasion, immediately after Grisha had come to pay him a visit at Tsarytsin, a poor carter, one of his most devoted followers, begged him despairingly for help. The carter's wife, it seemed, had been attacked by the devil, and only the monk-priest, by his powerful exorcism, could rescue her from the clutches of the Evil One. Iliodor started at once for his disciple's house, Grigori accompanying him. The carter's wife, a young, beautiful, and buxom woman, was rolling on the ground in convulsions, and uttering horrible, obscene cries. Iliodor did everything that an Orthodox priest can do in such cases, sprinkled the woman with holy water, bent over her and said the prescribed prayers, placed a big crucifix over her head, and adjured the devil until the sweat poured down his face. But the woman went on shrieking and rolling on the ground and showed no signs of improvement.

Then Grigori, who had hitherto looked on in silence, went up to Iliodor, clapped him on the shoulder, and said: "Come, *you* don't understand this business. Leave me alone with this sinful woman, and I will drive the devil of unchastity from her." Almost bursting with rage, the monk-priest silently turned and left the sick room, accompanied by the carter. He longed to beat Rasputin, so annoyed was he by this unseemly interference with his exorcism.

In the next room he talked to the husband of the unfortunate woman, spoke words of courage, and comforted and blessed him until the cries suddenly were silent. An anxious interval of waiting followed; then the pretty wife, with rosy cheeks and bright eyes, came smiling into the room; Grigori followed with a sly, triumphant smirk on his lips. "See," he cried in triumph, "I have driven the devil completely out of her!"

Iliodor shook with fury, but nevertheless turned at once to the carter and said: "Grigori Efimovich is a truly holy man, a miracle worker blessed by God." The carter threw himself at Rasputin's feet and kissed his hands in deep emotion. Next day the news of Grigori's cure spread all over Tsarytsin.

Chance willed it that, soon after, the devil attacked the niece of Madame Lebedeva, a rich merchant's wife. She had already heard of the cure of the carter's wife, and would have liked to send straight for Grigori. But, as she did not wish to slight the monk-priest, she begged him to drive the devil out of her niece, calculating that the holy Father Grigori would come with him.

Iliodor at once packed all the necessary apparatus in a case and started off, this time also accompanied by Grisha. Once again the sprinkling with holy water failed and the Biblical quotations and formulas of adjuration produced no effect, and at last Rasputin intervened, and demanded that Iliodor should leave the whole thing to him. The merchant's wife was secretly delighted at this turn of events.

Before beginning his work, Grisha declared that the room in which the patient was lying was entirely unsuitable for exorcising the devil. He examined the whole house, and finally ordered that the sick girl should be carried to an isolated room. This was at once done, and he shut himself in with the possessed girl.

N. IVANOV: CARICATURE OF RASPUTIN
"Russia's Ruling House"

RUSSIAN CARICATURES OF RASPUTIN
ABOVE—"*I drove him from the throne before you.*"
BELOW—"*We Nickolai, II.*"

This time the devil apparently did not give up the fight so quickly; for a long time passed without Rasputin's reappearance. Iliodor could not control his impatience, and several times went through all the rooms to the door of the isolated room. The girl was not crying any longer; everything was quiet; but still Grigori did not appear.

It was not until late in the evening that Rasputin left the sick room, and announced that he had at last succeeded in overcoming the evil spirit. The patient was in bed quietly sleeping. Her face was calm and peaceful, as if she were dreaming she was surrounded by angels.

After the news of this second miraculous cure became known in Tsarytsin, Grisha's fame grew enormously, especially when it was learned that this starets was none other than the celebrated Rasputin from St. Petersburg, the friend and adviser of the Tsar. The people of Tsarytsin, who for years had listened to Iliodor's preaching with fanatical piety, were now eager to pay homage to the new saint, and one deputation after another called at the monk-priest's house.

"The rascal, the lout, the sham saint!" cursed Iliodor to himself whenever one of these deputations appeared and asked to be allowed to testify to their veneration for the starets from St. Petersburg. But when the next day dawned, the monk-priest put on his finest vestments and went with Grigori from house to house. Everywhere, in the street and in the houses, Rasputin was received as a messenger from heaven. The people bowed to the ground before him, kissed his hands, and humbly begged for his blessing.

Iliodor could joyfully have struck this dirty peasant dead, seeing him receive the reverence of the whole town as a matter of course; but actually he joined in the universal chorus of praise, and loudly proclaimed that Grigori Efimovich was a true benefactor of humanity whom God had commissioned to advise and help the Tsar himself.

And so the cases of Grisha's debauchery and depravity increased, for as such Iliodor had at once recognized them. But he could not nerve himself to take any steps against the hated impostor, except that, on a sudden resolution, following the example of Bishop Hermogen, he turned round the picture of Rasputin which hung over his bed, so that the face of Antichrist was against the wall.

Antichrist had meantime thought out a new piece of deviltry with which to humiliate Iliodor: he suddenly declared his intention to start on a penitential journey from Tsarytsin, and demanded that he should be escorted out of the town with a ceremonial procession, and also that he should be given flowers and a valuable present on his departure. Iliodor once again raged inwardly at this imposition; but again he had not the courage to oppose Rasputin's will. He arranged a great procession, placed himself at its head, and escorted Grisha a fair distance on the road to Saratov; finally, he humbly wished him a good journey, and handed him a costly farewell gift.

Iliodor was not successful in freeing himself from the mysterious spell that emanated from Grigori Efimovich until the time when he travelled with Grigori to his home at Pokrovskoe. On the journey Grigori kept no guard on his tongue, and quite unconcernedly told him of his sinful life. It even seemed as if it afforded him special pleasure to speak of such loathsome things and to lead the ascetic monk-priest into temptation. He described at length and in detail how he had sinned with the Tsesarevich's nurse, and how she, along with Laptinskaia, the peasant woman, a beautiful princess, and some other women, had followed him to Verkhoture in summer. There he freely indulged himself in sin with them all, until the women and he "had overcome the flesh" and become "passionless."

Grisha spent much time in these narrations, and he continued them in the carriage, in the train, and even on the ship, as if he would never make an end. The strict monk-priest who, all his life, by rigorous asceticism, had struggled against the temptations of the senses, felt to his dismay that the devil who spoke from Grisha's mouth was gradually taking possession of him too. He gazed at the narrator with burning eyes, his mouth open in stupefied amazement; finally, when Rasputin asked him mockingly how he liked all this, Iliodor had to confess dejectedly that he had never let himself even dream of such things.

In his inmost heart the monk-priest now understood that

Grisha was one of those impious heretics belonging to the sect of the Khlysty, of whose diabolical sinfulness he had so often heard. Although this discovery did not then give him strength to make a final break with Grisha, it nevertheless helped him considerably in the end to acquire the necessary courage. During this journey another even more significant discovery was at last to free him entirely from Rasputin's spell, and to open up quite new and unexpected possibilities.

Iliodor had long known that the Tsar and Tsaritsa venerated Grisha as a holy man; but he was able now to convince himself by the evidence of his own eyes of the lengths to which this veneration went. Even before they arrived at Pokrovskoe Rasputin had said, in a boastful tone, that the Tsar looked on him as the Saviour, and how both he and the Tsaritsa bowed to the earth before him and kissed his hand. Grisha had remarked proudly on the boat: "The Tsaritsa has sworn to be loyal to me and to regard me as her benefactor and rescuer for ever." Then he added: "I am on such friendly terms with them that they are all at my beck and call."

In spite of all this talk Iliodor still clung to the hope that Rasputin was lying and exaggerating, and this idea served a little to calm his heart, which was bursting with jealousy. But how amazed he was when he came to Grisha's house in Pokrovskoe. Even the outside of this fine building made a great impression on him; the inside, however, surpassed all his expectations. It is true that there were the old modest peasant rooms, partly furnished with quite simple furniture; but among it stood luxurious, magnificent show-pieces, costly leather sofas, glass bookcases, sideboards full of valuable silver and cut glass. One room even contained a grand piano, gilt furniture, flowers, and palms. The whole upper story was carpeted with heavy Persian rugs and, on wall-brackets, stood portraits of the imperial family, the Grand Duchesses, Court dignitaries, and ministers, arranged according to rank, and all having flattering autograph dedications. There was a whole chest full of knick-knacks presented to their dear little Father by the imperial children; magnificent ikons hung everywhere, gifts from bishops, monks, nuns, and pious laymen. And the study! It looked like a minister's private room: a costly set of chairs upholstered in heavy leather occupied one corner; before the window stood a big oak writing-table, with a pile of papers, documents, telegrams, and letters on it.

Iliodor's eyes almost started from his head; for the first time he recognized the real power and enormous prestige of Rasputin, for all these things were not gifts from simple citizens; Grigori Efimovich could say exactly which member of the imperial house, which high State dignitary or admired beauty of the capital had presented each piece.

The whole stay at Pokrovskoe was a veritable martyrdom to Iliodor, for at every turn he met with fresh proofs of his antagonist's powerful position; and even during work in the fields or while fishing, Grigori kept telling him how prosperous he was, and what veneration he met with on all sides.

On the last evening before Iliodor's departure, Mikhail, the postman, brought a big letter that bore the imperial arms and seal. Rasputin read it through, stroked his beard contentedly, and informed his guest that it was an autograph letter from the Empress. This news gave the monk-priest no peace; in the middle of the night he rose, stole into his host's study, and searched the writing-table till he found the letter. Its contents made him furious, for in it the Empress, in urgent, almost imploring words, begged her "Friend" to come to Tsarskoe Selo at once, as the heir-apparent was ill again.

Iliodor was not content with reading this one letter; he rummaged through all the drawers, till he found a big bundle wrapped in blue checked cotton, which contained all the letters of the Empress and the Grand Duchesses. With feverish eyes he read these documents one after the other, and soon had to acknowledge that everything Rasputin had said about his position at Court was the simple truth.

But as an all-devouring jealousy flamed up in Iliodor's soul he felt the diabolical spell that had hitherto bound him to Rasputin fall away from him. Now at last he could hate his enemy freely and unrestrainedly. Now he would show him! From this time forth this vicious and impudent peasant would find he had an implacable enemy in him, the "great curser."

He appropriated a few particularly affectionate letters from the Empress and the Grand Duchesses; this was, of course, a theft and a sin; but it was done in the interests of truth and to save both the ruling house and the nation, and the end might justify his action. Next morning he left Pokrovskoe, firmly resolved to square accounts with Grisha, to unmask him, and reveal the full story of his depravity to the Emperor and the Empress themselves. For this purpose he went direct to St. Petersburg.

The monk-priest was fully aware of the difficulty of his undertaking. Had he not had to look on helplessly while good Father Feofan was immediately silenced when he tried to denounce Rasputin at Court? He had also a vivid recollection of the threatening air with which Grisha called after the Rector of the Theological Academy: "I'll show him!" It was certainly no chance either that Feofan, the Court preacher and confessor to the Empress, was suddenly dismissed from his high position and transferred as a punishment to Tauris.

Nevertheless, Iliodor was hopeful and sure of his case. Was he not called the "Knight of the Heavenly Kingdom"; was not he, the "great curser," known, feared, and honoured for his fearlessness? Was he, who had overthrown all-powerful governors and dared to defy chiefs of police and ministers and even the Holy Synod itself, to be afraid of denouncing this lout of a peasant, and opening the eyes of the sovereign to his real character?

* * * * *

Since that blessed night when the spell fell from him by Rasputin's writing-table, Iliodor had recovered his power of reviling, that sublime gift with which no one, since the time of the Old Testament prophets, had been so nobly endowed as he. He now cried aloud to all the world that Rasputin was a monster of iniquity, a child of hell, who deserved to be exterminated like the noxious vermin he was. Abuse and curses against Grisha poured from him in an inexhaustible stream, and he was able to bring ever fresh evidence of Rasputin's misdeeds and atrocious debauchery. He even told how he had looked through the keyhole in the house of Lebedeva, the merchant's wife, in Tsarytsin, and that what he saw there was anything but the struggle of a saint against the power of Satan!

And as for those everlasting "brotherly kisses" with which Rasputin greeted all women! Why did he kiss only the young and pretty ones, why did he never think of letting the Holy Spirit flow through his kisses to elderly matrons as well? He told the tale of Elena, the carter's pretty, voluptuous wife, whom Grigori Efimovich had completely entangled in his net; and how, during their journey together to Pokrovskoe, Grisha had tried to convert him to the heretical faith of the Khlysty; and, if anyone asked after the holy Father Grigori, Iliodor turned on the unfortunate man in a towering rage and cried: "A holy man, indeed! A holy devil is what he is!"

He went to Hermogen, who was then staying in St. Petersburg, to try to win him over to a joint campaign against the "holy devil," and, after his talk with him, he began to inundate with letters all the high dignitaries and even the Tsar himself. He also applied to Doctor Badmaev for the purpose of enlisting his influence with the Emperor. "I adjure you," he wrote to the Tibetan, "to break with Rasputin. His power is increasing every day; his army grows; his prestige with the people is visibly becoming greater. It is not my own fate that I am anxious about, but rather the fate of the imperial family. All this will lead to terrible scandal, perhaps even to revolution! For God's sake, shut Rasputin's mouth as soon as possible. Every day is precious!"

But, in a conversation with Hermogen, Iliodor declared, trembling with fury: "I want to see whether the imperial family will renounce this lout or not. What is the meaning of it all? Here we are dying for them, toiling for them, while they are carrying on God knows what with this licentious fellow!"

From the beginning the "miraculous idiot," Mitia Koliaba, had placed himself absolutely at the disposal of the "Knight of the Heavenly Kingdom" as a brother-in-arms. He had long been yelping, groaning, and growling in vain, and prophesying the most terrible disasters, through the medium of Egorov, the psalm-singer, if the peasant Grigori were not immediately banished. But no one paid any heed to his holy ravings. If Nikolai or Alexandra felt the need of oracles, they preferred to apply to Grigori Efimovich, who could see into the future better than

Mitia Koliaba, and who besides spoke in a generally intelligible, even too intelligible, language. The various mystical circles and salons, following the example of the Court, had also lost all interest in the miraculous idiot.

Thus it was not surprising that Mitia Koliaba agreed with a delighted croak to the request of Iliodor and Hermogen that he should support them in their campaign against the "holy devil." Soon a regular council of war was arranged, in which the bishop, the curser, the miraculous idiot, and the psalm-singer took part. Iliodor and Hermogen had previously attempted to enlist the aid of Shcheglovitov, the Minister of Justice; they paid a formal call on him, and asked whether it would not be possible to remove Rasputin by ordinary judicial means; but the Minister did not dare to embark on any measures against the powerful "Friend."

After they had found that no proceedings could be taken against Rasputin in this way, the conspirators resolved on a bold stroke in order to exact a solemn confession of sin and an oath of penitence from Grigori Efimovich.

Rasputin had just returned from a visit to the imperial couple in the Crimea when Iliodor called on him. He told the starets that Bishop Hermogen deeply regretted having opposed him, was longing to see him again, and begged him to come at once. Rasputin fell into the trap, and accompanied Iliodor to the Bishop's house where, besides the miraculous idiot, several witnesses, including two priests and—so as to provide for all contingencies—a journalist, were assembled.

Rasputin, noticing as he went in that Hermogen was not alone, at once suspected something wrong; but next moment Mitia Koliaba fell into a paroxysm of fury, and began to abuse the starets in stammering croakings like a madman, holding his stumps threateningly before his eyes. Rasputin, blazing with rage, turned on the idiot; but suddenly the gigantic Hermogen, swinging a large crucifix, stepped in between the two mutually cursing miracle-workers, and began to belabour Grigori Efimovich with the cross.

A tumultuous confused scuffle arose, during which Iliodor conducted an impressive speech for the prosecution, adorned with many quotations from Holy Scripture. Finally, they all fell on

Rasputin, beat him, and by frightful threats forced him to make a solemn confession of guilt. Then he was dragged into the adjoining house-chapel, and there made to swear by all the saints than in the future he would avoid all intercourse with the Emperor and Empress. There was nothing for the defenseless starets to do but to submit to all their demands. But, at the same time, he resolved to take a frightful revenge on his assailants.

Hardly had the conspirators released their victim than he rushed to the telegraph office and sent off a long wire to the Tsar at Yalta, in which he announced that Hermogen and Iliodor had instituted a murderous attack on him, but that he had, by God's help, been saved at the last moment.

But this did not satisfy Grigori's thirst for vengeance; he longed to pay his enemies back in their own coin. For this purpose he availed himself of Madame Golovina, making her telephone to Iliodor and invite him to come to see her next day; in the house of the old "Mother of the Church," the same trap as he had baited for the starets awaited the monk-priest.

Grigori Efimovich had collected round him the whole crowd of his women disciples, and, as Iliodor came in, he sprang at him and overwhelmed him with a flood of reproach and abuse. The indignant women simultaneously attacked Iliodor, and made as if to scratch his eyes out, so that the "curser" tried to escape with all speed. But at this moment the tall figure of von Pistolkors, Madame Vyrubova's brother-in-law, came up to him, and prepared to give him a sound thrashing. Iliodor had difficulty in reaching the door, and got out of the house pursued by a crowd of storming women.

A few days later an imperial edict arrived in St. Petersburg imposing severe penalties on both the ringleaders in the plot against Rasputin: Hermogen lost his bishopric, and was banished to a monastery in Lithuania, while Iliodor was shut up in the monastery of Floricheva Pustyn.

Iliodor was not long in escaping from his monastic prison and, as Russia was too hot to hold him, he fled to Norway, and settled there, in order to begin his real great campaign against the starets from that base. The chief thing he did was to write a libellous pamphlet entitled "The Holy Devil," in which he made a number of quite fantastic accusations against Grigori Efimovich, and also quoted a number of letters from the Empress and the Grand Duchesses, the originals of which were alleged to be in his possession. By means of these documents, most of which were glaring forgeries, he not only indicted his enemy Rasputin, but also opened a coarse attack on the whole imperial family and abused them in the most filthy fashion.

But he did not succeed in getting his book published immediately, for, at that time, Norway felt very little interest in Iliodor's revelations; so the manuscript remained for the moment in his drawer. He proceeded to engage in dangerous scheming and, from his safe retreat, planned an attempt on Rasputin's life.

There were still many fanatical followers of the exiled "curser" in Tsarytsin, and he used them for carrying out his plans. In 1913 a number of them had come together and resolved to try to revenge the injuries which had been inflicted on them and their revered monk-priest. With this object they concocted a definite plan to attack and overpower Rasputin; but they were imprudent enough to talk too much about their intentions, so that Grigori Efimovich was warned in time by one Sinitsin.

Again, in 1914, on Iliodor's express order, some of his followers formed a "committee of action," and discovered a hideous prostitute who had come down in the world, Kionia Guseva by name, a morbidly neurotic person, suffering from religious mania, whom it was not difficult to persuade to avenge Rasputin's many "vicious deeds." She went to Pokrovskoe and, on the pretext of making a pilgrimage, quartered herself on a peasant.

Some days passed before she found an opportunity of carrying out her plot; this did not happen till the 28th of June, a few days before the preliminaries of the World War. Rasputin had received a telegram from the Empress, and was hurrying to the street to give the answer to the postman, who had already left the house. Guseva, who had been prowling all the time in the neighbourhood of the house, went up to him, held out her hand, and begged for alms; the instant Rasputin put his hand in his pocket she drove the knife she held ready into his abdomen, crying shrilly that she had slain Antichrist.

Grigori Efimovich, by exerting all his strength, saved himself from falling, and pressing his hands over the gash, he fled into his house, where he at once collapsed. The assassin, who was carrying on like a mad woman, was secured with difficulty and placed under arrest.

Rasputin was found to be very seriously wounded. The doctor, summoned from Tiumen by telegraph, had, immediately on his arrival after an eight hours' drive, to perform a difficult operation on the patient in the big dining-room by the light of a few candles. A few days later he was moved to the hospital at Tiumen, where for weeks he lay between life and death.

The judicial inquiry into the case soon showed that the accused was more or less mentally deranged, and the legal authorities decided to stop proceedings and to confine her in an institution.

CHAPTER XIII

THE GREAT FISH SUPPERS

ONE foggy winter morning in 1914, as Rasputin, wrapped in thick furs, was driving along the Fontanka, his keen eye recognized in a car rushing past Prince Andronnikov, whom he had often seen but never spoken to. He immediately leaned out of the moving sledge, gesticulated violently with both hands, and cried at the top of his voice: "Nikolai Petrovich, stop a moment. *You've* come in the very nick of time."

The man thus appealed to stopped his car and examined the man in the sledge in amazement; but, search his memory as he might, he could not recognize him. Meanwhile, Rasputin had ordered his *izvoshchik* to stop, and, clumsily unrolling himself from his wrappings, he left the vehicle and rushed impetuously up to Nikolai Petrovich and embraced him. "Why do *you* look at me like that?" he cried. "Don't *you* know me then?"

"I think you are making a mistake," said the gentleman in the car. "I am Prince Andronnikov."

"That's right, my dear fellow; I know who *you* are. As for me, I am Grigori Efimovich Rasputin. Where are *you* going?"

"Home," replied Prince Andronnikov, his face visibly brightening.

"Well, look here," cried Rasputin, "I'll come with *you*. God himself sent me to *you* to-day; we have many things to discuss."

At this first meeting with Grigori Efimovich in the Fontanka, Prince Nikolai Petrovich recognized in a flash the full significance of the new acquaintanceship in all its bearings. Although he was not more religious than seemed expedient from business considerations, this time he honestly felt that God himself had really thrown Rasputin across his path.

"Where is *your* beautiful ikon-corner with the precious picture of the Mother of God?" inquired Rasputin the instant he entered the Prince's house. "I've been told *you* possess a regular little chapel."

Andronnikov eagerly conducted his visitor to his prayer-room, which actually did resemble a niche in a church; the starets at once fell on his knees and began a long prayer, in which his host joined with dutiful piety. At last he rose from his knees, and signed to the Prince that he too might cease. "Well, Nikolai Petrovich," he said, "now we have strengthened ourselves by prayer, and can confidently discuss our business!"

An animated conversation at once ensued in the Prince's drawing-room, which soon turned on Sukhomlinov, the Minister of War, whom Rasputin hated. He declared that Sukhomlinov had called him a beast, and must, therefore, be overthrown. Andronnikov fervently agreed with his guest, as he himself had had serious differences of opinion with the War Minister, and was overjoyed to hear that Rasputin was also ill-disposed towards him. Finally Andronnikov resolved to try to remove Sukhomlinov with Rasputin's help. He told his visitor all he knew of the defects and weaknesses of the minister, until at last Rasputin suddenly broke in with visible signs of impatience.

"Look here, my dear fellow," he cried, "it will be better if I come to *you* to-morrow evening. Have some fish prepared and order a few bottles of Madeira. Everything can be discussed much more easily over fish and wine. Such important things as those we have to speak of can only be blessed by a wholesome meal!"

Andronnikov gladly assented to this proposal, and took a devoted farewell of his powerful visitor, who, just as he was on the point of leaving the house, suddenly turned back, asked for writing materials, and scratched on a slip of paper the words: "*You* are a man of strong mind. *Your* strength lies in your mind." He handed the paper to the Prince, with the request that he should preserve it in memory of this first conversation; "For," said he, "we are going to be good friends."

Next night the starets appeared punctually for his fish supper. The Prince had made all the necessary preparations, had provided food and drink and also invited his friend Chervinskaia. Although a relative of Sukhomlinov's wife, she was on the worst possible terms with the family of the War Minister. She was an elegant woman with a good figure and fine eyes; but she already looked a little faded, as is not unusual with women who are approaching the end of the forties. She was also very witty and most excellent company, and it was a pleasure for any man of wit to talk to her. Moreover, she was distinguished by great discretion, and was a valuable ally in the present affair, because she was far more familiar with the affairs of the Sukhomlinov couple than even the well-informed Prince himself.

Rasputin was delighted to find a pretty woman there, and at once embraced her. Then he also kissed his host, had a few words with him, and took Madame Chervinskaia in his arms again. He occasionally liked to give a double greeting to women who pleased him.

The three sat down to table and began to discuss the details of the Sukhomlinov affair. The starets helped himself liberally, took one appetizing fish after another from the big dish, tore them to pieces with his hands in the air, picked the delicate flesh from the bones quite at his ease.

Madame Chervinskaia, on the contrary, her fish knife and fork between her long fingers, scraped the skin from every morsel before raising it to her mouth; but she hardly ate anything, for she kept thinking of fresh unsavoury details about the Minister and his wife, so that she did not get on very fast with her meal. The Prince, too, ate very sparingly; he was absorbed heart and soul in the matter in hand, and was contriving fresh plans and intrigues all the time. Grigori Efimovich, on the other hand, devoured one fish after another, drank several glasses of Madeira, felt very comfortable, and smacked his lips with content. Occasionally he would pause, and, with half a fish in his fist, remark that he would show Sukhomlinov. Then he brandished the fish threateningly for a moment, and buried himself in his meal again.

Sometimes, however, he would begin to talk on some quite irrelevant subject, for his mind was full of many important affairs; he did not like the conversation to linger too long on one theme, especially as he was convinced that even the most important things could be settled by brief sentences like "I'll see to it."

So he occasionally dropped the Sukhomlinov affair and began to talk of his relations with God, turning a bit of fish backwards and forwards in his fingers. He spoke of thorny problems of the soul and of faith, and here too uttered only a few brief, pithy sentences and then fell silent again. Both Prince Andronnikov and his friend, Madame Chervinskaia, were amazed at Rasputin's intelligence, and admired his religious competence.

Finally, the starets jumped up, wiped the wine from his beard, and left the table, repeating that he would deal with Sukhomlinov. He added in explanation: "I must tell you that 'Papa' and 'Mama' do everything I tell them." Whereupon he kissed Madame Chervinskaia, embraced his host, and hurried to the door, calling out as he went: "Merchants from Siberia are expecting me at the 'Villa Rode.' They have brought carpets for me and engaged gipsies." He hummed a few bars of the "Troika" song, made a few swaying dance steps, looked lovingly into the eyes of the lady, and disappeared.

* * * * *

More than a year passed. In the autumn of 1915 Madame Chervinskaia was paying a call on the newly appointed Director of Police, Beletski, from whom she had for some time been trying to secure the settlement of a petition. As she chatted with Beletski, a long, thin cigarette between her fingers, she remarked with apparent casualness: "Father Grigori came to a fish supper again with us yesterday. He told Nikolai Petrovich a great deal about the Emperor and Empress."

Beletski, who had hitherto been playing with his heavy gold watch-chain, and lending only half an ear to his visitor's conversation, pricked up his ears excitedly at the mention of Rasputin's name, asked for exact details of the conversation at the supper, and promised Madame Chervinskaia that her own affair would be favourably settled immediately. On saying good-bye he begged her to give his kindest remembrances to Prince Nikolai Petrovich, whom, alas! he had not seen for so long.

Senator Stefan Petrovich Beletski had recently, simultaneously with Khvostov's appointment as Minister of the Interior, risen to the dignity of a deputy-minister; he was entrusted with the supreme direction of the police, that is, with political espionage in particular. Since the Grand Duke Nikolai Nikolaevich and the "true Russian people" had abandoned Rasputin, Beletski had been one of the most skilful agents in the secret campaign against the starets, had supplied Colonel Balinski, the chief of the Grand Duke's Chancery, with almost daily reports of Grigori's debaucheries and drunken excesses, and, in this way, provided the "Nikolaevichi" and their wives with the material they collected so feverishly.

When Beletski heard from Madame Chervinskaia of the friendship between Grigori Efimovich and Prince Andronnikov, as a trained expert of the secret service he immediately saw the great possibilities which these fish banquets might offer him in the future. Here was an opportunity of being kept informed of all the private utterances of the starets, and the reports based on the material acquired in this way would be very welcome to the Grand Duke and the "true Russian people" in their attempts to oppose Rasputin. But apart from this private interest, Beletski saw how important such fish gatherings might be to him in the future, in his capacity as assistant to the Minister of the Interior, for the Ministry itself was exceedingly interested in being exactly informed about the intentions and plans of the all-powerful starets.

Beletski asked Prince Andronnikov to come to see him, having first ascertained from the official records his previous relations with the Ministry. To his satisfaction he found that the Prince had earlier been in receipt of regular subsidies, and had acted as a secret agent. So when Andronnikov appeared, he confined the conventional social forms to the minimum, exchanged a few cordial phrases with his visitor, and then proceeded straight to business in the manner of a Director of Police addressing one of his agents. In his singing, exaggeratedly melodious voice, he explained to the Prince his reason for sending for him:

"My dear Nikolai Petrovich, we have heard of your fish suppers with Rasputin. The Minister and I lay great stress on these fish suppers being held regularly in future, twice a week if possible; and we will permit ourselves from time to time to take advantage of your hospitality on these occasions. You know from experience that the Ministry is not stingy in such cases, and we shall be glad to pay the expenses of the meals you give Grigori Efimovich. In addition, you yourself can, of course, count on our gratitude."

Beletski went on to suggest that it was desirable that Madame Chervinskaia should be included in these social gatherings in order that she might tactfully lead the conversation round to "certain things" and a "few definite questions." Beletski closed his arguments with a further reference to the fact that the Ministry was not stingy, and gazed expectantly at the Prince with his round eyes that looked as if they were swimming in oil.

But Andronnikov also had experience with the Secret Service, and it seemed to him expedient not to trust to vague assurances of future gratitude and the like, but to demand a concrete equivalent for his services at the outset. So he replied that he was willing to accede to the wishes of the Minister's assistant, but that this time he could not under any circumstances accept compensation for his expenditure. On the other hand, he asked the Ministry to assist with the publication of his paper, *Golos Rossii*, in which journal he intended to give energetic support to the policy of the Ministers with whom he was on friendly terms.

Beletski understood the hint immediately, and soon a pact was concluded between the two men. Andronnikov left Beletski's office with a definite promise that the *Golos Rossii* would receive a liberal official subsidy, and that, in addition, Madame Chervinskaia could count on an adequate monthly salary while she participated in the princely fish suppers. In return Andronnikov pledged himself to have Rasputin to supper at least twice a week, to supply a detailed report of all he said, and occasionally to invite the Minister Khvostov and his assistant. In order to persuade the starets to visit Andronnikov regularly, it was arranged that the Prince should present him with a considerable sum of money—from the funds of the Ministry—at each of their meetings.

Although all possible precautions had been taken, Khvostov and Beletski felt somewhat anxious the first time they entered their car to be driven to one of Andronnikov's fish suppers. Beletski was only too well aware that, while he had Rasputin watched,

Rasputin also spied on him and, therefore, must be informed of his relations with the Grand Duke Nikolai Nikolaevich. Neither was Khvostov's conscience quite clear: the painful incident at Nizhni-Novgorod was, of course, practically forgotten since Khvostov had made it up with the starets by means of his fine bass voice; but a serious mistake in etiquette had crept in on the occasion of his appointment as Minister of the Interior. Full of impatient ambition, Khvostov had not waited for Grigori Efimovich's return from his expedition to Pokrovskoe, but had pushed on and carried through the appointment in his absence. This was a self-assertive act of a kind that Rasputin did not like, and so Khvostov looked forward to the fish supper with mixed feelings.

Immediately after the first greetings in Andronnikov's drawing-room the Minister's embarrassment increased still more, for the starets, his right hand thrust into his girdle, paced silently up and down the room and looked at fat Khvostov with unfriendly and searching glances. Even Prince Andronnikov, man of the world though he was, felt that things were beyond him, and he too was somewhat uncomfortable. Suddenly Rasputin stopped in front of Khvostov, looked him sharply and sternly in the eyes, and said: "Well, *you* were in a great hurry." Then he resumed his pacing up and down. A few more painful moments passed.

"*You* did not invite me to a meal that time in Nizhni-Novgorod," growled Rasputin in a low tone. "*You* behaved like a boor! And *you* were in such a hurry. And *you* too," turning to Beletski. But the latter had recovered his assurance in the interval, and poured out a shower of compliments and expressions of gratitude, in which Khvostov immediately joined. Prince Andronnikov also took the opportunity of bringing his social talents into play, and the three men gave Grigori Efimovich no further chance to speak. All talking at the same time, they thanked him with voices full of emotion for having come back, begged for his favour and his wise advice, and expressed the hope that he would always keep them on the right path and preserve them from mistakes. At this juncture Madame Chervinskaia appeared and asked them to come to supper. During the meal Rasputin's humour improved visibly, and, after drinking a few glasses of Madeira, he unbent so far as to say a few words in praise of Khvostov's bass voice.

As one fish after another vanished from the dish the gentlemen discussed various very important affairs of State. Khvostov, Beletski, and Andronnikov were very skilful, even at this first meeting, at putting this or that innocent question to the starets, and thus getting a fair idea of his intentions and plans. It is true that certain difficulties emerged that were inherent in the nature of a fish supper: if one of the politicians asked a question Rasputin went on eating, drank a glass of wine, wiped his mouth with the back of his hand, and only then gave his answer, which, in the circumstances, turned out most discreet and well considered. However cleverly Andronnikov's or Beletski's questions might be framed, the starets' replies were still cleverer, and all attempts to entice him into hasty or unconsidered speech proved fruitless. Soon all three, as they put their questions, had the depressing feeling that, as soon as he had finished his fish, Rasputin's reply would once again be cautious, reserved, and therefore useless for their purposes.

When the whole company retired to the drawing-room after supper, Andronnikov took the starets aside and disappeared with him for some minutes; as soon as they were through the door the Prince pulled out five hundred-rouble notes, and presented them to his guest, who buried them in his trousers pocket without looking at them. He begged Grigori to return the evening after next, and hinted that a similar sum would also be forthcoming then. Rasputin merely nodded, and the two returned to the drawing-room where, in their absence, Khvostov and Beletski had been giving Madame Chervinskaia detailed instructions. But it seemed as if the party could not feel at ease, for the lady suddenly rose and left the room on some trifling pretext. To Beletski's discomfiture fat Khvostov rushed after her. In the passage the Minister whispered to Madame Chervinskaia that she might also keep an eye on Beletski and note what he said to Rasputin behind his, Khvostov's, back. For any information on this point the Minister would show himself particularly grateful. Not until after this incident was the party re-united, and they talked on various political subjects for an hour longer. But, as they took their leave, Beletski took Madame Chervinskaia aside and asked her in confidence to report to him privately about the relations between Khvostov and Rasputin. Then they all kissed each other most affectionately and parted.

This noteworthy evening was the first of the series of historically important "fish suppers," which were soon to become a regular political institution. From that time onwards the most important affairs of State were more and more discussed and settled between the Minister, his assistant, and the "Friend" at such fish suppers. Although it was in the interests of all present to preserve the strictest secrecy about their meetings, rumours, and later, more and more definite accounts of them, began to circulate. It is easily understood that these secret conventicles were bound to rouse feelings of the most painful surprise, rage, and plain rebellion in all who saw their influence, if not their very existence, threatened by them.

* * * * *

The next fish supper to all appearances hardly differed from the preceding one. Again Rasputin, Khvostov, Beletski, Andronnikov, and Madame Chervinskaia sat talking round the well-spread table. With the exception of the starets, the appetites of all seemed to be very poor. While Grigori Efimovich steadily munched and chewed, the others talked to him with the greatest eagerness, to the neglect of the food in front of them. This was not to be wondered at, for in the course of this evening very important State business had to be settled: the dispute between Samarin, the Procurator of the Holy Synod, and Bishop Varnava about the canonization of John of Tobolsk.

Khvostov, Beletski, and Andronnikov endeavoured by adroit questioning to find out Rasputin's personal views on the matter. The Minister, in particular, had a strong interest in getting the quarrel settled in Varnava's favour and bringing about Samarin's retirement, for Samarin, as the representative of the Moscow nobility, was an opponent of Khvostov's. But to overthrow Samarin, Khvostov required the co-operation of the starets, and he was not yet sure whether he could count on it.

Varnava was, it was true, an old friend of Grigori Efimovich.

who had been instrumental in raising the simple monk to the episcopal throne. But a certain estrangement had taken place between the two, for Varnava, after his rise in rank, had noticeably drawn apart from Rasputin, a fact for which the starets was inclined to reproach him.

But the conversation with the starets on this subject again rather hung fire, and the inconveniences involved in the fish supper arrangement again became evident. Grigori Efimovich ate and ate, and thus was able to ponder over his answers. However, he at last dropped a word or two which let Khvostov and Beletski see that, although he had not yet quite forgiven his former friend Varnava for his present reserve, he was even more enraged at the haughty Procurator. Once he even flung the fish in his hands furiously on to the plate and shouted: "These distinguished nobles! What do they know of the Church and the holy faith? What we need in the Church are simple but pious men, who understand the people and whom the people understand! So Varnava pleases me better, even if I am sometimes thoroughly annoyed with him!"

That was enough. The party rose, gave each other a parting kiss, and went away satisfied. The Minister now knew that the days of his colleague Samarin were numbered.

Before the next supper the hosts had drawn certain inferences from their former experiences, and gave the starets meat dishes instead of fish, in the hope of speeding up the *tempo* of his replies. But this policy did not answer, for Rasputin left the meat untouched, showed his ill-humour quite plainly, and hardly spoke a word. So there was no help for it but to order to be served the fish dishes which had been prepared in case of emergency. And immediately a conversation on the Procurator and his probable successor developed. Khvostov had, in the interval, discovered a candidate agreeable to himself in the person of Volshin, a relative of his own; this man had, it is true, no experience fitting him for such high office; but, for this reason, would be a reliable tool in the hands of his patron, Khvostov. But it was by no means easy to secure Rasputin's approval of his candidature, for the former Procurator, Sabler, had been making despairing efforts to secure the favour of the starets and

THE GREAT FISH SUPPERS

the reversion of the vacant post. Beletski knew all about this, and during supper, found a most ingenious way of insidiously undermining Sabler's prestige with Grigori Efimovich. In the most innocent manner he brought the conversation round to the sects of the "Imiaboshtsy" and the "Onomatodoxy," which had been expelled from Athos, and for whom Rasputin, as he knew well, felt strong sympathy.

Grigori ate and listened in silence for some time. Then he pushed aside the clean-picked fish-bones, wiped his mouth, and said: "Yes, the Imiaboshtsy! When I was at Athos I found many clever and God-fearing men among them." Beletski then painted a dark picture of the terrible persecutions to which the Imiaboshtsy had been subjected during Sabler's tenure of the office of Procurator, and showed that Sabler had taken ruthlessly harsh measures against all the supporters of this doctrine, both open and secret.

Growing anger flamed in Rasputin's eyes. Suddenly he banged his fist on the table, crying: "So that's what Sabler's like? Well, I'll give it to him!" Khvostov at once joined in the conversation and pointed out the advantage of his candidate, Volshin; he particularly emphasized the fact that Volshin was ready to settle the painful dispute with Varnava about the canonization of John of Tobolsk by a compromise in Varnava's favour. Rasputin listened for some time in silence, cast searching looks at the Minister, tugged at his beard, and finally said that he would see Volshin and examine his soul.

At the next meeting the starets was in a very bad temper. "Pure good-for-nothings your agents are!" he attacked Beletski. "Lounging about the staircase all day, following me everywhere, but quite incapable of protecting me from stupid gossip. But just wait, you'll know me one day!" Then he became absorbed in his supper, and merely threw occasional furious glances at the Director of Police.

The latter did his best to appease Rasputin's wrath, and to find out what the trouble was. It was some time before Grigori Efimovich condescended to give any details, but when he did it appeared that a journalist called Davidsohn had written a gossiping article for the *Birzhevii Vedemostii* containing concealed allusions to Rasputin. This Davidsohn had made a special journey to Pokrovskoe to collect incriminating material against the starets, had wormed his way into Rasputin's family circle, and had even gone so far as to pay assiduous court to little Matriona, and had behaved as if he were her fiancé. In this way he had acquired some knowledge of Rasputin's habits, which he had expanded into a lengthy article.

The very next morning after Grigori's angry compliments Beletski sent to tell him that the matter was already settled, and that he would give the starets a full report that evening. At the next fish supper the ministerial assistant gave a full account of what he had done, which Grigori Efimovich followed with a satisfied smile, and such intense interest that he even forgot to eat.

"Immediately on arriving at the office this morning," said Beletski, "I proceeded to collect all the incriminating data about the past life of this Davidsohn. When I had enough I sent for the man, allowed him to cast an eye over my records, and handing him six hundred roubles from the secret funds, I intimated very strongly that he should give the question of further articles very careful consideration. Well, Davidsohn understood the hint, pocketed the six hundred roubles, and handed over his material in return. This afternoon I gave myself the pleasure of depositing this material for you, Little Father, with Madame Anna Vyrubova."

Grigori Efimovich beamed: "*You* are a good fellow, Stefan Petrovich!" he cried again and again. "*You* must be a minister." Khvostov was somewhat painfully affected by this remark and resolved that in future he would keep an even closer watch on his assistant. As he left the Prince's house he renewed his request to Madame Chervinskaia that she should give him the most detailed reports possible of conversations between Beletski and the starets.

* * * * *

Little by little a very comfortable atmosphere began to prevail in Andronnikov's dining-room. The party now knew each other pretty well, and no longer needed to observe such reserve. Beletski had counted on the growth of this sort of atmosphere when he made his pact with Andronnikov. It was for this reason that he had, so far, always restrained his chief from broaching the important but very ticklish subject of the opening of the Duma. Now the suitable moment seemed to have arrived.

The Duma was very close to the Minister's heart. From the moment of his appointment he had done everything in his power to have it convened. Since the outbreak of war the Russian National Assembly had been dissolved, a state of affairs quite in accordance with the wishes of old Goremykin, the Prime Minister, who had little desire to expose himself to the risk of violent parliamentary debates. Khvostov, on the other hand, the one aim of whose ambitious mind was to be Prime Minister himself, was endeavoring to involve Goremykin in just such inconveniences: on the assumption that the inefficiency of the Prime Minister would be made quite clear during the session of the Duma. Goremykin was not the man to weather a storm; he himself declared on all occasions that his real place was in a coffin under the ground.

But, in order to be able to convene the Duma, Rasputin had first to be won over, and that was likely to be anything but easy, as Khvostov well knew. For Grigori Efimovich, when Khvostov or Beletski had carefully tried to sound him, had more than once plainly expressed his aversion for the Duma. "Who sits in this Duma?" he challenged them. "Are they genuine representatives of the people? No. They're estate-owners, aristocrats, and rich men, but no real peasants."

It is true that the existing electoral regulations had, in fact, turned the original popular representative body into a class body, in which the peasantry had been forced into the background; although the starets knew and understood very little of this complicated state of affairs, he nevertheless felt that this Parliament would never support the only two questions which the peasants regarded as of importance, the conclusion of peace and the distribution of the large estates among the peasants. As, in addition, most of the members of the Duma, haughty deputies, landowners, and nobles, regarded Rasputin with hate and contempt, his attitude towards them was one of extreme hostility.

Khvostov and Beletski were very well aware of all this, and it was, therefore, only after considerable preparation that they dared to try to bring the starets round to favour the summoning of the Duma. The chief point in the preparations was to influence Rodzianko, the President of the Duma, in the desired direction, by conferring a high order on him on condition that he refuse to allow any attack on Rasputin in the Duma. It was not till he had in his pocket this promise from the President of the Duma, whom Grigori Efimovich particularly feared, that Khvostov began to bring pressure on Rasputin during one of the suppers at Andronnikov's house.

He started by laying stress on the importance for the whole Empire of again summoning the representatives of the people after so long an interval. As this argument obviously failed to make any impression on the starets, the Minister brought forward a stronger one, suggesting that any further postponement of the convocation of the Duma would be generally regarded as Rasputin's work, and would rouse great resentment against him. In accordance with a carefully pre-arranged plan, Beletski now intervened in the debate, and said with polite regret that, in the circumstances, it would, in future, be very difficult for the police to answer for the personal safety of the starets, as it might very easily happen that some fanatic or other would lay a plot against him. The summoning of the Duma, on the other hand, would have a very calming effect and divert all dangers. Finally, Khvostov mentioned Rodzianko's declaration, while Beletski assured them that he had talked with Protopopov, the Vice-President of the Duma, and that he, too, guaranteed a peaceful course for the session.

Rasputin listened to all these explanations without saying a word about his own opinion. It was not till he was leaving that he observed with a sly smile: "I will bear the matter in mind." Encouraged by these words, Khvostov, a few days later, departed for G.H.Q. with a fairly easy mind, to persuade the Tsar to summon the Duma.

But he was too late; old Goremykin had meanwhile discovered what was afoot, and had quietly taken steps to frustrate Khvostov's intrigues. To begin with, he formally deferred the resolution of the Council of Ministers, without which the decree summoning the Duma could not be submitted to the Tsar, and used the respite to do the very thing that the Minister of the Interior had done before him. He got into touch with Rasputin, and succeeded without much difficulty in making him once again change his mind about the Duma.

The result was that, at the next fish supper, Grigori Efimovich, on being asked what decision he had come to with regard to the Duma, quite briefly declared: "We have no need of the Duma at present." Nothing would turn him from this view, and, even after Andronnikov had presented him with a considerable sum of money, he repeated, as he went away, "We have no need of the Duma at present."

Khvostov was furious. His ambition gave him no peace, and, as the attempt to win Rasputin's support for his plans had failed so miserably, he took a new decision which seemed likely to enable him to attain his object. He tried to remove the starets from the capital for a time, in order to carry out his plans in his absence. So he drew up a fine memorial, setting out all the reasons which made it desirable that Rasputin should make a tour of inspection of Verkhoture and several other monasteries; such a tour, he explained, would silence all the slanderous rumours about the starets, and re-establish his prestige throughout the whole country.

In order to persuade Grigori Efimovich to undertake this journey, the Minister, after consulting Bishop Varnava, summoned the Abbot Martian from Tiumen, an old friend of Rasputin's, to St. Petersburg, so that he might use his influence with Grigori Efimovich. Martian arrived in the capital and declared his readiness to comply with the Minister's wishes, provided that he was made Archimandrite in return. Varnava had also made his cooperation conditional: he wanted to become an archbishop. Khvostov at once ran to his relative Volshin, who had meanwhile become Procurator of the Synod, and secured from him a promise that the demands of the two reverend gentlemen should be satisfied at the first opportunity.

Another fish supper took place, Varnava and Martian being present on this occasion. While the starets ate with his always hearty appetite they addressed him in turn, and begged him to undertake the tour of the monasteries. At the end of the meal

Martian and Varnava fell on Rasputin's neck, kissed him, and implored him until at last he agreed. Khvostov, with the most amiable smile, at once assured him that his Ministry would think it an honour to pay his travelling expenses, as the matter was an official one. Grigori Efimovich received this information with manifest pleasure, nodded approvingly, and, embracing the Minister, departed for the Villa Rode.

Next day Prince Andronnikov, in Khvostov's name, presented Rasputin with five thousand roubles for the journey, and the Minister now waited happily for the moment when Grigori Efimovich would leave the capital. But his preparations for the journey dragged themselves out most curiously: day after day passed, week after week, one fish supper succeeded another, and still Rasputin did not go. Finally Khvostov lost patience, and asked him, during their farewell embrace, when he was really thinking of setting out. The starets replied quite placidly that he had no intention whatever of going away.

Neither the Minister nor his assistant dared to say a word in reply; they left Andronnikov's house in silence; in silence they got into their car, and not till they were about a hundred paces away did Khvostov murmur in a low voice: "Believe me, Stefan Petrovich, we'll have to make away with this rascal!"

CHAPTER XIV

THE MURDERER WITH THE GUITAR

THE idea of murdering Rasputin had no sooner planted itself in Khvostov's brain than it took firm root there, and dominated all his actions. As he was Minister of the Interior and supreme Head of the Police and the entire surveillance service of the State, the departments under him burst into activity, and the plan of assassination passed through all the prescribed stages. Orders were issued and countermanded; conferences, meetings, discussions, and resolutions followed on and cancelled each other. It was as if the ponderous limbs of that anæmic colossus, the Russian bureaucracy, had set themselves in motion in order to take revenge on the full-blooded Siberian peasant for the provocative contempt he had displayed towards the Russian State; and this revenge was to be terrible. It was soon evident, however, that matters were to follow their usual course. The great plan, like a petty petition, passed through all the official departments; it led to a piling-up of documents, to excited questions, counter-questions, and discussions; but nothing happened.

Its beginning, it is true, seemed threatening enough. Khvostov argued as follows: The harm and danger of Rasputin's influence to the State and to Khvostov himself were becoming greater every day. His own position at Court was now sufficiently strong to enable him to dispense with Rasputin's support, while, on the other hand, the present state of affairs meant an infinite succession of dangers and annoyances. By making careful preparations for the murder it would easily be possible to avert all suspicion from themselves, and the advantages of the deed both for the Empire and for the Minister and his assistant would be obvious. Of course, money was of very little consequence in carrying through an affair like this, and the Ministry had ample funds at its disposal for such cases.

Beletski agreed with Khvostov, and pointed out that Maklakov, his chief's predecessor at the Ministry of the Interior, had also set his mind on the official removal of Rasputin. General Dumbadze, the Prefect of Yalta, had telegraphed to Beletski, in his then capacity of Director of the Chancery of the Ministry of Justice, to ask if he could count on official approval of the murder of Rasputin. Rasputin was to be enticed to an isolated castle on the sea-coast during his crossing from Sebastopol to Yalta, and there thrown over the cliffs. Beletski took the view that the Prefect's inquiry did not come within the province of the Ministry of Justice, but within that of the Ministry of the Interior, and, for this reason, he passed on Dumbadze's telegram to Maklakov, the Minister of the Interior. The Minister immediately got in touch with the Prime Minister, the Agency of the "Secret Protection," and the Department of the Governor of the Palace; but the last-named department was of the opinion that, as things were, the idea of removing Rasputin should be rejected for reasons connected with the dynasty. On mature consideration of all aspects of the question Maklakov decided to refuse Dumbadze the desired official approval, whereupon the assassination scheme fell through.

Khvostov listened with interest to his assistant's recital, and then developed his own plan. He proposed to entice Rasputin, by means of a false telephonic invitation, to the house of one of his female admirers. A car stationed there for the purpose would be waiting in Gorokhovaia, the chauffeur of which would be a police agent. Rasputin would unsuspectingly enter this car —to all appearances plying for hire—and drive to the lady's house. On the way there another agent, disguised as a policeman, would stop the car, and say that the street was closed for repairs. With this excuse the chauffeur could quietly turn into an unfrequented side street, and from there rush at full speed towards the city boundary. At a point arranged beforehand the car would slacken speed, two masked men would spring out, fall on Rasputin, render him insensible with a cloth soaked in chloroform, and strangle him with a rope they would have in readiness. The car would then drive as fast as possible to the coast, where the corpse would be buried in the snow, and washed out to sea in the spring.

Finally, the Minister gave his assistant strict orders to make all the necessary preparations immediately, to engage the car and reliable agents, and provide the cloth and the rope. When all the preparations were complete, Beletski was to furnish the Minister with an official report, so that the exact time of the murder could be fixed. Beletski accepted these orders, and took leave of his superior, saying that he would get in touch with the Chief of the "Special Police."

Beletski was extra-officially on intimate terms with Colonel Komisarov, the Chief of the "Special Police," and was thus able to communicate to him freely, not only the Minister's official orders, but also his own personal doubts about the affair. Beletski declared that he was an experienced official, had served in the police department under Stolypin, was assuredly no sentimentalist, and would naturally raise no moral objections to the Minister's plan. He understood only too well that Khvostov intended forcibly to clear the starets out of his way, because the latter had not obtained for him the title of Court Master of the Horse, and because he intended to make, not him, but State Councillor Stürmer, Prime Minister. Beletski himself had, in the past, repeatedly made exhaustive studies of the possibility of removing Rasputin, on behalf of General Bogdanovich's clique. If, therefore, he raised objections to Khvostov's designs, this was due to purely technical considerations. It was true that the murder of the starets would be regarded as a meritorious action in many circles of society, including the clergy and the Duma, and that its originators would gain great credit there; but, on the other hand, they would have to reckon with the vengeance of Rasputin's powerful followers, and they seemed to him very dangerous. Abuse of official authority was certainly justified when promotion or some other advantage might be expected from it; but, in this case, he feared the disadvantages would outweigh the advantages.

The worst of it was that Khvostov's plan was conceived in a dilettante spirit, and that the Minister, like the typical ex-provincial official he was, had entirely overlooked the real problems which a murder in St. Petersburg involved. In order to carry out this scheme a whole host of co-operators would be required, who would have to be made privy to the plot, and that alone was enough to wreck the whole thing. For agents were always unreliable when it came to really serious commissions. Moreover, Grigori Efimovich was perpetually watched by four different agencies, of which the spies of Globichev, those of Spiridovich's Court Agency, and the banker's agents worked entirely on their own, and kept a very close watch on each other. Khvostov attached no importance to all these difficulties, and, therefore, such an unskilfully laid scheme was doomed to failure.

The Chief of the "Special Police" listened attentively, and replied that he, too, had more than once occupied himself with plans for murdering Rasputin, and would be glad to co-operate to the best of his ability, within his circle of influence, in such a scheme. But he had special reasons for urgently warning his friend against co-operating with Khvostov in this affair. On account of the great goodwill that Beletski had always displayed towards him he was prepared to inform him confidentially of what he had learned through his agents of Khvostov's clandestine proceedings. The Minister had recently been emphasizing to everybody, including the Emperor, the fact that the surveillance of Rasputin and the measures for his safety were entirely in Beletski's hands. There was no doubt that the Minister was acting in this way so that he could afterwards throw all the responsibility for the murder he had planned on to his assistant's shoulders. Colonel Komisarov agreed with Beletski that the plot was dilettante in conception and quite impracticable. It was plain that Khvostov had gained his experience of administrative affairs not in the capital but in Nizhni-Novgorod.

After mature consideration of the whole situation Beletski and Komisarov came to the conclusion that it would be dangerous to give the Minister any serious support, as his methods were those of an uncivilized provincial bandit. Hence it was necessary to use all their resources to regulate future events in such a manner that the Minister's plans would prove abortive.

for there was no sense in risking one's own skin to further the selfish and underhand designs of Khvostov.

Beletski proposed to betray the whole scheme to Rasputin; but Colonel Komisarov advised against this course, as he did not wish, at this stage, to tie himself either to one side or the other. Besides, the Minister would then be in a position simply to deny the whole thing. They must try to get hold of a compromising document in Khvostov's own writing; unless they possessed such definite proof they could not venture on an open attack on the Minister.

Until that moment arrived, it seemed necessary to proclaim, outwardly at least, their complete agreement with Khvostov's plan and to fall in with his ideas, in order to be able to frustrate them at the proper moment. The chief thing was to gain time; and they decided to bring to the Minister's notice a number of difficulties and objections that must be got over before the plot proper could be carried out. Meanwhile every effort must be made to prevent any attempt on Rasputin's life, for the possibility of the Minister's becoming impatient, and perhaps tackling the murder in an extra-official way, had to be reckoned with.

The Chief of the "Special Police," therefore, gave his sub-chief immediate orders to double the number of the regular spies entrusted with the protection of Rasputin; and, while Colonel Komisarov was thus assuring himself that not a hair of Rasputin's head should be harmed, Beletski took upon himself the task of making it appear to the Minister that he was zealously preparing the execution of the murder, but that certain difficulties had arisen.

Accordingly, at their next conference, Beletski announced to the Minister that he had duly passed on his orders to Colonel Komisarov. He, Beletski, however, would take the liberty of suggesting that it might be advisable to pave the way beforehand for the murder of Rasputin by calling the Tsar's attention to the strong hostility felt by the country towards the starets, and to the fact that Rasputin had incurred much personal enmity by his sinful life, and that, besides, it was difficult always to look after his safety, as he often tried to escape the surveillance of the agents. If the Minister, in this way, more or less refused further responsibility for Rasputin's safety, no one could seriously reproach him if something actually did happen to the starets.

The Minister had to assent to this proposal, and instructed his assistant to look through all the records about Rasputin and draw up a memorandum which he could submit to the Emperor as a proof of Rasputin's vicious life and of the existence of strong hostility against him. Beletski immediately handed over the work to the director of his chancery, and the latter, in his turn, ordered his subordinates to study all the registers of the secret police that were available in the Ministry, and to compose an effective document from this material. This report Beletski laid before the Minister, drawing particular attention to the last part of the memorandum, in which, *inter alia*, the most recent reports of the agency on Rasputin's visit to Pokrovskoe were touched upon:

"12th July. About 8 P.M. Rasputin left the house with the wife of Soloviev, an official of the Synod, who had already visited him the day before. They both entered a carriage and drove to the forest, where they conducted themselves in an unseemly fashion, and did not return till after one o'clock. On the homeward journey Rasputin was very pale."

"13th July. After his bath, Rasputin went to the wife of the psalm-singer Ermolai, who was awaiting him at the window. He visits her nearly every day, as intimate relations exist between them. Then he received an officer's wife, embraced her in an improper way, and walked with her in the courtyard."

"18th September. Rasputin received a typewritten letter from St. Petersburg, which read: '*You* have great influence with the Emperor, and so we ask *you* to use that influence to have the Ministers made responsible to the people. If *you* do not do this, we will have no sympathy with *you* and will kill *you*. Our hands will not shake like Guseva's hand when she made an attempt on *your* life. We are ten and shall be able to find *you* wherever *you* may be.'"

Beletski pointed out that, after the murder, these last minutes would furnish a splendid alibi, for nothing could be simpler than to maintain that the removal of Rasputin was the work of this "group of ten."

The Minister took the memorandum to Tsarskoe Selo. On his return he summoned his assistant and the Chief of the "Special Police" to a joint conference, to fix a definite date for the murder. All the details of the plan were once more exhaustively discussed, and Beletski expressed the view that it would be desirable, for the sake of security and to provide for all contingencies, to arrange a kind of dress rehearsal of the murder, a method that had more than once proved advantageous. He reminded the Minister that, as appeared from the agents' reports, two jealous husbands, revolver in hand, had already forced their way into the starets' house. Beletski, therefore, thought that they ought to stage a similar scene and thus make it appear that Rasputin's life was threatened by jealous husbands.

But the Minister was too impatient to endure further delays, and the excessive caution of his assistant, which might perhaps be in order on other official business, excited his displeasure in this case. Next day, therefore, he asked Colonel Komisarov to come to see him alone, and appealed directly to him to carry out the plot against Grigori Efimovich with the utmost dispatch. In view of the many difficulties that had arisen in connection with the preparations for the murder by motor-car, Khvostov wished to alter his plan, and told Colonel Komisarov that he thought it would be best if Komisarov's own agents attacked and strangled Rasputin during a drinking bout.

The Chief of the "Special Police" dutifully expressed his admiration for this new scheme, but allowed himself to make the modest proposal that poisoning should be substituted for strangling, as poisoning would not involve admitting so many people to the secret. In his opinion it would be best if a case of poisoned wine were sent to the starets "as a mark of gratitude" in the name of some fictitious petitioner, on whom suspicion would at once be turned. Moreover, in this way no one would be let into the secret.

This plan pleased the Minister extraordinarily; he even invented an improvement on it. For the fictitious petitioner it would be preferable to substitute the name of the banker, Dimitri

Rubinstein, whom he hated. Then the police would know at once whom they had to deal with; Rubinstein would be arrested for the murder, and everything would go perfectly smoothly.

Komisarov objected that Rasputin, as soon as he received the wine, would telephone to thank Rubinstein, which would involve the discovery of the whole plot. To his regret the Minister had to acknowledge the justice of the Colonel's objections, and drop this part of the plan; but he ordered him, in any case, to prepare the poison immediately. He indicated, at the same time, that it was unnecessary to inform Beletski of this new plot, as he had already made the Minister nervous with his everlasting scruples. Komisarov said he was ready to see to the preparation of the poison personally, but that, in his opinion, it would perhaps be better to prepare it in the provinces, not in St. Petersburg itself. Accordingly, after hurrying to see Beletski and inform him unofficially of all these new decisions, he went by the next train to Saratov. On his return, Komisarov took from his attaché case several chemist's bottles containing powders of various colours, set them in a row on the Minister's desk, and declared that these were the strongest poisons available, and that he himself would try their effect that very night. Next morning he appeared and reported that his experiments had been successful, and that one of the preparations, in particular, had proved extraordinarily effective in killing cats. He described in detail the horrible agonies with which a cat, to whom he had administered a little of this powder, had died. The Minister listened contentedly and expressed the liveliest satisfaction.

Khvostov urged that the poisoning of Rasputin should take place as soon as possible, and Komisarov asked permission, now that everything was decided upon, to bring Beletski in again; he did not wish, he said, to be guilty of any offence against official regulations, and Beletski might regard his exclusion in that light. After some hesitation, Khvostov gave his sanction and Beletski was brought in. The conference ended with complete agreement between all the parties, and a decision to carry out the murder on the following Thursday night. The Minister indicated his desire to be present; but Beletski advised very strongly against this, and Komisarov also expressed warm objections, so that the Minister had finally to give up the idea. It was settled that the murder should be committed at the secret apartment in which Rasputin had for some time been regularly meeting Beletski and Komisarov and often Khvostov himself, since the earlier common meals at Prince Andronnikov's had for various reasons proved inconvenient.

On the morning of the day of the murder, the Minister received a succession of urgent reports from his agents, which showed that the fall of the Prime Minister, Goremykin, and the appointment of State Councillor Stürmer as his successor was imminent. Towards evening, official notice of the change came to the Ministry. Khvostov immediately sent for his assistant Beletski, but he was nowhere to be found. Then he sent to the secret apartment where the fatal meeting with Rasputin should have been taking place at that moment; but the house was found to be dark, empty, and shut. On receiving this information, Khvostov knew that both Beletski and Komisarov had betrayed him.

He began to cast about for someone else to help him with the murder. Suddenly he remembered the plot against Rasputin which the monk-priest Iliodor had set on foot, and which had almost succeeded. He discovered from one of his private agents, Rzhevski, that Iliodor was struggling with financial difficulties in Norway, and making vain efforts to find a publisher for his libellous pamphlet, "The Holy Devil."

Khvostov at once dispatched an express messenger to Iliodor, with a proposal to the effect that he was prepared to give the monk financial support on condition that he place his followers in Russia at Khvostov's disposal for a new attack on the starets' life. Thereupon a brisk exchange of telegrams took place between Iliodor and Khvostov; but, in the end, it proved necessary to send a special confidential agent to Norway with the money for Iliodor. After brief reflection Khvostov entrusted Rzhevski, who had already carried out similar business, with the task.

Beletski and Komisarov had at once discovered Khvostov's designs from their own spies, and had started counteraction. Beletski had, in his archives, incriminating material about almost every inhabitant of St. Petersburg, and documents that could send Rzhevski to prison for several years. With the help of these papers, he compelled the agent to obey his orders, and to furnish him with reports of all his conversations with Khvostov.

After consultation with Komisarov, Beletski decided to overthrow the Minister, for he was sure that, through the complicity of Rzhevski, he could procure a compromising document in Khvostov's own hand. For this purpose he ordered the agent to ask the Minister for an export permit for the money to be handed over to Iliodor. Khvostov made out the permit and Beletski had him where he wanted him.

He let the agent start on his journey in peace, but had previously arranged that certain steps should be taken at the Russo-Swedish frontier. When Rzhevski left the train at the frontier station, he was arrested on some pretext, searched, and brought back to St. Petersburg under escort; the export permit with Khvostov's signature had been removed during the search. A search of Rzhevski's flat in St. Petersburg was held simultaneously, and Beletski ordered a number of documents to be seized which were clear proof of the Minister's guilt. Armed with these documents Beletski hastened to Rasputin, to Stürmer, the new Prime Minister, to the Metropolitan Pitirim, and to Ania Vyrubova, and proved to them that Khvostov had intended to murder the starets.

Khvostov's position immediately became untenable; but he remained in office three days longer than his assistant had anticipated; he used these days to turn Beletski out of office and transfer him to Irkutsk in the most remote province of Siberia.

But before Beletski departed for his new sphere of service, he received a newspaper editor, and told him everything he knew about Khvostov's plots. This information was published immediately and caused an enormous sensation; by bribing a subordinate official, Beletski had prevented this newspaper from being notified of the ban placed by the Minister on the publication of any report on the Rzhevski case. The day after publication Khvostov was dismissed from office by the Emperor in the blackest disgrace.

* * * * *

During all this time the starets, amid his staff of police agents, spies, and hired assassins, went about his business and pleasures, unconcerned over the resentment, the intrigues, and the murderous schemes of his enemies, with a mind always calm and cheerful. For in Grigori's soul, even in the midst of the most complicated political business, still lived the indestructible, elemental strength of the Siberian steppes.

What means had not his adversaries already tried to injure, overthrow, and do away with him? How powerful these adversaries were, and how miserably all their efforts had ended! The Grand Duke Nikolai Nikolaevich had been one of his first followers at Court and had later wanted to "have him hanged"; now, somewhere, far away in the Caucasus, he was mourning the loss of his post of Commander-in-Chief of the Army. The beautiful "Montenegrins," at first Rasputin's enthusiastic admirers, might eat their hearts out: Grigori sat cosily, in their place, at the Empress's side.

And the three clerical dignitaries, the Archimandrite Feofan, Bishop Hermogen, and the dread monk-priest Iliodor, they had all paid dearly for their attempts to revolt against the starets, and were now condemned, in their various places of exile, to meditate on how dangerous it was first to create a new saint and then try to overthrow him!

If Rasputin had got the better of all these powerful personages, by whose support he had come to the Court, how easy it was bound to be for him to protect himself against his own creatures, the ministers and bishops he himself had raised to office and dignity. Grigori Efimovich could truly go to the telephone with an easy mind, call up Archbishop Varnava, who had intrigued against him, and say to him: "Now *your* motor rides are at an end. Go back home barefoot as *you* came! Off with *you*." He could be certain that after these words, the Archbishop would think twice before daring to enter upon any other schemes against him.

Nor did the starets need to worry much about the different gentlemen of the Duma and their revolt. It was, of course, annoying for him when Guchkov, the wholesale merchant, the Chairman of the Commission of National Defence, stormed against him in his fiery fashion, or when General Gurko, the President of the Zemstvo Union, cried that, though he would like to see a strong man at the head of the State, he did not want a "Khlyst." But, in the upshot, all this did not cause him much uneasiness, and his hair would certainly never grow grey on account of the savagely abusive speeches bald Purishkevich made in the Duma.

For Rasputin knew this man only too well, and could reckon him up to a nicety. Many a time had Purishkevich, the proud spokesman of the extreme Right, come to the starets' flat and meekly begged him for a ministerial post. But neither his bald head, nor the pince-nez on the too short nose under it, pleased the "peasant chancellor," nor yet the khaki-coloured field uniform of this "medical officer," who was ever urging on to further and even more barbarous bloodshed. Grigori Efimovich could not suffer this kind of phrase-maker, and he had obstinately refused to make Purishkevich Minister of the Interior. It was easy to understand, therefore, why Purishkevich afterwards regarded Rasputin as "Russia's greatest curse." When, later, one disaster at the front followed another, Purishkevich, the convinced monarchist, imperialist, and supporter of "war to a victorious end," could not very well ascribe the disastrous course of the campaign to the incapacity of the Russian army command; so, on every conceivable opportunity, he shouted from the speaker's platform in the Duma that "the dark powers," Rasputin and his clique, were responsible for the military failures, and that they must be removed, if the position of Russia were to take a turn for the better.

But what did the starets himself care for this hysterical bawling? Let Purishkevich storm as much as he liked about the "dark powers," the Tsar and Tsaritsa knew only too well what to think of the principles of the "true Russian people," and did not pay the slightest attention to any of the underhanded or open attacks and slanders directed against the starets.

Nor did Father Grigori worry over the terrible murder plots hatched against him in the private office of Khvostov. It was not that he went on unsuspectingly; he knew all about the masked men who were to strangle him in the motor-car, about the bribed secret agents, and the bottles of poison, for the spies entrusted with the task of keeping watch on him were on such good terms with him that they managed by discreet hints to warn him of all serious danger. But Rasputin was sufficiently well acquainted with the mutual hate, the jealousy, and the baseness of the different ministers, ministerial assistants, and chiefs of the various police services, to feel quite secure. With calm consciousness of the strength of his position, he trusted to the character of his enemies, and quite rightly judged that they would wring each others' necks before they harmed a hair of his head.

So when one day Beletski, breathing heavily in his agitation, visited him, and nervously twisting his gold watch-chain, disclosed to him in great detail Khvostov's "villainous murder plots," Grigori Efimovich burst into loud peals of ringing laughter, and his beard waved like a banner of victory. He had foreseen that this would be the end of it all! And when Beletski, by the revelation of the Rzhevski affair, made his superior's position impossible, and the latter, in his turn, dispatched his assistant to Irkutsk, it was one of the happiest moments of Rasputin's long rule over Russia. He saw contemptuously how the powerful apparatus of State, the whole accurately functioning machinery of espionage, intrigue, and violence, had suddenly come to a standstill, wrecked by its own baseness, and how the ambitious plots had been frustrated by the mutual mistrust and villainy of all concerned, without the starets himself having lifted a finger.

Later, as Rasputin sat comfortably at tea with Munia Golovina, her mother, and young Prince Felix Yusupov in the Golovins' drawing-room on the Winter Canal, he could think with satisfaction that God's will had opposed the intrigues and plots of his enemies, since the Almighty desired to preserve him unharmed for the good of the Emperor and the joy of his faithful women servants.

Munia Eugenia Golovina and her mother sat spellbound, their gaze fixed adoringly on the starets; their cheeks glowed, and they listened intently to his words with the enthusiasm of faith, for in both there was no shadow of doubt that their "holy father" was the reincarnate Redeemer Himself.

In everything Rasputin said, even though outwardly it was concerned with such worldly matters as the malicious intrigues of fallen ministers, these credulous women thought they saw a special sign from Heaven. The very fact that all the plots against the starets had failed, and that the wicked Khvostov had, in the end, been caught in his own snares, inevitably seemed to them a fresh proof that a protecting Providence stood between Father Grigori and his enemies.

Only occasionally did Munia Golovina's devoted and ecstatic gaze slip away from the starets to rest for a moment on young Prince Yusupov. Munia had long been grieved that Prince Felix, for whom she had a delicate and innocent attachment, refused to share her admiring love of, and faith in, Grigori Efimovich. She had tried again and again to bring the two into closer touch; this was, in fact, the real reason for her having invited the Prince to tea that afternoon. But, on this occasion, as so often before, Felix listened to the talk of the starets merely with politeness and forced attention, while Munia and her mother could read in his face obvious aloofness and even suppressed repulsion.

This caused the two ladies all the more concern because Father Grigori himself showed a sincere and positively paternal affection for Prince Yusupov. Ever since Rasputin had first made the acquaintance of this handsome young man in the Golovin drawing-room, his liking for him had steadily increased, and he had often tried to become more intimate with him. Although the Prince was close on the thirties, his whole appearance had something boyish about it. He was of medium height and very slightly built; his clean-shaven, oval face was pale and had deep circles under the eyes.

The Prince's manner was in harmony with his appearance. He was of a gentle, sweet, almost shy disposition, which had fascinated the starets from the start. Almost as soon as Grigori Efimovich met him, he went up to him and embraced him with sincere affection. And at later meetings, Father Grigori took every opportunity of saying a kind and friendly word to the Prince. With his amazing sensitiveness he had at once divined Munia's sympathy for Felix; when he said good-bye, he let his friendly glance travel from one of the young people to the other, and, turning to the Prince, said in a fatherly tone: "Hearken to her and she will be *your* spiritual wife. She has already told me much good about *you*, but now I see for myself that you suit each other." Later, too, the good Little Father often talked to Munia of his cordial affection for Felix, for her "little friend," as he usually called the Prince.

This "little friend," however, had never returned Rasputin's love. Even at their first meeting the way the dirty, uncared-for peasant behaved to the excited women who shuddered with awe before him, and embraced and kissed Munia without the least ceremony, roused his deepest indignation. Felix cherished for this young girl, who had been betrothed to his dead brother, a delicate and tender feeling which he hardly dared avow to himself; and now came this unwashed muzhik, who clutched Munia with his coarse hand, and kissed her fiercely on the mouth! At the sight the blood mounted to his head, and he was filled with a helpless, desperate fury.

Naturally he avoided anything that might vex Munia; but there came a time when an explanation could no longer be put off. Munia, zealously seconded by her mother, said that Grigori Efimovich was a saint, and, therefore, his kisses and embraces could not possibly be a sin, but rather a sanctification. This boundless reverence was quite incomprehensible to Yusupov, for however much he listened to the starets talking about matters of religion, it all seemed to him mere stupid, confused rubbish. But it was far worse when Grigori began to talk about his friendly relations with the imperial couple, and then, in a haughty and contemptuous tone, to favour them with his opinion of ministers, generals, and Court officials. All this wounded and infuriated the young aristocrat, and when he thought of how this "disgusting boor" went in and out of Tsarskoe Selo, he began to hate him with his whole heart.

Ere long, despite Munia's earnest pleading and efforts, he withdrew from all intercourse with Rasputin, and, for the same reason, he visited the Golovins less and less frequently. The enthusiasm of the girl who was to have married his dead brother for a creature like Rasputin became even more irritating and intolerable to him.

The profound repulsion the young Prince felt for Grigori Efimovich at that time, was later strengthened by Rasputin's increasing power. The public had previously divined rather than known this power; but now nothing else was talked of all over Russia and, wherever Yusupov went, he had to listen to fresh details about the inexplicable influence of the starets, while, at the same time, the wildest rumours were abroad about his life. Men were to be found everywhere, bearers of the most distinguished and noble names, princes of the Church and ministers, who had been personally insulted and humiliated, if not actually overthrown, by Rasputin, and, in their helpless fury, they cursed him, knowing all the time only too well that he merely made fun of their wrath.

Of all the reports that reached him about the "Friend," it was the stories of his dissolute life, his orgies with ladies of distinguished society, that affected Prince Yusupov most deeply. Whenever he heard a scandalous tale of this kind, there came to his memory the picture of Munia and himself sitting quiet, shy, and discreetly affectionate until this dirty peasant barged noisily in, seized Munia in his arms, and loudly kissed her on the mouth.

* * * * *

The grandfather of Prince Felix Felixovich Yusupov originally belonged to the lower ranks of the nobility and bore the name of Elston. He was, however, a handsome man, and succeeded in winning as his bride the only daughter of Count Sumarokov; soon after his marriage he received the Emperor's permission to add his wife's title to his own name, and to call himself Count Sumarokov-Elston. His name and rank descended to his eldest son, and he, in his turn, thanks to his handsome appearance, married the only daughter of Prince Yusupov, and, by imperial permission, assumed this title. The father of Prince Felix Felixovich was thus Prince Yusupov and Count Sumarokov-Elston.

The Yusupov family were of Tatar origin, and traced their ancestry back to that Yusup Mursa who, in the fifteenth century, was in the service of Tamerlaine; a later forebear of the Yusupovs was the Chamberlain of Peter the Great, and his descendants filled high offices in the State, as governors, senators, or ambassadors.

Both the grandfather and father of Prince Felix Felixovich had thus succeeded, by advantageous marriages, in rising rapidly to ever higher titles, and also to ever increasing riches. The Elstons were originally poorly off, but the Sumarokovs possessed great wealth. The riches of the princely house of Yusupov, however, were overwhelming, and these Felix's father acquired through his marriage with the sole heiress of the house. The palace of the Yusupovs, with its fabulous store of artistic treasures, formed a wonderful museum and contained, among other things, one of the most valuable collections of precious stones in the world; and the estates and the money of the Yusupovs were unlimited.

However, the brilliant rise of the Elstons did not reach its zenith until the marriage of young Prince Felix with Irina Alexandrovna, the niece of the Tsar. This imperial princess, the daughter of the Grand Duchess Xenia Alexandrovna and the Grand Duke Alexander Mikhailovich, fell in love with the handsome young Prince and, by this marriage, Felix Yusupov became a close connection of the Emperor himself.

Felix Felixovich lived the life of the most distinguished and richest men in Russia: by his marriage he had won to a powerful social position, and his fabulous riches gave him access to every pleasure and luxury of living. He had not only carried on the traditions of the Elstons, he had far surpassed their most audacious dreams, for neither his father nor his grandfather would have dared to think of marrying into the house of Romanov. Moreover, Irina Alexandrovna, Felix's wife, was one of the most beautiful women in St. Petersburg society, perhaps the most beautiful; and, for that reason alone, his marriage to her must have excited general admiration and envy in the Capital.

Yusupov had a friend who was slavishly devoted to him, the Grand Duke Dimitri Pavlovich, lieutenant in the third cavalry regiment of the Life Guards, the only son of the Grand Duke Pavel Alexandrovich. This inseparable friend of the Prince had not only the privilege of belonging to the imperial family, he was also regarded as one of the handsomest and most elegant of young men, and was idolized by the many noble officers of the Guards, who could be rapturous admirers of beautiful youths. Prince Felix Felixovich was also charmed by the girlishly delicate Grand Duke, and it was easy for him to win Dimitri's friendship, for Felix himself was young, handsome, elegant, supple, and of an amiable and fascinating nature. His high social position, his boundless wealth, his beautiful wife, and his beautiful friend, made of him the darling of St. Petersburg society, and everyone flocked and crowded round him wherever he appeared.

No one who is not rich, attractive, very young, and the centre of an admiring social circle, can have any idea how intolerably tedious riches, beauty, and popularity can be. Felix Felixovich had everything he could possibly want: he was master of the largest and most valuable collection of precious stones in the world, of palaces and castles and enormous estates; he had accomplished the highest that a man of noble blood, a descendant of the Elstons, could accomplish; he had won the hand of an imperial princess; his friend was the handsome, universally admired Grand Duke Dimitri. And yet for him this state of perpetual happiness, which hid nothing more in itself, which held out no promise of new experiences, which could offer him no further secrets, attractions, or excitements, was one of intolerable boredom and emptiness.

Like many other Russian aristocrats, Prince Felix did not avail himself of the possibility of filling his life with intellectual interests and, consequently, he was tormented by the painful boredom of the absolutely rich and absolutely happy person, the man to whom nothing is forbidden, and to whom, therefore, nothing any longer seems desirable. Inevitably, he began to feel his life of perpetual riches as a prison, from which there was no escape. His beautiful wife of imperial blood, his beautiful and elegant friend, the many adorers, male and female, and the handsome men and pretty women who flocked about him, were bound ultimately to seem like merciless warders, who kept him shut up in his prison of disconsolate boredom.

The poor can hope for riches, the unloved for love, and the lowly for elevation; but for the man who, like Felix Yusupov, is surrounded by enormous wealth, perpetual happiness, and unending pleasure, there remains no other outlet from his spiritual prison but crime. As the ray of light coming through his grating, so to the young Prince crime seemed the only hope of freedom. To commit a crime and once more taste a new, still unknown excitement, was a dream like the prisoner's dream of freedom.

But even this was more difficult for Prince Yusupov than for ordinary mortals: if he committed any petty crime, even if he killed a servant, a soldier, or a girl of the streets, he was well aware that his act would not produce any profound impression on his friends and acquaintances. Therefore Felix Felixovich must perform some greater deed, really to break into the tedious happiness of his empty life; the deed must be big and daring enough to stir both his own jaded blood and the whole country at the same time. Only a violent shock could win him release from the prison of his boredom, and therefore his crime must have a worthy victim.

In all Russia at that time there was but one man whom it would be difficult, worth while, and historically important to remove: that was Rasputin, the Friend of the Emperor and Empress, the powerful starets, who was worshipped as a saint by society ladies and revered by politicians, generals, and princes of the Church as the uncrowned ruler of the Empire. To murder Rasputin, that would be a feat truly great, historical, and worthy of Prince Yusupov!

* * * * *

The idea of escaping from his moral desert by the murder of Rasputin soon took complete possession of the bored young Prince. It was easy for him to find moral arguments to justify his decision; he had long sincerely hated Rasputin, as his sensitive nerves had, from the outset, revolted against the coarse, clumsy, and overbearing peasant. The more Yusupov thought about the starets, the more clearly did he feel that it was his duty to murder the man. Very soon his intention began to seem quite heroic; the idea of committing a murder "from idealistic motives" caused strange vibrations in his delicate soul, a mood of enthusiasm and ecstatic intoxication.

He was fortified in these feelings by everything he heard about Grigori Efimovich from his noble friends, grand dukes, courtiers, and officers. At every meeting with his equals, the young Prince was told further stories of Rasputin's dissolute and shameful life—of insults inflicted by the "peasant chancellor" on the highest dignitaries, of new appointments and dismissals brought about by him, and of disgraceful orgies with high-born ladies.

Soon, too, it came to his ears that Rasputin's membership of the Khlysty sect had been verified by the investigations of the Synod, although he himself had always denied it. There was no doubt that Rasputin had seized power on behalf of this sect and was ruling entirely in the light of that heretical doctrine. The advancement of the uneducated ex-gardener's boy, Varnava, to a bishop and archbishop, was nothing but mockery of the clergy by an impudent sectarian, for had not the starets himself said at the time: "The haughty and learned lords and bishops will be furious at my setting a peasant over them; but I don't care a rap for the bishops!"

Rasputin's habit of speaking of the highest clerical dignitaries in contemptuous terms—for example, he scarcely ever referred to Archbishop Vladimir except as "sheeps-head"—could be regarded as a sufficiently strong proof that he belonged to the Khlysty. And, as for his doctrine of sin and his preaching salvation through sensual debauchery! Only an accursed heretic would dare to say and do such things!

What a disgrace it was for Russia, once the stronghold of Orthodoxy, to be ruled by an adherent of this dark and loathsome sect! And how basely this Rasputin took every opportunity of showing his contempt for the aristocracy! The dislodgment of Samarin, the Procurator of the Synod, who had also been the leader of the Moscow nobility, was only the first blow: mad with victory, Grigori had since then given utterance, on every occasion, to the most infuriating remarks about the aristocracy and its worthiest representatives. Recently he had called out at a party: "Our aristocrats are always howling about 'war to a victorious end.' But they walk about Moscow and Petrograd, while out there the peasants are shedding their blood! Away to the trenches with them!"

Rasputin's great influence over the imperial couple agitated the whole of loyal society in the capital, for they saw in it a serious danger for the very existence of the monarchy. What would Russia come to if the all-powerful Tsar allowed himself to be led by the will of a common peasant?

Prince Yusupov also heard of the attempts made by persons belonging to the circle of Buchanan, the English Ambassador, to oppose Rasputin's influence. Some members of the imperial family belonged to this circle, and these had undertaken to bring pressure on the Emperor to get rid of Rasputin, and direct his policy in accordance with their wishes. But Tsar Nikolai replied to these remonstrances in the same way as he replied to those of all the other members of his entourage. He listened amiably at the beginning; but became more and more cold and reserved, and finally made his disagreement perfectly clear. Whenever complaints about Grigori's life were brought before the Emperor or the Empress, the reply was always the same: "People are hostile to him because we love him." It was evident that this peasant, whose only official title at Court was that of "Lampadary," was in truth the real ruler of the Empire.

It was frequently said that Rasputin owed his unshakable position not least to the frequent threat uttered in prophetic tones: "So long as I live, the imperial family will also live; when I die, they will also perish." The Tsaritsa, and even the Tsar, according to general report, believed in this prophecy, and this alone was enough to make them reject any idea of a separation from their "Friend."

But the obstinate way in which the imperial couple clung to Rasputin could not but seem extremely serious in the eyes of nationalistic noble circles, by reason of the multitude of veiled insinuations to the effect that Grigori Efimovich was a German spy. Of course, the censorship did not allow a word on this subject to appear in the newspapers; but occasionally the journals of the Right threw out hints that were at once understood everywhere and derisively commented on. For example, the *Novoe Vremia* once said that the Russian spring offensive had stuck in the *rasputitsa* (the season of bad roads). The censor overlooked the double meaning; but every other inhabitant of Petrograd understood what was meant.

Naturally, much in the stories and gossip about Rasputin was malicious exaggeration or pure invention; but to Prince Yusupov every report was welcome that branded the starets as a traitor and danger to the State. Once the Prince, out of his unspeakable boredom, had resolved to murder Rasputin, he found justification for his intention in all the rumours afloat about the "Friend." For a man who has got to the point of deliberately making up his mind to commit a murder is not very particular when it comes to providing "idealistic motives" for his act. For this purpose society gossip was good enough for the Prince.

It was true that Rasputin was not the first man in Russia to influence the sovereign in an unconstitutional way; neither was he the first to take bribes, hold orgies, and appoint and dismiss ministers from a personal, rather than an objective, standpoint. Grigori Efimovich, in his failings, was just like most of the men who both before and after him influenced the destinies of the Russian Empire. Nevertheless, it was not difficult for Prince Felix to work himself up to the conviction that Rasputin alone was to blame for all the trouble, and that the murder of this man was, not only a new excitement for his jaded nerves, but at the same time a national act of heroism, the freeing of the Tsar and the Russian Empire from the fatal "dark powers."

Yusupov himself soon believed quite sincerely in the justification of his designs which he had found in society gossip. He believed in it as sincerely as only an assassin from "idealistic motives" can delude himself about the loftiness of his crime. This overcame his last scruples, and he could proceed to make the necessary preparations for the deed.

* * * * *

The war had for some time been going from bad to worse; one defeat followed another; and the spirits of the people were visibly depressed; the Right radical imperialists, in particular, were in sheer despair. A culprit must be found at any cost on whom to cast the responsibility for the miscarriage of all the great plans.

The chief credit for discovering a scapegoat at the right moment belonged to Purishkevich. Since his hopes of a ministerial post had been disappointed, Purishkevich had been proclaiming on every conceivable occasion that Rasputin alone was to blame for the melancholy course of events, for the military disasters, and for the threatened collapse of the whole machinery of administration. Purishkevich was a passionate and gifted orator, so that his furious attacks on the starets in the Duma and the Press produced a considerable impression.

Towards the end of 1916, Prince Yusupov, reading a particularly violent attack of Purishkevich's, recognized that this Duma deputy was the very man to help him to carry out his great plan for freeing Russia from the "dark powers."

Purishkevich was active in the Russian Red Cross, and directed a hospital train of his own; it generally stood in Petrograd station, and Purishkevich had installed his office in one of the carriages. Prince Yusupov went to see him there, and communicated his plan for the murder of Rasputin. Purishkevich immediately became enthusiastic and promised the Prince his active co-operation.

The same evening another discussion took place. Prince Felix wished to give his friend, the Grand Duke Dimitri, the chance to take part in this great patriotic deed, for he could imagine that committing murder would be a welcome excitement to the Grand Duke, who, like him, was a warm admirer of Oscar Wilde's *Dorian Gray* and other books of the kind. He therefore proposed to Purishkevich that Dimitri Pavlovich should also be admitted to the conspiracy, and both agreed that this was very desirable. For the members of the imperial house were legally not subject to the ordinary authorities, but to the Tsar alone; this immunity extended to all the other participators in a criminal act in which an imperial prince was involved. Yusupov and Purishkevich, by dragging in the Grand Duke, assured themselves in advance against any serious annoyance from the police and the courts.

The Deputy, however, as a convinced monarchist, was enthusiastic about the proposal that a member of the imperial house itself should take part in the forcible removal of the "noxious creature," Rasputin; in this way a large part of the anticipated patriotic glory would accrue to the imperial family.

After the inclusion of the Grand Duke was decided, Purishkevich recommended that they should also persuade his assistant in the hospital train, the Polish physician, Doctor Lazovert, to co-operate, and make it his special task to provide the necessary poison; in addition, Sukhotin, a cavalry officer, and Yusupov's valet, Nefedov, were also to be initiated into the conspiracy.

The elegant Grand Duke was easily won over. Since serfdom had been abolished and the humanitarian prejudices of the West had taken root in Russia, there were really hardly any possibilities left of tickling the nerves of a Russian grand duke. Hunting and slaughtering animals could afford no permanent satisfaction; and it was no wonder that Dimitri joyfully seized the opportunity of "bringing down" a man. Moreover, the whole scheme had been thought out by Felix Felixovich, and the Grand Duke always did blindly everything his friend approved of. And was it not a patriotic act?

* * * * *

Yusupov's plan to murder Rasputin was based chiefly on Munia's and her mother's blind confidence and faith in people's goodwill. Felix Felixovich was well aware how vexed the Golovins had always been because he behaved with such cold aloofness towards their deeply revered Father Grigori, for had not the starets from the very start met his "little friend" with sincere and cordial sympathy? During the past year Munia had often tried to bring about a *rapprochement* between Yusupov and Rasputin, and Grigori had asked her more than once to invite him at the same time as the Prince.

Felix now recalled the evident liking the starets had for him and Munia's devoted affection; all this would help him to entice his victim into the trap. Of course, there were moments when Yusupov could not suppress an unpleasant feeling that it was not exactly honourable to abuse the trust of a lovable girl in this way, and, with her assistance, to approach an unsuspecting mortal for the purpose of treacherously murdering him. But such scruples always gave way rapidly before the conviction that he was committing this murder for "idealistic" and "patriotic" reasons, and that the "lofty" aim completely justified the hypocritical means.

Besides, this noble young man, who loved to intoxicate himself with "decadent" literature, already secretly tasted, with voluptuous anticipation, the special titillation of the nerves that lay in this very treacherousness. To attack his victim face to face, in a common, savage, and vulgar fashion was not to the liking of this refined young man. A crime, to suit him, must be contrived with a certain treachery and subtle perfidy. It was necessary, even in carrying out a murder, to display refined manners and taste, and thus show oneself to advantage in comparison with the many less civilized, unæsthetic, everyday murderers.

In accordance with these views, Prince Yusupov made arrangements to become intimate with Rasputin with the help of trustful Munia Golovina; the other conspirators were to make all the technical preparations in the interval, provide the poison and the heavy chains with which, after the deed was done, Rasputin's body could be weighted before it was sunk in the waters of the Neva.

Felix had practically ceased to visit the Golovins; but he took the earliest opportunity to call on them again and to display unostentatiously a certain interest in the starets. He let fall one or two remarks indicating that he would not be averse to meeting Rasputin again, as all that Munia and her mother had told him had awakened an impression that Grigori Efimovich was an estimable, almost a holy, man.

Accordingly, a few days after Yusupov, Purishkevich, and the Grand Duke Dimitri had finally decided on the murder, Munia rang up the Prince to ask him to come to tea with Rasputin next day. For an instant Felix was positively afraid at the ease with which his plan seemed to be succeeding, and at the lack of suspicion in Munia, who rejoiced over what, in fact, though she was unaware of it, was the delivery of the starets up to his would-be murderer in her drawing-room. Of course, the Prince, fortified by his "ideal" motives, overcame this slight attack of weakness almost instantaneously, and answered that he would be delighted to come.

When he entered the drawing-room next day, he found mother and daughter obviously excited, for to the two women Rasputin's coming meeting with the Prince was an important event. Soon the starets appeared. When he saw Felix his whole face beamed with joy; he hurried up to the Prince and embraced him. Towards his future murderer, Rasputin, who was generally so suspicious, acted as he never thought of acting to anyone else; he wooed Felix, he overwhelmed him with his awkward manifestations of affection, and tried to attract him by exaggerated cordiality and kindness. He had no suspicion that his "little friend" was cold-bloodedly dissembling, and he was honestly delighted at his apparent manifestations of sympathy.

Though Felix now behaved as if he were agreeably affected by Rasputin's friendship, in reality he experienced the same feeling of disgust as he had formerly felt for this muzhik. The way, too, in which Grigori talked to the two ladies and caressed them, once again made him nearly burst with rage; and the disagreeably paternal tone which Rasputin dared to adopt towards the Prince himself, his sympathetic questions—such as when was Felix thinking of going to the front—his arrogant utterances about the Court, and highly esteemed aristocrats, princes of the Church, ministers, and members of Parliament! "I have nothing to do," he cried, "but bang on the table with my fist for everything to go as I want it. This is the one and only way of dealing with you aristocrats! They cannot stomach my going in and out of the Palace in my muddy boots. They are so proud, and pride is the beginning of all our sins. He who would stand in the sight of God must first humble himself."

Yusupov was hard put to it not to show his anger. But a heroic deed had to be performed, and he smiled winningly at the starets and suffered his caresses. He felt that every embrace given, every affectionate word, brought him nearer to his goal, and that he was in this way insinuating himself more and more deeply into the confidence of his victim.

As Rasputin, called away by telephone, was preparing to depart, the Prince hurriedly arranged another meeting with him and Munia, in order to carry on the conversation as soon as possible. The following morning Munia rang up her "little friend" again and asked him, in Rasputin's name, to bring his guitar with him next time, as Father Grigori had heard that Felix could sing gipsy songs beautifully. At that moment Yusupov must have imagined that unseen powers were in alliance with him, for his delicate mind, so uncommonly susceptible to subtle perfidy, at once recognized what a weapon chance had placed in his hand.

The fact that Yusupov could sing gipsy songs, guitar in hand, to Rasputin, meant, as he saw clearly, the possibility of saving weeks and months of laborious work, and of reaching his goal in the shortest possible time. So that evening Prince Yusupov reached for his guitar as an assassin reaches for his weapon, and proceeded to the Golovins' house on the Winter Canal, where the unsuspecting starets, the trusting Munia, and her equally trusting mother were already longing for his arrival.

When they had all seated themselves at the tea-table, Rasputin fondled little Munia and then asked if Yusupov had really brought his instrument with him; and, on his answering "yes," begged him to sing something to him. Felix was quivering with disgust at the sight of the jolly peasant; but he gave him a friendly smile, took his guitar in his hand, and began some gipsy songs. Grigori Efimovich listened, leaning comfortably back in an arm-chair, and on his wrinkled face was a gleam of childish happiness and emotion. He asked for more and more songs, and Yusupov did not grow weary of singing airs gay and airs sad, touching the strings of the instrument with his delicate, carefully manicured fingers.

* * * * *

On the morning of December 16th (1916), Prince Felix took himself to his palace on the Moika to make the final preparations for the murder of the starets, which was to take place that evening. For the guitar playing had done its work well, and Yusupov had succeeded in insinuating himself completely into Rasputin's confidence. Since the evening when he had first played to him at the Golovins, Grigori Efimovich had treated him as his most devoted friend; Yusupov had also frequently visited him in the Gorokhovaia, and the starets was so extraordinarily happy over this that it seemed that love had struck him with complete blindness. Felix came and went as he liked in his victim's house, and even allowed himself, on the excuse of suffering from pains in the chest, to be treated with "miraculous magnetic strokings." But, at the same time, in conjunction with the rest of the conspirators, he was making every preparation for carrying out the murder.

As the scene of the crime, the conspirators had chosen an unused underground room in the Yusupov Palace on the Moika, which was undergoing alterations at the time. From this underground vault, betraying noises would not so soon penetrate to the outer world. The pretext by which the starets was to be lured to the palace had also been found: Grigori Efimovich had for some time cherished a wish to meet the wife of Prince Felix, the young and beautiful Irina Alexandrovna, and this fact was to form the last link in the chain of Yusupov's plans.

Although Irina Alexandrovna was not in Petrograd at all, but staying in the Crimea, Yusupov declared to the starets that his wife wanted him to go to see her, as she felt ill and would like him to treat her. Grigori Efimovich was delighted with this news, the truth of which he did not for a moment doubt, and gratefully accepted Yusupov's invitation for the evening of the 16th of December. Felix alleged that a late hour was desirable, as his parents were not well disposed to the starets, and were, therefore, to know nothing about this visit. Rasputin, usually so cautious and artful, had not the slightest suspicion even of this somewhat doubtful statement, so blinded was he by his affection; and he promised he would tell no one where he intended to spend the evening.

The underground room in which the murder was to take place had originally been a part of the wine cellar; but it was now adapted for use as a dining-room and the walls were papered. It had a stone floor, a rather low-vaulted roof, and two narrow windows, hardly above the street level, which looked out on the Moika.

Since the success of the whole plot depended on the room's

producing the impression of being always lived in, Felix had various pieces of good furniture brought from the store-room, carved wooden chairs upholstered in leather, tables, and cabinets, including one inlaid cabinet in exquisite taste, which contained a number of mirrors and little bronze pillars.

With the help of his servant Nefedov, Yusupov arranged the room as comfortably as possible, hung curtains at the windows, covered the stone floor with valuable Persian carpets and bearskin rugs, placed on the mantelpiece of the great red granite fireplace gilt tankards, old majolica plates, and ivory figures, and finally set in the middle of the room the table at which Rasputin was to eat the fatal meal. He ordered the servants to lay places for six people, and provide tea, cakes and wine. When all this was ready, the staff was to withdraw to the servants' quarters in a distant part of the house, and not leave them before next morning.

All these preparations took the best part of the day; and it was not until late in the evening that the hissing samovar at last stood on the table. The room, previously so unfriendly, now looked quite comfortable with the dark red curtains at the window, the many mats, and the flickering fire on the hearth. The other conspirators appeared; Doctor Lazovert put on rubber gloves, opened a box he had brought with him, which he said contained cyanide of potassium, and having rubbed some crystals between his fingers, he removed the upper layers from the chocolate cakes on the table, and scattered a large quantity over the under layers. He replaced the top halves, having made sure that the dose of poison was more than enough to kill a whole party.

Before the conspirators left the room, they took pains to produce the impression that several people had recently taken tea there. For this purpose they carefully disarranged the furniture, pushed back the chairs, pulled the mats a little awry, and poured some tea into the cups. Then they once more rehearsed the parts that each of them had to play during Rasputin's murder. The Grand Duke, who had been standing about idle most of the time, expressed a desire to be allowed a small share in the murder, but Purishkevich, loyal to the imperial house, on this occasion displayed his delicate feeling of the extent to which a member of the imperial family could take part in a crime, and put forward the view that an imperial prince could not stain his hands with dirty peasant blood, but might merely co-operate as a spectator of the murder. This opinion prevailed, and it was definitely decided that only Yusupov should regale the starets with poison, while the rest of the conspirators were to wait in the Prince's study over the underground room until everything was over. In order to scatter any trace of suspicion Rasputin might have, they were to put on the gramophone, to produce the illusion that there was a gay party of guests in the upper room.

Prince Felix himself then set off to fetch the victim of his hospitality. To prevent any other person's being admitted to the secret, Doctor Lazovert undertook to drive the car; Yusupov put on a big reindeer coat and hid his face under a black cap with ear-flaps. They entered the big car, which rolled away along the Fontanka in the direction of Rasputin's flat.

* * * * *

On the morning of the 16th of December, Rasputin, as on so many other occasions, came home very drunk. He felt extremely tired and cut down his day's programme as much as possible. At ten A. M., he went to the telephone to speak to Anna Vyrubova, and it cost him a great effort to force his heavy tongue to speak more or less distinctly. After this, he dispatched a few petitioners and went to the baths, accompanied by his agents, for his limbs were still heavy with wine. Towards midday, he welcomed his faithful little Munia, who had arrived while he was out, and then withdrew immediately to his bedroom to rest a little. He did not appear again until evening, when he went into the "Holy of Holies," where many of his women disciples were waiting for him, and read with pleasure a telegram announcing that the Tsar had appointed his protégé, Dobrovolski, Minister of Justice.

Munia inquired what he intended to do in the evening, as she would like to stay with him as long as possible; this day she felt it especially hard to have to part from her beloved starets. He explained with a mysterious and mischievous smile that he intended to go out; but refused to divulge his destination.

"I'll find out," said Munia tenderly, "and follow *you*, whether *you* like it or not."

Father Grigori answered jokingly: "No, my love, *you* cannot follow me where I am going to-day." He kissed her on the lips, made the sign of the cross over her head, and said, dismissing her: "God bless *you*, my darling, *you* must go now."

Munia took her leave and left the flat reluctantly; but he had wished it, and it would not have been right to resist or refuse to go. On the stairs she met Ania Vyrubova hurrying up to see Rasputin. Munia told her that Grigori Efimovich was thinking of going out that night, and was behaving very mysteriously. Would Ania be insistent and discover what he really intended to do?

Anna Vyrubova had come to bring the starets a holy picture from Novgorod, a present from the Empress. He accepted it with pleasure, and, going into his little room, added it to the many beribboned ikons and lit a little oil-lamp before it. Then he told Ania that the Minister of the Interior, Protopopov, had announced that he was coming to see him on important business, and would arrive very soon. When she begged him to tell her what he was going to do that evening, the starets, after a brief resistance, let her into the secret, for he well knew Ania's faithful devotion, understanding, and discretion. He informed her of young Prince Yusupov's invitation and of his request that Rasputin should say nothing to anyone, especially to the Golovins, about it.

This mystification made Anna Vyrubova indignant. She regarded it as an insult. If Yusupov and his wife were ashamed of receiving Rasputin openly and by daylight, he ought to refuse their hospitality altogether. But Grigori Efimovich described the childlike devotion that Prince Felix had recently shown him, and pointed out how he had been asked to cure the illness of the Princess Irina. It was impossible for him to refuse to do this, since God had granted him the gift of healing so that he could help the sick. After much resistance from Anna, he at last promised to put off the visit to another time. But he said this only so that the good Ania would leave him in peace, for he had quite decided to go to Yusupov's that night. There he would not only make the acquaintance of the beauteous Irina Alexandrovna and try his healing art on her; the attractive Felix had also faithfully promised to sing him gipsy songs. How could he give up an evening that promised such delights?

Ania could stay with Father Grigori only for a short time, as the Tsaritsa had asked her to come to see her again that evening to give her all the news of her dear "Friend." So she soon took her leave; but turned round again at the door to say beseechingly: "*You* won't go to Felix, will *you*, little Father? *You* have promised me."

When Rasputin was alone, he called the maid, a peasant woman, Katia Ivanovna by name, who had been in charge of his household for some time, and told her to get out the new blue silk shirt embroidered with cornflowers. He also ordered her to put a bright polish on his top-boots, as he wished to look his best that night. As he changed his clothes, he devoted great care to every detail of his costume, as if he had been going to the Easter festival at church.

When he tried to fasten the top button of his shirt, his clumsy peasant fingers would not perform their office. He struggled in vain in front of the long mirror, where his lady visitors adjusted their hair, hats, and clothing; he could not manage to fasten the damnably refractory button; and he cursed and blasphemed. Finally, like a big, helpless child, he ran to the kitchen and implored Katia to help him, because the stupid Princess Shakhovskaia had put far too big a button on his shirt.

At the moment Katia climbed on to a stool to fasten Grigori's shirt, the bell of the door at the back of the kitchen rang. Katia jumped down again, hurried to the door, and announced His Excellency the Minister Protopopov. Since Rasputin had appointed him Minister of the Interior in place of the treacherous Khvostov, Protopopov had been a regular visitor, and discussed with Rasputin the details of all important Government measures. He always came by the back stairway, and stole through the kitchen into Grigori's office with the utmost secrecy, so that no stranger should observe him. The other inhabitants of the house were quite aware of his identity; but knew that they were expected to preserve the strictest silence about his visits.

This time Protopopov seemed thoroughly upset when he came into the kitchen and greeted the starets. He was in a state of extreme agitation and trembled in every limb. His breath came in panting gasps, his sunken cheeks were as pale as death, and there was a wild glitter in his eyes. Rasputin could not help thinking for a moment that perhaps Protopopov's opponents were not so far wrong when they said that he was mentally deranged. But however that might be, he was honest and God-fearing, and that seemed to the starets to be the chief thing. So he clasped the Minister closely in his arms with a friendly smile, kissed him, and asked in a soothing tone: "What is the matter with *you* then? Have those louts in the Duma played *you* another trick?"

Whereupon he drew his visitor into the little room, where Protopopov once again fell on his neck and embraced and kissed him as if he were saying a last farewell. Then he began to address him in an agitated and uncontrolled manner: "Grigori Efimovich, I implore *you* never to go out alone the next few days. I have received orders that the agents are to watch *your* house with particular attention, as evil men are laying a plot against *you*. I entreat *you* to be cautious; don't take a single step unaccompanied, do not visit any public place, go nowhere, for I fear some evil."

Rasputin let the Minister finish his say. Truly a good and God-fearing man, this Protopopov, he thought, but often not quite right in the head. You had only to look at him to know that this time he was not to be taken seriously!

"*You* are a good creature, my friend," the starets said at last, cordially, "but take it from me, *you* are a little excited to-night." He calmly took Protopopov's arm, stroked it, and went on in a firm, confident voice: "Don't be afraid, I am in the hands of God, and except by the Lord's will, no one can do me harm. Go home now, my dear, and sleep well. I have still something important to see to."

The Minister was visibly calmed by these words: Rasputin's quiet and assured manner banished his anxiety for a moment. "Another new love?" he asked jokingly, as he departed; but Grigori Efimovich did not answer, and merely smiled and pushed him towards the back door. "Go, go, I have still to put on my things." Protopopov had scarcely left the flat when the bell rang again and "Sister Masha" came in. She was a tall, somewhat opulent-looking, fair-haired woman of about twenty-five, dressed in an elegant cloak, who had recently called on Rasputin rather frequently, and no one knew who she was. In the house she was generally referred to as "Sister Masha." The starets was impatient, dealt with his visitor rapidly, and dismissed her. He put out the light in his little room, so that it was lit only by the gold and yellow glimmer of the ikon lamps, and lay down on the bed in his clothes.

When his daughters and his little niece Aniushka, who had been spending the evening with friends, came back about eleven o'clock, they went to say good-night to Grigori before retiring to their pretty white rooms. They found him lying in bed fully clothed, his boots on his feet, and his eyes open. They felt a little alarmed at this unusual sight, and asked what he was going to do. Rasputin said nothing for some time, but at last replied: "I am going to visit the 'little one'; he is to fetch me at midnight. But, children, you mustn't tell anyone. Do you hear? No one must know anything about it, especially Munia." He put his finger to his lips, and threatened the girls with a joking gesture.

Somewhat later Katia also came into the room to see if the starets needed anything further. But he told her to go to bed, and not to trouble if someone knocked at the back door later. Katia departed; but she had noticed that something mysterious was afoot, and she made up her mind not to go to sleep for the moment, for she was very curious to learn what her master was going to do in the middle of the night. She had not long to wait. The bell of the back entrance rang sharply, and Katia heard Rasputin vainly trying to step softly in his heavy boots, as he went through the kitchen to open the door.

Katia stuck her head for an instant out of the alcove where her bed stood and caught a glimpse of her master's visitor for a second or two. He was a tall, slight man in a fur coat, with a black cap pulled well down over his face. He looked round anxiously and cautiously, as if he feared he was observed, and then asked softly: "Are *you* alone? Can anybody hear us?"

By his voice Katia recognized that the stranger was none other than the "little one" who had recently paid repeated visits to Rasputin. She did not know his name, but had heard that he was the husband of a grand duchess. The two men conversed in very low tones, and the servant was only able to hear Grigori Efimovich ask: "Why have *you* muffled yourself up like that?" The "little one" said something she did not catch, and then the starets took him by the arm and led him into his study. This exhausted Katia's interest in events, and she soon fell sound asleep.

When they were in the study, Grigori Efimovich said: "Protopopov was here to-night, and told me that wicked people want to murder me. Just let them try it; they won't succeed. Their arms are not long enough!" He put on his coat, opened a drawer and took out some money. Seeing Yusupov glance curiously at the bundles of banknotes lying in the drawer, Rasputin remarked: "My daughter Matriona is soon going to marry an officer; I shall be able to give her a fine dowry." He shut the drawer carefully and blew out the candle.

At that moment Felix was burning with shame over his own baseness. Here he was on the point of committing the most infamous of all deeds, enticing a defenceless man to his house on the pretence of hospitality, with intent to murder him there. For a second or two he even felt tempted to give up the whole plan; then he reflected that he would rather face the scorn of his victim than that of his fellow conspirators, and, calling to mind his "patriotic" aims, he conquered this fit of weakness.

When Grigori Efimovich had completed his preparations, he shut all the doors behind him, and, taking Felix affectionately by the arm, led him carefully down the dark staircase. Yusupov, with his bad conscience, felt that the starets was clasping his arm in a grip of steel; the darkness of the staircase confused and oppressed him, and it seemed an eternity before they at last got out of the house and entered the big field-grey car, where Doctor Lazovert sat at the wheel. During the journey Yusupov was very nervous, and glanced several times through the little window at the back to assure himself that the car was not being followed.

But the street was completely empty, and Doctor Lazovert drove to the Moika at a rapid pace by a circuitous route. At last he arrived, turned into the courtyard of the palace, and brought the car to a standstill by a side entrance.

* * * * *

The sound of the gramophone was heard from the first floor playing an American dance tune. Rasputin stopped in surprise, and asked: "What's that? Are *you* having a party?"

Felix tried to soothe him: "No, it's only a few friends with my wife. They will be going soon. Come into the dining-room for a little and drink a cup of tea with me."

Quite unsuspecting, Grigori Efimovich followed the Prince down the steps and examined the alleged dining-room curiously. He displayed a particular interest in the cabinet with the mirrors and little pillars; he opened and shut the little doors, and looked at the inside with childish pleasure. Then he accepted Yusupov's invitation and sat down at the tea-table.

A conversation ensued about common friends, the Golovin family, Anna Vyrubova, and finally the imperial couple. Felix, who in his nervousness felt all the time that something might make his guest suspicious, deliberately returned to Protopopov's warning, and asked why the Minister was so anxious.

"Well," said Rasputin, "I am a thorn in the flesh to a whole lot of people, because I always tell the truth. Your aristocrats are full of envy and malice. But why should I be afraid of them? They cannot get at me! They have had more than one go at it; but God has frustrated their infamous plans every time."

This speech seemed to Yusupov to be aimed at him personally, and it offended him so that his one thought now was to make an end of this peasant as quickly as possible. He poured out a cup of tea for the starets and handed him cakes; but he had not yet the courage to offer him the poisoned brown ones, and first put forward the harmless pink ones. Not till a few minutes later did he overcome his irresolution and, with polite cordiality, handed his guest the plate with the poisoned confectionery. Grigori Efimovich devoured several, one after the other.

Prince Felix awaited, trembling, some change in Rasputin's appearance, for, according to Doctor Lazovert, the cyanide was bound to act immediately. But the starets went on talking as if nothing at all had happened. Extremely disturbed, Yusupov went up to the tray on which stood the wine-glasses containing the poison, and asked Grigori Efimovich if he would taste some of the famous Yusupov wine from the Crimea.

With obvious pleasure Rasputin drained several glasses; his host stood before him, watching his every movement, and expecting each instant to see the starets drop dead; but the expression of his face scarcely altered. After a tense pause he rose, walked round the room, and then asked for more wine. Felix handed him another of the poisoned glasses; Grigori gulped down the wine, but this time, too, it had no visible effect. Host and guest now sat down opposite each other. In desperation the Prince racked his brain for the explanation of the failure of the poison. Had Dr. Lazovert tricked them all? Or had he made a mistake and used some other harmless preparation instead of the deadly drug? Or was Rasputin a super-man in vitality who could endure, without injury, a quantity of poison that would have killed on the spot a whole company of ordinary people? This seemed hardly credible. He gazed at his guest, and it seemed as if there was an expression of contempt and distrust in his eyes: Yusupov rose, went over to the wall, and took down the guitar that was hanging there. Grigori Efimovich smiled happily when he saw this movement, and begged him: "Oh, do play something, something gay. I love to hear *you* sing."

Prince Felix played and sang. In an insinuating voice, of exaggerated sweetness, he sang one gipsy song after another, and the starets listened with a smile. Whenever the Prince stopped, he at once asked him to go on, and his face was as pure as that of a truly saintly old man.

Meanwhile, however, the rest of the conspirators assembled in Yusupov's study had grown impatient, and began to make a noise with the object of urging the Prince to more rapid action. Rasputin looked up and asked what was happening up there.

"Probably it is my wife's friends getting ready to go," Felix answered with embarrassment. Then he added, happy at having discovered an excuse for leaving the room: "I will just go up and see what is happening." With these words he rose and hurried out, as the poison had had no effect, to fetch a pistol and put a bullet through the starets.

Rasputin looked after him placidly and affectionately; he was convinced that on his return Felix would immediately take up the guitar and sing to him again. Ah, how pleasant and delightful it was to listen to the singing of this lovable and attractive boy!

* * * * *

Katia Ivanovna, the maid, wakened as usual at five A. M. Before proceeding to the household duties of the day, she looked into her master's bedroom to fetch his clothes and boots for cleaning; but she found the bed empty.

It was not an unusual event for Grigori Efimovich not to be at home at this hour of the day; but the happenings of the night before, the strange behaviour of the starets, the mysterious, muffled visitor, and his whispered conversation with Grigori Efimovich all made Katia Ivanovna very uneasy. Seized with sudden alarm, she ran into the girls' room, roused Matriona from her sleep, and cried anxiously: "Maria Grigorievna, get up! I am afraid. Grigori Efimovich has not come home."

Matriona heard the words still half in a dream; but she at once recollected what her father had said the night before; she was annoyed by Katia's fears and muttered sleepily: "You stupid creature. Father went to see the 'little one'; probably he is spending the night there." This seemed to her to explain matters completely, and she turned over and fell asleep again immediately. At seven o'clock, however, she was roused again; Katia was standing by her bed frantic with terror, shaking her, and stammering in nameless fear: "The police."

This time Matriona became alarmed. She rose quickly, wakened her sister, and, throwing on a dressing-gown, went into the next room, where several detectives were awaiting her. They inquired where Grigori Efimovich had gone the previous night, and questioned all the other members of the household in detail about the events of the night before. Matriona told them that her father had said he was going to visit the "little one"; Varia and Aniushka confirmed this, and Katia also told them about the midnight visitor in the fur coat and the cap pulled down over his face. The police then sent for the concierge and the spies lounging on the staircase, and examined them; according to their reports, a big field-grey military car had driven up, a gentleman in a fur coat had rung the bell, and had gone up to Rasputin's flat by the back stair. After taking down all this information in their notebooks, the police went off without saying a word to the starets' anxious family of what it was all about.

Hardly had the officials gone, when Matriona hurried to the telephone and rang up Munia Golovina. Munia, however, soothed her and declared that, as Grigori Efimovich had spent the night at Felix Yusupov's, there was not the slightest ground for alarm; probably he had slept there and would come home quite soon.

About eight o'clock, the first petitioners arrived as usual; and at ten A. M. the waiting suppliants filled the reception-room; but Grigori Efimovich had not yet come back. The door of the mysterious little room into which he was accustomed to conduct his pretty petitioners stood wide open; someone had forgotten to shut it in her haste; and the petitioners were able to see every detail of this mysterious room, which now seemed ordinary, empty, and melancholy, without a trace of mystery or magic.

At ten o'clock the telephone rang as usual. All the petitioners knew that it was the call from Tsarskoe Selo. But, while usually the maid or one of the women disciples quietly took up the receiver and then called the starets, to-day the sound caused great excitement. Several people seemed to rush up to the instrument, and a confused noise of voices could be heard through the half-open door; this was soon shut and the conversation became inaudible.

The petitioners gradually began to feel somewhat uneasy: no one could explain the reasons for the starets' long absence, or the meaning of the excited hurrying to and fro of the household, or the whispering and general nervousness.

About eleven o'clock, Munia Golovina appeared accompanied by her mother. On hearing that Grigori Efimovich had not yet returned, she became as pale as death, and her thin girlish lips began to quiver. She declared her willingness to telephone at once to Felix Felixovich and, for this purpose, went out to a neighbouring fruiterer's, as she wished to avoid exciting any remark in the flat itself. She came back and reported that the Prince had gone out in the morning, and had not yet returned; she had only been able to speak to the valet, who declared that he knew nothing of the matter.

All the women sat in petrified silence round the table in the dining-room. Suddenly the telephone bell rang and Katia announced that Prince Yusupov wished to speak to Matriona. Matriona, in her alarm and agitation being in no state to do anything, old Madame Golovina went to the instrument. The other women heard a conversation in English carried on in an agitated tone. Then Madame Golovina returned to the table with her face deathly white, and whispered excitedly to her daughter that Felix maintained that Grigori had not been with him at all the previous night.

This information caused general consternation. The two girls and Aniushka confirmed each other's statement that Rasputin had expressly stated that he was intending to visit the "little one," and Katia had, beyond any doubt, recognized the midnight visitor as the "little one." Madame Golovina said very timidly that she must have made a mistake; but no one really believed it, and a feeling of helpless despair took possession of them all.

Another fearful silence ensued, and the hours crawled by with agonizing slowness. Then Katia suddenly appeared and announced that Bishop Isidor, who had been searching for the missing starets since early morning, had arrived in the company of a police official, and wished to speak to Matriona. Both men came in; the official had a large brown golosh in his hand, which he laid on the table in front of Matriona, and asked in a dry, official voice: "Are you the daughter of Grigori Efimovich Rasputin? Do you identify this golosh, size 10, Treugolnik make, as the property of your father?"

Matriona took the shoe in her hand, gazed fixedly at it for a second or two, and then, instead of answering, burst into despairing sobs. Varia, Aniushka, the Golovins, and the other women disciples hurried up, and they all recognized the golosh as Rasputin's property.

The police officer made vain efforts to continue his official investigations. He related how, about noon, the watchmen on the Petrovski Bridge had had their attention called to the matter by two workmen, and had discovered the golosh and several blood-stains on the ice between the third and fourth pillars of the bridge. Notice was at once sent to the police, and the district superintendent hurried to the spot; the golosh was fetched, carefully examined, and had now been brought for identification. Not a single person in Rasputin's flat paid any attention to the narrative of the police officer; the daughters of the starets were weeping despairingly; the women disciples were seized with hysteria, and the maid ran through all the rooms crying and wailing like a mad woman.

Suddenly the petitioners in the reception-room, who had been talking in whispers since morning, began to converse loudly and excitedly. The distinguished generals and officials who had come to beg for Rasputin's patronage tried to get away as quickly as possible, for they guessed that the police would come, and they did not wish their presence there to be officially remarked; and, as in any case it was to be assumed that Grigori Efimovich was dead, no one could say for certain who would in future decide the granting of places, offices, and dignities, and it was safer not to compromise themselves.

Most of the poor people, on the other hand, the peasants, petty officials, and needy petitioners, male and female, remained in the flat; some of them went to the door that led to the inner rooms, pressed the latch, and went in. Soon the rooms were crowded with people, half-curious and half-reverently amazed. The doors were wide open. People came and went, and lamentation, sobbing, and excited cries were heard everywhere.

Someone or other related in great excitement that the starets had felt a clear presentiment of death at the beginning of the month, and had said that he must soon die in horrible agonies because, in spite of his sins, he had been chosen as a sacrifice. Others again alleged that this time he had not wanted his son Mitia to go to Pokrovskoe for Christmas, and had said to him: "Mitia, don't go, *you* will never see me again; I shall not live to see the New Year."

The police appeared; secret agents opened all the cupboards, searched for papers, broke open the desk, sealed up several packages, and examined Rasputin's secretary. They looked for money, that fabulous wealth which Grigori Efimovich was supposed to have accumulated, and also for the Tsaritsa's letters, in order to be able to put them in a safe place. Some of the officials approached the visitors who had not yet left the flat and told them to go home. The uneasy crowd of poor people, some whispering, some raging, little clerks, soldiers, old women, and nuns, passed excitedly down the staircase, and disappeared into the misty twilight of the winter afternoon.

* * * * *

When Anna Vyrubova told the Tsaritsa on the evening of the 16th of December that Grigori Efimovich was intending to visit Yusupov, in order to make his wife's acquaintance, Alexandra replied in amazement: "There must be some misunderstanding. Irina Alexandrovna is not in St. Petersburg at all, she is in the Crimea."

Consequently the telephone message of the next morning about the mysterious absence of the starets immediately caused Anna Vyrubova some anxiety. As soon as Matriona Rasputin had told her that her father had not yet come home, Anna hurried to the Empress, and the two friends discussed at length the meaning of these strange events. The Tsaritsa had to go to her hospital; but, driven by anxiety, she soon returned to the Palace and called up Protopopov. The Minister had to inform her that a policeman, when passing the Yusupov Palace on his beat, had heard shots in the night. The matter had, however, not yet been explained. The Tsaritsa was mortally alarmed, and she had hardly the strength to instruct the Minister to make a strict personal investigation and report to her regularly.

The Emperor was at G.H.Q., whither Voeikov, the Governor of the Palace, as well as the majority of the aides-de-camp, had accompanied him, so that the Empress and Ania, helpless and with no one to advise them, were left entirely to their own devices. They hardly dared any longer doubt that the starets had met with an accident, and they were a prey to terrible fear. Alexandra could not grasp the idea that her only friend, the saviour of her son, her husband's most faithful adviser, could be dead. What would become of them all without the kindness, the love, and the ready help of Father Grigori? Amid innumerable enemies, evilly disposed and wicked people, he had been their one God-sent counsellor. Alexandra felt with perfect certainty that his death meant the ruin of the imperial family. Sobbing, she fell on Ania's neck; Ania alone could understand her grief in its fullness, for she, too, had lost everything by Grigori's death.

About midday the telephone bell rang, and Protopopov gave a detailed report of what the police investigations had so far brought to light. This information enabled the two women to form a clear picture of the events of the previous night.

A policeman patrolling the Moika heard, shortly after midnight, the report of several shots from the courtyard of the Yusupov Palace; he had immediately proceeded to the spot and met the Prince himself in the courtyard. In reply to his question whether anything had happened, the Prince had said with a smile that one of his guests, who was a little tipsy, had fired a shot in the air.

The official had not dared to doubt the statements of such a gentleman, but had saluted stiffly and gone away again. A little later, however, Yusupov himself had sent his steward to fetch him and bring him to his private office. There a gentleman in grey field-uniform was also present, and he suddenly turned to the constable, introducing himself as Purishkevich, member of the Duma, and told him that Rasputin, the notorious criminal and national danger, had just been killed; if the constable loved the Tsar he would preserve the strictest silence about the matter. The officer promised to do so, but had then done his duty, and immediately reported the occurrence to the district superintendent in charge.

In the morning a police commission had searched the Yusupov Palace; and there they came upon a broad track of blood that led up the staircase and across the courtyard. Yusupov tried to explain this by saying that one of his guests at the party the night before had killed a dog out of high spirits; the dead body of an animal was actually lying in the middle of the courtyard, but the authorities were able to ascertain immediately that the amount of blood was much too great to have come from the dead dog.

Protopopov told the Empress that, in view of all the circumstances, there could scarcely be any doubt that Rasputin had been murdered by Yusupov and his friends. An arrest was, however, for the moment out of the question, as the Minister had at once to explain, because a member of the imperial family was involved in the affair, which afforded a certain amount of immunity to the other persons concerned.

Only now did Alexandra recognize the full baseness of this murderous conspiracy and the cowardice of the murderers, who had dragged Dimitri Pavlovich into their plot, to secure themselves from punishment. Accordingly, when the murderers, one after another, protested their innocence to her, the whole situation was already quite clear in her mind. The Grand Duke Dimitri was the first to ring up and ask for permission to wait upon the Tsaritsa, who refused point-blank to see him. Soon afterwards Prince Yusupov telephoned, and made the same request. Alexandra sent a message to the effect that if he had any explanations to give, he should communicate them in writing.

Towards evening a letter from the Prince was actually delivered at the Palace, in which he again declared that Rasputin had not been at his house at all that night, and once again produced the fable about the shooting of the dog. The Empress was deeply indignant over this cowardice on the part of the murderer, and sent Yusupov's letter straight to Dobrovolski, the new Minister of Justice, for further official action.

In addition Alexandra wrote off in great agitation to her husband at G.H.Q. "We are sitting together," runs this letter of December 17th, 1916, "can imagine our feelings—thoughts—our Friend has disappeared. Yesterday A. saw him & he said Felix asked him to come in the night, a motor wld. fetch him to see Irina.—A motor fetched him (military one) with 2 civilians & he went away. . . .

"Our Friend was in good spirits but nervous these days. . . . Felix pretends He never came to the house & never asked Him. Seems quite a paw. I still trust in God's mercy that one has only driven Him off somewhere. *Kalinin* * is doing all he can. Therefore I beg for Voyeikov, we women are alone with our weak heads. Shall keep her to live here—as now they will get at her next.

"I cannot & won't believe He has been killed. God have mercy. Such utter anguish (am calm & can't believe it). . . ."

The same day the Empress also sent two telegrams to the Emperor:

"Send Voyeikov at once; we need his help, as Rasputin is missing since last night. We trust to God's mercy. Felix and Dimitri are involved in the affair."

"Protopopov is doing his best. Felix, who wanted to go off to the Crimea, has been detained. I long for your arrival. God help us in future."

A wire from the Empress, dated 18th December, reads:

"I prayed in the house Chapel. No trace yet found of Rasputin. The police are continuing the search. I fear that these two wretched boys have committed a frightful crime, but have not yet lost all hope. Start to-day, I need you terribly."

The 17th and 18th of December passed in despair and uncertainty, until at last Protopopov reported to the Empress that Rasputin's body had been found. After the discovery of the golosh on the Petrovski Bridge, the authorities at once had the ice on the Neva broken, and sent for divers. The divers soon recovered the body; Rasputin's arms and legs had been bound with ropes, and the corpse showed numerous bullet and knife wounds. In spite of this, Rasputin had clearly been still alive when he was thrown into the Neva, for one arm was half out of the rope and the lungs were full of water.

Immediately after the discovery the corpse was transferred with the greatest secrecy to the Veterans' Home at Chesma, which was situated outside the city on the way to Tsarskoe Selo; there Professor Kossorotov examined the body, and made a report on the wounds and the cause of death.

The Empress, on learning of the discovery of the body, ordered Sister Akulina, the nun who had been cured by Rasputin in

* The Empress's name for Protopopov.

the Okhtoi Convent, to perform the last offices of love for the dead. The nun watched the whole night by the murdered starets, washed him, and dressed him in fresh garments. Finally, she pressed a crucifix into his hands and also laid in them a farewell letter from the Empress.

"My dear Martyr," ran the Empress's last words to her Friend, "grant me your blessing to accompany me on the sorrowful road I have still to tread here below. Remember us in Heaven in your holy prayers. Alexandra."

Next morning Sister Akulina brought the coffin containing the last remains of the starets in a motor-car to Tsarskoe Selo. In order to prevent any public demonstration, the police had spread a report that the body would be taken to Pokrovskoe; but, in reality, the funeral took place on December 21st, a cold, foggy, winter morning, in the Park of Tsarskoe Selo. The coffin was interred in a plot of ground on which Anna Vyrubova had originally intended to build a home for invalided soldiers. The melancholy ceremony was attended by the Emperor and Empress, the Grand Duchesses, Ania, Protopopov, the two aides-de-camp, Loman and Maltsev, as well as by the daughters of the starets and Sister Akulina. Before the coffin was nailed down, Matriona laid on her father's breast the ikon which the Empress had brought from Novgorod; then the Court chaplain, Father Vassiliev, spoke the last blessing, and the mortal remains of Grigori Rasputin were laid in the earth.

In her desire to be surrounded by people who had sincerely loved her Friend, the Empress in the days that followed frequently summoned Rasputin's daughters to Tsarskoe Selo. Both she and the Grand Duchesses made every possible effort to comfort the two helpless girls, and the Emperor several times declared that he would be a father to them.

The hideous crime of which Grigori Efimovich had been the victim had from the beginning aroused the Emperor's extreme wrath and indignation. On his return from G.H.Q., he greeted the Court officials who received him with the words: "I am ashamed before the whole country that my kinsmen have stained their hands with this man's blood."

The Emperor subsequently approved all the measures which

his wife, in his absence, had ordered to be taken against the murderers. A strict watch was being kept on both the Grand Duke Dimitri and Prince Yusupov, and they were confined to their houses. Prince Felix had at once taken refuge in Dimitri Pavlovich's Palace, to which the police had no entry; there the two friends awaited their fate together. But, on this question, a bitter struggle developed between the imperial couple and the Grand Dukes' party. Nikolai had at once expressed the intention of punishing the culprits without mercy, a resolve which made the Grand Dukes furiously indignant. The Grand Duke Alexander Mikhailovich, in particular, did all he could to have the proceedings against the murderers stopped: he visited Dobrovolski, the Minister of Justice, shouted excitedly at him, and ordered him in a rude manner to quash the whole affair immediately. The Minister did not, however, allow himself to be intimidated; he cited the Emperor's express orders, and succeeded in forcing the Grand Duke to apply to the Tsar himself. With the Tsar he had such a violent altercation that his shouts could be heard several rooms away. The scene ended, of course, in the Tsar's showing him the door.

Nevertheless, Nikolai's weakness of will was again displayed on this occasion. He finally decided to abandon his original idea of severe penalties, and confined himself to banishing the Grand Duke to Persia and Prince Yusupov to a distant estate. Mild as this punishment was, it caused great bitterness among the Grand Dukes, and all the members of the imperial house petitioned for the revocation of Dimitri's banishment. But the Emperor merely wrote on the margin of the petition: "No one has the right to commit murder," and did not cancel his orders.

* * * * *

The "patriotic and heroic deed" of Prince Yusupov and his accomplices soon showed itself to be, as in reality it had been from the outset, a most contemptible action, a cowardly and treacherous murder. The attitude of the murderers after the perpetration of their crime stamped it as such. These "patriotic heroes" did not dream for a moment of confessing what they had done and publicly taking responsibility for it; on the contrary, they made feverish efforts to divert all suspicion from themselves, and told lies to ensure their own safety, regardless of conscience or honour. Prince Yusupov, the young nobleman, the relative of the Emperor, did not lose a moment in perjuring himself to the Empress, telling her lies and making statements whose lack of plausibility was immediately apparent. He preferred to reserve the truth for the memoirs he had already planned to write.

His fellow-conspirators behaved in the same way: neither the Grand Duke Dimitri nor the renowned orator Purishkevich was ashamed of persistently denying the obvious truth.

The sound instincts of the people at once recognized that here was no heroic deed, but an ordinary crime. Of course, the sensation-loving society of the capital applauded the murderers, and there were even a few instances of excited place-hunters and pompous bores accosting each other on the Nevski Propekt and exchanging congratulations on Rasputin's murder, for the systematic agitation in the Duma and the *salons* had done its share in giving Rasputin the reputation of being a criminal. All the people who had unsuccessfully tried to gain an appointment, a concession, or the dispatch of some shady bit of business through the agency of the starets now loudly proclaimed that the removal of Rasputin had freed the Empire from an incubus.

The effect on the peasants of the news of the murder was, however, quite different. To them Grigori Efimovich had always been one of themselves, the representative of the muzhiks at the Imperial Court, the only person to champion the real interests of the people amid all these rich and distinguished lords. The peasants had loved their starets, and they regarded his murder as a grave injustice and a grievous wrong. In all the thousands of peasants' cabins of Siberia there was mourning for the fate of Grigori, the peasant who had gone to St. Petersburg to tell the Tsar the truth, and who, for that reason, had been slain by the courtiers.

Many superstitious people in the provinces interpreted Rasputin's murder as a fatal omen, and with troubled faces quoted his prophecy: "If I die, the Emperor will soon after lose his crown."

CHAPTER XV

THE DEATH SHIP

THERE was serious agitation in the Putilov Works, the Baltic shipyards, and the Viborg quarter: the discontented workers were holding meetings and downing tools; speakers were inciting them to revolt and preaching a fight against the high cost of living, against the Government, even against the Emperor. The police asked for military assistance; but the troops dispatched in answer to this appeal fired on the police instead of on the strikers.

"What terrible times we are living in," writes the Empress to her husband on the 22nd of February, 1917. "I feel and suffer with you more than words can say. What can I do? I can only pray. Our true Friend Rasputin prays for us in a better world; now He is nearer than ever to us. But how I would love to hear Rasputin's soothing, comforting voice."

In the days and weeks that followed, the revolt grew from hour to hour. In Petrograd it was icy-cold; but there was no wood. People were starving; but there was no bread. The bakers' shops were besieged by the poor, who had to stand in long queues all night; more and more frequently the crowd lost patience and looted the bakers' shops. In these days the Tsaritsa must often have thought of Grigori's saying to the Emperor, shortly before his death, that the chief thing was to help the poor and hungry, "so that the people may not lose their faith in the love of their Tsar."

Now Rasputin was dead, his advice had not been taken to heart, and the consequences were everywhere apparent. The populace marched in great processions to demand bread and peace; nearly every day bloody collisions with the guard occurred on the Nevski Prospekt; police officers were knocked down or shot. The revolt was increasingly directed against the whole system, the Government, and the Tsar. The masses were singing the "Marseillaise," and turbulently demanding the resignation of the Government and the abdication of the Emperor. The Government was no longer able to cope with the situation; it dissolved; and the individual ministers sought refuge in flight. Next, the garrison mutinied, and even the troops of the Guards went over to the revolutionaries.

At this critical time the Emperor was at G.H.Q., far from Petrograd; at the first signs of unrest, he had remarked to his entourage that he was ready to abdicate if the people really wished it; he would retire to Livadia, and devote himself to his beloved gardening. But grave reports continued to come in from the capital, and he changed his mind as he had so often done before, and dispatched a hastily assembled army to Petrograd, with orders to put down the revolt by force of arms. But this army went over to the revolutionaries without a struggle, and the Emperor was obliged to recognize that his position had become hopeless. On March 15th, in the saloon of the Court train, which was standing at a little station between G.H.Q. and Tsarskoe Selo, he handed his formal abdication to the emissaries of the Duma.

On March 22nd the ex-Emperor, as the prisoner of the new Government, was taken back to Tsarskoe Selo, where his family had already been placed under strict military supervision. In the night of March 22nd and 23rd, a crowd of rebel soldiers broke into the Park of the Palace, tore open Rasputin's grave, seized the coffin, and carried it to the Pargolovo forest. There a great pyre was erected, on to which the decomposing body of the starets, soaked in petrol, was thrown and burnt.

* * * * *

For five months the imperial family lived as prisoners in the Palace of Tsarskoe Selo. On the evening of August 13th they were told by the Governor of the Palace to make all preparations for a journey, as the Provisional Government intended to transport them from Petrograd that very night. The Empress learned from one of the soldiers on guard that they were to be taken to Siberia, to the Tobolsk Government, and kept prisoners there for the present.

How very strange! That was the district to which Rasputin, her never-to-be-forgotten Friend, belonged; it was from there He had come to support them in all life's troubles! The Tsaritsa employed the last hours of her stay in the palace where she had passed "twenty-three happy years" in taking farewell of all she had held so dear. Finally, she wrote a few lines to her faithful friend Ania, who had for several months been a prisoner in the Fortress of SS. Peter and Paul.

"I know what a fresh and bitter grief the enormous distance between us will be to you. We do not know yet where they are taking us to: we are not to learn that until after we have started. How long they intend to keep us away is also unknown. But I fancy the journey will take us where you were not long ago. The transfigured spirit of our Friend calls us. . . ."

It was midnight before the imperial family completed their preparations for the journey. Then a visitor was announced, the new revolutionary ruler, Kerenski, the Minister of Justice. They assembled in the large semicircular reception-room, where the Minister informed them of the decision of the Provisional Government to dispatch "the family of the citizen Romanov" to Siberia.

At five o'clock in the morning, Nikolai, Alexandra, and the children entered a motor-car, and were driven under escort to the Alexander Station. On the 17th of August they arrived at Tiumen, where the steamer "Russ" was waiting to take them on to Tobolsk.

Next morning they learned that the boat was about to pass the village of Pokrovskoe; a feeling of unutterable melancholy took possession of them. How marvellously God had ordained that they, dethroned, humiliated, prisoners, should now pass by the place from which Grigori Efimovich had come to the Imperial Palace, a simple pilgrim in his heavy boots and poor sheepskin coat.

Very soon the clean little village, with the church on the hill and the broad, white roads appeared above the river bank. And there stood his house. With its two stories, it towered above all the other peasants' cabins. Gathered on the deck they all gazed at the village. Ania had been there several times on the Empress's behalf, and had seen everything; she had lived in Rasputin's house, slept on plain matting like himself and his family, and had gone daily to the banks of the Tura with him and the fishermen. Ania had told the imperial family many stories of Pokrovskoe and of the starets' life there. They recognized it all and were intimately acquainted with every detail.

Little Alexei gazed with special curiosity and excitement at the village, the houses of which were gliding past him. This then was that fairy-tale place with the mysterious stable and the talking horses, surrounded by the great steppes on which grew flowers, each of which had a soul just like people! This was the place of which dear, kind Father Grigori had told the sick boy so many stories, and of which he had said: "Everything, all this fairy-tale country, belongs to *your* Papa and Mama, and will one day belong to *you* too." But now Alexei was a big boy, and knew that Papa, Mama, and he himself were poor exiled prisoners, and that the fairy-tale country of Siberia no longer belonged to them.

The boat had long passed the little village; but they went on talking of Grigori and recalling all he had been, all he had done and said. The Empress remembered the words which Ania had repeated to her long before the terrible disaster: he was passing the Fortress of SS. Peter and Paul with two of his women friends, when he suddenly stopped and cried in a voice full of deep emotion: "I see many tortured creatures, whole masses of people, great heaps, crowds of bodies! Among them are many grand dukes and hundreds of counts. The Neva will be red with blood."

How strange that sounded now, when his prophetic words had been fulfilled! They looked back once again to where Pokrovskoe had disappeared behind a bend in the river, and prayed the little prayer Grigori Efimovich had taught them. The steamer moved slowly on. In the distance the outline of the Kremlin of Tobolsk gradually took form in the twilight of the late summer evening. The ship that was bearing the last Emperor of Russia and his family to their unknown fate glided slowly downstream into the half-darkness of evening.

APPENDICES

SOURCES AND BIBLIOGRAPHY

In addition to private accounts and information supplied by people who knew Rasputin, the author has made use of the following sources of information:

A. DEPOSITIONS, REPORTS, AND LETTERS OF DOCUMENTARY IMPORTANCE

ALEXANDRA FEDOROVNA, THE TSARITSA. *Letters to the Tsar.* State Publishing Office, Moscow. 1923.

ALEXANDRA FEDOROVNA, THE TSARITSA. Telegrams to the Tsar dated 17th, 18th, and 19th December, 1916.

ANASTASIA NIKOLAEVNA, THE GRAND DUCHESS. Letters to Rasputin, 1908–1909.

ARNOLDI. *Notes on the Sectarians in the Kostroma Government.*

BELETSKI, S. P. *Grigori Rasputin.* Moscow, 1923.

BUCHANAN, GEORGE. *Meine Mission in Russland.* Berlin, 1926.

BULATOVICH (THE PRIEST-MONK ANTONIUS). *The Justification of Faith in the Name of God.*

BULATOVICH (THE PRIEST-MONK ANTONIUS). *The Justification of Faith in Invincible Power.*

DIANUMOVA, E. *My Meetings with Rasputin.* Petrograd, 1923.

ELISAVETA FEDOROVNA, THE GRAND DUCHESS. Telegram to the Grand Duke Dimitri Pavlovich and Princess Yusupov dated December 18th, 1916.

Extraordinary Commission of Investigation set up by the Provisional Government. Minutes of meetings, 1917:

Depositions of the Ministers, Count P. N. Ignatiev, A. N. Khvostov, N. A. Maklakov, A. D. Protopopov, I. G. Shcheglovitov, and N. B. Shcherbatov; the Deputy-Minister A. N. Verevkin; and Prime Ministers V. N. Kokovtsov, B. V. Stürmer, and I. L. Goremykin; Generals P. G. Kurlov, V. F. Dzhunkovski, A. V. Gerasimov, E. K.

APPENDICES

Klimovich, N. I. Ivanov; A. I. Spiridovich; Colonei M. S. Komisarov; V. N. Voeikov, Governor of the Palace; I. T. Manasevich-Manuilov; Anna Alexandrovna Vyrubova; Olga Vladimirovna Lokhtina; N. E. Markov.

GILLIARD, P. *Zar Nikolaj und seine Familie.* Vienna, 1921.

ILIODOR (SERGEI TRUFANOV). Letters about Rasputin.

ILIODOR (SERGEI TRUFANOV). Letters to Badmaev.

ILIODOR (SERGEI TRUFANOV). *The Holy Devil. Golos Minuvshchago.* No. 3. Petrograd, 1917.

ILIODOR (SERGEI TRUFANOV). Petition about Rasputin presented to the Court Chancery. January 1st, 1912.

KOMAROV-KURLOV, GENERAL. *Das Ende des russischen Kaisertums.* Berlin, 1920.

Letters and Reports of Dr. Badmaev. Moscow, 1926.
  (a) Letters of Badmaev to Rasputin and Iliodor. 1912.
  (b) Report by Badmaev to the Tsar dated February 17th, 1912.
  (c) Report by Badmaev on the Treatment of the Heir-Apparent, dated October 9th, 1912.
  (d) Letters of Badmaev to Anna Vyrubova dated February 24th, 1916 and March 9th, 1916.
  (e) Letters of Badmaev to the Tsar dated March 24th, 1916.
  (f) Letters of Badmaev to the Tsar dated April 22nd, 1916 (enclosing a pamphlet entitled "*The End of the War*").
  (g) Letters of Badmaev to Anna Vyrubova dated September 9th, 1916.
  (h) Report by Badmaev to the Tsar on the composition of the Council of Empire, dated December 26, 1916.
  (i) Letter of Badmaev to the Tsar dated February 8th, 1917 (enclosing a pamphlet entitled "*The Wisdom of the Russian People*").
  (j) Letter of Badmaev to the Tsar on the Murman Railway, dated February 20th, 1917.
  (k) Letter of Badmaev to Alexander III on the tasks of Russian Policy in the Far East, the Trans-Siberian railway scheme, the Chinese and Christianity, and the

SOURCES AND BIBLIOGRAPHY

possibility of annexing Mongolia and Tibet to Russia, dated February 13th, 1893.

(*l*) Report by Count Witte to Alexander III on Badmaev's Far Eastern proposals.

(*m*) Letters of Badmaev to Alexander III, dated July 2nd, 1893 and October 26th, 1893.

(*n*) Report by Badmaev to Alexander III dated February 22nd, 1895, on the Japanese-Chinese war and the tasks of Russian Asiatic policy.

(*o*) Letters of Badmaev to Nikolai II, dated March 2nd, 1895 and April 30th, 1895.

(*p*) Report by Badmaev to Nikolai II on his journey to China and Mongolia, dated January 15th, 1897.

(*q*) Report by Badmaev to Sukhomlinov, Chief of the General Staff, enclosing a draft of a proposal for a railway to the Mongolian frontier (joint proposal of Badmaev and General Kurlov).

MELNIK, TATIANA. *Memories of the Imperial Family and their Life before and after the Revolution*. Belgrade, 1921.

MINERVIN (PRIEST). Memorial submitted to the Public Prosecutor of Nizhni-Novgorod in 1850 on Radaev, the Khlysty prophet.

Ministry for Foreign Affairs, Petrograd. Documents concerning Events preceding the Outbreak of War. State Archives.

Minutes of the Investigation of Rasputin's murder by the Special Police (Colonel P. K. Popov):

Depositions of Rasputin's niece, Anna Nikolaevna; his daughters, Varvara Grigorievna and Matriona Grigorievna; M. I. Golovina; M. M. Yuravleva; I. I. Potekina; F. A. Korshunov; F. Yusupov; F. Kusmin (bridge watchman); V. F. Kordiukov (watchman); I. I. Nefedov (servant of Prince Yusupov); I. I. Bobkov (porter of Prince Yusupov's palace).

NARISHKINA, ELIZAVETA, ex-Mistress of the Court. Notes. (MSS. in possession of the author.)

NIKOLAI II. Diaries (edited by S. Melgunov). Berlin, 1923.

N. N. "At Grigori Rasputin's," *Novoe Vremia*, Nos. 1290 and 1298. 1912

N. N. Anonymous letter to Prince Yusupov, signed "The Voice of the People" and dated January 3rd, 1917.

N. N. "Anna Vyrubova and Grigori Rasputin." *Petrogradskaia Gazeta*, March 23rd, 1917.

OLGA NIKOLAEVNA, GRAND DUCHESS. Letters to Rasputin. 1909.

PALÉOLOGUE, MAURICE. *Am Zarenhof während des Weltkrieges*. Munich, 1926.

PALEY, PRINCESS. *Souvenirs de Russie*. Paris, 1923.

PREOBRAZHENTSEV. *Confessions of a Former Sectarian*. Magazine of the Bishopric of Tula. 1867–1869.

PROTOPOPOV, A. D. Letters to Badmaev, 1903, and telegrams dated April 16th, 1903 and July 7th, 1903.

PROTOPOPOV, A. D. Order No. 573 of the Ministry of the Interior on the judicial examination of Rasputin's murderers.

PURISHKEVICH, V. N. *Diary*. Verlag National Reklama, Riga.

RASPUTIN, GRIGORI EFIMOVICH. Letters and Telegrams to Badmaev.

RASPUTIN, GRIGORI EFIMOVICH. Letters and Telegrams to the Tsar.

RASPUTIN, GRIGORI EFIMOVICH. *My Thoughts and Observations*. Brief description of a Journey to the Holy Places and the Thoughts on Religious Subjects Inspired by it. Moscow, 1911.

RASPUTIN, MATRIONA GRIGORIEVNA. Diary.

RASPUTIN, MATRIONA GRIGORIEVNA. *The Truth about Rasputin*. Verlag Alt-Russland, Hamburg.

Record of the Burning of Rasputin's Body, March 11th, 1917 (old style). Revolutionary Museum, Leningrad.

Records of the Secret Supervision of Rasputin from January 1st, 1915 to February 10th, 1916. State Archives, Moscow.

Records of the Procurator of the Holy Synod on Rasputin's affiliation to the sectarians. State Archives, Moscow.

ROSTOVSKI, D. *Investigation into the Sectarians, their Aims and Actions*. Moscow, 1824.

RUDNEV, V. M. President of the Commission for the Investigation of the Administration of the former Imperial Ministers. Results of the Investigation. Moscow, 1917.

SOURCES AND BIBLIOGRAPHY

SERGUEEV, I. (PRIEST). Investigation of the Khlysty Sect. Memorial to the Synod. Rumiantsov Museum, Moscow.

SHUKOVSKAIA, V. A. Notes. (MSS. in possession of the author.)

VASSILCHIKOV, MARIA, former Lady-in-Waiting to the Tsaritsa. Notes and Diary. (MSS. in possession of the author.)

VYRUBOVA, ANNA. *Glanz und Untergang der Romanoffs.* Vienna, 1927.

WITTE, COUNT. *Erinnerungen.* Verlag Ullstein, Berlin. 1923.

YUSUPOV, F. *How I Killed Rasputin. Sunday Chronicle,* May to June 1927. London.

YUSUPOV, F. Letter to the Tsaritsa dated December 30th, 1916.

B. BOOKS ON RASPUTIN AND OTHER LITERATURE

(Those marked * are purely tendencious works without documentary value.)

* ALMAZOV, B. *Rasputin und Russland.* Vienna, 1923.

ARNDT, A. *Das Sektenwesen in der russischen Kirche. Zeitschrift für katholische Theologie.* Innsbruck, 1890.

BARZOV, N. *The Hymns of the People of God.* Publications of the Russian Imperial Geographical Society. St. Petersburg, 1871.

BEKHTEREV. *Rasputin and Society Ladies. Petrogradskaia Gazeta,* March 21st, 1917.

BETSKI, K., and PAVLOV, P. *The Russian Rocambole.* Leningrad, 1919.

* BIENSTOCK. *Raspoutine.* Paris, 1917.

BONCH-BRUEVICH, V. *The World of the Sectarians.* Moscow, State Publishing House, 1922.

DOBROTVORSKI, I. *The People of God.* Kazan, 1869.

DOLGORUKI, ST. *La Russie avant la Débâcle.* Paris, 1926.

DÖLLINGER, F. *Beiträge zur Sektengeschichte des Mittelalters.* Munich, 1890.

DUBENSKI, D. *What Led to Revolution in Russia. Ruskaia Letopis,* vol. iii. Paris, 1922.

EVREINOV, N. N. *Rasputin.* Leningrad, 1924.

GEHRING, J. *Die Sekten der russischen Kirche.* Leipzig, 1898.

GEIBEL-EMBACH, N. VON. *Russische Sektierer. Zeitfragen des christlichen Lebens,* vol. viii, no. 4. Heilbronn, 1883.

GROSBERG, OSCAR. *Grigori Rasputin's Ende. Einkehr,* July 27th to August 3rd, 1924. Munich.

HARNACH, A. *Das Mönchstum, seine Ideale und seine Geschichte.* 1886.

HIPPIUS, ZINAIDA. *La maisonnette d'Ania. Mercure de France,* August 1923. Paris.

* KANTOROVICH. *Alexandra Fedorovna Romanova.* Moscow, 1922.

KESSEL, J., and IZVOLSKI, H. *Les Rois aveugles.* Paris, 1925.

KLEINMICHEL, COUNTESS. *Souvenirs d'un monde englouti.* Paris, 1927.

MURAVIEV. *Geschichte der russichen Kirche.* Karlsruhe, 1857.

NASHIVIN, I. *Rasputin* (Novel). Leipzig, 1925.

* OMESSA, CHARLES. *La secret de Raspoutine.* Paris, 1918.

PFITZMAYER, A. *Die Gottesmenschen und Skopzen in Russland.* Schriften der Akademie der Wissenschaften. Vienna, 1883.

PFITZMAYER, A. *Die neue Lehre der russischen Gottesmenschen.* Vienna, 1883.

PFITZMAYER, A. *Die Gefühlsdichtung der Chlysten.* Vienna, 1885.

PHILARET. *Geschichte der Kirche Russlands.* Frankfurt-a-M., 1872.

PROTOPOPOV, G. *Study of the History of the Mystical Sects in Russia.* Publications of the Clerical Academy of Kiev, 1867.

SEVÉRAC, J. B. *La Secte Russe des Hommes-de-Dieu.* Paris, 1906.

SMILG-BENARIO, M. *Der Zusammenbruch der Zaren-Monarchie.* Vienna, 1927.

TAUBE, O. VON. *Rasputin.* Munich, 1923.

TOLSTOI, A. N. and SHCHEGOLEV. *Rasputin* (Play). Heidelberg, 1926.

INDEX

Abdication of Nikolai II: 370.
Academy of Sciences: 73.
Academy of Theology: 52.
Adrianov (Prefect, Moscow): 276.
Akulina Nikichkina, Sister: 208, 222, 224, 365ff.
Alexander I, Tsar of Russia: 113.
Alexander II, Tsar of Russia: 78, 91.
Alexander III, Tsar of Russia: 78-79, 91, 92, 97, 109, 113, 125, 126.
Alexander Mikhailovich, Grand Duke: 93, 337, 367.
Alexandra Fedorovna, Tsaritsa of Russia (Consort of Nikolai II): 70 (ch. V *passim*), 130 (ch. VI *passim*), 172, 193, 272, 273, 290, 297, 300, 308, 331, 332, 351, 352, 356, 362ff., 369 (ch. XV *passim*).
Alexandrovna, Princess Irina (wife of Prince Felix Yusupov): 337, 348, 351, 362.
Alexei, Tsesarevich (son of Nikolai II): 74, 81, 120, 129, 130 (ch. VI *passim*), 371ff.
"All Russian Union": 109, 133.
Anastasia Nikolaevna, Grand Duchess: 144, 289, 366, 371ff.
Anastasia Nikolaevna ("the Montenegrin"): 93, 111, 114, 122, 132, 290, 331.
Andronnikov, Prince Nikolai Petrovich: 102ff., 201, 305 (ch. XIII *passim*).
"Aniushka" (Anna Nikolaevna, niece of Rasputin): 193, 354, 358.
Antoni the strannik: 124.
Aronson (sculptor): 223.

Augustin, Bishop: 189.
Avelan: 73.

Badmaev, Petr Alexandrovich (Shamzaran): 125, 130, 132, 147, 150, 170.
Badmaev, Zaltin: 127.
Balinski, Colonel: 309.
Bark (Minister of Finance): 107.
Bashmakova, widow: 134, 181.
Basilevskaia: 188.
Beethoven: 75.
Belaev (War Minister): 102.
Beletski, Senator Stefan Petrovich (Chief of Police): 105, 185, 223, 233, 239, 272, 276, 308 (ch. XIII *passim*), 322ff., 333.
Belkovski: 190.
Berchik (Mme. Vyrubova's man-servant): 149.
Bermann, Katarina: 189.
Bogdanovich, General: 232, 323.
Bok, Councillor von: 183.
Brussilov, General: 163.
Buchanan, Sir George (British Ambassador): 341.
Bulygin: 89.
Burdukov (Imperial Master of the Horse): 106, 148, 201.
Burning of Rasputin's body: 370.

Central Committee of the True Russian People: 65.
Chekhov: 75.
Chervinskaia, Mme.: 189, 306ff.

Danila Filipich (founder of the Khlysty): 19, 21, 38.
Daria Ossipova: 120, 123, 150.
Davidsohn (journalist): 315.

Derevenko (attendant on Alexei): 82, 130, 156.
Derevenski (singer): 188.
Dianumova, Elena or Lenochka ("Frantik"): 187, 223ff., 227, 277ff.
Dimitri Pavlovich, Grand Duke: 337ff., 364, 367.
Dobrovolski (secretary to Rasputin; later Minister of Justice): 189, 235, 350, 364, 367.
Dolgorukaia, Princess: 108, 148, 212.
Dolina: 220.
"Donon" (restaurant): 196, 198, 273.
Dostoevski: 66, 75, 107, 114, 122.
Duma—question of opening: 195, 317ff.
Dumbadze, General: 322.
Dunia (Rasputin's maid): 184 (ch. VIII passim), 201 (ch. IX passim), 241 (ch. X passim).
Durnovo: 73.

Egorov: 122, 150, 300.
Elena (carter's wife of Tsarytsin): 293ff.
Elisaveta Fedorovna, Grand Duchess (sister of the Tsaritsa): 87, 290.
Elston, Count Sumarokov-: 336.
Ermolai, Mme.: 326.

Fedorovski Sobor (Church of the Life Guards): 112, 115, 145.
Feofan, Father: 54ff., 62, 118, 133, 292, 331.
Filipov: 198.
"Frantik" (see Dianumova, Elena).
Fredericks, Count: 73, 98, 99, 148.

Gapon (priest): 86.
Gar, Maria: 188, 189, 197.
Gibbs, Mr. (Court tutor): 74.
Gilliard, P. (Court tutor): 8, 74, 176.
Ginsburg, Baron: 223.
Glazov, Nikolai: 183, 198.

Globichev (Chief of Secret Service): 181, 190, 192, 324.
Gogol: 75.
Golos Rossii: 310.
Golovina, Mme.: 171, 187, 189, 210, 245ff., 344, 356, 360.
Golovina, Maria Eugenia ("Munia"): 188, 189, 196, 210, 227, 246ff., 333, 344ff., 350, 356, 359.
Goremykin, I. L. (Prime Minister): 92, 276, 317ff., 329.
Grazhdanin: 107.
Gregubova (prostitute): 198, 200.
Guchkov (Chairman of the Commission of National Defence): 331.
Gurko, General (President of the Zemstvo Union): 332.

Hermogen, Bishop of Saratov: 56, 292, 300ff., 331.
"Holy Devil, The" (pamphlet): v, vii, 303, 329.
Holy Synod: 61, 286.

Ignatiev, Count Alexander Pavlovich: 109.
Ignatiev, Countess: 3, 109, 122, 134, 148, 235.
Iliodor (Sergei Trufanov): v, vii, 59, 209, 260, 277, 292ff., 329ff., 331.
"Imiaboshtsy" sect: 315.
Isidor, Bishop: 360.
Ivanitskaia: 197.
Ivanov (agent): 192.

John of Kronstadt: 59, 113, 132, 150, 277.
John of Tobolsk: 313.

Karavia, Mme.: 185.
Katia (sempstress): 182, 189, 200.
Katia Ivanovna (Rasputin's maid): 352, 354, 358.
Kerenski: 371.
Khlysty ("Men of God"): 18ff., 26, 29, 47, 203, 241, 297, 332, 340.

INDEX

Khodinski Field tragedy: 83, 88.
Khvostov, A. A. (Minister of Justice): 275.
Khvostov, Alexander Nikolaevich (Minister of the Interior): 107, 108, 128, 168, 239, 269, 276, 308ff., 321ff., 333, 352.
Kionia Guseva (would-be assassin of Rasputin): 303, 326.
Kleigels, General: 197.
Klepikov: 81.
"Knight of the Heavenly Kingdom" (see Iliodor): 59.
Knirsche: 189, 197.
Kokovtsov, V. N. (Prime Minister): 81, 153.
Komisarov, Colonel M. S. (Police Dept.): 190, 193, 201, 323ff.
Kossorotov, Professor: 365.
Kovariski: 197.
Kreuz, Countess Olga: 196.
Krüdener, Frau von: 101.
Kurlov, General P. G.: 61.
Kuropatkin (Minister for War): 117.

LAPTINSKAIA: 196, 296.
Lazovert, Dr.: 344, 349ff., 355ff.
Lebedeva (merchant's wife of Tsarytsin): 294ff.
Leikart, Mme.: 185.
Lerma-Orlova: 197, 232.
Livadia (Crimea): 75, 301, 370.
Lokhtina, Mme. (Olga Vladimirovna): 209, 212, 249ff.
Loman (aide-de-camp): 147, 366.

MAKARI (holy starets): 24, 33.
Maklakov, R. A. (Minister of the Interior): 105, 232, 322.
Maksakov, Sub-Lieutenant: 219.
Maltsev (aide-de-camp): 147, 366.
Mamontov, Senator: 185, 188.
Manasevich-Manuilov, I. T.: 129, 189, 197, 227, 239.
Manus, Ignati Porfirievich: 106, 217.
Maria Alexeevna: 219, 222.
Maria Fedorovna, Tsaritza of Russia (mother of Nikolai II): 80.
Martian, Abbot (of Tiumen): 198, 274, 319.
"Masha, Sister": 211, 354.
Meksasudi, Colonel: 230.
"Men of God": see Khlysty.
Meshcherski, Prince: 107, 229.
Militsa Nikolaevna ("the Montenegrin"): 93, 111, 114, 115, 122, 132, 160, 243, 247ff., 290, 331.
Mitia Koliaba (or Kozelski): 121, 150, 300.
Mitinskaia: 189.
"Montenegrins, The": (see Anastasia Nikolaevna and Militsa Nikolaevna).
Muraviev-Amurski, Count: 116.

NATIONAL SCHOOL of Tsarskoe Selo: 184.
Nefedov, I. I. (valet to Yusupov): 344, 349.
Neumann, Mendel (engineer): 220.
Neustein, Mr.: 182, 183, 185.
Nikita, King of Montenegro: 93.
Nikitina, Lydia: 170, 189.
Nikolai II, Tsar of Russia: 70 (ch. V passim), 130 (ch. VI passim), 193, 221, 272, 273, 289, 297, 300, 308, 318, 326, 330, 332, 341, 350, 356, 362ff., 369 (ch. XV passim).
Nikolai Nikolaevich, Grand Duke (uncle of Nikolai II): 93, 114, 160, 163, 165, 290, 292, 309ff., 331.
Nikon, Patriarch: 28.
Nilov, Admiral: 100, 106, 107, 147.
Nizier-Vachot (see Philippe): 116.

OBOLENSKI, Prince: 92, 122.
Obolenski, Princess: 80.
Obrasov (officer in the Guards): 274.
"Old Believers": 28.
Olga Nikolaevna, Grand Duchess: 74, 143, 289, 366, 371ff.
"Onomatodoxy" sect: 315.
Orbeliani, Princess: 94.

Orlov, Prince: 71, 100.
Ossipenko (secretary to Pitirim): 189, 195, 197, 199, 200, 239.
Ott, Professor (Court Doctor): 117.

PALÉOLOGUE, Maurice (French Ambassador): 7, 8, 90, 95, 161.
Papus (Dr. Encausse): 124.
Pavel Alexandrovich, Grand Duke: 337.
Pecherkin, Mikhail: 16.
Pestrikov: 198.
Peter Nikolaevich, Grand Duke: 93, 114, 135, 290.
Petr, Father: 44ff.
Petr Alexeevich (Peter the Great), Tsar of Russia: 21, 22, 336.
Petrov, Andrei: 22.
Pets (riding-master): 233.
Philippe, "Doctor" (Nizier-Vachot): 115, 124, 132, 136.
Pistolkors, Alexandra von: 187, 197, 245.
Pistolkors, von: 187, 245, 302.
Pitirim, the Metropolitan: 195, 197, 239, 287, 330.
Plehve (Minister of the Interior): 87, 89, 104.
Pobedonostsev (Procurator of the Holy Synod): 114, 119.
Pogan (agent): 220.
Pokrovskoe, Siberia: 3, 11ff., 26, 33ff., 139, 147, 153, 186, 187, 271, 274, 297, 316, 371.
Polakova, Nastia (singer): 279.
Popermann: 185, 197, 199.
Popov (agent): 192.
"Potemkin" mutiny: 89.
Prokopi Lupkin: 22.
Protopopov, A. D. (Minister of the Interior): 170, 214, 318, 351, 352, 362ff.
Purishkevich, A. N. (deputy): 269, 332, 343, 345, 349, 363, 368.
Putianin, Prince (aide-de-camp): 147.

RADAEV: 22, 38.
Rashevski: 108.

Rashkovski: 117, 229.
Rasputin, Anna Egorovna (mother of Grigori): 14, 33.
Rasputin, Efim Andreevich (father of Grigori): 11ff., 33, 38.
Rasputin, Grigori Efimovich: passim.
Rasputin, Matriona (Maria Grigorievna): vi, 149, 204, 212, 248ff., 354, 355, 358, 366.
Rasputin, "Misha" (brother of Grigori): 13.
Rasputin, Mitia (son of Grigori): 361.
Rasputin, Praskovia Fedorovna (wife of Grigori): 16, 34, 38, 212.
Rasputin, Varvara (Varia) Grigorievna: 149, 212, 354, 358, 366.
Reshetnikov, Mme.: 277.
Richter: 73.
Rodzianko (President of the Duma): 318.
Rosen, Baroness: 108, 148.
Rubinstein, Dimitri: 106, 185, 191, 201, 235, 327.
Russian National Assembly: 317.
Russo-Japanese War: 81, 86, 126, 229.
Rzhevski (agent): 329, 333.

SABLER (Procurator): 314.
Saikin the boxer: 60.
Samarin (Procurator of the Holy Synod): 313, 340.
Sandetski, Staff-Captain: 188.
Sazonov (Minister for Foreign Affairs): 101, 162, 166.
Schneider, Fraülein (Court tutor): 74.
"Seleni" (see Manus): 107.
Serafim of Saratov: 78, 118.
Sergei Alexandrovich, Grand Duke: 87, 89, 93.
Shakhovskaia, Princess Tatiana: 74, 188, 196, 199, 212, 352.
Shcheglovitov, I. G. (Minister of Justice): 301.

INDEX

Shcherbatov, Prince N. B. (Minister of the Interior): 275.
Shervashidze (Steward): 105.
Shishkin, Gavrila: 218, 220.
Shukovskaia, Vera Alexandrovna: 241 (ch. X *passim*): 284ff.
Simanovich (secretary to Rasputin): 184, 188, 203, 235, 237.
Simeon of Verkhoture, Saint: 145.
Sinitsin: 303.
Snarski, Mikhail Otsupa-: 239.
Soloviev, Mme.: 188, 189, 326.
Spiridovich, General A. I.: 146, 190, 324.
"Standard" (Imperial yacht): 76.
Stankevich (governor of Tobolsk): 275.
Stolypin (Prime Minister): 87, 89, 168, 323.
Strauss, David Friedrich: 113.
Stürmer, B. V. (Prime Minister): 169, 181, 198, 232, 323, 329, 330.
Sukhomlinov (War Minister): 102, 105, 168, 306ff.
Sukhotin (cavalry officer): 344.
Suslov, Ivan Timofeevich: 21, 30, 38.
Svistunov (agent): 192.

Taneev, Alexander (Keeper of the Privy Purse): 90, 94.
Tatarinov, Colonel: 185.
Tatishev (banker): 197.
Taube, Freiherr von: vi.
Tenisheva, Princess: 187.
Terekhov (agent): 192.
Terekhova, Eugenia: 198, 218.
"Thoughts on My Pilgrimage": 173ff.
Tincheva, Miss (Court governess): 146, 289.
Tobolsk: 17, 34, 57, 67, 77, 151, 159, 187, 370.
Tolstoi: 66, 75, 85.
Trepov: 89, 158.
"True Russian People, Union of the" (see also "All Russian Union"): 109, 151, 157, 168, 292, 310, 332.

"Truth about Rasputin, The": vi.
Tsarskoe Selo: 62, 69, 70 (ch. V *passim*), 138, 155, 190, 191, 197, 201, 239, 327, 359, 366, 370.
Tschaikovski: 75.
Tsushima disaster: 86, 89.
Turgenev: 75.
Turovich: 189.

Utilia (masseuse): 182, 190.

Varnava, Bishop: 102, 151, 187, 189, 235, 277, 313ff., 319, 331.
Varvarova (actress): 188, 199.
Vassiliev, Father (Court chaplain): 145, 160, 366.
"Villa Rode" (restaurant): 185, 190, 197, 270, 273, 274, 308, 320.
Vishniakova, Maria (Court nurse): 74, 130, 139, 146, 212.
Vladimir, Archbishop: 340.
Voeikov, Vladimir Nikolaevich (Governor of the Palace): 98, 100, 218, 362, 365.
Volshin (Procurator of the Holy Synod): 314ff., 319.
Vorontsov, Countess: 80.
Vostorgov (priest): 67.
"Vriag" (ship): 159.
Vyrubov, Lieutenant: 95.
Vyrubova, Ania (Anna Alexandrovna Taneeva): 70, 71, 74, 76, 77, 88, 94ff., 129, 149, 154, 158, 169, 172, 187, 189, 193, 201, 210, 222, 246ff., 276, 302, 316, 330, 351, 356, 362ff., 371.

Wilde, Oscar: 343.
Winter Palace Massacre: 86, 89.
Witte, Count: 85, 100, 104, 136, 230.

Xenia Alexandrovna, Grand Duchess: 337.

"Yar" (restaurant): 273, 276, 279.
Yazininskaia: 197.
Yuravleva, M. M. (concierge's wife): 182, 189, 199.

Yusupov, Prince and Count Sumarokov-Elston: 336.
Yusupov, Prince Felix Felixovich: 8, 162, 333 (ch. XIV *passim*).

ZABLIN, General: 101, 106, 107, 147.
Zaborovski, Mileti: 17.
Zipiagin (Minister): 118.

Printed in the United States
44897LVS00001B/99-100